ADA IN ACTION
With Practical Programming Examples

ADA IN ACTION
With Practical Programming Examples

Do-While Jones

WILEY

John Wiley & Sons, Inc.

New York • Chichester • Brisbane • Toronto • Singapore

Copyright © 1989 by John Wiley & Sons, Inc.

All rights reserved. Published simultaneously in Canada.

Library of Congress Cataloging in Publication Data:

Jones, Do-While
Ada in action.
Bibliography: p.
1. Ada (Computer program language) I. Title
QA76.73.A35J66 1989   005.13'3   88–33785
ISBN 0-471-6078-8

Printed in the United States of America

10   9   8   7   6   5   4   3   2   1

This book is gratefully dedicated to God, in the hopes that it will be used

> *for attaining wisdom and discipline;*
>   *for understanding and insight;*
> *for acquiring a disciplined and prudent life,*
>   *doing what is right and just and fair;*
> *for giving prudence to the simple,*
>   *knowledge and discretion to the young—*
> *let the wise listen and add to their learning,*
>   *and let the discerning get guidance—*
> *for understanding proverbs and parables,*
>   *the sayings and riddles of the wise.*

(Proverbs 1:2–6 New International Version)

CONTENTS

ADA IN ACTION
With Practical Programming Examples

INTRODUCTION

This book is not intended to teach you the Ada programming language. You should already be familiar with Ada syntax and semantics. My goal is to share with you the experiences I've had using Ada in engineering applications. I hope these pages will help you avoid some common pitfalls. Most of all, I hope I can help you fill your bag-of-tricks with some reusable Ada routines.

1.1 ORGANIZATION AND CONTENT

The rest of this book is divided into four main topics. The first topic is numeric considerations. The examples in Chapter 2 illustrate the things you need to think about whenever your program does nontrivial calculations. This includes obvious things such as how many bits you will need for integers and what floating-point data type to use, but it also includes some things you probably haven't been exposed to before. The idea of letting the compiler check the consistency of the dimensional quantities in equations is a new innovation made possible by the Ada language.

Another difficult problem most programs have to deal with is the user interface, so this is the second topic. People aren't as predictable and consistent as mechanical devices, which makes user interfaces difficult to design. This is an area with a lot of potential for reusable software. Chapter 3 is full of utility routines that I think you will find very useful.

Contrary to what you've often heard, the whole is *more* than the sum of its parts. Even if you have all the pieces, they aren't worth much if you don't know how to put them together. Chapter 4 shows several examples of small-scale programming and one example of more rigorous software engineering, which is the third topic.

The last topic is testing. I saved it for last because writing code is easy; making sure it works correctly is hard. Over the years I've used a variety of methods to check code, and Chapter 5 talks about them.

A quick peek at the back of the book shows there are hundreds of pages of examples of Ada source code. The first examples are simple, and they get more complex as you read toward the end of the book. "Complex" has come to mean "difficult," but that's not the case here. The later examples are properly called complex because they were composed by combining the smaller building blocks found near the beginning to create bigger, more powerful building blocks. This means the book will be easiest to understand if you read it from front to back without skipping around.

When choosing the examples, I didn't try to go through the list of Ada reserved words and come up with an example for each one. If I did, the first example would have an *abort* statement in it, the second would show how to use the *abs* operator, and so on. These contrived examples wouldn't do much more than show syntax, which you should already know.

Contrived examples often do things in strange ways just for the sake of illustrating a point, and this sometimes teaches bad programming habits. For example, recursion is often demonstrated by recursively computing N factorial $(N! = N*(N-1)!$ until $N = 1)$. That's a good way to show recursion, but a terrible way to compute N factorial. Students often miss the point of the example. If the homework assignment is to write an excellent program to compute N factorial, guess how most of the students will do it. (Hint — They don't use a loop!)

I used practical examples with real applications, so the examples determined which Ada features were demonstrated and their order of appearance. This approach gives the most exposure to the most commonly used Ada features and less emphasis on the less important ones. The only two Ada features that didn't get a fair shake from this approach were tasking and access types.

There are so many things that need to be considered when using tasking, I might be able to devote almost an entire book to it. I wanted to avoid any discussion of tasking because I didn't want to get started on a topic I didn't have space to adequately explain. (It turned out that I couldn't completely avoid the subject of tasking, so you will find a brief example in the *VMS* package.)

Access types are most useful for solving problems in very specialized areas. The only time I've ever needed to use access types was for an artificial intelligence (AI) problem. My AI example is an excellent showcase of access types, but it requires too much technical AI background to fit in this book, and it isn't quite ready for publication yet. That's why you won't find any examples of access types in this book.

1.2 FIGURES AND LISTINGS

All the figures and listings are at the back of the book for easy reference. Despite their location, they are meant to be read right along with the text. Package specifications include comments that tell what the routines do and how to use them. Comments in the package bodies tell how the algorithms work. I generally don't repeat this information in the body of the book. The body of the book tells what the other alternatives were and why I made the decisions that I did. If you don't read the figures and listings when they are first mentioned in the text, you might not understand the discussion.

There is a distinction between figures and listings. Both contain code, but the code in the figures is not intended to be used in your application programs. Some of the figures are examples of what *not* to do. Other figures are examples of correct style but are intentionally incomplete (to avoid obscuring the main point of the figure with necessary but extraneous details). Listings, however, are complete. They have been compiled and tested on at least one validated Ada compiler and may be useful in your application programs. The source code for all the listings (but not the figures) can be separately purchased on a floppy disk.

1.3   COPYRIGHT

It would be foolish for me to write a book revealing many of my software secrets and then say to you, "You may buy this book only if you promise never to use any of the code I'm going to show you." It would be even more foolish of you to buy the book under those conditions. I expect (and want) you to use the code shown in the listings. If you make a bundle of money doing that, good for you. You will not owe me any royalties.

You may *not* copy or publish any parts of the text (including the figures and listings) without permission. The copyrights for all this material are the property of John Wiley & Sons, Inc. The copyright notice must remain in the source code.

1.4   LIABILITY

As far as I know, there are no errors in the listings, but I have no control over them once they leave my computer. There may be a typesetting error, or you may miscopy the listings. The source-code disk may be defective, or your disk drive may introduce undetected errors when reading it. You may modify the listings in some way that introduces an unexpected side effect. You could compile them with a defective compiler. There may be a strange run-time dependency in your computer that my computer doesn't have. There are all sorts of things that could go wrong, over which I have no control.

Since I have no way of knowing how you are going to use the code, what compiler you are going to use to compile it, what target machine it will run on, or how you are going to modify it, I can't guarantee that it will work in your application. You may use my code at your own risk, but you have to take the responsibility for the consequences yourself.

1.5   Ada NOT ADA

Everyone reading this book should know that ADA is the American Dental Association and Ada is a programming language named in honor of

Ada Lovelace, the first programmer. Ada was born in 1815, and that's the reason the Ada Language Reference Manual (LRM) is named MIL-STD-1815A. In light of this distinctly feminine background of the language, I consistently use feminine pronouns when referring to Ada. To avoid confusion, I use masculine pronouns for humans (programmers and users) of either gender.

NUMERIC CONSIDERATIONS

Granted, there are some programs that don't have to do extensive mathematical calculations, but as a general rule, computers have to manipulate numbers to get results. This chapter is devoted to things you have to consider when working with numbers.

2.1 *POOR_COORDINATES* PACKAGE

Embedded computers often have to convert from rectangular coordinates to polar coordinates to track a target or compute an intercept trajectory. Real applications generally use three-dimensional geometry, but to keep the example as simple as possible, I have used only two dimensions. The *POOR_COORDINATES* package shown in Figure 1 is typical of how a beginning Ada programmer would write the code. It isn't a terrible package, but it could be a lot better.

There are several good things in Figure 1. Credit must be given for recognizing that transformations between coordinate systems are common to a variety of embedded computer applications, and putting them together in a library package makes them available for reuse by future programs. It was perceptive to recognize the need for data types representing rectangular and polar data points, and those type definitions certainly belong in the *POOR_COORDINATES* package. It is highly commendable that comments are used to tell us that the distances are in feet and the angles are in degrees. The package specification is in its own file, so it can be compiled separately. These are all good software engineering practices that are usually taught in introductory Ada classes.

2.1.1 Control of Integer Data Length

Even so, there is a fatal flaw in the *POOR_COORDINATES* package specification. There is likely to be trouble if this package is developed on a host computer and then recompiled for a different target. Suppose the software is developed on a VAX. Since the VAX is a 32-bit machine, VAX Ada compilers naturally use 32 bits for the predefined type *integer*. The distance (in feet) that can be represented by 32 bits is nearly a round-trip from the earth to the moon.

The predefined *integer* type doesn't always have to be 32 bits. The Meridian and Alsys Ada compilers for 8086-based machines use 16 bits for *integer*. The distance (in feet) that can be represented by 16 bits is equivalent to just over 6 miles. That often isn't enough. Programs that use the *POOR_COORDINATES* package may work on a VAX, but not on an 8086, because the number of bits in the predefined *integer* type is machine dependent.

The Ada Language Reference Manual allows compilers to predefine families of integer data types with names like *integer*, *long_integer*, *long_long_integer*, *short_integer*, and *short_short_integer*, but it doesn't say how many bits to use. A *long_integer* on an IBM PC has the same number of bits as an *integer* on a VAX.

2.2 *STANDARD_INTEGERS* PACKAGE

Whenever it matters how many bits there will be in an integer, you should always specify the range yourself. If you try to do this locally in your program, then you might have some trouble interfacing with a library unit. Consider Figure 2, where package *X* has declared a 16-bit integer, and package *Y* has declared a 16-bit integer, and procedure *P* wants to use both packages. The types *X.Whole_numbers* and *Y.Whole_numbers* aren't the same type as *Whole_numbers*, so an Ada compiler will give an error similar to the one shown in Figure 2.

The problem can be solved by using the package *STANDARD_INTEGERS*, given in Listing 1. It declares some useful integer types of known ranges, which can be shared by everybody. I didn't use a representation clause to specify the number of bits because I don't really care how many bits the computer uses. If a 32-bit computer finds it easier to use a whole 32-bit word to store an 8-bit value, that's fine with me. The important thing is to set the allowable range of values. Whether the computer has to use partial words or multiple words isn't of any concern unless it causes a performance limitation. (If I expect to run short of space or time, then I will make representation suggestions to the compiler, but under normal circumstances that isn't necessary.)

The *SLIGHTLY_BETTER_COORDINATES* package in Figure 3 shows how to use *STANDARD_INTEGERS* to solve the machine-specific range problem.

2.2.1 Shared Data Types

Since *Integer_16* is declared only once, any package or procedure that is compiled in the context of *STANDARD_INTEGERS* can use it. Figure 4 shows how packages *X* and *Y* and procedure *P* can share *STANDARD_INTEGERS.Integer_16*.

Engineering application programs often have one package that defines some data types that will be shared by many units. That's a consequence of the effect we saw in Figure 2, and it is an intentional feature of the Ada language. It's good to force the definition of a type to be in one place rather than allowing duplicate definitions to exist in several places.

There's a chance that some, but not all, of the duplicate definitions would get changed when fixing a bug (creating even more bugs). The single definition of a shared data type insures that all modules will be working with the same kind of data. Putting all the type definitions in a single package makes them easy to find.

There is a danger, however, in creating one monster type-definition package. Monsters usually try to take over the world, and type-definition packages are no exception. If you put all your type definitions in one package, sooner or later practically every module depends on it. Then every module must be recompiled whenever a new type is added to the monster.

It is usually better to have several, smaller type-definition packages, and let the application program use whatever packages it needs. For example, you might have a package *BRITISH_UNITS* with data types *Feet, Pounds, Seconds*, and so on, that you have used on several projects. If you are assigned a new project that needs metric types as well, don't add the new metric types to *BRITISH_UNITS*. If you do, you will have to recompile everything that uses *BRITISH_UNITS*. Instead, write a new package *METRIC_UNITS* with types *Meters* and *Newtons* in it. Don't put *Seconds* in *METRIC_UNITS*, because it already exists in *BRITISH_UNITS*, and Ada will try to keep *BRITISH_UNITS.Seconds* distinct from *METRIC_UNITS.Seconds*. If your program needs *Newtons, Meters*, and *Seconds*, compile it in the context of both *BRITISH_UNITS* and *METRIC_UNITS*.

Some data types are more naturally defined in a special package, rather than in a general package of data types. For example, it makes more sense to define *Rectangular_points* and *Polar_points* in *POOR_COORDINATES* (as was done in Figure 1) than it does to put them in *BRITISH_UNITS* and then compile *POOR_COORDINATES* in the context of *BRITISH_UNITS*. If *POOR_COORDINATES* was modified to use floating-point types instead of *Integer_32*, then you would have to recompile *BRITISH_UNITS* and dozens (maybe hundreds) of modules that depend on *BRITISH_UNITS*. Leaving *Rectangular_points* and *Polar_points* in *POOR_COORDINATES* allows you to change their definition without affecting many unrelated modules. You only need to recompile the few modules that depend on *POOR_COORDINATES*. That's a better approach to take.

2.3 NONEXISTENT *STANDARD_FLOATS* PACKAGE

Since I use a package called *STANDARD_INTEGERS*, it is logical for you to assume I have also written a package called *STANDARD_FLOATS* with data types *Float_7* and *Float_15* defining seven- and fifteen-digit real numbers. I haven't and don't intend to, because I don't think it is a good idea. To explain why, I need to tell you a little personal history.

I went to school long ago, in the years B.C. (Before Calculators). In those days you could easily spot an engineering student by the slide rule dangling from his belt like a sword. The slide rule was his weapon for slaying the dragons he encountered daily. It was a mechanical device with numbers and lines etched on it, which was used for multiplying, dividing, and computing trigonometric functions. It gave three-digits of precision, and you had to keep track of the exponent in your head.

Three digits let you express numbers from 00.0 to 99.9, so the best accuracy you could get from a slide rule was 0.1%. That never bothered civil engineers when they calculated the maximum load a bridge could stand, because they knew better than to design the bridge with only a 0.1% safety factor. The limited accuracy of calculations forced engineers to be conservative and to use a little bit of common sense.

I fear that younger engineers, lacking that heritage, have gone digit crazy. A fourteen-digit calculator has a subtle way of seducing people into unrealistic conclusions.

2.3.1   Type *float* Default Precision

Ada's predefined type *float* can be any number of digits selected by the implementer. Generally, hardware considerations or software-compatibility issues limit the available choices. For example, VAX/VMS has standard floating-point representations that have 6, 9, 15, and 33 digits of precision, so Ada maps all user-defined floating-point types onto one of those representations.

I have not yet found an implementation that uses fewer than six digits for the predefined type *float*. I maintain that six digits is plenty of resolution, and I am skeptical of designs that claim to require more.

Suppose we want to represent angles in units of degrees using floating-point numbers. If we use six digits of resolution, we need three digits to represent whole degrees up to 360, leaving three digits for fractional degrees. Angles can be resolved to 0.001 degree. Will this precision yield good enough accuracy? In real applications it better.

Let's say that you are using these angles in some avionics software that slaves the infrared seeker on a missile to a position determined by the aircraft radar so the missile can lock onto the target. If this system requires 0.001 degree accuracy to work, it means that the radar and missile pylon have to be aligned to the aircraft body to within 0.001 degree. Do you think a sailor on an aircraft-carrier (who has been on combat alert and hasn't had much sleep lately) can do that on a rolling aircraft-carrier deck in a few minutes? Even if he can, will it still be aligned after a catapult launch and an arrested landing? Don't kid yourself. If you design a system that can't tolerate a 0.001 degree error, it is never going to work in combat.

Can anyone argue that it is ever necessary to compute the sine of an angle to fifteen decimal places? Sines are used as scale factors. For example, **DISTANCE_NORTH : = RADIAL_DISTANCE * Cos(BEARING);**. Does the scale factor really need to be accurate to 0.0000000000001%? Was *RADIAL_DISTANCE* measured with that accuracy? Care to figure out how accurately you have to measure the *BEARING* to maintain that accuracy?

The reason I don't have a *STANDARD_FLOATS* package is that I don't believe in designing programs that need floating-point numbers with better resolution than one part per million. There may be applications in research laboratories that need higher precision, but in my applications the input data is only good to "slide-rule accuracy." I use the default type *float* because the compiler has probably selected the representation that gives the fastest computational speed.

2.4 *DIM_INT_32* PACKAGE

STANDARD_INTEGERS solves machine-specific range problems, but there is another dragon to slay before we are completely safe. We need to protect our program against dimensional-unit errors.

Figure 5 uses a package called *DIM_INT_32*. It is a skillful blend of derived types, private types, and a generic unit. We are about to embark on the derivation of that package. I've let you peek ahead because I wanted to give you a glimpse of how easy and valuable it is to use dimensional units. The derivation of this package is not trivial, but once derived it is simple to use. All you need is one context clause and one type definition for each kind of unit you want to use. The benefit you reap is the detection of dimensional inconsistencies at compile time.

2.4.1 Type Checking

Have you spent many hours debugging a program before you discovered the angular argument to a trigonometric function was expressed in degrees instead of radians? Has a misplaced parenthesis ever caused one of your equations to produce strange results? Most of these kinds of errors can be detected at compile time if dimensional data types are used.

For example, consider the equation **DISTANCE := (INDI-CATED_AIR_SPEED + WIND_SPEED) * TIME;**. This equation will be correct only if the variables use consistent units (i.e., *DISTANCE* in feet, the two speeds in feet per second, and *TIME* in seconds). If *TIME* is in milliseconds, *INDICATED_AIR_SPEED* is in knots, and *WIND_SPEED* is in miles per hour, then *DISTANCE* can't possibly be correct. Even if consistent units are used, you won't get the correct answer if the parentheses are missing, because the multiplication operation has higher precedence than addition.

If the compiler knows that two variables of type feet per second added together produce a result of type feet per second, and if it also knows that a variable of type feet per second multiplied by a variable of type seconds produces a result in feet, then the compiler can check the dimensional consistency of an equation for you. If you leave out the parentheses in the example above, the compiler will know that *WIND_SPEED* multiplied by *TIME* gives an answer in feet, and feet added to *INDICATED_AIR_SPEED* (in feet per second) won't give a correct answer in feet.

Ada's built-in type checking enables her to automatically check the dimensional consistency of all your equations at compile time, if you simply declare the variables to be dimensional units.

Let's look at Figure 5 closely to see how this is done. It uses a package called *DIM_INT_32*, which contains a dimensioned 32-bit data type called *Units*. *Feet* and *Meters* are both new types derived from *Units*. The variables *A*, *B*, and *C* express distances in feet, but *X*, *Y*, and *Z* express distances in meters. Lines 13 and 14 of Figure 5 show that Ada's type checking will allow addition of distances in the same kind of units, but will prohibit you from accidentally adding distances in mixed units. If you really want to add a distance measured in feet to a distance measured in meters, you can use *Units_Convert* to tell Ada you really want to do that, and she will automatically multiply by the proper scale factor.

2.4.2 Derived Types

A derived type has all the allowable values and operations of its parent type, but is an entirely different type. You can derive a type from any other type. You may wonder why I derived the type *Feet* from the type *Units*. Why not just derive it from *integer*?

Suppose I wrote **type Kilograms is new integer;**. This would create a new data type that could have any value from *integer'FIRST* to *integer'LAST*. It would also have all the integer operations defined for it. You could add two objects of type *Kilograms* and get a result of type *Kilograms*. You could not, however, add an object of type *Kilograms* to any other type object, integer or otherwise. This gives us some of the protection we desire.

Deriving *Kilograms* from *integer* does not give us a complete solution. *Kilograms* could be multiplied by *Kilograms* to get an incorrect answer in *Kilograms* because integers can be multiplied together, and so that property is automatically derived from the parent. Although Ada always allows you to add new operations to a data type, she never lets you take away operations derived from a parent. We can't derive dimensional units from the predefined *integer* data type and then remove unwanted operations. We have to start with a data type with fewer operations than we need, and add more operations to it.

2.4.3 Private Types

Private types have no predefined operations except assignment, equality, and inequality. Those are useful operations for dimensional data types, so we are glad to inherit them. But private types don't have an addition operation defined for them. Therefore, we have to specially define addition for private types.

I published a package called *DIMENSIONAL_ UNITS* in the spring of 1987[1] and put it in the Ada Software Repository.[2] This package used private types as the parent types for integer and floating-point dimensional units. It bothered me, however, that I lost automatic range checking for dimensional data types. That is, I couldn't define a data type *Kelvin* that automatically detected impossible (negative) temperatures.

I also didn't like the excessive size of the *DIMENSIONAL_ UNITS* package. I put both integer and floating-point data types in the package, so programs that needed only integer types also picked up some dead code associated with floating-point types.

The *DIMENSIONAL_ UNITS* package worked fine, but there was room for improvement. The two generic packages (and their instantiations), which you are about to see, include those improvements. They allow you to add range constraints and to separate the integer data types from the floating-point data types, so you can selectively obtain the data types you need.

The *Range_ Checking_ Example* in Figure 6 shows how Ada can detect impossible values. In the declarative region, I instantiated the generic *FLOAT_ UNITS* package to get a new package called *TEMPERATURE*. I put range constraints on it by specifying *MIN* and *MAX* values. The *MIN* value is absolute zero on the Celsius scale. The *MAX* value is arbitrary. I could have used the default value, but you wouldn't have known what that value that was. I picked 32_ 000.0 for no particular reason.

---

[1] Do-While Jones, "Dimensional Data Types," *Dr. Dobb's Journal of Software Tools*, No. 127, May 1987, pp. 50–62.

[2] The Ada Software Repository is a collection of files containing reusable Ada components. These files are maintained by Richard Conn on a computer named SIMTEL20. SIMTEL20 can be reached by anyone who has a computer on ARPA/MILNET network and File Transfer Protocol (FTP). See Richard Conn's *The Ada Software Repository and the Defense Data Network*, published by New York Zoetrope, 838 Broadway, New York, NY 10002.

In the body of the code I have three assignment statements, each enclosed in a block structure with an exception handler. You can consider them to be *if-then-else* structures. If the assignment statement succeeds, then the following line is printed. If the attempted assignment raises *CONSTRAINT_ERROR*, then the program jumps to the exception handler and prints the line found there. The lines of output appended to the end of Figure 6 show Ada found the errors when I ran the program.

2.5   GENERIC *INTEGER_UNITS* PACKAGE

Listing 2 shows the generic *INTEGER_UNITS* package. Take some time here to read through it before we discuss it.

2.5.1   Generic Parameters

There are three generic parameters. The first is the integer type. The four logical choices for this parameter are *integer*, *Integer_8*, *Integer_16*, and *Integer_32*. Of these, *Integer_32* is the one I generally use. I would use the others only in those applications where (1) the range of values is small enough to be represented by 8 or 16 bits, (2) there is a significant speed advantage associated with a smaller size, and (3) speed is important to that application.

Notice that I didn't make *Integer_32* the default data type. That's because Ada doesn't allow a default for a generic type. Notice too, that I can't instantiate this package for type *float* because the type is *range* <>. The *range* <> must always be replaced with an integer type.

The other two generic parameters are *MIN* and *MAX*. I expect that most of the time you will want the full range of values, so I made the default range as large as possible. There are times when you may wish to restrict the range, and the *MIN* and *MAX* parameters give you the option of doing that.

2.5.2   Type Conversions

There are three type-conversion functions named *Type_Convert*, " + ", and "−". They all do the same thing. They all add units to a pure number. That is, they change "5" to "5 feet." Assuming that *DISTANCE* has been declared to be of type *Feet*, where *Feet* has been derived from an instantiation of this package, it would not be legal to say **DISTANCE :=** **5;**. That's because 5 is a *universal_integer*, and *DISTANCE* is derived from a private type. The private type happens to be an integer but that is irrelevant. Ada sees them as different types and that's exactly what I want. I want to make a distinction between *Feet* and pure numbers.

Somehow we have to be able to jump the barrier between *Feet* and pure numbers. The *Type_ Convert* function does that. We can say **DISTANCE** := **Type_ Convert(5)**; and Ada will know that we mean 5 feet. I usually use the long phrase *Type_ Convert* because I want to make it obvious that I am dimensioning a number. Sometimes, however, that makes a program line awfully long, and distracts from other things in the line that I feel are more important. In those cases I use the " + " or "−" operator to do the same thing. (*Note*: the Meridian AdaVantage version 2.1 compiler sometimes has trouble differentiating the " + " type convert from the unary + operator. It generates an error message, which is easily eliminated by replacing the " + " with *Type_ Convert*.)

There is one other type conversion routine, called *Dimensionless*. It is the opposite of the three routines we have just discussed because it removes dimensional units instead of adding them. I'm going to delay the discussion of this function for a moment because it will make more sense after we have discussed dimensioned arithmetic.

2.5.3 Dimensioned Arithmetic

Most of the arithmetic functions are self-explanatory. It should be obvious why you need the common operators like addition and subtraction, so let's skip over them. Things don't get interesting until we get down to the multiplication and division operators.

Conspicuously absent is **function "*"(LEFT, RIGHT : Units) return Units;**. That's because the product of two dimensioned quantities has different dimensions. (5 feet × 2 feet is not 10 feet, it's 10 square feet.) Multiplication is legal only when one of the numbers is a pure (dimensionless) number. (5 × 2 feet = 10 feet.) The pure number can be on the left or right side of the multiplication operator, so there are two definitions of multiplication of a dimensioned quantity times a pure number.

There are three division operators. The first division operator divides a dimensioned quantity by a dimensionless number, yielding a dimensioned result. (For example, 10 feet / 5 = 2 feet.) Ada's predefined division operator for integer types truncates toward zero, rather than rounding. Therefore, 9 feet / 5 = 1 foot.

Unlike multiplication, division isn't symmetrical. Dividing by a dimensioned quantity changes the units. (1_000_000 / 1 *Second* = 1 *Mega_ Hertz*.) That's why there isn't a mixed division operator with *Integer_type* on the left and *Units* on the right, as there is for multiplication.

The second division operator divides two dimensioned quantities (feet/feet, for example) and returns a dimensionless result. Just like Ada's predefined integer division, the result is truncated toward zero rather than rounding.

It is possible that you would like to get an exact ratio. The third division operation does that. The third division operation can be used to divide 10 feet by 3 feet to determine that the ratio of the lengths is 3.333 to 1. If the predefined type *float* doesn't have enough digits of precision for you (which I think is unlikely), the *Dimensionless* function (described later) can be used to get more precise results.

If you want a division routine that will round instead of truncate, use the third division routine to get the exact ratio and do an explicit type conversion to an integer type. (Explicit integer type conversions automatically round the result for you.) For example, if X and Y are of type *Feet*, *INT* is type *integer*, and F is type *float*, you can say **F := X/Y; INT := integer(F);**.

Rem and *mod* and all the relational operators work just as you would expect them to, so let's move on to the *Dimensionless* function.

2.5.4 Removing Dimensional Units

The *Dimensionless* function is the inverse of *Type_ Convert*. It converts dimensioned quantities to pure numbers. It should be used with caution because it defeats the strong type checking we have worked so hard to achieve. Normally you would use it inside a special arithmetic function. For example, if you want to write a function that divides objects of type *Feet* by objects of type *Seconds* and produces a result in type *Feet_per_sec*, you will have to use *Dimensionless* to convert to pure numbers for the intermediate calculations and then use *Type_ Convert* to change the result into *Feet_per_sec*. Figure 7 shows how to do this. The *Dimensionless* function could also be used to find a high-precision ratio, as in Figure 8.

One of the most common uses for the *Dimensionless* function is for output. You can't instantiate the *TEXT_IO* package, *INTEGER_IO*, for any dimensional data type, such as *Feet*, because *Feet* is a private type, not an integer type. (I wouldn't instantiate *INTEGER_IO* even if I could, but that's a story we will save for the section on user interfaces.) A good way to print a dimensioned integer is shown in Figure 9. An even fancier way is shown in Figure 10. (These examples use the *IMAGE* attribute, but you will see something even better than the *IMAGE* attribute in the *ASCII_ UTILITIES* package.)

2.5.5 Generic Bodies

Let's return to Listing 2 again. This is one of the rare instances where I put the package body in the same file as the package specification. Normally I separate the package body from the specification. I can't always do that with generic packages. The Ada language specification expressly allows vendors to require all generic parts (bodies and subunits) to be in a single file, and some vendors have taken advantage of that. That's a real nuisance for programmers, but it apparently makes it much easier for vendors to implement generics.

The package body is trivial, even if lengthy. In general, each function body just converts its argument to the *Integer_type*, does the operation, and converts the output to the appropriate type.

2.5.6   Instantiation

Generic packages need to be instantiated before they are used. I instantiated the package for 32-bit integers, put it in a library, and called its instantiation *DIM_INT_32*. You've seen it used in five of the last six figures. Now it is time to see the package itself. Its simple listing is given in Listing 3. It uses integers with a 32-bit range, regardless of the target computer. Since I did not include values for *MIN* and *MAX*, the default values (*Integer_32'FIRST* and *Integer_32'LAST*) are used.

2.6   GENERIC *FLOAT_UNITS* PACKAGE

The *FLOAT_UNITS* package, shown in Listing 4, is almost identical to the *INTEGER_UNITS* package. Therefore most of the comments about the *INTEGER_UNITS* package equally hold true for the *FLOAT_UNITS* package. Let's just concentrate on the differences. First, Listing 4 is instantiated for a type described as *digits <>* instead of *range <>*. This means we can instantiate it for any real type.

Second, the limits *MIN* and *MAX* are real numbers instead of integers. I chose to give *MIN* and *MAX* fixed defaults rather than an attribute. I gave serious consideration to letting the defaults be $-1.0 *$ *SAFE_LARGE* and *SAFE_LARGE*, and finally decided against it. There was no compelling argument to make a decision one way or another, and I finally picked $\pm 1.0e25$ as the limits because I felt they will cover most real applications and they are less than the published limits for the type *float* for all the compilers I use. If you need an exceptionally large range you can always instantiate this package with any limits the compiler can support. Using fixed values instead of attributes guarantees that the default limits will be the same no matter which compiler is used, so it is less likely that there will be an unpleasant surprise when programs are moved from one computer to another.

2.6.1   Division, Remainder, and Modulo Operators

Normally if you take the ratio of two real numbers, you want a real result. There are times, however, when you want the old elementary-school definition of division. ("How many times does X go into Y?") For example, "How many complete revolutions has an object made if it has turned 25.89 radians?" You might also want to know the orientation of an object that has turned 25.89 radians. A division operator that returns an integer ratio, and a modulo operator that takes a real argument, would be helpful in converting 25.89 radians to 4 revolutions and 0.76 radians. Ada does not define division of two real numbers with an integer result, nor does she have *rem* and *mod* operators for real types. That's not a major problem. It was easily solved.

I started with *INTEGER_UNITS* package and converted integer types to floating-point types. I left the two common division operators (**function** "/"(**LEFT : Units; RIGHT : Float_type) return Units;** and **function** "/"(**LEFT, RIGHT : Units) return Float_type;**) clustered with the other common arithmetic operators, but simply for cosmetic reasons, I moved **function** "/"(**LEFT, RIGHT : Units) return Integer_type;** to the end of the list of arithmetic operators, next to *mod* and *rem*. (It put the division operator close to the comment that describes its use.) Then I wrote the bodies of the integer division, *rem*, and *mod* operators. (*INTEGER_UNITS* just used the predefined Ada operators. Since the equivalent operators don't exist for real types, I had to write them myself for *FLOAT_UNITS*.)

When I first wrote this package, I used *integer* for the result of the integer ratio. That was a bad idea because, as the broken record says, the range of *integer* depends on the implementation. Then I decided to use *STANDARD_INTEGERS.Integer_32*. That wasn't a good idea either, because I don't expect ratios to be large and it seems silly to burden a 16-bit computer with double-precision arithmetic to calculate a number less than one hundred.

I finally did the smart thing. I added a fourth generic parameter, *Integer_type*, and let the programmer make the best choice based on the application.

2.6.2 *First* and *Last* Functions

When I talked about the *INTEGER_UNITS* package, I intentionally avoided mentioning the *First* and *Last* functions because I wanted to wait until now to discuss them. Both *INTEGER_UNITS* and *FLOAT_UNITS* have *First* and *Last* functions.

If you have done much Ada programming, I'm sure you've found how valuable the *FIRST* and *LAST* attributes are. You have probably come to take them for granted. If I didn't provide you with the *First* and *Last* functions, it would be distressing to discover that a dimensioned data type such as *Celsius*, has no *FIRST* or *LAST* attributes.

There are two reasons why Ada won't allow you to write a statement like **ABSOLUTE_ZERO := Celsius'FIRST;**. The first is that even if

type Celsius is new DIM_INT_32.Units;, then type *Celsius* is a *private* type, not an integer type. The fact that type *Units* is represented by a 32-bit integer doesn't matter. *Private* types do not have *FIRST* and *LAST* attributes, no matter how they are represented.

The second reason is that if **type Celsius is new DIM_FLOAT.Units;**, then type *Celsius* is a *private* type that is represented by a type (*float*) that doesn't have *FIRST* and *LAST* attributes to begin with!

The *First* and *Last* functions provide a way of obtaining the *MIN* and *MAX* values used to instantiate the *INTEGER_UNITS* or *FLOAT_UNITS* package. They aren't quite as clean as actual attributes, but at least it is possible to declare **ABSOLUTE_ZERO : constant Celsius := Type_Convert(TEMPERATURE.First);** (regardless of whether *TEMPERATURE* is an instantiation of *INTEGER_UNITS* or *FLOAT_UNITS*).

2.7 *DIM_FLOAT* PACKAGE

It was convenient to instantiate the *FLOAT_UNITS* package for the predefined types *float* and *STANDARD_INTEGERS.Integer_32* and put it in the program library. I called this instantiation *DIM_FLOAT*. It is found in Listing 5. The Meridian AdaVantage version 2.1 refused to instantiate *Integer_type* for 32-bit integers, so I used the version shown in Listing 6 on the Meridian compiler.

2.8 NONEXISTENT *NUMERIC_UNITS* PACKAGE

The two packages *INTEGER_UNITS* and *FLOAT_UNITS* are so similar, it is tempting to ask, "Why not combine both into a single generic package that can be instantiated for either integers or real numbers?" I must admit I was seduced into trying this, but I quickly recognized the error of my ways and escaped from the trap. I'll show you how I started, so you won't get tricked into trying the same thing.

I wrote a generic package called *NUMERIC_UNITS* for a type described as *private*. This package could have been instantiated for any numeric type. If I did this, I would also have to supply some arithmetic operators because private types don't have predefined arithmetic operations. Part of the package specification is shown in Figure 11.

As it turns out, Figure 11 isn't very practical. Notice that I haven't supplied any default values for *MIN* and *MAX*. I can't, because numbers like *integer'LAST* and 1.0e25 aren't private-type values. That means an instantiation would always have to supply the limits. That's a minor inconvenience. The real showstopper though, is an ambiguity in the division operators. If I worked long and hard enough, I think I could come up with a way to keep the division operators straight. I'd probably have to replace the "/" operators with distinct functions with names like *Float_Result_Division* and *Integer_Result_Division* and instantiate the package very carefully. The only way you can really appreciate the problem is to fool around with it yourself and see what problems you run into.

Suppose you do figure out how to get the universal *NUMERIC_UNITS* package to work. What have you gained? It won't do anything you couldn't do by instantiating the integer or real versions already discussed.

There is one possible advantage for combining the two packages. Whenever there is a good reason to change the *INTEGER_UNITS* package, the *FLOAT_UNITS* package should *probably* be changed for the same reason. It might be easier to maintain the single *NUMERIC_UNITS* package than to maintain both *INTEGER_UNITS* and *FLOAT_UNITS*, so combining the two packages might make maintenance easier.

There are two possible disadvantages. The maintenance considerations discussed in the previous paragraph may really be a disadvantage. It might not be true that changes made to the *INTEGER_UNITS* package should also be made to the *FLOAT_UNITS* package, so coupling the two packages might cause bugs or maintenance difficulties. It will certainly be more difficult to instantiate the *NUMERIC_UNITS* package because of the limit and division-operator problems.

The conclusion is that you waste an awful lot of engineering time (that is, money) for a questionable improvement if you combine *INTEGER_UNITS* and *FLOAT_UNITS* into a single generic package. The combined package is elegant, but elegance for elegance sake doesn't make sense in the engineering world. It is better to keep the *INTEGER_UNITS* and *FLOAT_UNITS* packages separate.

2.9　NONEXISTENT *FIXED_UNITS* PACKAGE

Since I have written an *INTEGER_UNITS* package and a *FLOAT_UNITS* package, it is reasonable to expect me to have written a *FIXED_UNITS* package. I haven't. There were two reasons why not.

First, the *FIXED_UNITS* package requires some options that can't easily be selected using generic parameters. Sure, I could use generic parameters for the number of digits, minimum values, and maximum values, but there are more decisions that need to be made. For example, sooner or later you will have to convert the value to a character string of many digits. Do you want to separate digits by commas, periods, or underlines? There are even more difficult decisions to be made regarding the location of the decimal point after arithmetic operations. I just couldn't guess what you would want, so I didn't try.

Second, I don't think the *FIXED_UNITS* package is necessary, and it might not even be a good idea. If I wrote a *FIXED_UNITS* package and included it with *INTEGER_UNITS* and *FLOAT_UNITS*, then it would encourage people to use *FIXED_UNITS* when they probably should use *INTEGER_UNITS* or *FLOAT_UNITS*. I don't like to encourage the use of fixed-point arithmetic.

2.9.1 Problems with Fixed-Point

You might be tempted to use Ada's predefined fixed-point type to represent certain kinds of physical quantities, such as dollars. That's not a good idea. Suppose you write **type Dollars is delta 0.01 range -10_000_000.00 .. 10_000_000.00;**. You might be surprised to discover that the precision isn't exactly to one cent. The LRM allows *Dollars'SMALL* to be 1/100 or 1/128 (or any other fraction smaller than 1/100). If it uses 1/128, then there could be a roundoff error of a few cents if a long column of numbers is added.

There is an optional pragma you could use to specify *Dollars'SMALL*, but it might not be supported on the compiler you want to use. Even if it is, whenever you depend on pragmas to make your program work, you are asking for portability problems.

The LRM gives the vendors so much freedom when it comes to implementing fixed-point types, you can't be sure what you are getting. DEC Ada just uses a 32-bit integer and interprets the LSB as the delta value. That means DEC Ada could perfectly represent the type *Dollars* just described but could not represent *Big_Bucks* if **type Big_Bucks is delta 0.01 range -22_000_000.00 .. 22_000_000.00;**. This is because that declaration exceeds the range of values that can be represented by 32 bits.

I have never found a situation where Ada's fixed-point data type was useful. If I need nine or fewer digits of range, with one digit of absolute accuracy, then I can use *Integer_32*. Just for the sake of argument, suppose there was a situation where I needed 50 digits of range with one digit of accuracy. The implementation of Ada's fixed-point type probably wouldn't be sufficient to support that many digits anyway. Even if it did, I couldn't be sure I would get accurate results from it.

2.9.2 Custom Fixed-Point Types

If I did have an application where I needed exceptionally high accuracy, I would write a package that used a private data type to represent the large, fixed-point numbers. It's so easy to write, I usually assign it as a problem in my beginning Ada class. There are three ways that students commonly solve the problem.

Most students use the same Binary Coded Decimal (BCD) approach that 4-bit hand-held calculators use. This involves creating an array of digits that represents the number. Arithmetic operators process the numbers one digit at a time, just as you would if you were adding or multiplying two long numbers using paper and pencil. They use hidden variables with names like *CARRY*, *BORROW*, and *PARTIAL_PRODUCT* to hold some intermediate results. A Boolean variable tells if the value is positive or negative, and another integer tells where the decimal point is.

It isn't very efficient to use a 16- or 32-bit computer to process numbers 4 bits at a time, so some students use an integer to represent a group of three or four digits. The technique is basically the same as BCD, but the computer processes several digits at a time, so it is more efficient.

Perhaps the most difficult part of these two approaches is converting arrays of digits to character strings and vice versa. This sometimes leads a third group of students to use a character string as the private type representing the long number. They still process the data one digit at a time, but instead of arrays of integers they use arrays of characters and define special operations that work on characters.

2.9.3 *FIXED_UNITS* Exercise

If you like, you can try to write a *FIXED_UNITS* package. Start with the *INTEGER_UNITS* specification and make a few modifications. (You don't have to make it generic if you don't want to.) You will have to replace the definition of the private type with something that can represent many digits. You can use one of the three approaches just suggested or come up with something totally different. You will probably want to replace the *Type_Convert* and *Dimensionless* functions with *Image* and *Value* functions (similar to those found in the *ASCII_UTILITIES* package in the next chapter), because you can't use numeric types to represent all the values you want to represent. (If you could, you wouldn't need the *FIXED_UNITS* package.)

If you want to be able to multiply a monetary figure (which has two decimal places) by 6.5% sales tax (three decimal places), then your private type will have to have a *floating decimal point* so it can represent numbers to two or three (or any other number) decimal places.

If you allow a floating decimal point it raises some interesting problems. For example, if you subtract 0.123 from 0.9, you will have to move the decimal point before you find the difference. Once you have performed the subtraction, should the answer be 0.777 or 0.8?

The problems associated with fixed-point arithmetic make it more trouble than it is worth. I think you would be better off to avoid fixed-point arithmetic whenever you can.

2.9.4 Fixed-Point Computers

Ten or fifteen years ago, before floating-point coprocessors were common, some computers were designed to use fixed-point binary numbers. A fixed-point computer does surprising things if you don't know how it works. For example, a computer that uses integer arithmetic will multiply 0100_2 times 0010_2 and yield the expected result 01000_2 ($4 * 2 = 8$). When a fixed-point computer multiplies 0100_2 times 0010_2 the answer is 00001_2 ($1/4 * 1/8 = 1/32$). That's because integer machines assume a binary point to the right of all the bits, while a fixed-point machine assumes a binary point to the left of all the bits.

Fixed-point computers are no longer in vogue, but they are still in some military systems. An Ada compiler for a fixed-point target computer *might* take advantage of certain machine features if you declare real data types to be fixed-point types with deltas that are a power of two. I haven't used an Ada compiler for a fixed-point computer, so I don't know what it does, but you may want to look into it if you find yourself in that situation.

2.10 *TRIG* PACKAGE

The dimensioned numbers we have developed can be put to good use in a math package I call *TRIG*. The *TRIG* package specification shown in Listing 7 gives your Ada programs new levels of reliability and transportability.

It is more reliable because it is impossible to provide the wrong argument to a trigonometric function. I'm sure any reader who has written programs involving sines and cosines has tried at least once to take the sine of an angle expressed in degrees using a function expecting an input in radians, or vice versa. An even more common mistake is multiplying by *PI_OVER_180* when the angle should have been divided by that factor, or vice versa. Those days are gone forever if you use the *TRIG* package.

2.10.1 Type-Naming Convention

The *TRIG* package creates two data types, *Deg* and *Rad*, which you can use for angular variables. I could have called these data types *Degrees* and *Radians*, but that violates a simple convention I use when deriving dimensional units. Whenever I derive a dimensional unit from *INTEGER_UNITS*, I spell the units out completely. If the dimensional unit is derived from *FLOAT_UNITS*, then I use an abbreviation. Therefore, I know immediately that type *Feet* is an integer data type, but type *Ft* uses real numbers. This means I can tell its range and precision without having to search through the code to find out if the unit was derived from *INTEGER_UNITS.Units* or *FLOAT_UNITS.Units*. The convention is easy to remember because both abbreviations and real numbers have dots in them. Since the *TRIG* package uses real numbers, rather than integers, I used *Deg* and *Rad* for the type names.

2.10.2 Overloaded Function Names

Notice there are two overloaded versions of *Sin*. That is, there are two different functions with the same name. One *Sin* function works for type *Rad* and the other works for type *Deg*. When you declare an angular object, you assign its dimensions by making it type *Rad* or *Deg*. When you call for the sine of that angle, Ada will automatically select the correct *Sin* routine from the *TRIG* package based on the data type. When you take an inverse function, the *TRIG* package will automatically return degrees or radians, whichever is correct. If *ANGLE_1* and *ANGLE_2* are expressed in different units, you can always say **ANGLE_1 := TRIG.Convert_Units(ANGLE_2)**; and you will get the correct result, no matter which one is in degrees and which one is in radians. (If *ANGLE_1* and *ANGLE_2* already are the same kind of units, both degrees or both radians, Ada will tell you so at compile time with a fatal-error message.) You won't need any more *PI_OVER_180* constants cluttering up your program.

2.10.3 Portability

The *TRIG* package also makes your programs more portable because it can be used as a standard math package. You were probably surprised when you discovered Ada has no predefined math package. That may seem strange for a military programming language, but it makes good sense. Since Ada is strongly typed, you would have to have separate math functions for every real data type. Since the number of distinct real data types is unbounded, that would be a lot of math routines. A standard generic math package could be instantiated for each real data type (the way *FLOAT_IO* is), but that doesn't completely solve the problem. Some machines have an optional math coprocessor. Ada would have to have multiple versions of the math library, some that would use the coprocessor and others that wouldn't. Furthermore, some applications may need immediate answers good to three decimal places, while other applications need higher precision and have all the time in the world to compute the answer. If Ada had a built-in, standard math library, a trade-off would have to be made, and the resulting math routines would be good for some applications but not good for others.

These are all good reasons for leaving the math routines out of the Ada language. I wouldn't have it any other way. Compiler vendors, however, wisely recognized that most of us programmers often use math functions in our application programs. Furthermore, we want to solve the problems we are being paid to solve, not to reinvent the sine function. We would abuse their sales representatives if they didn't include a math library as part of the programming environment, so today most compilers come with a math library. You will probably find a package called something like *MATH_LIB* or *GENERAL_MATH* in the system library.

Math libraries often cause portability problems. They generally have different names for the library as well as for functions. For example, the square root function might be called *Sqr* or *Sqrt*. Some of math libraries are generics and some have already been instantiated. Some math libraries have two functions, *Sin* and *Sind*, for taking sines in radians and degrees. Other libraries only have a radian sine function. Suppose your program used *Sind* to find the sine of angles expressed in degrees, and you transported it to another system that used *Sind* for a double-precision sine in radians. How long would it take you to find that bug?

I run into these problems a lot because I use so many different Ada compilers. I solved the problem by using the *TRIG* package as a shell over the underlying math library. Once I get the *TRIG* package ported to a new system, then all my other programs can be transported without any math modifications.

The *TRIG* package specification remains the same on every system, but the body has to be specially tailored for each system. Listing 8 shows the *TRIG* package body for the DEC compiler. It simply calls the corresponding VAX/VMS math library routine for each function. The *TRIG* package body for the Meridian compiler in Listing 9 uses a slightly different approach, just for the sake of illustrating a different way of doing it. (Mathematicians know the method I used in the Meridian body is inferior, and we will talk about that much later when I show you how the routine was tested.) I pretended that there wasn't any *Cos* or *Tan* function available and derived them from the *Sin* function. (If you are using an embedded computer, you might just have a sine lookup table, or a coprocessor that only computes sines.) In the fall of 1987, Alsys did not officially provide a math library. The Version 3.2 distribution disk contained a math library contributed by a customer. Listing 10 uses that unofficial Alsys math library. No matter what the package body implementation is, the package specification doesn't change, and that makes all the programs that use the *TRIG* package portable.

2.10.4 Reciprocal Functions

When I wrote this package, I had to decide what to put in and what to leave out. I chose to leave out the reciprocal functions (cosecant, secant, and cotangent). I can't remember the last time I used one of these, so it didn't seem worth the memory space to put them in. If I had put them in, they probably would have just returned *1/Sin*, *1/Cos*, or *1/Tan*. If the application program used the secant in an equation like **X := Y*Secant(THETA);**, it would compute **X := Y*(1/Cos(THETA);**, which involves an extra operation and an extra function call (unless the optimizer takes them out). It would be better to simply write **X := Y/Cos(THETA);**. (Dividing by *Secant(THETA)* would be even more foolish.) I decided it was better to leave out the reciprocal functions than be tempted to use them.

This *TRIG* package may not exactly fit your needs, but it is built in such a way that you can modify it to do exactly what you want. You can derive *Deg* and *Rad* from any floating-point type you desire. You can change the body to use any desired algorithm. Since it isn't part of the language, you are free to do whatever you want.

2.10.5 Special Cases

I made some decisions concerning special cases, and those decisions might not be appropriate for your application. Since the *TRIG* body is given in source code, you are free to change it however you like.

The first special case is the tangent of 90 degrees. The theoretical value is infinite. DEC Ada raises the exception *FLOAT_MATH_LIB.FLOOVEMAT*. I could have handled this by simply raising *NUMERIC_ERROR* in its place and let the application program figure out how to handle it, but instead I decided to return a very big number. The problem is, how big is "very big?" I decided that since I had previously decided limits for *DIM_FLOAT*, I might as well use the same maximum and minimum here. I return *DIM_FLOAT.Last* for the tangent of 90 degrees, and *DIM_FLOAT.First* for the tangent of 270 degrees. If that's not appropriate for your application, feel free to change it.

The second special case is the two-argument arctangent where both arguments are zero. What is the bearing from the origin to the origin? It is undefined. You could say that it is a stupid question that doesn't deserved to be answered, but consider this: People who are trying to drop bombs on you generally try to fly right over your head, and sometimes they succeed. When that happens the elevation is 90 degrees and the azimuth is *Atan(0.0,0.0)*. It could be an important moment in your life and you want the right answer. If you are flying an airplane and pull a vertical loop, there are moments when you are flying straight up or straight down, so your heading is *Atan(0.0,0.0)*.

My first approach to the problem was to define *Atan(0.0,0.0)* to be 0.0 because I wanted to avoid raising an exception. That drove an aircraft simulation nuts when it tried to simulate a loop if the aircraft wasn't

flying due north or due south. I decided it was better to raise the
INVALID_ARGUMENT exception and let the application program handle it. (The aircraft simulation program handled it by using the previous
heading, and that worked fine.) Your situation may require a different
solution, and you are free to do whatever you like with the source code.

2.10.6 Which Way is Up?

The four-quadrant arctangent function is a common cause of programming errors because it is easy to confuse the arguments. To help you
appreciate the problem, let me try to confuse you.

Suppose a position is expressed in polar coordinates. The distance
from the origin is 10 and the angle is 30 degrees. If we need to convert
this to cartesian coordinates, we compute $X = 10 * \cos(30) = 8.66$. Then
we find $Y = 10 * \sin(30) = 5.00$. No problem. But suppose we want to
convert that point back to polar coordinates. Do we use *Atan(8.66,5.00)*
or *Atan(5.00,8.66)*?

The common convention is that *Atan(A1, A2)* returns the arctangent of
A1/A2, so the first argument should be the *Y* component and the second
argument should be the *X* component. So, if the *X* coordinate is 8.66
and the *Y* coordinate is 5.00, the correct angle is found by computing
Atan(5.00,8.66).

Now, what is the bearing of a target 8.66 miles east and 5.00 miles
north? You think it is *Atan(5.00,8.66)*? Think again! *Atan(5.00,8.66)*
yields 30 degrees, but the correct answer is 60 degrees.

Mathematicians compute the angle of a point in polar coordinates
by measuring counterclockwise from the horizontal axis, as shown in
Figure 12. Anyone who has ever used a compass (especially pilots and
radar operators) knows 0 degrees is north and 90 degrees is east. Angles
are measured clockwise from the vertical axis, as shown in Figure 13.
Therefore, the bearing to a target 8.66 miles east and 5.00 miles north is
given by *Atan(8.66,5.00)*.

That is why I called the arguments to the *TRIG.Atan* function
EAST_OR_Y and *NORTH_OR_X*. This makes it easier for me to
remember the correct parameter associations.

Things get even worse in three dimensions because there are so
many different right-handed coordinate systems. Mathematicians like to
use *X* (right), *Y* (ahead), and *Z* (up) vectors. Airborne systems like to
use *NORTH, EAST, DOWN*. Ground-based systems like to use *EAST,
NORTH, UP*. Body-referenced coordinates can be *X',Y',Z'* or *X'',Y'',Z''*
where the major body axes could be aligned with any of those vectors,
depending on the programmer's whim.

Fortunately, Ada allows you to define enumeration types that specify
body directions in meaningful terms. If you want to use an array to

represent a three-dimensional velocity in body coordinates you can do the following:

```
type Body_Coordinates is (BOW, STARBOARD, KEEL);
type Velocities is array(Body_Coordinates)
  of Feet_per_second;
MISSILE_SPEED : Velocities;

MISSILE_SPEED(BOW) := (some_value);
```

You don't have to use arrays to represent three-dimensional quantities. For example, you could use a record like the following one to represent the attitude of the missile.

```
type Attitudes is
  record
      PITCH, YAW, ROLL : Degrees;
  end record;
MISSILE_ORIENTATION  : Attitudes;

MISSILE_ORIENTATION.PITCH := (some_value);
```

In any case, you can avoid confusion by avoiding the use of the ambiguous X, Y, and Z labels for each axis.

2.11 *COORDINATES* PACKAGE

This chapter began by looking at a poor specification for a coordinate-transformation package. It is fitting to end the chapter by applying all we've learned to make it better. Figure 14 shows an improved version of the package specification.

Most of the improvements will show up in the package body, so there isn't too much difference between Figure 14 and Figure 1. The comments telling us that linear distances are measured in feet and that angles are in degrees have been eliminated because they say the same things that the component declarations say. (Ironically, some code-quality metric tools might tell us that the original version is better than the improved version because the original version has more comments.) Replacing the comments with dimensioned data types may not make much difference to human readers, but it makes a big difference to Ada because she can read data types and she can't read comments. This lets her check dimensional consistency. On a large program she is more likely to find errors than a human would.

2.11.1 Comments

Adding comments to an Ada program can be counterproductive, so it is worthwhile to talk about how to comment an Ada program. Many of you have been taught that the more comments a program has, the better it is. That just isn't true. For example, if your program includes the statement **X := A + B;** and you comment that line with the phrase **– –Add A to B to get X** you have made the program worse, not better.

What's wrong with adding a comment like that? Two things are wrong. First, you have repeated information. Whenever you do that, you create an opportunity for contradiction and confusion. Suppose the program doesn't work properly because a third term, C, has to be added to X. Someone discovers the error and changes the code but forgets to change the comment. Then when another maintenance programmer looks at the code to solve another problem, he will get confused because the comment contradicts the code. He may figure the comment is correct and take C out of the equation.

Second, too many frivolous comments can clutter your program so much, you can't easily find the important comments. Once a comment is in a program, it enjoys all the respect and status of any other comment in the program. There is no easy way to tell good comments from bad comments. I've occasionally used a text editor to remove all the comments from someone else's program because there were so many frivolous comments, I couldn't easily find the executable lines of code. In doing so, I probably lost some valuable information, but that information was already lost in the clutter.

Since it is practically impossible to remove bad comments from a program, the only solution to the problem is to not insert them in the first place. Every organization seems to have some internal standard for a header block of comments. These header blocks include things such as the module name, a brief description of what it does, who wrote it, when the last revision was made, and so on. I have my own format, which you have seen in the listings, but I don't insist on any particular header format. Header blocks aren't a problem. They generally contain important information, and since they are at the beginning of the program they can easily be skipped if they don't. Use whatever style of header you like. The comments sprinkled through the listing are the ones that are likely to cause problems.

The nature of the Ada language makes many comments unnecessary. For example, it is important to know which modules depend on each other. In some languages it might be appropriate to include comments telling about these dependencies. This doesn't make sense in Ada because the dependencies are shown by context clauses (i.e., **with LIBRARY_ UNIT;**) and separate clauses (**separate(Main_Program)**). Ada requires these clauses to be at the beginning of every compilation unit, so you don't have to search through the code to find them. If you refrain from excessive *use* clauses, then dot notation will make dependencies obvious in the executable code. For example, if your program is calling the procedure *Normalize* from the package *LIBRARY_UNIT*, your statement will be **LIBRARY_UNIT.Normalize(X);** and there is no need to comment that *Normalize* is found in *LIBRARY_UNIT*.

One thing Ada doesn't do is force you to include information about source file names. This makes it possible for you to write a body stub like **procedure Accumulate is separate;**, which doesn't tell the name of the file containing the source code for *Accumulate*. Ada doesn't care what the name of the source file is. Some Ada implementations may record that information in the library as a courtesy to you, so you can write automatic recompilation tools, but it isn't required by the language. Even if the information is in the library, you shouldn't force the maintenance programmer to run a library utility to find it. Always follow a separate clause with a comment like − − **File ACCUM.ADA**, so people will know where to find the source code.

Ada package specifications provide a top-level view of the services the package provides without a hint at how it works. The comments should be consistent with this policy. Comments describing the implementation of subprograms have no place in a package specification. I like to let subprogram declarations serve as headings. Then I follow them with comments describing what the subprogram does. Sometimes I include samples of how the subprogram should be used. If it can raise an exception, it is important to include comments telling that the subprogram may raise that exception and under what circumstances that might happen. When a package declares user-defined exceptions, I always include comments below the exception declaration that tell what subprograms can raise the exception. I try not to repeat what conditions cause that exception to be raised because that information should be in the comments describing the subprogram. (If many subprograms can raise the same exception, I sometimes save space by using comments below the exception to describe the conditions that cause the exception to be raised and let the subprogram specifications refer to the comments below the exception handler.)

Unlike package specifications, Ada package bodies shouldn't include descriptions of what the subprograms do. At best, those comments would exactly duplicate the comments in the package specification. At worst, they would contradict those comments and confuse the reader. Most often they would have no effect because a rational person wouldn't think to look in a package body for comments describing the purpose of a subprogram. Package bodies should contain comments describing how the subprograms work. These comments shouldn't describe what you are doing because that should be obvious from the code. If you find you need to comment a line like **P** := **GI** − **E;** you should rewrite it as **PROFIT** := **GROSS_INCOME** − **EXPENSES;** to eliminate the need for the comment. Never write a comment that could just as well be expressed as executable code.

Comments should describe why you are doing something. For example, if the package body says **for PORT in 1..MAX_PORTS loop** ... the comment should not say **− − Do the following statements for every input port**. Instead, just before the loop there should be a comment saying **− − We need to check all the input ports to see if any new messages have been received**. This tells the reader why the loop is there and what it is trying to accomplish, rather than the obvious fact that it is a loop.

Good programmers always indent *if* statements and control loops to show structure. They recognize how white space can improve readability. Blank lines can also do the same thing. If a group of three to ten lines cooperate to do a particular operation, use blank lines to separate those statements from the surrounding code. It has the same effect as breaking an essay into paragraphs. When you have isolated a few statements into a paragraph, it usually is appropriate to begin that paragraph with a comment to serve as a topic sentence. This not only helps the maintenance programmer understand your program, it helps you write better code because you will occasionally discover that one of the statements in the paragraph doesn't fit with the topic sentence. This is usually an indication that it belongs someplace else.

Ada will check everything in your program except the comments. That means you have to pay particular attention to them yourself. Be sure that you don't have a lot of useless comments cluttering up your code. Don't use a comment to repeat something that is expressed in Ada statements. Wisely use comments to point to important information, like the name of the file containing a subunit or the names of all the subprograms that can raise a user-defined exception. Use comments near a subprogram declaration to tell what that subprogram does. Use comments inside a subprogram body to describe why it is doing what it is doing. Use comments and white space inside a subprogram body to break it into logical processing steps. If you need comments inside a subprogram body to explain how it works, you need to ask yourself why that isn't obvious from the code, and perhaps rewrite the code to make the comment unnecessary.

2.11.2   Other Improvements in *COORDINATES*

The derivation of type *Feet* forces the distances to be expressed as 32-bit integers (or longer integers with constraints limiting them to 32-bit range). The original version only told us that distances were expressed as integers, but did not fix their length. It used different lengths on different systems. The improved version is more consistent.

The real differences show up in the package bodies. Figure 15 shows the poor version. It works, but it has some problems. Most of the problems have to do with transportability. There is the previously mentioned problem of undefined integer size, and also a reliance on a package found only in the Meridian Ada compiler library. Fortunately, Figure 15 has used dot notation rather than a *use* clause, so a text editor can search for *MATH_LIB* to find all the potentially nonportable statements.

The original package is cluttered with conversion constants (*RADIANS_TO_DEGREES* and *DEGREES_TO_RADIANS*). These are places where errors are likely to creep into the code. It also includes logic to figure out which quadrant to use. At best, this logic was copied out of one of several other application programs that needed a four-quadrant arctangent. At worst, it was written from scratch and took several iterations to get all the bugs out. In either case, it took some duplication of effort.

Figure 15 has some nasty surprises in it. First, it blows up for points more than 8.78 miles from the origin. Although 32 bits can almost represent the number of feet in a round-trip to the moon, 32 bits can only represent 46,340 feet squared. The declaration **R_SQUARED : integer;** is inadequate even on 32-bit machines. Second, the four-quadrant logic returns an angle of 270 degrees when *NORTH* and *EAST* are both zero, instead of raising an *INVALID_ARGUMENT* exception.

The improved version in Figure 16 is much shorter and cleaner. It uses 32-bit integers no matter what computer it is running on, and it is directly transportable to any system that has the *TRIG* package on it. It is shorter because the four-quadrant arctangent is in the *TRIG* package (where it belongs). The reuse of *TRIG.Atan* saves time and improves reliability because the four quadrant logic does not need to be developed and tested again.

In a large program there might be several times when distances are multiplied to compute an area. Then I would write a function that multiplies two distances in *Feet* and returns a floating-point type *Sq_ft*. I would also write a function that takes the square root of an object of type *Sq_ft* and returns *Feet*. In this little example, distances are only squared once, so it isn't worth the trouble to write a special function. Instead, I move into the dimensionless number domain to calculate the square root of the sum of the squares. Since Ada can't check these statements for me, I bracket them with comments to draw my attention to them.

The final version of the *COORDINATES* package gives us a library unit that defines all the data types the application program is likely to need. It defines *Feet* for linear distances, *Rectangular_points* for Cartesian coordinates, and *Polar_points* for polar coordinates. (A realistic version of this package would use three-dimensional coordinates and would also include more dimensional data types.)

This package specification should be given careful consideration, because most of the other modules in the application program will depend upon this package for type definitions. If you change *COOR-DINATES*, you will have to recompile every module that depends on it. That's a two-edged sword. You won't want to add data types to the package because you cut yourself every time you do, suffering the pain of recompilation with every change. But the sword also protects you because it tells you which modules need to be reexamined in light of your recent change in type definitions.

2.11.3 *use* Clauses

I avoid *use* clauses whenever practical. Special emphasis should be placed on the word *practical* because it was intentionally chosen instead of *possible*. It is always possible to avoid a *use* clause, but I feel there are times when it isn't practical.

I like to avoid *use* clauses because I like to remind myself which package defined the type or subprogram. It shows me exactly where the dependencies are. My general rule is, don't use the *use*.

There are exceptions to the rule. Some packages, like *TEXT_IO*, are so common that I don't need to be reminded about them. A statement like **TEXT_IO.new_line;** is no more informative than **new_line;**, so I commonly **use TEXT_IO;**. But, if I have added a line like **TEXT_IO.put_line**("Section 1 entered"); for diagnostic purposes, then I retain the dot notation to make it easy to take the diagnostic line out.

Another package that is so common it doesn't need dot notation is *STANDARD_INTEGERS*. There is real motivation for **use STANDARD_INTEGERS;** because it makes arithmetic visible. That makes it possible to write **X := Y + Z;** if *X*, *Y*, and *Z* are all *STANDARD_INTEGERS.Integer_32*. If you don't use a *use* clause, you have to write **X := STANDARD_INTEGERS.**"+"**(Y,Z);**. I think that distracts from the program logic, especially if it is part of a complex equation. True, you could use renaming declarations to rename all the arithmetic functions, but that is longer and no clearer than the following *use* clause and comment.

```
use STANDARD_INTEGERS;
-- makes 32 bit arithmetic operators visible
```

I/O UTILITIES

One of Ada's unusual features is that she has no I/O instructions. That's because Ada was originally designed to be a language for embedded computers. Embedded computers typically don't have the same kind of peripherals as general-purpose computers do. The output peripherals on embedded computers are usually things like missile control surfaces and high explosives. Inputs come from infrared seekers, doppler filter banks, and push buttons. If Ada had the usual I/O services, it would be necessary to design a warhead with the same software interface as a card punch.

Since it is impossible to predict appropriate interfaces for all the bizarre I/O devices Ada is likely to use, she was given language features that make it possible to design custom I/O services. Packages, tasking, and the low-level interfaces described in chapter 13 of MIL-STD-1815A, can be used to interface Ada to anything you can imagine.

Embedded computer applications are unique, so it is unlikely I could write reusable embedded-computer I/O routines with broad appeal. General-purpose applications, on the other hand, often involve an ASCII interface to a CRT terminal. This section, therefore, contains some I/O routines I think you will find useful in general-purpose applications. Although these packages don't often apply directly to embedded-computer applications, the lessons learned from this section do.

3.1 *ASCII_UTILITIES* PACKAGE

I/O often involves ASCII data. File names are specified by ASCII strings. Numbers are displayed as a string of ASCII characters. Users enter a sequence of ASCII digits that must be converted to numbers. The *ASCII_UTILITIES* package (Listings 11 through 16) contains some handy routines that manipulate ASCII data.

3.1.1 *IMAGE* Attribute

Ada has a predefined attribute called *IMAGE*, which takes a discrete value (an integer or an enumeration value) and converts it to an ASCII character string. It simplifies I/O operations because you can **put(integer'IMAGE(X))**; to output the integer *X*, without having to instantiate *INTEGER_IO*.

I often find it annoying that the *IMAGE* attribute for integers adds a single blank space on the beginning of the string when the number is positive. This causes problems when I try to insert numbers in the middle of a line of text. If I leave a space before the number, then it appears that there are two spaces in front of positive numbers. If I don't leave a space, then a negative number appears to be hyphenated to the word immediately before it.

The *IMAGE* attribute for integers also has the sometimes annoying characteristic of returning a string with an unpredictable length. When it converts a number to a character string, it uses only as many characters as it needs. This often is desirable because it frequently is necessary to insert a number in the middle of a line of text, and it would look funny if there were lots of leading spaces. There are other times, though, when you want the number to be converted to a string with a certain number of characters regardless of the value of the number. For example, when converting the internal representation of 14 February 1988, to the eight-character string "02/14/88" for output, you want two characters each for the month, day, and year. As another example, you might want to give the file containing the data from flight number 375 the name "FL00375.DAT". You will need a routine to convert flight numbers to a five-character string with leading zeros.

Later in this section, you will see a package called the *VIRTUAL_TERMINAL*. The first version of this package body depended on the *IMAGE* attribute. To move the cursor to line seven, column fifteen, it was necessary to generate the string *ASCII.ESC* & *"[7;15H"*. Figure 17 shows all the trouble I had to go through to get rid of leading spaces and adapt to the variable length strings produced by the *IMAGE* attribute.

These little quirks in the *IMAGE* attribute make it awkward to use in many applications, so I wrote the *Image* function in *ASCII_UTILITIES*. It does the same thing the *IMAGE* attribute does for integers, but it gives me the control I need over the length of the string and leading characters. Figure 18 shows how much easier it is to use the *Image* function than the *IMAGE* attribute.

Many people are surprised to discover the *IMAGE* attribute is not defined for the type *float*. That's because the attribute is defined only for discrete types, and type *float* is not a discrete type. I can understand why the LRM didn't require an *IMAGE* attribute for all data types, because the image of a composite data type can be complicated, especially if it is a record that has components that are composite data types. That doesn't mean it is impossible to define an *IMAGE* attribute for composite data types. In fact, Ada debuggers have to be able to display the contents of composite data types, and I have seen a couple that use aggregate notation to do that.

The lack of an *IMAGE* attribute for real data types is a nuisance if you want to output real numbers. You have no choice but to instantiate *FLOAT_IO*. Since I don't often use *TEXT_IO*, I didn't like that choice. Compilers are starting to get to the point where they can eliminate dead code, so linking all of *TEXT_IO* just to get a couple of string conversions may not be as bad as it used to be, but I still don't like to do it. The *Fixed_Image* and *Float_Image* functions in *ASCII_UTILITIES* give you better alternatives than instantiating *FLOAT_IO*.

The *Fixed_Image* function will display a floating-point number in fixed notation. You can select the number of characters before and after the decimal point. If you don't specify these values, the default is the minimum number of characters before the decimal point and two characters after it.

The *Float_Image* function displays real numbers in exponential form. I thought about designing it so that it would allow you to specify the number of digits before the decimal point, but decided against it. When people output numbers in exponential form, they don't normally stick them in the middle of a line of text, and they don't normally want a variable number of digits before the decimal point. Numbers printed in exponential notation usually appear in columns on printouts, and I suspect people often just glance at the single digit in front of the decimal and at the exponent, to get an idea of the magnitude of the number. The numbers should neatly line up in the columns, so I precede the number with a leading space if it is positive. There isn't any way I can predict how many digits should be printed after the decimal point, so I made that a parameter. (I set the default to five digits to enforce my disposition toward six-digit floating-point numbers.)

I considered a single image function that would figure out if the user wanted fixed- or floating-point format, just as *FLOAT_IO* does. I decided not to for three reasons. First, combining the two routines results in a more complicated, and therefore less reliable, routine. Two simple routines are less likely to contain an error and are easier to test than a single complicated one. Second, combining two similar but different routines sometimes forces some design trade-offs. For example, I wanted an *AFT* default of 2 for fixed format and 5 for exponential format. If I combined them I would have had to pick 2 or 5, or force the programmer to supply a value every time it is used. Third, the two names *Fixed_Image* and *Float_Image* make the program more readable. The reader doesn't have to know to look at the *EXP* field to see if it is zero or not, to tell him if the number will be printed in fixed- or floating-point format.

I considered making all the image functions in *ASCII_UTILITIES* generic but decided not to. There isn't any need for generics. The *Dimensionless* functions can be used to convert dimensioned data types to *Integer_32* or *float* and normal type conversions can be used to convert other special numeric data types to *Integer_32* or *float*. Then the appropriate image function can be used on the equivalent *Integer_32* or *float* value.

There isn't a predefined *IMAGE* attribute that will convert an integer from 0 to 9 (or 0 to F in hexadecimal) to the corresponding ASCII character. This would be a handy attribute to have if you wanted to write a utility program that outputs files in octal or hexadecimal, or you wanted to print address locations in octal or hexadecimal. Several years ago I published a function in the *Journal of Pascal, Ada & Modula-2* that fills this need. In those days I called it *ASCII_Code_For*, but to make it consistent with the other similar functions in *ASCII_UTILITIES*, it is now called *Image*. This function doesn't let you specify the length of the return string because it doesn't return a string, it returns a single character. Instead, it has a second parameter to let you specify the numeric base. This is necessary for it to check for digits out of range.

3.1.2 Qualified Expressions

There is one minor disadvantage to renaming the *ASCII_Code_For* routine to *Image*. It causes a compile-time error when you do something like the following:

```
TEXT_IO.put(Image(X,8));
```

Error messages are different for every compiler, so I can't tell you exactly what your compiler will say, but it will almost certainly contain the word "ambiguous." The problem is that *TEXT_IO.put* is overloaded for strings and characters. The *ASCII_UTILITIES* package contains two functions called *Image*, one of which returns a string and the other a character. Ada can't tell whether you want to convert *X* to an eight character string and output the string, or if you want to convert *X* to an octal character and output the character. You have made an ambiguous statement and she refuses to try to guess what you mean.

There are three simple solutions. The first is to change the name of the character *Image* function back to *ASCII_Code_For*. I don't like that solution. (If I did, I wouldn't have changed it in the first place.) The second solution is to break the statement into two statements, making it clear what you want to do. For example, if you want to print an eight character string image, you could do the following:

```
   S : string(1..8);
begin
   S := Image(X,8);
   TEXT_IO.put(S);
```

If you wanted to convert *X* to an octal digit you could do it this way.

```
   C : character;
begin
   C := Image(X,8);
   TEXT_IO.put(C);
```

I prefer a third solution, which uses a qualified expression. The qualified expression is a rarely used Ada feature, but it comes in handy in situations like these. It is a way for you to tell Ada what you really mean. In this case it looks like the following:

```
TEXT_IO.put(string'(Image(X,8)));
```

or

```
TEXT_IO.put(character'(Image(X,8)));
```

The function *Image(X,8)* can return either a string or a character. By enclosing it in parentheses and qualifying it with a type, you tell Ada which one you want. Knowing the type of data returned by *Image*, she can select the correct *put* procedure.

3.1.3 *VALUE* Attribute

The *VALUE* attribute is the inverse of the *IMAGE* attribute, and it is also useful for I/O operations. For example, you can use **get_line(TEXT, LENGTH); X := integer'VALUE(TEXT(1. .LENGTH));** to read an integer value from the terminal.

I have no complaint with Ada's standard *VALUE* attribute for discrete types, so I haven't written another version of it. The deficiency is that *VALUE*, like *IMAGE*, is only defined for discrete types. Ada does not have a *VALUE* attribute for real numbers.

If she did, I probably wouldn't like it. Ada would probably be fussy about the format, just as she is for real literals in a program. That's fine for programmers. If a programmer wants to specify a real value, he should be smart enough to know the correct syntax. You can't expect that kind of knowledge from a user. If you write software for military applications, you have to remember that the lack of a degree in computer science does not disqualify someone from joining the ranks of enlisted personnel. If you prompt a marine with "Enter the distance to the enemy position (in miles)", you had better be prepared to accept "12" as an answer. If you insist on "1.20e01" the marine is more likely to smash the weapon to bits than to figure out what you mean by "Data Entry Error!".

The *Value* function is complicated because it accepts any reasonable input and converts it to a floating point number. Real computer scientists will probably find this tolerance offensive, but that's the way it has to be in the battlefield. (If I were writing this function for use in a compiler, I would have required strict Ada syntax. You are permitted, even encouraged, to modify the *Value* function to make it less tolerant if that would make it more appropriate for your application.)

There is a *Value* function in *ASCII_UTILITIES* that converts a character in the range '0'..'9' or 'A'..'F' to a number from 0 to 15. It is the inverse of the single character *Image* function. It checks to make sure the input character is valid for the numeric base specified. The default is, of course, base ten.

You shouldn't need a qualified expression to distinguish the two value functions because both the input and output types are different. It is hard to imagine an ambiguous situation that might occur naturally, although I'm sure you could create one if you are devious enough.

3.1.4 Short-Circuit Control Forms

I want to draw your attention to the short-circuit control forms in Listing 16. Somewhere near line 40 you will find a section of code that looks like

```
-- reject special cases
if I < S_LAST then
   if S(I..I+1) = "-." or S(I..I+1) = "+." then
     case S(I+2) is
        when '0' .. '9' =>
           null;
        when others =>
            raise CONSTRAINT_ERROR;
     end case;
   end if;
end if;
```

This section of code is designed to accept representations such as "$-.7$" and "$+.05$" but to reject "$-.e$" and "$+.$". The variable *S_LAST* represents the last nonblank character in the string and will be equal to *S'LAST* if there are no trailing blanks.

Suppose the string is "   +.". The pointer *I* has skipped over the leading blanks and is pointing to the plus sign. It is true that $S(I..I + 1) =$ "$+.$". When the *case* structure tries to evaluate $S(I+2)$, which is outside the range of *S*, a *CONSTRAINT_ERROR* will be raised. That's fine, because that's what I would do if $S(I+2)$ existed and was not a digit. The *CONSTRAINT_ERROR* isn't a problem, rather it is a beneficial side effect that I have taken advantage of.

That isn't always the case. Consider this section of code just a little farther down the listing. I have replaced the short-circuit control form (*and then*) with the usual *and* statement to illustrate a potential problem.

```
-- compute whole part
if S(I) = '.' then
   WHOLE := 0.0;
```

```
else
  FIRST := I;
  while I <= S_LAST and S(I) in '0'..'9' loop
    I := I+1;
  end loop;
  LAST := I-1;
  WHOLE := float(Integer_32'VALUE(
    S(FIRST..LAST)));
end if;
```

This part of the routine finds the first and last characters of the whole part of the number. That is, if the number is "−123.45", the routine will leave *FIRST* pointing to the number 1 and *LAST* pointing to the number 3, so *S(FIRST..LAST)* will be the string "123". This will work without error. Suppose, however, the string was "123". *FIRST* points to the 1, but *CONSTRAINT_ERROR* might be raised looking for the 3.

The problem is in the statement *while I <= S_LAST and S(I) in '0'..'9' loop* when *I = S_LAST+1*. If the program tries to evaluate *S(S_LAST+1)* to see if it is in '0'..'9', *CONSTRAINT_ERROR* will be raised. You can't be sure the program will check *I <= S_LAST* and realize the whole expression must be false before finding the character in *S(S_LAST+1)* because section 4.5 paragraph 5 of the LRM says that they are "evaluated in some order that is not defined by the language."

The solution is to use the short-circuit control form. The statement *while I <= S_LAST and then S(I) in '0'..'9' loop* tells the computer to evaluate *I <= S_LAST* first, and then evaluate *S(I)* only if the first part is true. You will find several examples of the short circuit control form *and then* in the *ASCII_UTILITIES.Value* function.

3.1.5 Character Conversions

If you ask a user to input a file name, you may need to convert it to all upper-case (or all lower-case) letters. You might want to write a spelling checker, which finds words in a dictionary file, and you don't care if the words are capitalized or not. You may want to remove the underscores from the image of an enumeration type before printing it. The *ASCII_UTILITIES* package contains routines called *Upper_Case*, *Lower_Case*, and *Change* that will do this for you.

These text processing functions can be used in combination to make an enumeration output look prettier. For example, a poker program may have an enumeration type with the value *THREE_OF_A_KIND* that must be displayed. The *IMAGE* attribute first converts it to the string *"THREE_OF_A_KIND"*. The *Lower_Case* string function can then convert all the letters to lower case, and the *Change* string function can replace the underlines with blank spaces. This produces "three of a kind". If you like, you can use the *Upper_Case* character function to capitalize the first character to get "Three of a kind".

3.1.6 Ada Strings

Ada's fixed strings are hard for some people to get used to. If you are used to programming in other languages, you probably think dynamic (variable length) strings are essential. I thought so. That's why I published an improved version of Sylvan Rubin's dynamic string package.[1,2] But the more I used dynamic strings, the more I realized they were a bad idea. I discovered that, sooner or later, you had to decide how many characters the string could hold. Discovering it later usually caused trouble. I abandoned the use of dynamic strings and now exclusively use fixed strings.

When using fixed strings, it occasionally is necessary to add spaces to the end of a short string to fill out a variable that was declared as a longer string. It might also be necessary to truncate a long string to make it fit in a shorter string. The *String_Copy* procedure was designed to do this.

String_Copy can be useful when dealing with enumeration images. For example, if **type Colors is (RED, GREEN, BLUE);** and you use *Colors'IMAGE* to convert a value to a character string, the result may be 3, 4, or 5 characters. If you want the result to always be five characters, you can do the following:

```
type Colors is (RED, GREEN, BLUE);
  X : Colors;
  S : string(1..5);
begin
  String_Copy(FROM => Colors'IMAGE'(X),
              TO   => S);
```

Consider the poker example again. The value of the hand might be *NOTHING, A_PAIR, TWO_PAIR, THREE_OF_A_KIND, A_STRAIGHT, A_FLUSH, A_FULL_HOUSE, FOUR_OF_A_KIND, A_STRAIGHT_FLUSH,* or *A_ROYAL_FLUSH*. The length of the image of the value could be six to fifteen characters long. Figure 19 shows how the text-processing functions can format the output for display. (Note that Figure 19 shows what you will get if you direct the output to the printer, and what you *should* get if you direct the output to a CRT screen. I discovered that something in MS-DOS or my EGA card substitutes

[1] Dr. Sylvan Rubin, "Dynamic String Functions in Ada," *Journal of Pascal, Ada & Modula-2*, Vol. 3, No. 6, Nov./Dec. 1984.

[2] Do-While Jones, "Ada Dynamic Strings Revisited Part 2," *Journal of Pascal, Ada & Modula-2*, Vol. 5, No. 3, May/June 1986.

blanks for nulls, because all the commas line up vertically if I look at the output on the CRT.)

3.2   *MONEY_UTILITIES* PACKAGE

Money is an important part of our daily life, and naturally it becomes a subject of a variety of accounting programs. There are programs that compute the mortgage payments, tax liabilities, and interest on savings, to name a few. The *MONEY* package (Listings 17 and 18) is useful for Ada programs that do financial calculations in American dollars. It is included in this section because it contains *Image* and *Value* functions, needed for input and output of monetary figures.

Notice that the *MONEY* package builds on the concepts introduced in the previous section. We don't want to multiply dollars times dollars to get dollars squared, and if we did, we certainly wouldn't want to assign it to an object of type *Dollars*. Therefore, we should use a dimensioned data type to represent monetary values. The question is, which one?

Fixed-point is a logical choice to represent dollars, but I explained why that isn't a good idea when I told why I never wrote a *FIXED_UNITS* package. A floating-point data type could be used to represent dollars. If we do that, the accuracy will vary with the size of the amount because there will be a fixed number of bits to represent the whole number of dollars plus the fractional dollars (cents). Therefore the dollar figures would be accurate to a certain percentage, but not to a certain number of cents. The accuracy is much worse than expected if calculations compute a small difference between large sums of money. Floating-point isn't a good choice for representing money.

Practical arguments aside, the real reason you shouldn't use a fixed- or floating-point data type to represent money is that money is a discrete quantity rather than a continuous one. If money was specified in terms of ounces of gold instead of individual pennies, then a real variable would be appropriate for money. When working with money, we are really dealing with a finite number of individual, countable things, so an integer representation is the philosophically correct one.

If we decide to use an integer data type to represent cents, then we must decide how many bits to use. Sixteen bits would allow us to represent values from −$327.68 to $327.67. That's far too small. Thirty-two bits range from −$21,474,836.48 to $21,474,836.47. While this isn't sufficient range to represent national budgets, it is certainly large enough to figure the mortgage on any house I am likely to buy.

Having made this decision, the *MONEY* package declares a data type, *Cents*, which is a dimensioned 32-bit integer. It also provides *Image* and *Value* functions to convert between strings and *Cents*. Notice that even if I had written the *ASCII_UTILITIES.Image* and

ASCII_UTILITIES.Value as generic functions, I could not have instantiated them for type *Cents* because I want to be able to use a decimal point, a dollar sign, and commas in the string.

The *Width* function tells the string size required to represent the value. This is essential for declaring strings of the proper size.

Figure 20 is a simple program that demonstrates how to use the *MONEY* package. It prompts the user to enter the price of an item, the sales tax rate, and prints the total cost to the customer. This isn't a terribly useful program, but it does show how to declare objects of type *Cents* and shows how to input and output them.

Cents is derived from *Units* in *INTEGER_UNITS*. I can multiply *Cents* by dimensionless integers, but I can't multiply them by dimensionless real types because there isn't a multiply operator for *Units* times *float* in *INTEGER_UNITS*. That wasn't an oversight. I once had a floating-point multiply in *INTEGER_UNITS*, but I decided to take it out. I wanted to force myself to think about how to handle the fractional results that are likely to occur.

When *PRICE* is multiplied by *RATE*, the resulting *TAX* may include fractional pennies. In California, sales tax is rounded to the nearest cent. If I lived in a state that insisted on rounding any fraction of a cent of sales tax to the next higher cent, I could have written that into the multiplication algorithm shown in Figure 20.

The body of Figure 20 shows how I used the *Value* function in *MONEY* to convert the user's entry from a character string to the *PRICE* in *Cents*. If you compile and run this example you might have some fun trying experiments. You will find that you can enter a price of $5.00, $5, 5, 5.0, $05.00, or several other ways you might imagine. The *MONEY.-Value* function lets you embed dollar signs and commas in the price. If you try to enter a tax rate with a dollar sign in it, you will get a *CONSTRAINT_ERROR*. That's because the rate is a pure number, interpreted by *ASCII_UTILITIES.Value*, not *MONEY.Value*.

I didn't want to make this example too complicated and distract from the use of the *MONEY* package, so I didn't check for errors (like negative tax rates). If you want to fool around with this example, you might try detecting the presence of a percent sign in the *TEXT* string and dividing the *RATE* by 100 only if the user entered a percent sign.

I put a block structure in the middle of the *Sales_Tax* program just to show you how you could use *MONEY.Width* to declare a string like *TAX_STRING*. I don't normally do that. I usually create the strings on the fly, as I did when I printed *COST*. (There I didn't bother to create *COST_STRING*. I just put the *MONEY.Image* function inside the *put* procedure.)

I used *TEXT_IO* as a user interface in this example. I followed every *get_line* with a *new_line*. That may or may not cause a blank line after each input, depending on your operating system. If you leave the *new_line* calls out, you may (or may not) have superimposed input prompts. This is just one of many problems you will discover if you try to use *TEXT_IO* as a user interface. Fortunately, you don't have to use *TEXT_IO* if you don't want to. That's our next topic.

3.3   *TEXT_IO* PACKAGE

When most Ada programmers think of I/O, the first thing that comes to mind is *TEXT_IO*. Although Ada doesn't have any built-in I/O instructions, the language designers realized that Ada would be used for more applications than just embedded computers. They knew many general purpose applications would require interfaces to common peripherals (disks and terminals), so they filled Chapter 14 of the LRM with some standard I/O packages. These packages, such as *TEXT_IO*, are provided for your convenience. You may use them if you like, but you don't have to.

I often use *TEXT_IO* in the code examples I publish. This should not be considered an endorsement of *TEXT_IO*. The fact is, I don't like *TEXT_IO* very much. I use it because all Ada programmers are familiar with it. If I used *SCROLL_TERMINAL* or *FORM_TERMINAL*, the unusual user interface would distract readers from the point of the example.

3.3.1   What's Wrong With *TEXT_IO*

I don't really have many complaints with *TEXT_IO* as an interface to text files, but it makes a terrible user interface. *TEXT_IO* treats the user's terminal just like a file, and that creates input problems. Files never make mistakes, so they don't need a rub-out key. Files never enter passwords that they don't want echoed to the screen. Files never want to insert or delete text. Files never want to clear a screen or move a cursor. Files never realize the program has run amok and try to send an unsolicited *CTRL-C* to stop the process. Users often want to do all of these things, but *TEXT_IO* won't let them because it wasn't designed to support users.

The second problem with *TEXT_IO* is that it is heavily dependent upon the host operating system. That means it works differently on different computers, which makes it difficult to move programs from one computer to another. For example, a program containing the line **TEXT_IO.put_line(OUTPUT_FILE,"Some Text");** may write "<LF> Some Text<CR>" or "Some Text<CR><LF>", depending on how the operating-system service writes lines of text. This causes minor, but annoying, problems when you write a file on one computer and try to read it on another.

You get some nastier surprises when you instantiate *INTEGER_IO* for integers and then call **get(X)**; to read the integer *X*. Suppose while entering *X*, the user types the wrong character and uses the rub-out key to delete it. Some operating-system calls will respond to the editing command and pass the corrected number *X* to *INTEGER_IO* for processing. Other operating-system calls will just leave the rub-out character in the middle of the string of digits. *INTEGER_IO* will recognize that rub out is not a decimal digit and raise *DATA_ERROR*, which at best will prompt the user to enter the number again.

Even if the user doesn't make a typing error, there are still problems. *INTEGER_IO.get(X)* will read all the characters up to, but not including, the end of line marker. These characters will be correctly converted to the number *X*, but the input buffer pointer will be sitting just in front of the end of the line marker. If you then call *get_line(TEXT,LENGTH)*, it will return a null string. You have to remember to write **get(X);skip_line;** every time you get an integer.

Since input-data editing may or may not be done by the operating system called by the *get* procedure, you never can tell if *CTRL-X* will erase a whole line or if backspace will be the same as delete. These things all combine to frustrate the user and make Ada appear to be a user-hostile language.

I got fed up with *TEXT_IO* in a hurry and wrote a set of replacement user interfaces. These packages are called *VIRTUAL_TERMINAL*, *SCROLL_TERMINAL,* and *FORM_TERMINAL.* They don't have a lot of state-of-the-art bells and whistles (like graphics and pop-up windows) because they have to run on "glass teletype" terminals, but they do provide a portable, consistent, friendly user interface.

3.4 *VIRTUAL_ TERMINAL* PACKAGE

Terminals are notoriously inconsistent when it comes to control codes. They all have different control sequences for clearing the screen and moving the cursor. The *VIRTUAL_TERMINAL* hides all these differences. The package specification is shown in Listing 19.

3.4.1   Guaranteed Functionality

As you can see, it supports a screen with 79 columns and 23 lines. Everybody knows terminals always have at least 80 columns, but the terminal's response after the 80th column has been printed is uncertain. Some terminals stay at column 80 and overprint the last character entered. Other terminals automatically generate a carriage-return/line-feed sequence and go to the next line. Often the action after the 80th character is programmable. On the other hand, all terminals treat columns 1 through 79 the same. I was willing to sacrifice one column to avoid portability problems. That's also the reason why I used a conservative 23 lines, even though common American terminals have 24 or 25 lines. A 23-line, 79-column screen is the most guaranteed functionality I can expect from every CRT.

The *VIRTUAL_ TERMINAL* has 4 cursor control (arrow) keys, 20 function keys, and the *INSERT, DELETE, TAB* and *BACK_ TAB* keys. Not all terminals have all these keys, so provisions have been made for control characters to simulate these 28 special keys. I'm aware that many terminals have more special keys than these, but I'm designing for maximum portability, not maximum performance. Even with this limited capability and designing the package with portability in mind, .there are problems porting the *VIRTUAL_ TERMINAL* to DEC terminals on VAX/VMS. (These problems are described in a later section.)

The 20 function keys are converted to two-character control strings. Each string begins with *CONTROL-F* and is followed by a character '1' through '9' or 'A' through 'K'). The remaining eight keys are converted to a single control character. (Refer to the *get* procedure specification in Listing 19 to see what they are.) Therefore, those 8 keys can be simulated by entering the control code. For example, if a keyboard lacks a *DOWN* arrow key, the user can use *CONTROL-D* instead.

3.4.2 Information Hiding

The *VIRTUAL_ TERMINAL* specification gives you a procedure that clears the screen, as well as procedures that position the cursor. These procedures hide the control sequences used by the physical terminal from the application program. This information hiding is the key to portability.

The *VIRTUAL_ TERMINAL* needs three services from the underlying operating system: (1) send a single character to the screen, (2) get a character from the keyboard without echoing it, and (3) find out if there are any unprocessed keystrokes. Every operating system does this differently, and the *VIRTUAL_ TERMINAL* body hides these differences from any application program that uses it.

3.4.2.1 Alsys *VIRTUAL_ TERMINAL* body.

If you are using the Alsys compiler on an IBM PC AT compatible system, these three services are all provided by the Alsys *DOS* package. The *VIRTUAL_ TERMINAL* package body that works for Alsys programs is shown in Listing 20. The procedure *DOS.Display_ Char* sends a character to the display. The procedures for clearing the screen and moving the cursor can use *DOS.Display_ Char* because it will pass all ASCII characters (even *ESC*) to the display. (I point this out here because it is different from the Meridian implementation of the *DOS* interface.)

The function *DOS.Read_ Kbd_ Direct_No_ Echo* gets characters from the keyboard directly (that is, without interpreting control sequences) and without echoing them to the screen. The *get* procedure uses this function to fetch keystrokes. It converts the special keys to the standard control keys before passing them to the application program.

The *Keyboard_ Data_ Available* function simply renames *DOS.- Kbd_ Data_ Available*. Notice I didn't use the *rename* statement because I would have had to have put that in the package specification. I wanted to keep the package specification the same for all implementations and just change the body. I hope that the global optimizer will remove the double call for me. (It doesn't really matter if it does or doesn't because human reaction time is much slower than the few wasted microseconds in the double function call.)

The control procedures use the *put* procedure to send terminal-specific control codes. For example, *Clear_ Screen* uses *put* to send the control string *ASCII.ESC* & *"[2J"* to the screen. The cursor control procedures build similar strings and use *put* to send them to the display. The exact form of the control string depends on the hardware you are using, so you will probably have to change the escape sequences if you are using a different terminal. That's why you need different bodies for different systems.

The *Move_ Cursor_ To* procedure is interesting. It needs to construct the control string *ASCII.ESC* & *'['* & *L* & *';'* & *C* & *'H'*, where *L* is the string representation of the *LINE* number and *C* is a string representing the *COL*. There can be no embedded blanks. You've already seen Figure 17, which shows all the trouble I had to go through to move the cursor before I had the *ASCII_ UTILITIES.Image* function.

The *get* procedure is a little more complicated than you might expect. It clearly does a lot more than just get the keystroke. It has to check to see if the keystroke is one of the special keys. If it is, then *get* converts it to the standard control code. On the IBM PC AT the special keys are sent as a two-character code. The first code is always 00 and the second code is a unique number. For example, the *LEFT* arrow key is 00 75. The *RIGHT* arrow key is 00 77. The *get* procedure recognizes the 00 as a special-key flag and then reads the second number to find out which key it is.

If the special key is a function key in the range from 1 to 20, the *get* procedure returns *CONTROL_F* and stores the number (1 to 20) in a hidden variable *F_ KEY*. The application program can get this number by calling the function *Function_ Key*. It is possible that the terminal doesn't have function keys, and the user simulated the function key by pressing *CONTROL_F* followed by a letter or digit. Since the computer is probably faster than the user, there is a danger that the application program will recognize the *CONTROL_F* input and call *Function_ Key* before the user has a chance to press the letter or digit. That's why

F_KEY is reset to 0 each time it is read. If the *Function_Key* function finds that *F_KEY* is 0, it knows the user hasn't pressed the letter or digit yet and waits to read the next keystroke.

3.4.2.2 Meridian *VIRTUAL_TERMINAL* body.

The Meridian version of the package body is shown in Listing 21. It shows how different two implementations on the same machine can be. Instead of a general-purpose package like the Alsys *DOS* package, Meridian sells several special-purpose utility packages. If you know a lot about MS-DOS, you can use the *INTERRUPT* package to access MS-DOS directly. That may be too complicated for some programmers, so Meridian has some less flexible, but simpler, user-interface packages. Two of these packages are *TTY* and *CURSOR*.

The *TTY* package calls *put* to send a single character to the display. It seems to be just like the Alsys *DOS.Display_Char*, but it isn't. If you try to use *TTY.put* to send *ASCII.ESC* & *"[2J"* to the display to clear the screen, it won't work. It filters out the *ESC* and just writes *[2J* on the screen. Similarly, *ASCII.ESC* & *"[C"* won't move the cursor right one space. That's why I had to use special routines like *TTY.Clear_Screen* and *CURSOR.Right* in the Meridian body.

The *TTY.get* procedure is similar to the Alsys *DOS. Read_Keyboard_Direct_No_Echo* function. The *TTY.get* procedure has two Boolean parameters, *DIRECT* and *NO_ECHO*, which must both be set to *TRUE* to achieve the desired effect.

Finally, the *TTY.Char_Ready* function is effectively renamed to *Keyboard_Data_Available* by enclosing it in a function body.

If you look at the *Move_Cursor_To* procedure and compare it with the Alsys version, you will see an offset has been subtracted. That's because Alsys counts rows and columns starting with 1, and Meridian starts counting at 0. If you carefully compare the two bodies, you will find additional small differences. The important point to make is that all of these differences would appear in every application program if they weren't carefully confined to the *VIRTUAL_TERMINAL* body.

3.4.3   Visual Attributes

Terminals usually have different visual attributes. That is, the characters can be bright or dim, blinking or steady, normal or reverse video. An interesting exercise is to make a copy of *VIRTUAL_TERMINAL* Version 1 and rename the copy Version 2. Then modify Version 2 to include attribute-setting procedures called *Use_Bright, Use_Dim, Use_Blinking,* and so on. You may want to add Boolean functions *Is_Bright, Is_Dim,* and so on that tell the current status of the visual attributes.

3.4.4 *VIRTUAL_TERMINAL* Uses

The *VIRTUAL_TERMINAL* can be used for screen-oriented displays. It is handy whenever you want to move the cursor all over the screen and write text fragments in different places. You'll see an example of this later in this section in the *FORM_TERMINAL.Create* procedure.

Although the *VIRTUAL_TERMINAL* can be used as an end product, that isn't really its main use. The *VIRTUAL_TERMINAL* is most valuable as a portable foundation that can be used as the base for a more useful terminal package. You are about to see two such packages, *SCROLL_TERMINAL* and *FORM_TERMINAL*. These two packages are built on top of *VIRTUAL_TERMINAL*, so it isn't necessary to have different bodies for every implementation. If you can port the VIRTUAL_TERMINAL to work with a different physical terminal or different operating system, then you have ported *SCROLL_TERMINAL* and *FORM_TERMINAL* as well.

3.5 *SCROLL_TERMINAL* PACKAGE

The *SCROLL_TERMINAL* is a portable, general purpose interface. It is called "scroll" because new data is printed at the bottom of the screen, causing old data to scroll off the top.

3.5.1 Reusability and Consistency

The user interface often is one of the most complicated parts of an application program. That makes it an important candidate for reuse. After all, isn't it better to reuse the components that are hardest to write than to reuse trivial ones?

Auto manufacturers recognize that people are creatures of habit, so they put controls where people expect them to be. Maybe the steering column isn't the best place for the turn signal, but any automaker who moved it to a "better" place would have trouble selling cars. Unfortunately, many programmers don't have the same good sense that automakers have. Every time they write a program, they redesign the user interface. Sometimes they use *TAB* to advance to the next item on a menu, other times they use the *RIGHT* arrow key to do that. Sometimes backspace acts as a delete, other times it doesn't. It can drive a user nuts.

Windows are becoming popular and are starting to put an end to unique interfaces. When application programs use commercially available window products, they not only benefit by reusing tested user interfaces, they also present a familiar interface to the user. A complete window package with graphics and a mouse interface is too complicated to be included in a book of intermediate Ada examples, but *SCROLL_*

TERMINAL gives you the same benefits of reuse and consistency. It is a simple, standard user interface which can be used by a variety of application programs.

3.5.2 Layering

Often it is a good idea to build device handlers layer upon layer. That's what I've done here. The *SCROLL_TERMINAL* (Listing 22) is built on the *VIRTUAL_TERMINAL*, which hides hardware specific differences. There is no need for special *SCROLL_TERMINAL* bodies for each of the different implementations. The *SCROLL_TERMINAL* has the same number of lines and columns as the *VIRTUAL_TERMINAL* and propagates the *VIRTUAL_TERMINAL.PANIC* exception by renaming it. Therefore, the application program doesn't need to know that there is a *VIRTUAL_TERMINAL* under the *SCROLL_TERMINAL*.

3.5.3 *SCROLL_TERMINAL* Features

The *SCROLL_TERMINAL* boasts features you won't find in *TEXT_IO*. It lets you check the keyboard to see if the user has entered any keystrokes, and you can flush the type-ahead buffer to discard any entries that may have been typed (but not processed) before the prompt was displayed. You can turn the character echo on or off. There are several new *get* procedures that return strings of the proper length (padded with blanks if necessary). The new input routines include a prompt, like a BASIC input statement. (If you don't want a prompt, then use the null string as a prompt.)

The *SCROLL_TERMINAL* has an interesting way of handling default responses. It works like this: The screen shows the prompt and the default response. If you press *RETURN*, it takes the default. If you begin typing a new response, the default is automatically erased. If the default is almost exactly what you want, you can edit the default response.

The *LEFT* and *RIGHT* arrow keys can be used to move the cursor without changing the characters underneath the cursor. If the keyboard doesn't have arrow keys, *CONTROL-L* and *CONTROL-R* can be used as *LEFT* and *RIGHT* arrow keys. *BACKSPACE (CONTROL-H)* deletes the character to the left of the cursor and moves the cursor back one space. *DELETE (CONTROL-E)* erases the character covered by the cursor. *INSERT (CONTROL-A)* adds characters at the cursor location without destroying any existing text.

Whenever you press *RETURN*, the entire response showing on the screen is taken, regardless of the cursor position. (You don't just get the characters to the left of the cursor.) This was done at the request of a customer who insisted on a constant policy of "what you see is what you get."

The *SCROLL_TERMINAL* also generates an exception called *NEEDS_HELP* whenever the user presses the question-mark key. This is an important feature you will see demonstrated often in the later programming examples.

3.5.4 Compatibility

Even though I don't like *TEXT_IO*, I know there are a lot of application programs that have already been written using *TEXT_IO* as the user interface. Therefore, I should make it as easy as possible for those programs to use *SCROLL_TERMINAL* instead of *TEXT_IO*. The routines with *TEXT_IO* names (*put*, *put_line*, *new_page*, *get_line*, and so on) are identical to *TEXT_IO* so existing programs that use *TEXT_IO* for a user interface can use *SCROLL_TERMINAL* instead simply by substituting **with SCROLL_TERMINAL; use SCROLL_Terminal** for **with TEXT_IO; use TEXT_IO;**.

3.5.5 Hiding Details in the Package Body

The package body is shown in Listing 23. It makes a distinction between cursor positions and column numbers. The column number can be from 1 to 79 but the cursor can be at position 1 to 80. This was done so the cursor will always be to the right of the character just entered. The application program doesn't need to know about *Cursor_positions*, so this data type is hidden in the package body.

3.5.6 Coupling

If one module affects another module, those two modules are said to be *coupled*. If modules are too tightly coupled, then there are major maintenance problems. When you change one module it forces you to change another, which is coupled to another, so that other module must also be changed. The ramifications of a single change ripple through the whole system. Too much coupling is bad.

If you take the extreme position that all coupling is bad, then you can never build a working system because all the modules in a system have to work together to achieve the goal. They can't do that if they are completely independent.

The coupling quandary is like networking computers. Many people want their computers to be networked (coupled) together so they can share data, but as soon as they do that they run risks. A network failure could keep them from accessing vital data. A hacker could break into one part of the network and gain access to the whole network. When computers are networked, you want to control the coupling so authorized users can safely pass data (even if part of the network fails), but unauthorized users can't get at any of the data. The same is true of coupling software modules. You need controlled coupling.

One of the best ways to control coupling between modules is to pass all information from one to the other using parameter lists. This method allows Ada to check for consistency between modules and helps programmers see how modules are coupled. I pass information between modules using parameter lists whenever I can, but there are some times when this isn't practical. The *SCROLL_TERMINAL* body is a good example.

There are three variables in the package body that are used to couple several routines together. *COLUMN_NUMBER* tells where the cursor is. *TAB_STOPS* remembers how many columns there are between tab stops. *ECHO* is used to decide if input characters should be echoed or not.

Let's look at *ECHO* first. All of the input procedures need to know if they should echo characters to the screen as they are typed. We could do that by adding one more parameter to all of the input procedures. This Boolean parameter would tell the input routine if it should echo or not. You could put this parameter last in the list and give it a default value of *TRUE*. It wouldn't be too awkward, but you would force every application program that ever needs to control the echo to keep track of the echo status itself.

I elected to add *Echo_On* and *Echo_Off* procedures to the *SCROLL_TERMINAL* body to make it easier on the application program. Since the normal mode is *Echo_On*, the elaboration of *SCROLL_TERMINAL* always calls *Echo_On*. The application program can call *Echo_On* or *Echo_Off* whenever it wants and does not need to remember the current echo status.

The method works by coupling the *Echo_On* and *Echo_Off* procedures to all the *get* procedures, using the shared variable *ECHO*. In so doing, I intentionally violated a software quality assurance guideline that says, "There shall be no hidden couples between modules." If management got really nasty about it, I could get rid of the *ECHO* variable and clutter all the input routines with Boolean parameters, without doing too much damage to the overall design.

The situation isn't so simple with *COLUMN_NUMBER* and *TAB_STOPS*. These variables provide a straight-forward (hidden) way of coupling the output procedures. Look at what has to happen.

The procedure *put* has to do more than just output characters. It also has to keep track of the cursor position. It has to do this so it can expand *TAB* characters. If the character to be printed is a printable character, it generally prints the character and moves the cursor to the next location. The one exception is when the cursor is at column 80. Then the *new_line* procedure is called, the character is printed in the first column of the next line, and the cursor moves to column 2.

Nonprintable characters are handled specially. *CARRIAGE_RETURN* sets the cursor and the *COLUMN_NUMBER* back to column 1. *LINE_FEED* and *BELL* are sent to the display without affecting the *COLUMN_NUMBER*. *TAB* is sent as one or more spaces (until *COLUMN_NUMBER* is a multiple of *TAB_STOPS*). Other nonprintable characters (*ESCAPE*, for example) are replaced by *BELL* characters to prevent programmers from trying to send terminal-specific control sequences to the screen. (The *SCROLL_TERMINAL* is a portable package. If it lets terminal-specific codes through, then you can't be sure an application program can be ported to another system.) The procedure *Set_Col* acts like a *TAB*, except it spaces over to the specified column regardless of *TAB_STOPS*.

So *Set_Tab*, *Set_Col*, *new_line*, and *put* are all coupled through *COLUMN_NUMBER* and/or *TAB_STOPS*. I'm a really clever fellow, so I probably could figure out a way to pass *COLUMN_NUMBER* and *TAB_STOPS* all over the place using parameter lists, but what a maintenance nightmare that would be!

The guideline is correct. You should generally avoid using shared variables as hidden couples between modules. The guideline shouldn't be considered to be absolute. There are times when the guideline should be violated. Some would argue that the *SCROLL_TERMINAL* body is a module, and that *Set_Tab*, *Set_Col*, *new_line*, and *put* are cohesive parts of one module, so the guideline hasn't been violated. That's just avoiding the issue. You have to recognize that there are rare instances when it is better to use hidden coupling than visible coupling.

3.5.7 Module Partitioning

The *SCROLL_TERMINAL* package body is broken into two files (Listings 23 and 24). The first file contains the main part of the package body, and the second file is the *Get_Response* subunit. The package body is five pages long, and the subunit is five pages long. If I left *Get_Response* in the package body, then the body would have been ten pages long, and that is too long.

Some people would say that even five pages is too long, and I generally agree with them. I try to keep each compilation unit to three pages or less, but I don't have a fixed rule, "Thou shalt not write any compilation unit longer than three pages." Guidelines have to be tempered by common sense.

I could have reduced the size of the *SCROLL_TERMINAL* body by turning *put_line*, *New_Page*, *Set_Col*, *Set_Tabs*, and several other small procedures into separate units. That might have made the body small enough to satisfy someone's software quality assurance guideline, but would that really be an improvement? Does it really help to break *SCROLL_TERMINAL* up into a dozen files, many of which contain procedures with only six statements? The file headers would take up more space than the executable code! (That's not a disk space problem, it is a visual clutter problem. The code gets lost in the boilerplate "information" people unconsciously skip over.)

I'm not arguing in favor of big compilation units. There are good reasons for keeping compilation units small. When compilation units get large, it is hard to find a particular piece of code. Often a module is too large because it is trying to do too many things at once; it should be broken down into several smaller modules that each do a single thing. Whenever you have a module over several pages long, you should seriously consider dividing it into smaller pieces.

Partitioning the code into smaller modules is a good idea most of the time, but there comes a point where partitioning hurts more than helps. I have friends working on a project where management insists that every subprogram must be a separate module. If I wrote *SCROLL_TERMINAL* for that customer, I would have to treat *Set_Tabs* as a configuration-controlled module complete with pseudocode description, structure chart, data dictionary, formal walkthrough, requirements traceability, module test plan, and integration test plan. (My friends' project is currently one year behind schedule, is about to announce another year schedule slip, is way over budget, and has no end in sight. I think I know why.)

3.5.8   Limited Name Space

Another factor you need to consider when partitioning a program into modules is that the more modules you have, the more module names you need to make up. You may think I'm joking, but when you have a big program with several hundred modules, it gets tough to find a name that is short, meaningful, and hasn't already been used. This is a serious problem in Ada because subunit names can't be overloaded.

The *SCROLL_TERMINAL* body has two overloaded subprograms called *put*. One *put* takes a character as a parameter, the other takes a string. Both exist blissfully in the package body. I can make either one of them a subunit, but if I try to make both of them separately compilable subunits, I can't do it. I would have to rename one, hide one in yet another package, or think of something else equally clumsy. Sometimes it may be better to let a module get a little bigger than the guidelines suggest, rather than be forced to do something creative to a procedure name to resolve a name clash so you can use separate subunits.

The *SCROLL_TERMINAL* body and *Get_Response* subunit are long, but I don't think they would be improved any by more partitioning. Partitioning would just make configuration management more difficult because you would have so many more files with strangely named modules in them.

3.5.9 The Top is at the Bottom

Ada makes it easy to write programs from the top down, but when you are finished writing it you will find the top-level logic is at the bottom of the listing. You can see this when you look at the *Get_Response* subunit.

Ada needs to have all the minute details described to her before she is willing to look at the big picture. In the *Get_Response* subunit, she needs to be told all about *Beep, Forward, Backup,* and so on, before she will even consider the main sequence of statements. My human mind balks at this. I can't help thinking, "Why are you telling me about this *Beep*? What has *Forward* got to do with getting a response from the user?" I find it much easier to understand a listing by going to the end and working backwards.

With this in mind, let's skip all the way down to the main *begin* statement in Listing 24. The program begins by setting the *INSERT_MODE* to *FALSE*. This means characters entered will type over existing ones, rather than shoving existing characters to the right to make room for a new character to be inserted at the cursor location. Then the *DEFAULT* response is put in a temporary *BUFFER*, and the *BUFFER* is displayed if the *ECHO* is enabled. If the *ECHO* is disabled, then blanks are displayed instead. Writing the contents of the *BUFFER* (or blank spaces) to the screen moves the cursor to the end of the *BUFFER*. X is a scratch variable used to keep track of where the cursor is, so it is set to the end of the *BUFFER*. Then the *Backup* procedure is called as often as necessary to move the cursor back to the beginning of the *BUFFER*. *Backup* automatically adjusts X and the *COLUMN_NUMBER*.

All of these actions happen in the twinkling of an eye. You probably won't see them unless you look closely at the screen or are using a 1200 baud modem. To the casual observer, the default appears and the cursor is sitting at the beginning of the default. The program is now sitting at the **VIRTUAL_TERMINAL.get(C);** line, waiting for the user to enter a character.

The first character the user enters may be special. If the user presses *INSERT (CONTROL_A)*, the *INSERT_MODE* is set to *TRUE*. This allows subsequent characters to be added to the beginning of the default. If the first character entered is *DELETE (CONTROL_E)*, the first character of the default is erased but the remainder of the default remains. If the first character is a *RIGHT* arrow *(CONTROL_R)*, the cursor moves one space to the right, without affecting the default characters under the cursor. If the first character is the *RETURN* key, the *DEFAULT* response (visible or not) is returned as the user's input and the subunit is done.

Often the first character will be none of the above. In that case, the default response is erased and the first character is processed as a normal keystroke input. The default is erased by filling the *BUFFER* with blanks and writing the *BUFFER* to the screen. This puts the cursor at the end of the *BUFFER* again, so *Backup* needs to be called to move the cursor back to the beginning of the *BUFFER*. Since no characters have been processed yet, *SIZE* (the number of valid characters in the buffer) is set to 0.

After the initial character is entered, the program goes into a loop that gets a character and processes it. The *Process_Character* procedure puts the keystrokes in the *BUFFER* and sets *DONE* to *TRUE* when the user presses *RETURN*. The *DONE* flag is used to exit the loop. When this happens the *BUFFER* and the *SIZE* are passed back to the main program and the cursor is moved to the beginning of the next line.

That is the top level description of the logic flow. It gives a general description of what *Get_Response* does. Suppose we want more detail about the *Process_Character* routine. We go to the next lower level by backing up in the listing.

The *Process_Character* procedure is found just before the main begin. *Process_Character* is always called after the user has entered the character *C*. A case structure decides what to do with *C*. For example, if the *C* was the *RETURN* key, then all that needs to be done is to set *DONE* to *TRUE*. If it was a *BACKSPACE* character, then *Rubout* the character to the left of the cursor.

If you backup again and look at the *Rubout* procedure you can see that it checks to make sure there really is a character to the left of the cursor. If so, it calls *Remove* to remove the character from the buffer. If not, it just makes the terminal *Beep* at the user, so all his coworkers will know he did something stupid.

Suppose someone gave you the *Get_Response* subunit and asked you to draw a picture of it, using your favorite form of structure chart. The top-level diagram would show what happens in the main sequence of statements. One of the items drawn under *Get_Response* would be *Process_Character*. If you drew a diagram of *Process_Character*, it would have *Rubout* hanging from it. If you drew a diagram of *Rubout*, it would have *Remove* and *Beep* under it.

In general, the closer you get to the top of the listing, then the closer you get to the bottom of the structure chart. This even extends to the context clauses because they name utility packages and subprograms that appear at the very bottom of the structure chart (if they appear at all).

3.6 *FORM_TERMINAL* PACKAGE

Most of the programs I write use *SCROLL_TERMINAL* as the user interface, but there are some instances where I need some special features the *SCROLL_TERMINAL* doesn't have. Those applications need a *FORM_TERMINAL*.

The *FORM_TERMINAL* package is more sophisticated than the *SCROLL_TERMINAL*. In some instances it is a much easier interface for the user to use, but it puts a little more burden on the programmer. This is an unavoidable consequence of the law of conservation of energy. It takes a certain amount of work to get a job done. Some of the work has to be done by the user and some has to be done by the programmer. The more work the programmer does, the less the user has to do and vice versa. A programmer has to work hard to come up with an easy user interface.

The complete *FORM_TERMINAL* consists of nineteen listings. That's too much to tackle at once, so let's begin by looking at the first six listings (25 through 30). They provide most of the functionality of the *FORM_TERMINAL*. The last thirteen listings (31 through 43) are only used to create and modify forms and will be discussed later.

3.6.1 When to use the *FORM_TERMINAL*

The *FORM_TERMINAL* is useful for those applications where a sequential data-entry interface (such as the *SCROLL_TERMINAL*) is not appropriate. For example, suppose you used the *SCROLL_TERMINAL* for an income tax program. The *SCROLL_TERMINAL* would force the taxpayer to answer far too many questions in a prescribed order. Suppose the taxpayer got to Line 31 and realized he had made a mistake on Line 14. It is too late to go back and fix it. He would have to start all over and answer all the questions again. The taxpayer needs a way to go back and change an answer. The *FORM_TERMINAL* allows him to do that because he can fill in the blanks in any order. The data is not passed to the application program until the user is satisfied with the way the form looks.

I saw another excellent example of a good use for the *FORM_TERMINAL* when I went to see my insurance agent a few days ago. I wanted to make some changes on my car insurance. He sat down at his computer and typed in my name, and a screen full of information appeared. It showed my name, address, birthday, vehicle type, coverage limits, and who knows what else. The agent was able to move the cursor to the proper field, made the change to the coverage I wanted, and pressed a button. The computer figured my new premium. If he had used the *SCROLL_TERMINAL* to do that, he would have had to have reentered my name, address, birthday, and so on. It would have been a real pain.

3.6.2 Consistency

Despite its advantages in situations like these, the *FORM_TER-MINAL* isn't as good as the *SCROLL_TERMINAL* for user dialogs.

Because of this, programs that use *FORM_TERMINAL* often use *SCROLL_TERMINAL,* too. (The *FORM_TERMINAL* examples you are about to see use the *SCROLL_TERMINAL* for help messages.) It would be terribly frustrating if the *FORM_TERMINAL* wasn't consistent with the conventions already established for the *SCROLL_TERMINAL*. The editing keys must work the same for both interfaces. If they don't, the user will wonder why the *INSERT* key works some times but not other times.

All of the keys that work for *SCROLL_TERMINAL* work exactly the same way for the *FORM_TERMINAL*. The *FORM_TERMINAL* also uses four more keys. The *UP* and *DOWN* arrows mean "previous form" and "next form." The *TAB* and *BACK_TAB* keys mean "next field" and "previous field."

It was tempting to use some of the IBM PC keys, like Pg Up, Pg Dn, Home, and End for the *FORM_TERMINAL*. I chose not to because some terminals, like the Televideo 910, don't have these keys. I wanted to keep the mental remapping of keys down to a minimum. I didn't want to have to remember that function key F5 is Pg Dn on a Televideo 910.

No matter what hardware is used, the *FORM_TERMINAL* always works the same, because it is built on the *VIRTUAL_TERMINAL*. No modifications are required to port it to an environment that already has the *VIRTUAL_TERMINAL* package running. That's good, because the *FORM_TERMINAL* is extensive and makes heavy use of cursor control keys. It would be difficult to rehost if it were built directly on host operating-system calls.

3.6.3 Abstract Objects

The *FORM_TERMINAL* is an example of a package representing a single object. It is an electronic representation of a special piece of paper called a form. Let's describe the properties of a form and see how they are represented in Ada.

I'm sure you've had experience with all kinds of forms. For example, income tax forms, employment applications, an application for a driver's license, and so on. What do all these forms have in common?

First, they all have a limited size. There are only so many characters you can fit on a single page. If all the information won't fit on a single page, you need a multiple-page form. In the *FORM_TERMINAL* package specification (Listing 25), I've defined the size of a single page with the subtypes *Line_numbers* and *Column_numbers*. This size is related to the size of the terminal screen because you need to be able to see the whole page all at once. I've made the form one line shorter than the number of lines on the screen, so I can use the bottom line for status and instructions that aren't part of the form. It may be that you can't fit all the information you need on a single form, but that happens with paper forms, too. The solution is the same for the electronic form. Use more pages if necessary.

The second thing you notice about a form is that it is divided into parts. Some of these parts have information preprinted on them. Other parts are blank so the user can enter data. The *FORM_ TERMINAL* calls these parts "fields." Protected fields are those printed parts the user can't change. Unprotected fields are the blanks he can fill in. Unlike paper forms, this electronic form can have a default response in an unprotected field.

Paper forms sometimes have numbered fields. That's because you sometimes need to refer to a particular field. In version 1, I numbered the fields on the form, but I found it hard to remember what numbers referred to each field. In version 2, I chose to give every field a 20-character name. The *FORM_ TERMINAL* uses a subtype *Field_ names* to represent the names of the fields.

Clearly there will be at least two things we will want to do with these fields. We will want to print instructions and default responses in some of them, and we will want to read what the user has written in the blanks. The *get* and *put* procedures allow us to do this. We can *put* a text string to any field we name, or we can *get* a string from any named field.

There are other, not so obvious, things we need to do with a form. One is simply to display it. More often, we want to display the form and give the user a chance to update the information on it. The *Display* and *Update* procedures let us do that.

The two parameters, *CURSOR_AT* and *NEXT*, in the *Update* procedure need a little explanation. *CURSOR_AT* lets us place the cursor in any unprotected field. This is the first field the user should want to change. Generally, it will be the first unprotected field in the upper left corner of the form. Each time the user presses the *RETURN* or *TAB* key, the cursor will move to the next unprotected field. If the user presses the *BACK_ TAB* key, the cursor moves to the previous unprotected field. The cursor will never appear in a protected field because protected fields contain things the user is not allowed to change.

When the user moves the cursor off the bottom of the screen (using the *RETURN* or *TAB* key in the last field, or using the *DOWN* arrow anywhere on the form), the *Update* procedure knows the user is finished with this form and wants to go on to the next page (if any). When this happens, the *NEXT* parameter is *TRUE*. It may be, however, that the user wants to go back to a previous page. He can do this by pressing the *UP* arrow, or using the *BACK_ TAB* key until he moves the cursor off the top of the page. In this case *Update* returns with the *NEXT* parameter set to *FALSE*. This should be interpreted as a request to go back to the previous form and update it again.

This idea of multiple pages brings up an interesting design decision. How do you keep track of multiple page forms? In version 1, I had a *limited private* type called *Forms* and declared arrays of *Forms*. All the *Forms* were in memory at once, and I could move forward and backward by simply incrementing or decrementing the index. The problem was that I was using a less efficient internal representation of the form than I use now, and I could only get three forms in memory at once. Furthermore, version 1 of the Alsys compiler didn't realize it didn't have enough memory for a fourth form, and wrote it over my code.

The representation of forms used in version 2 (although not the most compact form possible) takes much less space than version 1 needed, so I suspect I could hold as many forms in memory as necessary under normal circumstances. I was afraid, though, that someday I would have an application that required more forms than there was room for. This could happen because I needed lots of forms, or because the code segment of the program used up almost all of the memory space. I decided it was safer to keep just one form in memory at a time, and keep the others on disk. (This has a side benefit. If there is a power failure, I lose only the information on the form currently being updated.)

The decision to store forms on disk required *Read* and *Write* procedures to be included in the package. This means the application program needs to know the names of the files containing the forms. I have a generic *FILE_SYSTEM* package that hides path names and makes it easy to port programs to different operating systems, but it is too complicated to include in an intermediate-level book. It is not necessary to use a special file system, however. You can use a simple file name. (You will see how this is done in a later figure.)

There are several things that could go wrong when using the *FORM_TERMINAL*. You might try to read a file that doesn't exist, write a form to a full disk, get a form from a file that doesn't exist, or read a form from a file that doesn't really contain a form. The exceptions *READ_ERROR, WRITE_ERROR, ASSIGNMENT_ERROR*, and *LAYOUT_ERROR* are raised in these situations. Except for *WRITE_ERROR* (the disk is full), these exceptions probably won't happen after you have debugged your application program.

There are two other exceptions that could happen under normal circumstances. These are *PANIC* and *NEEDS_HELP*. Both of these exceptions are raised at the user's whim, and no amount of debugging can prevent them. The *PANIC* exception is raised whenever the user says to himself, "Oops! I didn't want to do this. Let's quit." The *NEEDS_HELP* exception is raised whenever the user presses the question-mark key because he doesn't know how to answer the question. The *NEEDS_HELP* situation is a classic example of a puzzling problem to many new Ada programmers, so let's digress for a moment and talk about it.

3.6.4   Exception Handling

The common complaints about Ada's exceptions are (1) the exception
does not include a status code telling the type of error, and (2) it is not
possible to return to the place the exception was raised. These aren't
really problems. They simply are features Ada doesn't need. People
who criticize Ada for these "deficiencies" could be compared to sailors
criticizing an automobile for not having a sail and a bilge pump.

People who don't know how to use Ada exceptions usually find themselves in the dilemma shown in Figure 21. This example lets the user
enter a name and address and echoes it back. There is a possibility that the user will raise the *NEEDS_HELP* exception by pressing
the question-mark key. When this happens, the dilemma is that the
NEEDS_HELP exception doesn't tell us which of the three questions
confused the user, and we couldn't get back to that question even if we
knew where we wanted to go.

The usual solution is to structure the program as shown in Figure
22. By encapsulating each query in a separate procedure, it is possible
to separate the exception handlers. Each exception handler gives an
appropriate help message and then recursively calls the appropriate input
routine. This is a good solution because it keeps the exception handler
close to the point where the exception will be raised, and it keeps the
error routines from cluttering the main program. I recommend using this
solution whenever possible.

Unfortunately there are cases where this solution won't work. We are
faced with such a situation when we use the *FORM_ TERMINAL* instead
of the *SCROLL_ TERMINAL* to get the name and address. Consider the
Form_ Dilemma shown in Figure 23. *ADDRESS.DAT* is a file containing
the data necessary for drawing a simple name and address form on the
screen. We will look at the contents of this file in a few pages. Right now
all you need to know is that it defines a form that prompts for name,
address, and city, and it tells where these fields should appear on the
screen. *Form_ Dilemma* fetches the blank form from *ADDRESS.DAT*,
lets the user update it, extracts the name and address from the form, and
echoes it to the screen. It works fine unless the user *NEEDS_HELP*.
Then we are back to another variation of the usual dilemma. We are in
the exception handler, don't know why, and don't know how to get back.
What are we to do?

A horrible solution is shown in Figure 24. We will see a much
better way to solve the problem in a moment, but we must suffer
through this bad example just to see what's wrong with it. I call this
the *FORTRAN_ Mentality_ Solution* because FORTRAN teaches people
to program this way. Some Ada critics claim you *have* to solve the problem this way. If that were true, they would be justified in their criticism.
But let's not damn Ada for their ignorance.

The *FORTRAN_Mentality_Solution* is to rewrite *Update* somehow to eliminate the *NEEDS_HELP* exception and replace it with a *STATUS* variable. Every time the procedure is called, you must check the *STATUS* variable to see if the procedure completed correctly. There are two problems with this. First, it forces you to depend upon every application programmer who will ever use the *Update* procedure to remember (or care enough) to check the *STATUS* variable. Second, it adds overhead every time you use it, to make sure the procedure completed correctly.

The *FORTRAN_Mentality_Solution* requires several *GOTO* statements. Ada doesn't normally need *GOTO*s. The *GOTO* is included in the LRM for no other reason than to allow you to convert poorly structured FORTRAN into poorly structured Ada. That's what I've done here. Please don't consider this an endorsement of *GOTO*s. Remember, this is the wrong way to solve the problem.

The right way to solve the problem is shown in Figure 25. It is similar to the usual solution because it uses a block structure to encapsulate a routine that is likely to raise an exception and provides a local exception handler for the routine. This eliminates the need to go back to the point of the exception because we haven't really left the point of the exception. In this case, that's only half the solution. We still have to figure out why *NEEDS_HELP* was raised.

Ada doesn't provide any way for me to pass the *WORKING_FIELD* number back along with the exception. Even if she did, it wouldn't do me much good because the application program thinks in terms of the names of the fields, doesn't know the fields are in an array indexed by an integer, and doesn't know *WORKING_FIELD* is the index. (If I let the application programs know this, I don't dare ever change the representation of a *FORM* for fear it will mess up a critical application program someone else wrote.)

Application programs using the *FORM_TERMINAL* will know about *Field_names* because they use them to *get* and *put* data, and position the cursor. The application programmer needs to know the name of the field being processed when the *NEEDS_HELP* exception is raised. The real key to the solution is having the foresight to include the *Confusing_Field* function in the *FORM_TERMINAL* package. Whenever the *NEEDS_HELP* exception is raised, the application program can call the *Confusing_Field* function to find out the name of the field that was being processed when the exception was raised. This is similar to checking a status variable, but the difference is that you only do it on those rare occasions when the exception occurs.

To do this I had to move the *WORKING_FIELD* number out of *Update* (where nobody but *Update* can use it) and put it in the *FORM_TERMINAL* body. Here other *FORM_TERMINAL* subprograms have access to it. The *WORKING_FIELD* variable is shared by *Update* and *Confusing_Field*. *Update* reads and writes it. *Confusing-Field* reads it and converts it to the corresponding *NAME*, which is what the application program needs to know.

The *Confusing_Field* function not only gives the application program all the information necessary to handle the exception, it also leaves me free to change the internal representation of the *FORM*. Suppose there was a compelling reason for me to change to a linked list (which uses an access type *FIELD_POINTER* instead of the integer *WORKING_FIELD*) to represent a *FORM*. I could do this with full assurance that I wouldn't have to rewrite any application programs that use *FORM_TERMINAL*, provided I put *FIELD_POINTER* in the package body and I modify the *Confusing_Field* function to convert *FIELD_POINTER* to a field name.

3.6.5   Keep Shared Variables Hidden

You might be tempted to do the same thing by declaring the shared variable in the package specification. Then you wouldn't need a subprogram to get at it. That's asking for trouble because who knows what stupidity lurks in the minds of the application programmers who will come after you. Somebody might assign it to 0 before calling your routines, check it on completion to see if it is 0, and call an error routine if it isn't. Maybe the initial value of 0 will mess up your routine. Maybe your routine normally changes it, even if there isn't an error. Protect yourself (and your good name) from them. Keep the variable hidden in the body and let others use it only in a controlled way using routines you have written yourself.

There is another reason for keeping the shared variable out of the package specification. If the shared variable is in the package specification, you have lost the ability to change internal representations. Suppose *WORKING_FIELD* was in the package specification, and you changed to a linked-list scheme that uses *FIELD_POINTER*. Then every application program that used *WORKING_FIELD* wouldn't work any more and would have to be rewritten.

So, the general lesson is this: Whenever something goes wrong and you have information you need to pass back to an application program, store that information in a variable declared in the package body, instead of a subprogram body. Then write another subprogram in that same package that can return the information to the application program in the most useful form.

3.6.6   Reuse by Copy

You may have noticed that the *Get_Form* subunit (Listing 27) is strikingly similar to the *Get_Response* subunit (Listing 24) in the *SCROLL_TERMINAL*. These two routines are too different to be derived from a common generic unit, but too similar to start completely from scratch. I simply made a copy of *Get_Response* and used a text editor to change it a little to create *Get_Form*.

There are major differences between the two units. You can easily find them using a file comparison utility program. Most of the differences aren't worth much discussion. The *FORM_TERMINAL* doesn't need to check the *ECHO* flag, because it isn't designed to be used in applications where it shouldn't echo the response. It doesn't have to worry about how many characters the user has entered, because the *SIZE* of the blank field on the form is constant. But even though there were significant differences, I still saved time and effort by editing a copy of an existing unit instead of starting from scratch.

The difference that is worth talking about in detail has to do with the parameter list. *Get_Response* passes *DEFAULT*, *TEXT*, and *LENGTH* as parameters. When the user presses the *RETURN* key he is done, and that's all there is to it. The *FORM_TERMINAL* is more complicated because the user can end his response by saying he wants to go to the *NEXT_FIELD*, *PREVIOUS_FIELD*, *NEXT_FORM*, or *PREVIOUS_FORM*. That explains why *Get_Form* has to return one of those *Actions*. The parameter list of *Get_Form* clearly shows this, but it isn't even remotely obvious how *Get_Form* knows what the prompts and defaults are or how it returns the user's responses.

3.6.7   Global Variables

The *Get_Form* reads data from and writes data to a (dare I say it?) global variable called *FORM*. I know how some of you feel about global variables. I feel the same way. It is usually a bad idea to use a global variable because it obscures the coupling between modules. If several modules write to the same global variable, and it is found to contain the wrong value, it is sometimes hard to determine which is the guilty module. Suppose two modules communicate through a global variable. If you decide to change the meaning of the value in both of those modules, you will get unusual and difficult-to-locate errors if you have forgotten that a third module also uses that variable.

You don't see me using global variables very often. In this case, however, I feel justified in using them. True, I could pass an object of type *Forms*, but that seemed awkward. It wouldn't explicitly show the prompts, defaults, and response, so it didn't really provide any more information than using the global variable. Since there is only one object of type *Forms*, I can't possibly get it confused with any other object of the same type. The application program can't see *FORM*, so it can't corrupt it.

The *FORM* is indexed by *WORKING_FIELD*, which I definitely don't want to pass as a parameter because there is a possibility that an exception might be raised. (If *WORKING_FIELD* is passed as a parameter, I can't guarantee it will be the correct value if *NEEDS_HELP* is raised.) It seems strange to me to pass *FORM* as a parameter yet index it with a global variable. The exception argument also holds for the *FORM* itself. If the user *NEEDS_HELP*, I can be sure the global variable *FORM* contains the user's partially edited form. If *FORM* is passed back as a parameter and the user *NEEDS_HELP*, there's no telling what is in *FORM*. Maybe it is the virgin form that existed before the user started editing it. Maybe it is the partially edited form. Maybe it is garbage, pointed to by whatever number happened to be in the stack frame when the exception was raised. This is just one of those rare cases where a global variable makes more sense than a passed parameter.

3.6.8   A Package Can Be an Abstract Object

Perhaps the most important concept in Listing 26 is the data type *Forms*. By declaring *Forms* in the body rather than the specification, I have made it even more private than *limited private*. Application programs can declare objects of type *limited private*, but they can't even declare objects of type *Forms* because it isn't visible to them. If they can't declare objects of type *Forms*, what good is it? Plenty, but you may have to change the way you think about objects.

You are probably used to packages that contain objects. This time the package itself is an object. The package represents something that has a value. When you write **FORM_TERMINAL.put(SOME_FIELD,"Some Text");** you are actually assigning a value to a component of that object. You can read it back using the statement **FORM_TERMINAL.get(SOME_FIELD,STRING_VARIABLE);**. That's why you don't need to declare objects of type *Forms*. The package itself is the form.

3.6.9   Discriminated Records

Type *Forms* is a discriminated record with three components. It consists of a number of fields, an array of that number of fields, and an image of the screen. We will soon see that discriminated records are a little difficult to work with, but they solve an important problem. They avoid the need to guess how many fields there will be on the form.

Looking at the *FIELD* component, we see that it is an array of *Field_specs*, where each specification tells the name of the field, what line it is on, where it begins and ends, and if it is protected or not. The text showing on the form is not part of the field specification. Instead, it is stored in a two-dimensional array of characters called a *SCREEN*. Since many of the characters are blank, there is a potential for saving some space by storing text in the *Field_specs* and doing away with the

SCREEN. (This requires nested discriminated records, and I didn't want to get that complicated.)

Version 1 of the *FORM_TERMINAL* didn't use a discriminated record. It used an ordinary record, and one component of the record was a fixed-length array of *Field_specs*. A constant *MAX_FIELDS* set the size of this array. At various times this constant was 30, 60, or 100. When I tried using 30, I ran into trouble because I often wanted more than 30 fields on the form. When I tried 100 fields, it used up so much memory I only had room for one form in memory. I finally settled on 60 as a reasonable compromise, but I always worried it would be too large or too small.

The discriminated record lets me declare an array of fields that is exactly the right size. The problem is that I have to know how many fields will be on the form before I declare it, and I have to change the entire form in one shot if I want to redimension it. That's not a trivial problem, but it is far from impossible. If you have worked with discriminated records before, you have probably run into this difficulty. Maybe you gave up. If you did, you'll be glad to see this solution.

For those of you who have not run into this problem, let me quote three pertinent parts of the LRM.

> For a variable declared by an object declaration, the subtype indication of the corresponding object declaration must impose a discriminant constraint unless default expressions exist for the discriminant. (Section 3.7.2 paragraph 8)

> If the type of an object is a type with discriminants and the subtype of the object is constrained, the implicit initial (and only) value of each discriminant is defined by the subtype of the object. (Section 3.2.1 paragraph 12)

> Direct assignment to a discriminant of an object is not allowed; . . . The only way to change the value of a discriminant of a variable is to assign a (complete) value to the variable itself. (Section 3.7.1 paragraph 9)

Here are three examples to show what those three parts of the LRM mean in practice. I've written these examples as procedures, so you can compile them to see what error messages your compiler generates.

Figure 26 shows that an object must be constrained when you declare it. This constraint can be explicitly shown, as in *FIRST_NAME* or *WHOLE_NAME,* or it can be the default, as shown in *LAST_NAME.* *MY_NAME* is illegal because it has no explicit constraint and it has no default constraint.

Figure 27 shows that constraints can be changed only when the object is declared with a default constraint. Since *LAST_NAME* was declared without an explicit constraint, that constraint can be changed. Notice that it is the object declaration, not the type definition, that counts. *WHOLE_ NAME* is of type *Default,* so it has a default constraint, but we didn't use the default when we declared it. When we declared **WHOLE_ NAME : Default(14)**; we told Ada we want *WHOLE_ NAME* to always have a fourteen-character *TEXT* string, and she takes us at our word. If we change our mind later, it's just tough luck.

The moral of the story so far is, "If you want to be able to change a discriminant of an object, the type definition must include a default value and the object declaration must use that default."

Finally Figure 28 shows us that even under the special circumstance when we can change the discriminant, we may only change it in a particular way. We can't change the discriminant alone, we must change every component of the object at once. The only way to do that is with an assignment statement. We can assign the value of another object of the same type to it, or we can assign an aggregate (but not a slice) to it.

The rest of the lesson is, "You either set the discriminant to the correct (constant) size when you declare the object, or you declare the object without a constraint and change the whole object at once." The two ways to change an object all at once are to assign all the components using an aggregate, or assign it to another object of the same type (even though it has a different constraint).

Of course there was a reason for this long explanation. The *FORM_ TERMINAL* needs to read a discriminated record from a disk file. In general, this means it needs to change the size of a discriminated record currently in memory and read new data into it. The preceding discussion was designed to impress upon you how tricky this is.

3.6.10   Reading Discriminated Records from a File

Data is stored in a file similar to the one shown in Figure 29. This is the *ADDRESS.DAT* file we first saw in the *Form_ Dilemma* program (Figure 23). The first line of the file contains the number 7 because there are seven fields on the form. Each of the seven field specifications begins with the header "– – data – –". The six lines following each header tell (1) the name of the field, (2) the line the field appears on, (3) the first column of the field, (4) last column of the field, (5) whether it is protected or unprotected, and (6) the text that appears in the field. You can't tell it from the figure, but the field names have been padded with spaces to make them exactly twenty characters long. The lines that appear to be blank actually contain the correct number of blank spaces needed to fill the first through last columns of the field.

The *Read* subprogram (Listing 28) opens the input file and reads the first line. This line contains the number of fields in the *FORM*.

Then it calls a function, *Stored_Form*, passing it the number of fields as a parameter. The function *Stored_Form* declares an object *TEMP* of type *Forms*, with the discriminant set to the proper size. It reads the information from the file a line at a time and builds up *TEMP* a piece at a time (but it never changes the discriminant because it was the correct value to begin with). When it is all assembled, TEMP is returned as the result and assigned to *FORM* all at once. So, reading a discriminated record from a file isn't difficult if you know how to do it.

3.6.11 Discriminants May Not Save Space

The motivation for using a discriminated record was to save space. If there are only three fields on the form, why bother to define *Field_arrays* big enough to hold a hundred *Field_specs*? In theory, we could save memory space by using a discriminated record, declaring *Field_arrays* to hold only as many *Field_specs* as necessary. In practice, it may not work that way. The LRM permits an implementation to allocate enough space to accommodate the maximum possible discriminant. The discriminated record may actually take more space than an ordinary record with a few empty fields. For example, an early version of Listing 26 declared *Forms* the following way:

```
type Forms(FIELDS : positive := 1) is
  record
    FIELD : Field_arrays(1..FIELDS);
    SCREEN : Screens;
  end record;
```

This worked on the Meridian Ada compiler but raised an exception on the DEC Ada compiler, presumably because DEC Ada tried to allocate space for

```
FIELD: Field_arrays (1..positive'LAST);
```

and didn't have enough memory space to do it. I solved the problem by introducing a subtype that limits the maximum number of arrays.

```
subtype Field_numbers is positive range 1..200;
type Forms(FIELDS : Field_numbers := 1) is ...
```

This appears to be exactly the same as defining *Forms* using an ordinary record.

```
type Forms is
  record
```

```
        FIELDS : positive;
        FIELD : Field_arrays(1..200);
        SCREEN : Screens;
   end record;
```

Both take exactly the same amount of memory space (on some implementations). The difference only appears in Listing 28. There you find the following statements:

```
function Stored_Form(SIZE : positive)
     return Forms is
   TEMP : Forms(SIZE);
```

I think that calling *Stored_Form(10)* will allocate space for ten *Field_arrays* instead of two hundred, and therefore saves a little space, but I can't be sure of that.

Compilers vendors have taken different approaches to implementing discriminated records. You can't depend on every validated Ada compiler to implement discriminated records exactly the same way. This means you can't count on discriminated records to use the minimum required space, and that could cause portability problems if you use discriminated records.

If I had it to do all over again, I might not have used a discriminated record because of their unpredictable nature. I was tempted to rewrite the *FORM_ TERMINAL* using an ordinary record and a generic parameter *MAX_ FIELDS*, or perhaps use *access* types to build an unbounded linked list of *Field_ specs*. I decided not to because it would have left me without an example of discriminated records.

3.6.12   Use *Read* as a Pattern for *Write*

Unless this is your first week on the job, I'll bet you've witnessed this scenario several times. Data from an important test had to be recorded in real time and analyzed immediately after the test. The project engineers carefully devised a format for recording the data on tape. The test was performed and data was recorded using that format. The tapes were taken to the data processing people, and project management anxiously awaited the results. Weeks later nobody had seen any reduced data. The data processing people still had not figured out how to read the tapes yet! The project engineers blamed the data processing section. The head of the data processing department defended his people and tried to put the blame on the project engineers. Why does this happen?

It is easy to see how this could have happened with the *Read* procedure. The first thing it does is read the number of *Field_arrays* from the first line of the file and create a discriminated record the proper size to hold the data. Suppose I hadn't written the number of *Field_arrays* to the first line of the file. I could have thought that it isn't necessary to waste a line on writing that information because it is possible to find the number of fields by reading the file and counting the number of times the "– – data – –" header line appears. If I had done that, I would have had to read the whole file to find out how many field specifications it contains, create a form the proper size, and then read the file again to put the data in the form. (Or I could save all the data in memory from the first pass through the file and then transfer it to the form if there is enough memory space.) If I had written the *TEXT* in each field before writing the *FIRST* and *LAST* column numbers, it would have been much more difficult to read the form from the file. If I had made either of these stupid decisions when I defined the file format, the data wouldn't have been lost. I still could have read the file with a little extra effort.

Writing a file is easy. You can write anything in any order without any problems. Reading a file can be difficult because you often need to know certain pieces of information before you can process others. So, the first rule for establishing a file format is, "Write the routine that gets the data from the file before you write the routine that puts it there." After you have done this, you can use your *Read* routine as a pattern for your *Write* routine.

Look at Listing 28, which contains both the *Read* and *Write* procedures. Let's compare *Read* to *Write*. The first thing *Read* does is *Open* a file, so the first thing *Write* does is *Create* a file. The next thing *Read* does is to read the number of fields on the form, so *Write* must write the number of fields on the form before writing anything else. *Read* uses that number to set the limit on a loop that reads a header, *NAME*, *LINE, FIRST, LAST, PROTECTED*, and *TEXT*, so *Write* should also set up a loop that writes those things in that order. *Read* ends by closing the file, so *Write* should end that way, too. The only thing *Read* does that doesn't correspond to something *Write* does is the error checking. (That's because *Read* can't be sure the file it is trying to read really contains a valid form.)

The *Read* routine in Listing 28 is more complicated than most file-reading routines because it needs the *Stored_Form* function to create a discriminated record. In many cases a file-reading routine is a simple loop or straight line program. In those cases you can create a *Write* routine from a *Read* routine simply by using a text editor to change all occurrences of *get* to *put*, and then make some other minor changes (change *Open* to *Create*, for example). But whether you copy and edit the *Read* source file or just use a printed copy of the *Read* source code as a guide for writing the *Write* source code, the principle is the same.

Pick a format that is easy to read, write the *Read* routine first, and then use that as a pattern for the *Write* routine.

3.6.13 ASCII Data Files

You perhaps noticed that I used ASCII (rather than binary) format for the *FORM* files. Not only that, I wastefully put only one data item on each line. Binary files generally use less disk space and are faster than ASCII files. In this case the ASCII files are probably small enough to fit in a single disk sector with room to spare, so an ASCII file probably isn't any bigger than a binary file. The time it takes to convert those few words from binary to ASCII and back is negligible. In cases like these, I always prefer ASCII to binary files because I can easily display, print, and edit them.

If I try to write a *FORM* to a file and then read it back, and it doesn't work, how do I know what went wrong? Did it write the file correctly and fail to read it? Or did it write the file incorrectly? It is easy to print an ASCII file and see. Of course there are utility programs to dump and patch binary files. You can examine blocks of hexadecimal listings and find out what data was written to the file, but that's not as easy as looking at ASCII files with one data item per line. So even if I know I'm eventually going to be dealing with huge files, I usually start developing the file I/O routines with ASCII representations of dwarfed files. After they are debugged, I switch to binary and test the routines again with small files. Then I try them with the big files.

A computer can easily count lines to determine which numbers are associated with each variable, but I can't. I had some difficulty figuring out which numbers represented lines and columns, especially if I was interested in a field specification near the middle of the file, so I added header lines that said "– – data – –" at the beginning of each field specification. They stick out like a sore thumb and make it easy for me to visually see where each field specification begins.

The *Read* program could ignore the "– – data – –" lines, since they convey no information. This is easily done using *skip_line*. I decided not to skip them, but to use them as parity checks instead. Every time I would normally have skipped the header line, I read it and make sure it really says "– – data – –". If it doesn't, it means the file has been corrupted, the *Read* routine has gotten out of sync, or the file doesn't really contain a form. In any of those cases, I don't want to continue trying to read the form, so it raises the *READ_ERROR* exception and quits.

3.6.14 Storing Boolean Values in a File

I've seen a message on an electronic bulletin board saying that a particular implementation of *TEXT_IO* has a bug in it that prevents it from

properly storing Boolean types when *ENUMERATION_IO* is instantiated for Boolean types. I'm not sure if that's true or not. (Perhaps that
person just wasn't using it correctly.) What I am sure of is that they
were trying to use *ENUMERATION_IO* to store a Boolean value, and I
don't think that's a good idea.

The *Read* and *Write* routines store the Boolean variable *PROTECTED*
in an external file without instantiating *ENUMERATION_IO*. They simply use the character *P* to indicate protected fields and *U* to indicate
unprotected ones. What could be easier?

If your really have your heart set on writing *TRUE* and *FALSE*, you
can use the attributes *boolean'IMAGE* and *boolean'VALUE* to convert
between Boolean values and text strings, just as I used *integer'IMAGE*
and *integer'VALUE* to do the same for numbers. I don't see any reason
to use four or five characters where one will do the job, but you may
have a good reason. Consider this, however. When you look at the ASCII
representation of the file, *TRUE* and *FALSE* don't tell you much. They
just tell you something is true or false. If you see a *TRUE* in a file, does
that mean the field is unprotected? You have to think about it. If I
were going to use several characters instead of just one, I would write
PROTECTED or *UNPROTECTED* to the file, not *TRUE* or *FALSE*.

3.6.15   One Compilation Unit Per File

By now you must have noticed that I almost always put just one compilation unit in a file. I could have combined all 19 *FORM_TERMINAL*
listings in a single file. That would have made it easier for you to compile the *FORM_TERMINAL*. You could just submit that one file to the
compiler and go visit your coworkers at the water cooler. Ten minutes
later, you could return to your terminal and see if it was done yet.

There are two good reasons not to combine several compilation units
in one file. The primary one is that you have to recompile a whole file
at a time. If the file contains ten long compilation units and you change
one, then you waste time recompiling nine units that haven't changed.

The secondary reason is that separate files allow you to make it easier
to find particular compilation units. If there is something wrong with
the *Display* routine, it is easier to look in Listing 29 than to search a
huge listing looking for it. (This reason for separating compilation units
isn't as compelling as it once was, because modern software engineering
environments make it possible for anyone associated with the project to
electronically search any file for anything, but I still think it is a good
idea to try to keep files small.)

Everyone who has completed an introductory Ada course should have
had it pounded into his head why package specifications should be sepa-
rated from package bodies. I shouldn't need to tell you that using separate

files for the package body and specification allow you to make changes to the body without making units that depend on the specification obsolete. I won't insult your intelligence by reminding you of that.

You don't need to combine compilation units in a single file to compile them all at once. Every operating system has something equivalent to a shell script (perhaps a ".BAT" file, or ".COM" file) that lets you execute a sequence of commands at once. Whenever I have a software component like the *FORM_TERMINAL* that is spread out over several files, I just write a script that compiles them all in the correct order.

There are times, however, when you have to break the "one unit per file" rule. Some Ada compilers require all parts of a generic package or subprogram to be in a single file. On those compilers you don't have any choice but to put multiple compilation units in the generic file. Since I know that is a potential portability problem, I always put all the components for a generic unit in one file, whether the compiler I am using requires me to or not.

3.6.16 Encapsulating Details in One File

Listing 28 is another example of when to break the rule. It contains two separate subunits, *Read* and *Write*, even though they aren't generic.

Normally, I try to encapsulate design details in a single compilation unit. The format of the file containing a *FORM* is a design detail I would like to confine to one location. If possible, I would like to make only one compilation unit dependent upon the external file format, so any changes to that format will require me to recompile only one unit.

In this case, *Read* and *Write* both need to know the external file format. Since the file format affects both *Read* and *Write*, any changes made to the format affect both subunits. There isn't any practical way I can see to encapsulate the format in just one unit. If you change one subunit without changing the other, it will cause problems.

Ada's compilation-order rules sometimes help out, but not this time. If you change the *FORM_TERMINAL* body, Ada will realize that *Read* and *Write* are obsolete and need to be recompiled; but since *Read* and *Write* are both subunits of the body, you can change and recompile either without making the other one obsolete. Ada won't automatically tell you that you have to change and recompile the other subunit.

Since I couldn't encapsulate the external file format in a single subunit, I did the next best thing: I encapsulated it in a single file. If I modify one of the units, I'm bound to notice the other one and remember that it has to be changed, too. This isn't foolproof. It is possible to open the file, change the format in one subunit without changing the other, and recompile the file, but it's hard for me to imagine someone who could do that accidentally.

Putting both subunits in the same file not only reminds me to make the same changes in both, it also makes it easier to use a text editor to cut and paste patches to both subprograms at once.

Encapsulating the external file format in a file with two subunits gives us the flexibility to change the external format without affecting any other part of the program. If we want to use binary external form instead of ASCII, we can change the *Read* and *Write* routines, and all our changes are confined to one source file. Whenever we compile that file, we automatically compile a matching pair of routines. We never have to worry about accidentally compiling the old ASCII format *Read* and the new binary format *Write*.

3.6.17 Formatted I/O

I've hated formatted output ever since I first encountered a FORMAT(F6.2) statement 22 years ago. You would think that after all these years it would have gotten easier, but it hasn't. It is still easy to make a mistake when counting spaces, so column headings don't line up correctly! I never seem to get it right the first time.

Laying out a two-dimensional form is even a greater hassle than laying out one-dimensional column headers. The *FORM_TERMINAL* requires you to count rows, columns, and string lengths. Everything has to be exactly right or else *CONSTRAINT_ERROR* will raise its ugly head.

The difficulty of formatting the display on the screen almost led me to a fatal design error. This error is so common and so important, it is worthwhile to devote the next subsection to it.

3.6.18 The Danger of Improvement

It's ironic, but sometimes you can improve a good product so much that it becomes useless. Several examples quickly come to mind. There was a word processing program that dominated the CP/M market in the late seventies. The manufacturer added many features to this good product and released the new, improved version. The resulting product was so slow and difficult to use that it got terrible reviews in computer magazines, and other word processors tore the market away from it. There are two real-time operating systems that came out in the seventies that are suffering the same fate. Too many good products have failed because they've been improved too much. Some people can get upset and nasty when I criticize their products, so I'll pick on my own *FORM_TERMINAL* and show what almost happened to it.

The original *FORM_TERMINAL* consisted of six files that looked a lot like Listings 25 through 30. It did not have the capability of creating or editing forms. I used a text editor to create the external file containing the field specifications. As I pointed out, that was a nuisance, but it only had to be done once for each form I created, and I only created ten different kinds of forms. Each time I did it, it took less than an hour, so I spent less than 10 hours total time creating files with the text editor.

The *FORM_TERMINAL* is such a useful user interface, I wanted to be sure to include it in this book. I realized that its most serious deficiency was the laborious procedure required to create the form file. I decided to add the *Create* procedure, which would make this much easier. Well, after several days I got the *Create* procedure working, and it only increased the size of the *FORM_TERMINAL* package from six files to ten files. (Listings 31 through 34.)

I used the *Create* procedure for a while, and realized that it forced the user to start from scratch every time a new form was needed. If you wanted to correct an error in a form or make a second form almost exactly like another form, you had to start from scratch. I needed a way to edit an existing form, so I wrote the *Edit* procedure.

The Edit procedure is spread out over eight files (Listings 35 through 42), and brought the total number of files in the *FORM_TERMINAL* to eighteen. Needless to say, it took considerable time and effort to get this feature working.

I discovered that while using the *Create* or *Edit* procedure it was possible to produce a form containing errors. I needed *Error_Recovery* to allow me to recursively call the *Edit* procedure until the form was error free. One more small file (Listing 43) brought the total to nineteen files in the *FORM_TERMINAL* package.

I used the *Make_Form* and *Edit_Form* programs (Listings 44 and 45) and discovered that the first call to *Error_Recovery* raises *STORAGE_ERROR* on my IBM PC AT clone. The publication deadline was getting close, and *FORM_TERMINAL* didn't work anymore. I was panic-stricken.

Finally I got the *FORM_TERMINAL*, as shown in Listings 25 through 43, to work on a VAX (and also on a PC if you don't make recursive errors). Most of your application programs won't use *Create*, *Edit*, or *Error_Recovery*. That means thirteen of the nineteen source files create dead code that will have to be removed by an optimizer (if you have one).

Looking back, I see countless hours spent writing slick utility programs that save a few minutes. I was tempted to remove *Create* and *Edit* from the package specification, then remove all the code associated with them and never tell you about them. That's less embarrassing to me, but I'd rather have you learn from my mistake. The whole sordid package is there for you to see.

It is easy to get seduced into doing more than you should. From time to time it is a good idea to ask yourself, "Is this really worth it?" Sometimes you have to admit you made a mistake and go back to an older version.

One easy way to return *FORM_TERMINAL* to its original small size is to use the *Edit* and *Create* stubs in Listings 46 and 47. If you compile these two small stubs, they write error messages if you should ever try to *Edit* or *Create* a form. I don't expect any of your application programs to call these routines, so they produce dead code, but it is not nearly as much as produced by the real *Edit* and *Create* routines. The better way, of course, is to edit the package specification and body to remove all references to *Create*, *Edit*, and *Error_Recovery*.

If I could live my life over again, I wouldn't have written the *Edit* and *Create* procedures; but the fact is that I did write them, and there are some lessons that can be drawn from them. Let's look at them.

3.6.19   Creating a New *FORM*

Create takes most of the work out of designing a form. You still need to decide what the form should look like, but the Create procedure does all the counting of lines and columns for you.

I wanted to make *Create* an independent program outside the *FORM_TERMINAL* package, but it needs to know about *Field_specs* and the *SCREEN*. I would have to make those internal details visible to all programs outside the package if the *Create* procedure was outside the package. I don't want clever application programmers directly manipulating the *Field_specs* and the *SCREEN*. Putting the *Create* procedure inside the package allows me to keep those details hidden from application programs.

The *Create* procedure asks you if you need instructions. If you do, it gives you a screen full of explanation. After you have read this, it covers the screen with '~' characters. The wiggles are there to help you see how much space you have to work with. (They won't appear on the form you create.) You can use the arrow keys to move the cursor around wherever you want, and type whatever you like. Keep doodling around until the form looks like you want it to. If you make a mistake, just type over what you have already done.

Eventually, the form will look like you want it to. When it does, it is time to tell the computer to store it. In general, you do this by pointing to the beginning and end of each field with the cursor and using function keys to indicate if it is protected or not. Each time you do this, the program will ask you to give the field a name. Every field must have a unique name and must fit on a single line. Remember there is the concept of *next field* and *previous field*, so be sure to specify them in the correct order (just as you must specify enumeration types in the correct order). Usually you will want to start with the field in the upper left corner and work to the right and down, but that isn't necessary. (If you want to really baffle a user, you can start at the bottom and work up!)

You point to the beginning of a field by moving the cursor to the first position in the field and press F1 or F2. Press F1 if this is to be a protected field the user can't modify. Press F2 if it is an area where the user is expected to enter data. Use the *RIGHT* arrow key to move the cursor to the last character in the field. (You can use the *LEFT* arrow key if you overshoot the end.) When the cursor is at the proper place, press F3. The computer stores the line number, the first and last column numbers, and the text contained in those columns. (The text could be a prompt, a default response, or blank spaces.) It also stores whether this field is protected or not. All that remains for you to do is to give it a unique name of twenty characters or less. You do this by typing the name at the prompt at the bottom of the screen and pressing the *RETURN* key. (*Note*: you may use significant embedded blanks and underlines, but all lowercase letters will be automatically converted to uppercase.)

After you have entered a field name, the cursor returns to the end of the field you just entered, and you may enter the next field. When all the fields have been entered, press F10.

The *Create* procedure leaves the form in memory. You probably want to write it to a disk file. The *Make_Form* program (Listing 44) shows you how to do this. It doesn't do much more than call *FORM_TERMINAL.Create* and *FORM_TERMINAL.Write*.

3.6.20   Character Substitution

When I designed the *SCROLL_TERMINAL*, I chose the question-mark key as a help request. I couldn't imagine anytime a user would answer a question with another question, so I decided the question-mark key should always raise the *NEEDS_HELP* exception. I kept the same convention in the *FORM_TERMINAL*. There were no problems until it came time to create a form.

It is likely someone will want a form to display a prompt with a question mark in it. How can someone create a form containing a question mark when pressing the question-mark key always raises the *NEEDS_HELP* exception? The solution (near the end of the *Process_Keystrokes* procedure in Listing 33) was to substitute the escape key for the question mark. I don't like to map keys to other functions, but in this case, it seemed like the best way to solve the problem.

3.6.21   Long Strings

Sometimes string literals won't fit on one line. Suppose you want to print a string that is 60 or 70 characters long. The print statement might appear at a point in the program where there are several levels of indentation, and you may be using dot notation, and your word processor may insist on saving a generous right margin. There isn't room to put **SCROLL_TERMINAL.put_line("70 characters here");** on one line. The text editor inserts a carriage return somewhere in the string literal, and Ada generates an error saying something about an unterminated string.

I ran into that problem in Listing 32. The help messages wouldn't fit on a single line. The simple solution was to break the messages into two strings (one string on each of two lines) and print the catenation of the two strings. You can use this trick whenever a string literal won't fit on a single line.

3.6.22 *in out* Mode

I am ashamed to say that in my desperation to try to get the complete *FORM_TERMINAL* package to fit on a PC, I saved space by intentionally misusing the *in out* mode in Listing 33. That was a really bad thing to do. Let me explain why.

Lazy programmers always use *in out* mode to avoid those annoying error messages Ada generates when you misuse an *in* or *out* mode parameter. Ada warns you of those errors for your own good. Using *in out* mode to suppress them simply prevents you from detecting the error at compile time and makes it appear at run time, when it is much more difficult to detect.

Pardon my FORTRAN, but Figure 30 shows what can happen if you don't pay attention to parameter modes. This is a fragment of a program I wrote for a client in FORTRAN because he didn't have an Ada compiler for his computer. FORTRAN treats all parameters the way Ada treats *in out* mode parameters. *TIME* is expressed in milliseconds, and I wanted to convert it to *HOURS, MINUTES,* and *SECONDS* so I could display the time in "HH:MM:SS" format. The program did strange things because the value of *TIME* was corrupted by the *SPLIT* subroutine. For example, if the value of *TIME* was 34,644,822 before calling *SPLIT*, the display correctly showed 09:37:24, but the value of *TIME* was changed to 24,822. It took me most of a day to figure out what went wrong.

If I had written the routine in Ada, it would have looked like Figure 31. Since I thought I was just reading *TIME* and not changing its value, I would have declared it to have *in* mode. Ada would have spotted my error at compile time. Then I would have rewritten it as shown in Figure 32. If I had used *in out* mode for all the parameters in Figure 31, Ada would not have caught the error, and I would have had the same problem I had in FORTRAN.

Notice the solution in Figure 32 requires the declaration of an extra variable. I didn't want to do that in Listing 33 because *Form_specs* take up lots of space. To be brutally honest, I was using *DATA* as a global variable, but pretending to pass it as a parameter. I should have made *DATA* an *out* parameter because *DATA* is produced by *Get_Field*. Then I should have declared a local variable of type *Form_specs* and copied it to *DATA* at the end of the procedure. (In fact, that's what I did in the original version. I had to take out the extra variable because it caused *STORAGE_ERROR* to be raised on the PC.)

Legitimate use of *in out* mode is rare. It should only be used in those cases where you are passing a variable to a routine and you expect that routine to somehow modify it and return the modified value back to you. If you use *in out* mode to avoid declaring an extra variable, your program may work, but it may confuse a maintenance programmer. He may spend hours trying to figure out where the calling program created the original value (it really didn't) or where the calling program will use the transformed value (it really doesn't). You shouldn't mislead someone into thinking a routine transforms a value if it simply uses it or produces it.

3.6.23   Editing an Existing *FORM*

I sometimes became very frustrated with *Create* because I would almost be finished with a complicated form and would make a little mistake. There was nothing I could do except start all over again. There was no way to edit the form.

If you have a complicated form with many fields, and you just want to add one more field, swap the position of two fields, or correct a spelling error in a prompt, you can't fix it with *Create*. *Create* will make you enter the entire form from scratch. That's a lot of unnecessary work, and it gives you too many chances to make a mistake.

The *Edit* procedure can be used to make changes to the *Field_specs* or *SCREEN*. The *Edit_Form* program, Listing 45, uses the *Edit* procedure to make it easy for you to make minor changes in the form.

3.6.24   *null* Exception Handlers

Students often make an amusing mistake when they are first exposed to exceptions. They think they need to handle every exception in every routine. If they don't know what to do, they put a do-nothing exception handler at the end of the block.

```
begin
   -- some code here
exception
   when others => null;
end;
```

I generally come down pretty hard on the student because he is telling Ada, "I don't know what went wrong, so just ignore it and proceed to the next block as if everything is OK." I used to say there is never a time when a *null* statement is an appropriate exception handler. Now I say it is *almost* never appropriate. I used one in Listing 45.

The *FORM_TERMINAL.Read* procedure will raise *LAYOUT_ERROR* if it reads a form into memory from a file and then discovers an error in it. A LAYOUT_ERROR should be rare, and will probably force most programs to terminate abnormally. The *Edit_Form* program is a special case. When it reads a form from a disk there is a good chance there is a *LAYOUT_ERROR* in it. (That's why we want to edit it!) If we only allow the program to read good forms, then it isn't much use to us.

Notice that the *Edit_Form* procedure encloses the **FORM_TER-MINAL.Read(FILE)**; statement in a block and provides a local exception handler for that block. The exception handler ignores the *LAYOUT_ERROR* and lets the program proceed normally. Any other exception, like *READ_ERROR*, is not ignored and is handled by an exception handler at the end of the program.

3.7 PORTING THE I/O INTERFACE TO VAX/VMS

Ada solves many portability problems, but there are always a few problems moving software from one system to another. These problems can be reduced if the program is written with portability in mind, but they can never be completely eliminated.

Almost all of the software in this book was developed on an IBM PC AT clone, using the Meridian Ada compiler. Moving to a genuine IBM PC AT with the Alsys compiler was no trouble at all. Most of the software was moved to a VAX running the DEC Ada compiler under VMS without any modification. The only real trouble was moving some of the I/O routines to the VAX. That's not unusual. I/O typically causes portability problems.

At first it might seem surprising that some things that are easy to do on a microcomputer are hard to do on a minicomputer. A minicomputer is more powerful, but power does not always imply ease of use. A jack-hammer is a powerful tool, but it is easier to use a less powerful 16 ounce clawhammer for small jobs (like hanging a picture). The VAX is powerful, but for a small job, like a custom terminal interface, a smaller computer is easier to use.

There are two major differences between the PC and the VAX. The first difference is the number of users that are simultaneously supported. DOS on the IBM PC is a single-user operating system. This means it was designed to make it as easy as possible for the programmer to get direct access to system resources (disk files, terminal, printer, and so on). VMS is a multiuser system designed to prevent users from interfering with each other. It does this by preventing direct access to system resources. The only way VMS lets you use system resources is through an operating system call that gives you limited access. When you are trying to directly control a peripheral, small single-user operating systems work for you, large multiuser operating systems work against you.

The second difference is that the DEC software is tightly coupled to DEC hardware. DEC terminals are not general purpose dumb terminals—they have been specially designed to take some of the burden off DEC software. This specialization results in improved performance under normal circumstances, but it lacks the flexibility needed for non-DEC applications.

Limited access provided by the operating system and specialization of the hardware are typical problems encountered whenever software is ported from one system to another. This isn't a unique problem with VAX/VMS. It happens all the time. That's why it is important to try to hide I/O details in a package that provides a consistent virtual interface regardless of the underlying system. If you don't, you fight the same battle every time you port another application program.

3.7.1 *VMS* Package

The VMS operating system doesn't want to encourage you to exchange individual character data with the terminal (it isn't as efficient as block transfers), so those system services don't exist. That's why I had to write a package similar to the Alsys *DOS* package, containing the three subprograms I needed. I called this package *VMS*. It is shown in Listings 48 through 51.

3.7.2 Raising Exceptions

The *VMS* package has to call some system services. These services return with a status variable telling if the operation was successful. I don't know enough about the VMS operating system to know why the service request would fail, but I do know that I probably don't want to ignore the failure and try to proceed anyway. I need to do something about the failure, but I don't know what. In cases like these it is a good idea to raise an exception and let the next higher level worry about it. (The technical term for this is "passing the buck.")

If I raised a predefined exception, like *CONSTRAINT_ERROR*, it would really confuse someone if the error ever happened. I need to declare a user-defined exception unique to this problem. I decided to call it *VMS_IO_ERROR*. That's not a very descriptive name. It doesn't tell what the problem is. It would be better to call it *TERMINAL_OFF_LINE*, or something like that. I couldn't do that because I don't know what the problem is. All I know is that it is somehow related to a VMS I/O system service.

If I declared this exception in the package body instead of the specification, then the *VMS* subprograms could still raise it. The exception would propagate out of the package as an anonymous (unnamed) exception, because names inside a package body aren't visible outside the body. The application program would need an anonymous exception handler for this exception. (For example, **when others** = > **Do_Something_Appropriate;**). Since the application program doesn't know about it, it probably won't provide a handler for it, so the program will terminate with an unhandled exception if it is ever raised.

I was really tempted to do this, because I believe *VMS_IO_ERROR* has to be a fatal error resulting in the immediate termination of the program. I resisted the temptation because it isn't my place to decide the fate of someone else's application program. If I leave the exception buried in the body, a client will only see that the package *VMS* contains three subprograms and think that it doesn't raise any exceptions. What a nasty surprise when the program bombs with a cryptic error message like "unnamed exception raised at PC = 00AF0166 never handled."

Placing the exception in the package specification warns the client that the exception can occur. The client can decide what to do about it. I doubt that there is much that can be done, because when VMS dies, it cuts down on your options in a big way. Perhaps the client knows a clever solution. I don't want to deny the client the option to recover from the error.

3.7.3 *CONTROL-C* Powder Keg

Unfortunately, VMS isn't as generous with options as I am. Whoever wrote the QIO service decided that nobody would ever want to pass *CONTROL_C, CONTROL_Y*, or *CONTROL_Z* back to a main program. Whenever a user presses one of these three control keys, the QIO service diverts the program flow to a VMS default handler that is reluctant to give control back to your program.

This is a serious problem on two counts. First, it forced me to pick a different character for the panic button. (I picked the exclamation point for no particular reason.) Now users have to remember the panic button is *CONTROL_C* on the PC, but it is *!* on a VAX. I could solve this problem by changing the IBM PC versions so that the exclamation point is the panic character on those versions, too. That would make the user operation consistent regardless of the system, but it wouldn't solve the second part of the problem. Old timers like me are used to using

CONTROL_C as a panic button. Whenever things run amok, we hit *CONTROL_C* by force of habit. The VMS intercept of the *CONTROL_C* leaves the user program running and removes any possibility of the user regaining control.

There is a LIB$DISABLE_CTRL VMS service that might be used to disable *CONTROL_C* and *CONTROL_Y*, but it doesn't seem to do anything about *CONTROL_Z*. I tried to add it to the package body, but it got really messy. This isn't supposed to be a book about quirks in VMS, and these things don't really have much to do with Ada, so I decided to leave them out. If there is a VMS wizard among the readers of this book who can write an improved version of this package that isn't beyond the comprehension of mere mortals, I will be glad to include it in the next edition of this book. In the meantime, we just have to live with the danger.

3.7.4 Operating-System Limitations

Situations like this one often lead to criticism of Ada. The charge is that Ada doesn't have enough low-level capability, or Ada's run-time system is inadequate. This isn't an Ada problem, it is an operating system problem. The *CONTROL_C* problem doesn't exist on DOS, and I would have the same problem on the VAX if I were writing this in FORTRAN, C, or assembly. The fact that my Ada program doesn't handle *CONTROL_C* on VAX/VMS isn't because Ada is inadequate—it's a VAX/VMS limitation. If you can show me a VMS FORTRAN program that gets unfiltered characters from the keyboard, I bet I can show you how to do it in Ada using the same technique. Ada just makes operating system limitations more visible because Ada programs attempt more ambitious projects. (Can you imagine trying to write the *FORM_TERMINAL* in FORTRAN?)

3.7.5 *INPUT* task

Listing 49 shows the VMS package body. The input subprogram bodies simply call entries in a task called *INPUT*. A complete treatment of tasks is beyond the scope of this book, so I was hoping to avoid the subject completely, but VMS forced me to use this one. Here is a quick overview of this particular task.

The *INPUT* task (Listing 50) has three entries: *Keypush*, *Ready*, and *Get*. It is normally suspended, waiting for one of those three entries to be called. *Keypush* is an asynchronous system trap (AST) entry. It is asynchronous because it happens whenever a user presses a key. (That is, it doesn't always happen at a certain point in the program.) It tells the *INPUT* task that it must process the input character so the user can press another key. You can consider it to be the input port of a buffer between the asynchronous input from the user and the synchronous requests for data from the application program. The *Get* entry point is the output port of the buffer. It waits to supply data to the program until the program asks for it, or makes the program wait until data is available. (It synchronizes the data with the program.) The *Ready* entry point tells the application program if there is any unprocessed data in the buffer or not. This is useful in programs that can be doing other things while waiting for data. The program can poll the *Ready* entry point periodically and process input data (if it is there) at its convenience.

The *INPUT* task is filled with "secret sauce" unique to VMS. It would have taken me forever to figure this out myself, but fortunately Lee Lucas and Dave Dent had to solve this problem before I did, and I was able to take advantage of their work. They didn't come up with this all by themselves. They adapted an earlier program by Dee DeCristofaro for their use. I say this not only to give credit where credit is due (and shift blame away from myself if this is a dumb way to do it), but also to make a software engineering point. Even in those cases where software can't be reused without change, modular programming can make it easier to adapt software from one application to another. Lee and Dave structured their software in such a way that I was able to easily recognize the parts I needed and could extract them for my use.

DEC Ada comes with two unique packages for interfacing with VMS system services. The main one is *STARLET*. (The name simply means that some of the DEC programmers like to name software modules after constellations, stars, planets, and so on.) If you want to print a copy of the *STARLET* package specification, be sure you dump it to a high-speed line printer with a nearly full box of paper. I might have named the package *NOT_KITCHEN_SINK* because that is one of the few things it doesn't contain. Despite all that, it doesn't include the definition of *Cond_value_type*, so a second package, *CONDITION_HANDLING*, is needed too.

Finally, there is a package called *SYSTEM* that gives the definition of address types, and other system-dependent declarations. Section 13.7 of the LRM allows some special features to be added to this package. The DEC version includes conversions of addresses and integers to unsigned long words, and a function *Or*, which acts as a bit set operation.

The task body *INPUT* just glues pieces of these DEC-specific packages together. The task begins by calling *STARLET.Assign* to assign the user's terminal, called *SYS$COMMAND*, to a *CHAN-NEL*. When it does this, it assigns a value of *STARLET.Channel_type* to the local variable *CHANNEL*. It also assigns a value of *CONDITION_HANDLING.Cond_value_type* to a variable called *ASG_STATUS*. A Boolean function called *CONDITION_HANDLING.Success* knows how to examine the *ASG_STATUS* and decide if the operation was successful or not. The *Assign* operation should always succeed, so the *Success* function should always return *TRUE* when it examines *ASG_STATUS*. If it doesn't, the *INPUT* task raises *VMS_IO_ERROR* and gives up. (I've never seen that exception raised, and hope I never will.) Once the channel is assigned, it is ready for use. It need not be assigned again.

It may bother you that we don't know what the type or value of *CHANNEL* or *ASG_STATUS* is. It shouldn't. We don't need to know if these are integers, strings, or enumeration types. Keeping this information hidden from us prevents it from distracting us. If we knew *CHANNEL* was an integer, we might get lazy and just assign it the value of 27 instead of using *SYS$COMMAND*. That might work when we logged on at our usual terminal, but not when we logged on at another one.

After the terminal is assigned to a channel, the task enters a loop that tells the VMS operating system to get a keystroke from the keyboard, waits for keystroke, and then gives it to the client program. This loop continues as long as the *VMS* package is in scope. Since the *VMS* package is normally *with*ed by *VIRTUAL_TERMINAL*, which is *with*ed into a package like *SCROLL_TERMINAL*, which is *with*ed into the main program, the loop continues until the main program ends.

When the loop begins, no data has been received yet. Therefore, the variable *NEW_DATA* is set to *FALSE*. This fact will be used to guard an entry point later in the task.

The *STARLET* procedure *Qio* starts an I/O operation and returns immediately without waiting for completion. The operation uses the *CHANNEL* that was assigned to *SYS$COMMAND*, and the function to be performed is to read a virtual block. This function is modified by *IO_M_NOECHO*, which tells it not to echo the characters to the screen as they are received. Furthermore, the *IO_M_NOFILTR* tells it not to interpret *CONTROL_R*, *CONTROL_U*, or *DELETE* as editing characters, and it passes them along to the task. (Alas, it still filters *CONTROL_C*, *CONTROL_Y*, and *CONTROL_Z*, as we have already mentioned.)

The success of the *Qio* procedure is stored in *QIO_STATUS*, and it is interpreted by *CONDITION_HANDLING.Success* just as the *ASG_STATUS* was. The status of the operation (presumably values like *ready, pending, in progress, complete,* or *transfer count*) is stored in *QIO_IOSB*, which is of type *STARLET.IOSB_type*. *QIO_IOSB* will have a transfer count of 0 the first time it is read, but later, after the user has pressed a key, the transfer count will be 1. The value of this variable will change as the result of a direct memory-access operation, or perhaps as the result of an interrupt service routine.

The pragma *Volatile(QIO_IOSB)* tells the optimizer that *QIO_IOSB* can change without program intervention. Without that pragma, an optimizer might realize that it had already read *QIO_IOSB* and saved the value in a register. It would keep rereading the register and always find the same result.

KEYINPUT is a string, where the *Qio* procedure will put the input data. Normally this string is several characters long for efficiency, but I want to process each character individually, so I made the string one character long. The parameters *P1* and *P2* tell the *Qio* procedure where the string is and how long it is.

The *ASTADR* parameter in *Qio* is the address of the *Keypush* entry. When the user presses a key, *Qio* will transfer the value of the key to *KEYINPUT(1)*. Then *Qio* calls the *Keypush* entry to let the application program know there is new data in *KEYINPUT(1)*.

After the *Qio* operation has been successfully initiated, the task enters an inner loop. This inner loop allows three alternatives. It can (1) accept a *Keypush*, (2) report that no keys have been pressed yet, or (3) *terminate*. The second alternative can happen multiple times. The first alternative can happen only once because it sets *NEW_DATA* to *TRUE*, which exits the inner loop. The last alternative, *terminate*, can happen only once.

Eventually the user will press a key, and the task will enter a second inner loop. It is strikingly similar to the first inner loop, except its first alternative is to accept a *Get* instead of a *Keypush*. The second inner loop ends when the *Get* entry is called. The *Get* entry copies the input character to the *out* parameter and sets *NEW_DATA* to *FALSE* to exit the loop. The outer loop calls the *Qio* procedure again and the cycle repeats.

Most of the time, the *INPUT* task is suspended, waiting for something to happen. When the main program ends, it will be sitting on a *select* statement that includes a *terminate* alternative, so it will end when the main program ends.

3.7.6 *OUTPUT* Package

The *OUTPUT* package (Listing 51) looks a lot like the *INPUT* task. In fact, originally the source file was created by editing the *INPUT* task source code. Let's look at the differences.

The obvious difference is that it is a package, not a task. Since the first version was derived from a copy of *INPUT*, it used a second task for *OUTPUT* and it worked just fine. I could have left it a task, but I elected to change it to a package.

I think it is better not to use a task, not because of the task-switching overhead, but mostly for a philosophical reason. Tasks should be reserved for independent, concurrent activities. The *INPUT* task deserves to be a task because it can be considered to be a separate program continuously scanning the keyboard so the main program doesn't have to.

If I were sharing a printer with other users, it would make sense to make *OUTPUT* a task that buffers output characters, checks for printer availability, and sends the characters when the printer is ready. That would allow the main program to continue processing even though the printer isn't available. That isn't the case here. I'm sending this data to the user's terminal, which should always be available. Generally, I'm sending a prompt and waiting for the user's response. There is no sense running ahead to look for a response before the prompt is sent. So OUTPUT shouldn't be a separate thread of control. It is just another step in a sequential process.

That's why the *put* procedure uses *STARLET.Qiow* instead of *STARLET.Qio*. The *w* stands for wait. I don't want to run ahead until the output character is on its way to the user. I have to wait until the character is sent, so I might as well give up the processor and let someone else use it.

3.7.7 Enforcing Order

Why isn't *put* just a procedure? Why did I stick it in a package? The key is in the last few lines of the package. The output channel has to be assigned before data can be sent to it.

This raises a portability issue. I want to port all my programs developed under DOS to VMS, and none of my existing application programs assigns the output channel because it isn't necessary on DOS. If I didn't hide this channel assignment in the elaboration of some package, I'd have to change all my application programs to port them to VMS.

Even if there wasn't a portability problem, there would still be a compelling reason to stick *put* in a package. There is a procedural order that must be enforced: First assign the output channel once, then use it many times. If I didn't use a package, I would have to depend on every application programmer that ever uses the VMS package to remember to assign the output channel before use. If the application programmer forgot to do that, who knows what error would happen. I have to make sure the procedures are called in the correct order.

When an application program running under VMS uses *SCROLL_TERMINAL* it *with*s in *VIRTUAL_TERMINAL*, which elaborates the package *VMS*, which elaborates *OUTPUT*, which runs *STARLET.Assign*. All this happens automatically, so the application program doesn't have to remember to assign the output channel. Furthermore, it all happens before the application program gets control, so the application program can't write to the output before it is assigned.

Tasks can also be used to enforce order. The *INPUT* task assigned the channel first and then used *select* statements to assure that *Get* was not accepted until after a key was pressed.

I think failure to consider order of execution is a major problem in Ada programming. I suspect this is because most programmers are used to writing single-task programs that automatically enforce order because they have a single thread of control, so they aren't used to thinking about it. Programmers who are used to writing programs with multiple tasks are more likely to think about it, but they may be tempted to rely on secret things they have discovered about their operating system's scheduling algorithm, because that's the way they've always done it. Their programs aren't likely to be portable.

The Ada language does contain features that enforce an order of execution. The *INPUT* task and *OUTPUT* package are examples of how to use these features. Use them wisely.

3.7.8   Hardware Limitations

There is also a hardware interface problem on the VAX. If you are using a VAX, you are almost certainly using a VT52, VT100, VT220, VT240, or something that emulates a DEC terminal. When you look at all those extra keys on the right side of a VT100, and the row of function keys across the top of the VT220, you would think there would be no problem making it compatible with the *VIRTUAL_ TERMINAL*. Although a DEC terminal appears to have all the capability you need, it doesn't. Many of those keys don't get past the keyboard. For example, function keys F1 through F5 on a VT240 are dedicated to *Hold Screen, Print Screen, Set-Up, Data/Talk*, and *Break*. Pressing these keys makes the terminal do something, but it sends nothing to the computer, so no amount of clever software can process them. The *INSERT* and *DELETE* keys don't exist on a DEC terminal, either.

The situation is a little better if you use a dumb terminal instead of a DEC terminal. The Televideo 910, for example, has fewer keys than a DEC terminal, but most of them produce unique codes. Even so, there are still a few problems. The *DOWN* arrow key on a TV910 produces the same ASCII code as the *LINE_ FEED* key. Therefore, you really don't have a *DOWN* arrow key, you just have two *LINE_ FEED* keys with different legends on the key cap, and there is no way for software to tell them apart.

The possibility of missing keys is the reason the *VIRTUAL_ TER-MINAL* package specification defines special control codes. A terminal may not have an *INSERT* key, but it will certainly have a control key and an *A* key, so to add text the user can press *CONTROL-A* to simulate the *INSERT* key. Even if the terminal doesn't have a *DELETE* key, the user can press *CONTROL-E* to erase characters. The *VIRTUAL_ TERMINAL* package will work on any terminal, but it may be awkward on some terminals because they don't have the required keys.

The *FORM_TERMINAL.Create* procedure is more awkward to use on a DEC terminal than on an IBM PC because function keys F1, F2, and F3 don't exist on the DEC terminal. *FORM_TERMINAL.Create* uses F1 to mark the beginning of a protected field, F2 to mark the beginning of an unprotected field, and F3 to mark the end of either. When creating a form on a DEC terminal, you have to use *CONTROL_F* followed by a 1, 2, or 3 to simulate those missing keys. The program works, but it isn't as convenient as it would be if those function keys existed.

If you port the virtual terminal to your physical terminal, you may have some unused keys that produce unique codes. You may want to define these keys to replace missing keys. Just modify the *VIRTUAL_TERMINAL* package body so the unused keys get mapped to the control codes specified in the package specification. (If you do this, it might be confusing if you ever change terminals, but that's a price you might want to pay for convenience.)

3.7.9 DEC *VIRTUAL_TERMINAL*

Despite all these problems, it is possible to port the *VIRTUAL_TERMINAL* package to DEC Ada. The DEC version is shown in Listings 52 and 53. In theory, I shouldn't have to change the package specification, but I did because of the way VAX/VMS handles control characters, and because my *VMS* package may want to raise an exception that the PC version doesn't need to raise. Since I wrote the *VMS* package to look a lot like the Alsys *DOS* package, the *VIRTUAL_TERMINAL* package body for VAX/VMS is almost identical to the Alsys body.

All I/O specific code is confined to the *VIRTUAL_TERMINAL* package. The more powerful *SCROLL_TERMINAL* and *FORM_TERMINAL* packages are built on top of the *VIRTUAL_TERMINAL* package. Therefore, once the *VIRTUAL_TERMINAL* is running on VAX/VMS, the *SCROLL_TERMINAL* and *FORM_TERMINAL* can be ported to VAX/VMS without modification.

3.8 *VIRTUAL_PRINTER* PACKAGE

If you have ever tried to use *TEXT_IO* to send data to a printer, you know you have to know the name of the printer to open it. If you are using DOS on a PC, there is a good chance the printer will be connected to *LPT1*, but it doesn't have to be. On VMS the printer could be on just about any port, so you can't assume *TXA7:* will always be the printer port. (In most cases it won't.)

3.8.1   What's Its Name?

What are you going to do if you want to write a program that sends
data to a printer? You could ask the user the name of the printer every
time. That's a bad idea because it is a nuisance to the user, and the user
might not even know the name of the printer port. You could code the
printer port name right into your application program, but that can cause
maintenance and portability problems. Suppose the central computing
facility reconfigures the system and moves the printer to another port.
You would have to search through all your application programs to find
every place you have named the printer port. You would have to do the
same thing if you wanted to use your programs on another computer.

My solution is to write a package called *VIRTUAL_PRINTER* (Listing
54), which has the name of the printer hidden in the body. If you ever
need to change the name of the printer port, you just have to change
the name in the *VIRTUAL_PRINTER* body, recompile it, and relink any
application programs that use it. You don't need to recompile the affected
application programs, because they depend on the *VIRTUAL_PRINTER*
specification, and you've only had to change the body. All you have to
do is relink them. (An Ada programming environment ought to be able
to give you a list of all units that depend on the *VIRTUAL_PRINTER*
package specification, so you will know which programs to relink.)

3.8.2   Printer Quirks

The *VIRTUAL_PRINTER* body is also a good place to take care of
printer quirks. Many years ago, I ran across a printer that used an
escape sequence instead of the normal ASCII form-feed character to
advance to the top of a page. There may not be any of those printers around anymore, but if there are, you can put some code in
the *VIRTUAL_PRINTER* body that substitutes the appropriate escape
sequence whenever it receives a form feed.

The first printer I attached to my IBM PC AT clone was my old,
reliable Microline 83 printer, which had served my CP/M system for five
years. It was configured for 1200 baud serial operation, and I put it on the
COM2 port. Modern printers buffer several thousand characters, but in
1982 serial printers only buffered a line or two. At the end of each line,
the Microline 83 used an RS-232C control signal to tell the computer
not to send any more data because it was busy printing the data in the
buffer. My new computer expects the printer to use *CONTROL_Q* and
CONTROL_S to tell it when to start and stop sending data, and it must
not bother to check the RS-232C control lines. Consequently, the first
character of a line would sometimes be sent while the printer was still
printing, and wouldn't get into the print buffer.

This is not a new problem. The original teletypewriter terminals took a long time for the print cylinder to return to the first column. They used a 20 milliamp current loop, and didn't have any extra control lines in those days. Since they didn't have any way of telling when the print cylinder was ready to print again, they routinely sent a few null characters after every carriage return. Nulls aren't printed, so it doesn't matter if they get lost or not. (Now you know why electronic bulletin boards sometimes ask you if you require any nulls.) Figure 33 shows that I solved my problem in exactly the same way.

When I bought my Epson LQ-850, I put it on the parallel port *LPT1*. All I had to do was make the changes shown in Listing 55, and all my old programs would send data to my new printer.

You will almost certainly have to write your own *VIRTUAL_PRINTER* body, but it shouldn't be too difficult. All you have to do is know the logical name of the printer.

3.9   *SCROLL_PRINTER* **PACKAGE**

Just as the *VIRTUAL_TERMINAL* provided a portable base for the *SCROLL_TERMINAL*, the *VIRTUAL_PRINTER* is the base for the *SCROLL_PRINTER*. The *SCROLL_PRINTER* specification is shown in Listing 56, and the body is in Listing 57. It's basically just the *SCROLL_TERMINAL* with the input parts removed, so there isn't any more that needs to be said about it.

PROGRAMMING ISN'T SOFTWARE ENGINEERING

The difference between programming and software engineering is like the difference between gardening and farming. You could say the difference is the size of the effort, but there is really more to it than that.

Farming isn't just gardening on a large scale. You can't use the same techniques for farming that you would if you were gardening. Any farmer who tries to plant his crops using nothing more than a shovel, rake, and hoe is not going to succeed. Farming requires more powerful tools. A farmer needs a tractor.

Gardening isn't just farming on a small scale. You can't use the same techniques gardening that you would use if you were farming. I shouldn't try to use a tractor to plant my six tomato seedlings. It would be more trouble just getting the tractor into my backyard than it would be to dig six holes with a shovel. The amount of money I save growing my own tomatoes wouldn't pay the maintenance on the tractor.

Even though there are differences between gardening and farming, there are some fundamental principles that don't change. Regardless of the size of the effort, you still need to provide the plants with adequate nourishment, water, and the right amount of sunlight. Things that you learn about soil preparation will be useful to you regardless of whether you are gardening or farming.

Software engineering isn't just programming done by more people over a longer period of time. You need different techniques for "programming in the small" and "programming in the large." In this section you will see several examples of small programming projects and one example of software engineering. Some of the techniques that work for small programming projects aren't adequate for large projects. Some of the techniques necessary for large projects are too awkward for small projects. Some basic principles (like the ones discussed in the previous sections on numeric considerations and I/O utilities) hold for both programming and software engineering.

I'm sure you wouldn't try to plant a 40 acre farm with just a shovel, nor would you be foolish enough to try to use a tractor to plow a 5 by 10 foot backyard garden. Most people intuitively know when an area of land is too big to shovel or too small to plow. Unfortunately, many people lack that same intuition when it comes to software development. They have one method, and they use it regardless of the size of the project. Using software engineering techniques on a small program leads to just as much trouble as using simple programming techniques on a large project does. You will save yourself a lot of grief if you can recognize when to shovel and when to plow.

You are about to see several little software tools that are examples of programming. They took a few hours to write and debug. I didn't spend weeks planning them; I just started writing with a vague goal in mind. As I got closer to the goal, my vision became clearer. I used the programs and then made minor modifications to improve them. That is an appropriate approach to take for small projects.

If the project is large, seat-of-the-pants programming won't work. You don't just sit down one afternoon and write the operational flight program for the space shuttle. You can't just say to yourself, "I'm not really sure what this space-shuttle software should do, but it will come to me if I just wing it." Big programs require software engineering. The *Draw_Poker* program is a small example of a big program, and it shows some of the things you have to do differently when working on a large project.

I wish I could give you a simple rule like, "Use simple programming techniques for projects less than 1,000 lines of code, and use software engineering for larger projects," but I can't. There isn't a clear-cut boundary between big and small that can be expressed in lines of code. Even if there were, it wouldn't do you any good because you don't know how many lines of code there are in the program until it is finished, and then it's too late.

Still, there are ways to tell when a project warrants software engineering. Ask yourself, "Is this program likely to require long-term maintenance? Will there be people on salary who will be responsible for improving this program and correcting bugs? Is this a program that will take several man-years to develop?" If the answer to these questions is yes, then you should use software-engineering principles. If not, applying rigorous software-engineering discipline will simply make a small project cost as much as a large one, with little or no benefit.

4.1   THE *Show* TOOL

I was doing a job for a client, using his Alsys Ada compiler on his IBM PC AT. It was my first experience with Alsys Ada and my first experience with PC-DOS. I discovered that when you compile SOMEFILE.ADA, and SOMEFILE.ADA has errors in it, Alsys Ada will write the errors to SOMEFILE.LST without displaying them on the screen. Alsys gives such complete error messages that every error produces a paragraph that describes the error and suggests how to correct it. SOMEFILE.LST can easily contain two or three screens full of error messages.

Since I was inexperienced with PC-DOS, I tried to display SOME-FILE.LST the same way I would on VMS. I used the command *TYPE* SOMEFILE.LST. The DOS *TYPE* command does not pause when the screen fills, and text written to the screen isn't limited by a 1200 baud modem, so the whole error file flashed across the screen in a blur. I had to use *CONTROL-S* and *CONTROL-Q* to interrupt the transmission of text to the screen, and I had to have very fast reflexes.

I've had some limited experience with UNIX, so I tried *MORE* SOMEFILE.LST. That appeared to crash PC-DOS, so I had to reboot.

(It didn't really crash, but the symptoms were the same as a crash. The explanation of what really happened is best delayed for a little while.)

In desperation, I read the PC-DOS documentation. The section on the *TYPE* command told me there were no switches I could set to display one screen at a time, and there was no cross-reference to the *MORE* command.

I knew it was easy to write a program to display one screen of data at a time, because I had done it years ago in 8080 assembly language. I decided to rewrite it in Ada. I called the first version of that program *Show*, and you can find the listing for it in Figure 34. It prompts the user for the file name, opens the file, then does a loop 22 times that gets one line from the file and writes that one line to the screen. It prompts the user to "Press RETURN for the next screen," and jumps back to the loop that copies 22 lines to the screen. It does this until it hits an end of file mark.

4.1.1 Named Loops

Let's digress for a moment, and talk about named loops. I will sometimes use a comment to describe what a loop is doing, but I don't name a loop unless I'm going to use an unusual exit from the loop. The label *MAIN:* in Figure 34 should draw attention to that loop.

The problem is that I have nested loops. The inner loop executes 22 times, and the outer loop executes as often as necessary, until there is no more data to display. I could begin the outer loop with **while not End_Of_File(FILE) loop** if I were certain every file would have an exact multiple of 22 lines in it. In general, that won't be true. The end of the file will almost always be reached after a partial screen has been displayed. If I just write **exit when End_Of_File(FILE);** , that will get me out of the inner loop, but not out of the outer loop. The program would prompt the user to press RETURN, then go to the top of the outer loop again, where I would have to check for the end of file again.

The chicken way out is to never check end of file, let the program run until it raises an exception, and quit in the exception handler. That works, but it requires some intuition on the part of a maintenance programmer to figure out how the program ends (unless you reveal the trick in a comment). I find that solution artistically offensive because it looks sloppy and careless. Besides, exception handlers should be used for unusual error conditions. A finite length file is not unusual or erroneous.

The assembly language version handled the problem by checking for end of file at the point corresponding to the *exit* statement. If it found it was at the end of the file, it jumped to a statement corresponding to **Close(FILE);** . (Jump is the assembly language equivalent of GOTO.) I certainly didn't want to endure the shame of using a GOTO in an Ada program, so I didn't use that solution either.

Naming the outer loop is the clean solution to the problem. The **exit MAIN when End_Of_File(FILE);** statement takes us down to **end loop MAIN;** as soon as we run out of data. It clearly shows the maintenance programmer the condition required to leave the loop and is considered a normal exit.

4.1.2   Command Tail

Now let's return to the story of the development of the *Show* tool. I wasn't happy with the program because it still wasn't as good as the assembly language version. When I used the Ada version, I had to wait for the program to prompt me for the file name. The assembly language version let me type a single command, **SHOW SOMEFILE.LST**, and automatically extracted the file name SOMEFILE.LST from the command line without my having to enter it in response to the prompt.

The Ada LRM doesn't specify a standard way to get the rest of the command line. In all fairness to Ada, I should point out that most other languages don't do that either, because it is beyond the normal scope of the language. It is really an operating-system function.

I looked through the Alsys documentation and found a package called *DOS* that includes a function *Get_Parms* that fetches the command tail for you. It wasn't exactly what I wanted, because I wanted something that was an exact replacement for the *get_line* procedure already used in the *Show* program. I knew I would have portability problems if I used *Get_Parms* in *Show* and tried to move *Show* to another system, because *Get_Parms* is a special function Alsys was thoughtful enough to provide with their compiler. It almost certainly wouldn't exist in any other Ada implementation.

4.1.3   Compiling Library Procedures

I decided the best approach would be to write the procedure *Get_Command_Line*, shown in Figure 35. It produces a string and a length, just like *get_line*. All the implementation specific code is confined to one place, and does not infect all the application programs that need to read the command tail. Once this procedure is compiled and stored in the Ada library, every application program that needs to read the command line can use it. Novice Ada programmers think that only packages can be compiled and reused as library components. That's not true. This is an example of a procedure that can be compiled once and reused often.

4.1.4   Unconstrained Strings

Implementation specific routines are usually tricky, and Figure 35 is no exception. The *Get_Parms* function returns an unconstrained string *L* characters long, where *L* depends on the number of characters typed after the command name. I want to write **LENGTH** := **L; TAIL(1..L)** := **DOS.Get_Parms;** . The problem is, I don't know what *L* is. The incredibly clever solution is to make the function call an input parameter to the *Extract* function. **Extract(DOS.Get_Parms, TAIL, LENGTH);** associates the string returned by *DOS.Get_Parms* with the formal parameter *S_IN*. The *LENGTH* attribute yields the value of *L*. Notice that I couldn't write **S_OUT(1..L)** := **S_IN;** because *L* is an *out* parameter and can't be read. That's not a problem because I can use the *LENGTH* attribute as often as I want.

I thought that trick was pretty clever, until I read a column by Ben Brosgol. He knew an even easier way to use the Alsys *DOS.Get_Parms* function. (He has an unfair advantage over me. He works for Alsys!) When you declare a constant string, you don't need to declare the bounds, because the bounds can be determined from the value you assign to the constant, even if that value is an unconstrained string returned by a function. I incorporated his idea into my procedure and came up with Listing 58.

4.1.5 Using Library Procedures

The *Show* program was compiled in the context of the *Get_Command_Line* procedure, as shown in Figure 36. *TEXT* and *LENGTH* come from *Get_Command_Line* if the user enters a file on the command line, or from *get_line* if he doesn't. (I like the way VMS prompts for missing parameters, so I usually include that feature in my routines.)

4.1.6 Porting *Show* to Other Systems

Soon after I wrote the *Show* program, I bought an AT clone of my own and Meridian Adavantage Version 1.5 compiler to go with it. I decided to port the *Show* program to my computer. As I expected, Meridian had a utility that could fetch command line arguments, but it didn't look anything like the Alsys *Get_Parms* function. "No problem," I thought, "I'll just enclose it in a different version of *Get_Command_Line*."

My first attempt at doing this must have looked a lot like Figure 37. I compiled *Get_Command_Line* and then compiled *Show*, linked them, and tried the resulting executable code. There was something wrong with it. The main program *Show* was fully debugged, so the error, of course, was in *Get_Command_Line*. I thought I knew what was wrong with *Get_Command_Line*, changed it, and recompiled it. I tried to relink it with *Show*, but the compiler (correctly) told me that *Show* was obsolete. *Show* was compiled in the context of *Get_Command_Line*, and since I had changed *Get_Command_Line*, Ada couldn't be sure *Show* was still valid. I recompiled *Show*, linked, ran the program, and it still didn't work. I modified *Get_Command_Line* again, recompiled it, then had to recompile *Show* again, and so on. Eventually I came up with the form you see in Figure 37, but it was frustrating having to recompile *Show* every time.

It happened that I was evaluating the Gould APLEX Ada compiler running under the MPX-32 operating system at the time. I decided to try to transport the *Show* program to it. I was not very well acquainted with MPX-32 or APLEX Ada, and I knew I was going to have to recompile *Get_Command_Line* a million times before I got it working. That didn't bother me. I expected that. What bothered me was that I was going to have to recompile *Show* every time, even though I knew it was correct and never changed it.

I wished I had put *Get_Command_Line* inside a package. Then I could have compiled the package specification, compiled *Show*, and compiled the package body containing *Get_Command_Line* last. Then I could recompile the body as often as it took to get it working, and *Show* wouldn't need to be recompiled because it wouldn't be obsolete. (*Show* would depend upon the package specification, not the body.) Then I realized the value of a widely ignored Ada feature. You can separately compile a procedure specification.

4.1.6.1 Compiling Procedure Specifications.

Ada programmers tend to forget that procedures and functions have specifications and bodies just like packages and tasks do. Ada requires you to compile the specification of a package or a task before you compile its body. She lets you omit that step, however, when compiling nongeneric procedures and functions. We almost always take a shortcut when compiling subprograms by compiling the subprogram body without compiling the specification first.

Sometimes taking a shortcut turns out to be longer, and porting *Get_Command_Line* to the Meridian environment is an example of such a situation. But I learned my lesson before porting *Show* to MPX-32. I compiled the package specification shown in Listing 59. There's not much to it, but it saved a mountain of work. After compiling Listing 59, I compiled the *Show* procedure and my first attempt at the *Get_Command_Line* body. It didn't work of course, but when I changed and recompiled it, I was delighted that I didn't have to recompile *Show*. It took me several iterations before I got *Get_Command_Line* right, but I only had to compile *Show* once. The correct *Get_Command_Line* body for APLEX Ada running on MPX-32 is shown in Figure 38.

4.1.6.2 Porting *Show* to VAX/VMS.

Porting *Get_Command_Line* to the VAX/VMS environment was the most difficult. First there was the problem of finding a system service that would get the command line. That wasn't a trivial task. DOS is described in three paperback books with a total thickness of about four inches, but VMS is described in a series of big, orange, three-ring binders that take 5 or 6 feet of shelf space. That means there's a lot more haystack to find the needle in. To make matters worse, the needle was cleverly disguised. It was called *Get_Foreign*, which doesn't immediately suggest suitability for fetching the command line.

Once you find this service, you have to figure out how to interface with it. DEC has some special pragmas, *Interface* and *Import*, that allowed me to associate the LIB$GET_FOREIGN service in the system library with the *Get_Foreign* procedure specification. Listing 60 shows how this was done.

The final problem is using it. If you compile and link it with the *Show* procedure, it produces an executable module. The normal way to run an executable file is to type *RUN* SHOW. In this case, however, we want to type *RUN* SHOW SOMEFILE.EXT. If you do that, it complains about TOO MANY PARAMETERS. I suppose *RUN* calls LIB$GET_FOREIGN to find out what to run, and is expecting only one parameter. When it finds two, it generates an error message.

The magic VMS trick is to use an alias. If you type $SHOW := = $MY_DISK:[MY_DIRECTORY]SHOW.EXE (where MY_DISK and MY_DIRECTORY represent the actual path to the executable file), then you can type SHOW SOMEFILE.EXT and it will work (because you don't have to use RUN to run the program). It is convenient to put this command in your login file, so you don't have to remember to type it before you try to SHOW something.

This is an awfully brief explanation, but remember it doesn't have anything to do with Ada. These are features of VAX/VMS that are mentioned here just because they are necessary to port the *Get_Command_Line* procedure to VMS. If you want to know why these things work, take a course on the VMS operating system, or talk to your local VMS wizard. (I'm lucky to have Dave Dent around to find these VMS features for me.)

4.1.7 Library Procedure Summary

You can separately compile a single library procedure or function without having to put it into a package. (Most people must not know this because I've seen package specifications with nothing but a single subprogram specification in them.) When you do this, you freeze the interface. Then you can recompile the body over and over again, and Ada will check to make sure you have used exactly the same formal parameter list. As long as you don't change anything in the parameter list, you can make as many changes in the body as you like without making units that depend on the specification obsolete.

4.1.8   Common Command Names

Remember how I thought typing *MORE* SOMEFILE.LST caused DOS to crash? We are about to run into that same problem again, and this time we will see that command names can sometimes get you in trouble.

I was particularly frustrated because I was using so many different operating systems. They all used different names for deleting files. I could never remember if I should *ERA*, *DEL*, *DELETE*, *rm*, *KILL*, or *VOLMGR*. On one system *LIST* would type a file, on another it would display the directory. It was driving me nuts! I decided I wanted to try to standardize utility names. Since I was using UNIX then, I decided to rename the *Show* program to *More* to match the UNIX name. Since it was going to have a UNIX name, I also wanted it to work like the UNIX version.

4.2   THE *More* TOOL

The UNIX *more* command pauses after each screenful (22 lines), printing "– – More – –" at the bottom of the screen. If the user types a carriage return, one more line is displayed. If the user types a space, another screenful is displayed. If the user types an integer, that number of lines is printed. If the user hits *d* or *CONTROL-D*, 11 more lines are displayed. The UNIX version also has nine command line switches, but since I've never used any of them I didn't bother to implement them. (That's left as the proverbial exercise for the reader. See the UNIX documentation for a description of the nine unimplemented options.) The *More* program is shown in Listing 61.

When I tried to run *More* on the PC, I ran into a name clash. DOS already has a command called *MORE*. It differs from the UNIX *MORE* because DOS *MORE* has to be used as a filter. That is, you can say *TYPE* ANYFILE.EXT |*MORE* and it will show you a screen full at a time, but if you type *MORE* ANYFILE.EXT it just sits there waiting for you to enter data from the keyboard, which it will display one screen at a time. When that happened, I thought the system crashed.

I could have left the name of my program *Show*, but that doesn't solve the problem. I had fallen into the habit of typing *MORE* ANYFILE.EXT on the UNIX system and occasionally did that on DOS. So, I used the DOS *REN* command to rename *MORE.EXE* to *DOSMORE.EXE*. Then, when I ran my version of *More* it did not clash with the existing DOS program of the same name. If I want to use the original DOS *MORE* program, I can still enter a command such as *TYPE* ANYFILE.EXT |*DOSMORE*.

The moral of the story is that users expect certain results when they do certain things. It is hard for them to remember that the same command does different things depending on the context. Sometimes users can work around the problem by renaming commands or creating aliases, but they shouldn't have to. Whenever you write a program that has a direct interface to a human user, be sure you are consistent with what that user is accustomed to.

4.2.1 Multiple Loop Exits

Respectable loops have one entry and one exit point. To be perfectly proper the exit point is at the beginning or end of the loop. Some people allow the exit point to be in the middle of the loop, but they do so at the risk of being snubbed by elite programmers. A close inspection of Listing 61 shows that it ends with a loop containing (shudder!) two exit points, and one of them is in the middle. How could anyone with a name like Do-While do such a thing?

The software guideline restricting all loops to *Do-While* or *Repeat-Until* structures has merit. Certainly I'm not advocating a return to long loops full of GOTOs that twist a tangled trail through torturously tightened tentacles. Those structures are as hard to understand as they are to read. Loops that enter at the top and exit only at the top or the bottom are much easier to understand and maintain than something that looks like a nervous giant squid.

I am prepared to argue, however, that there are special instances when the most maintainable loop has multiple exits. Furthermore, I submit that the *More* program is one such instance. I think it is much cleaner than the single exit from the nested named loops in the *Show* program.

The two exit loop in the *More* program more closely describes what is really happening than the nested loops in the *Show* program do. Specifically, it displays some lines of text on the screen, and if it has displayed all there are to display, it quits. If there are more lines left, it lets the user decide how many more he wants to see. If he doesn't want to see any more, the loop ends. The loop is so short, it is easy to find all the exit points.

If I had coded the *Display* and *get* routines in-line instead of using procedure calls, then I would agree that the two exits are hard to find, and I would submit to any number of lashes with a wet noodle. Instead, the *Display* routine hides the confusing fact that there is another loop reading and writing one line at a time. The *Show* procedure might have less trouble passing a code walkthrough, but I believe *More* is better.

4.3 THE *Write* TOOL

Every time I get a new, better computer, it is always harder to do the things I used to do so easily on my old, obsolete computer. On my old CP/M computer, I had an 8080 assembly language program called *Write* that printed files on the printer. It put a title at the top of the page, a page number at the bottom, and never printed on the page perforations. It would double space the listing, too, if I asked it to. I was disappointed when I discovered I couldn't do the same thing on my "advanced technology" clone.

The DOS *PRINT* command prints files, but it just copies them straight to the printer with no headers or page numbers, and it doesn't even skip over page perforations. I bought a well-known word processor from a major software house and thought I could use it to print flat ASCII files. I can, but it sure is a nuisance. The command sequence to print a single-spaced file is

```
<ESC> TRANSFER LOAD FILE.EXT <CR>
<ESC> FORMAT DIVISION PAGE-NUMBERS YES <CR>
<ESC> FORMAT DIVISION MARGINS 0 <TAB> 0
<TAB> 0 <TAB> 0 <CR>
<ESC> PRINT PRINTER
<ESC> QUIT NO
```

That doesn't put titles on the top of every page. (I know there must be a way to get titles, but I haven't figured out how yet.) If I want to double-space it, I have to do all of the above, plus <SHIFT-F10> <ESC> FORMAT PARAGRAPH <TAB> <TAB> <TAB> <TAB> 2 <CR> somewhere in the middle.

Oh, how I longed for the good old days when I could WRITE FILE.EXT! It didn't take too long for the frustration level to build to the point where I translated my *Write* program from 8080 assembly language to Ada. Figure 39 shows the first version of the *Write* program, and Listing 62 shows the final version.

4.3.1 Error Recovery and Help

Figure 39 was a direct translation from assembly to Ada. It didn't have any help features, because I wrote the program for my own use and didn't need them. When I decided to publish it, I knew other users might press the question-mark key to get help, so I had to include *NEEDS_HELP* handlers. I suppose I could have put one big help procedure at the end of the program that explained every option, but then the user would have to read all the answers and figure out which one answers his question. I prefer to give the user short, pertinent explanations that help solve the immediate crisis.

What managers and programmers often fail to realize, is that a major portion of a program with a user interface will be devoted to error recovery and help messages. Everyone expects a routine that asks the user for the first page number to include some statements that convert a string to an integer. They often don't realize there must also be some statements that know what to do when the user says the first page number is "banana". Look at how much of the *Write* program is devoted to error recovery! Compare Figure 39 to Listing 62 to see how short the program could be if I left all the error recovery routines out.

The final typesetting process may change the exact number of lines in these two versions of the *Write* program, but before reformatting them to make them fit on the printed page, the original version was 57 lines and final version was 145 lines. That means 57 of the lines in *Write* are doing the work, and 88 lines are just there for error recovery. That's a 154% increase in program size to make the program user-friendly. The 154% figure isn't an absolute constant. The amount of expansion depends on the number of questions you ask the user, and how verbose each help message is, but it isn't unusual for programs with extensive user interfaces to more than double in size when error recovery and help messages are added. Take that into consideration when you are estimating the size of a software project, and don't be naive enough to think that error recovery will be 2% of the total software effort!

4.4 THE *Line* TOOL

Meridian now has an Ada Development Interface (ADI) that integrates a smart editor with the compiler. If you compile a file that has an error in it, you can push a button and the cursor will move to the point in the source code where the next error is. AdaVantage Version 1.5 didn't have that feature. If you compiled a file that contained errors, it would write a message to the screen telling you that line number X in SOMEFILE.ADA contained a certain error. You could call up the EDLIN editor and go to line X to see what it was. Sometimes the error was really in line $X-1$ (a missing semicolon, for example), and the compiler didn't recognize the error until line X. Sometimes the real error was many lines earlier. (For example, proper use of a variable that was improperly declared generates an error message pointing to the line using the variable, not the line declaring it.)

I decided I would like to be able to type LINE X SOMEFILE.ADA and see that line on the screen. The more I thought about it, the more I realized I really wanted to see a few lines before and after line X. So, I wrote the *Line* program shown in Listings 63 and 64.

Although the *Line* program was written in response to a specific need (to display lines containing errors), it isn't limited to that single use. You can use it to browse through any file for any reason.

4.4.1 Multiple Arguments

The *Line* program needs two arguments on the command line (a line number and a file name). The *Extract* subunit extracts these two pieces of information from the command line and returns them as separate parameters. This forced me to make some design decisions. Which argument should come first? What should I do if the user enters the arguments in the wrong order?

My first reaction was that the file name should be the first argument and the line number should be the second one. This makes sense from a programmer's point of view because the file has to be opened before the program can start looking for a particular line. It also seemed consistent because *More* and *Write* both have filenames immediately following the command.

I wrote the *Extract* routine to take the file name first, used the program for a while, and found I kept making mistakes. If I wanted to see line 15 of SOMEFILE.ADA, I naturally typed LINE 15 SOMEFILE.ADA. It wasn't natural to type LINE SOMEFILE.ADA 15. (Since it's usually right to not split an infinitive, analogy suggests that I shouldn't separate 15 from LINE.) From a user's point of view, it makes more sense to put the line number first, so I changed the order in *Extract*.

4.4.2 Error Tolerance

I put the arguments in the order that seems right to me. Who's to say that every user will feel the same way. If it is natural for them to put the file first, they will usually enter the arguments in the wrong order. That's an easy error to detect. Only one of the fields will be the image of an integer, so that field must contain the line number. If the program detects the incorrect entry, the program could respond with the error message, "You have entered the arguments in the wrong order. The correct syntax is LINE N FILENAME.EXT."

The user might respond to this error message with a respectful genuflection and say, "Oh, I'm so sorry. Please forgive me. I promise never to make that mistake again." Users like that may exist, but I've never found one. Most users will say, "If you're so darn smart, and know that the arguments are reversed, why don't you just do what I want?" The point is well taken. If a program is smart enough to recognize the error and can tell the user exactly how to correct it, can't it just as well be smart enough to fix the error itself?

This kind of tolerance is almost unknown in user interfaces, but perhaps the *Line* program may start a trend. Instead of insulting the user, it simply complies with any poorly stated command. If the user enters the two arguments in the correct order, it works. If the user enters the two arguments backwards, it works. If the user forgets to enter the file name, it asks for the file name. If the user forgets to enter the line number, it asks for the line number. If the user doesn't enter either, it asks for both. There's no need to be nasty when it's so easy to be nice.

4.4.3 Presuming Too Much

If a software component is going to be reusable, it can't presume too much about how it will be used. A case in point is the *Get_Command_Line* procedure for the Meridian system. It presumes too much and that makes it awkward to use.

The Alsys and DEC versions of *Get_Command_Line* are built on general routines that return the whole command line. Alsys and DEC didn't make any assumptions about how anyone would want to use the command line. They just give you the command line and let you do whatever you want with it.

Meridian assumed that anyone who wants the command line will want to break it down into individual arguments, so they tried to do the programmer a favor and split it apart for him. Their *ARG* package tells you how many arguments there are, and passes an array of arguments back. That's really handy if that's exactly what you want to do. If it isn't, then it becomes very clumsy.

I've written a routine, which doesn't appear in this book (because it doesn't teach any new lessons), called *Search* that searches a file for a text string. It is invoked by the command SEARCH FILENAME.EXT "A STRING WHICH MAY CONTAIN PUNCTUATION, SPACES, AND WHO KNOWS WHAT ELSE!". The Meridian *ARG* package returns this as thirteen individual arguments, but there are really only two (*FILENAME.EXT* and the text string). I have to go to the trouble to put together the things that Meridian has taken apart.

That's not a terrible ordeal. Listing 65 shows how to do it. It's inefficient for *ARG* to take apart the command string and then make *Get_Command_Line* put it back together so *Line.Extract* can take it apart again, but that's what happens if you make your lowest-level utility routines too specific.

4.5 THE *Search* TOOL

Let's talk about the *Search* program some more. The command line contains a file name and a text string. The *Search* program searches that file for every occurrence of the string, and prints a list of all the line numbers containing that string. It's a handy tool for authors who are building the index for a book. Quality assurance folks can use it to search through code for *gotos* and *abort* statements. Students can use it to search through source code to find examples of particular Ada constructs. After *Search* gives you a list of line numbers, you can use *Line* to look at those lines in context.

I can see I have created an insatiable desire to have this marvelous tool. You can't wait to turn to the back of the book to find the source listing. Don't bother. It isn't there.

4.5.1 I've Seen That Before

I took the *Search* program out of the text because I thought most readers would say, "I've seen that before!" You must have noticed the striking similarity of *More*, *Write*, and *Line*. They are really three variations of one basic program (*Show*). They all take data from a command line, open a file, and display the contents in a slightly different way. *Search* is just a fourth variation on the same theme. The only difference is that it contains a Boolean function that tells if a string is contained in a line. If you can write that function, then you can edit *Line* into *Search* without much difficulty. Why don't you try it and see for yourself?

4.5.2 Keep Selling the Same Software

It isn't unusual to find yourself in a job where you keep doing essentially the same thing over and over again. If you ever write one missile simu- lation, it is a good bet you will write more in the next year or two. If you write a compiler program, there is a good chance your boss will tell you to write another one (for another language or the same language on a different computer) as soon as you get finished. Rarely does one work on a compiler one day and a missile simulation the next. Companies and individuals keep selling the same basic product.

When I wrote the *More*, *Write*, and *Line* programs, I was able to do them quickly because I already developed all the building blocks I needed by the time I finished the *Show* program. This is what modularity and reusability is all about. I almost always start a program by making a copy of an existing program, deleting parts I don't need, and adding some new code. If you find yourself starting from scratch every time you write a new program, you are doing something wrong. Whenever you start a new program you should ask yourself, "What program have I previously written that I can use for a starting point?" You ought to be able to think of several possibilities, unless you are doing something totally new. (You can't turn a compiler design into a missile simulation, but you should be able to edit a compiler into a pretty printer much faster than you could write a pretty printer from scratch.) If the answer to your question is,

"Well, I could use program *X*, but it would take much too long to modify it," then you deserve to be beaten severely for the bad job you did on program *X*. It shows that program *X* is not modular or maintainable.

Of course the ultimate in programming excellence is when everyone in your group writes such good code that you can use each other's code. Some people say that will never happen, but I don't think it is unrealistic to expect people to be able to write code good enough to share with a friend. I get by with a little help from my friends. (Dent, Leif, and Lucas—in alphabetical order.)

The way to make big money and impress your boss with your tremendous productivity is to build on what has already been done. People will say, "Isn't that amazing! Jones wrote the *More* program, and the next day he wrote the *Write* program, and the day after that he wrote the *Line* program, and on the fourth day he wrote the *Search* program. Four different programs in four days! What a genius!" The truth is I wrote one program and sold it four times. As long as I keep my mouth shut, everybody is happy and I'm rich.

4.6   *Draw_Poker*, VERSION 2

The *Draw_Poker* program developed in this case study is an improved version of one I published several years ago. This program was developed using a more rigorous design strategy than *Show*, *More*, *Write*, and *Line* used. It was developed using Software Engineering.

4.6.1   Software Engineering

Software engineering differs from programming in several areas. Software engineering requires more planning than ad hoc programming. A wise person once said, "If you don't know where you are going, you will wind up someplace else." This is especially true of software engineering. You really have to know where you want to go.

Of course, just knowing where you want to go isn't enough. You also have to know how to get there. Software engineers use a methodology to arrive at the goal.

> Meth-od-ol-o-gy. 1: a collection of methods, rules, and superstitions used as a substituted for intelligence. 2: a particular procedure or set of procedures used to turn a difficult problem into an impossible one.

Software engineers are often devoted to their favorite methodology with a zeal that exceeds the enthusiasm of all but the most fanatic member of a religious order. That makes it difficult to carry on a rational discussion about specific methodologies.

The primary difference between software engineering and programming is the level of documentation. Software engineering requires you to document (1) requirements, (2) analysis, (3) design decisions, (4) error reports, (5) test results, and (6) configurations.

Some of these topics fall outside the scope of a book about Ada, but we can at least touch on some of them, particularly when we talk about how they affect Ada.

4.6.2   Military Standards

The current military standard for Defense System Software Development is DOD-STD-2167A. It supersedes MIL-STD-1679. I'm not going to talk about those two specifications, because this book describes techniques I have found to be valuable. Those specifications have good intentions and present a theoretical method for software development, but in practice, I've never seen them do anything but increase cost, cause schedule delays, and result in inferior software.

There will certainly be some who will say that the development of the *Draw_Poker* program does not satisfy the requirements in 2167A. My response to that charge is, "That's right. I make no attempt to satisfy those requirements."

4.6.3   Goals and Requirements

The first thing you have to do is recognize the difference between a goal and a requirement. The goal is what you want or need to do. A requirement is an intermediate objective that must be achieved to reach the goal. I am amazed at how often people focus on requirements and lose sight of their goals.

I first realized how dangerous it was to focus on requirements when I was reviewing a proposal for a target detecting device. The engineer presenting the proposal began his speech by saying, "The requirement is to design a complicated, multi-level interrupt-driven, microprocessor-based target detecting device." I interrupted him, saying that I couldn't believe that was his requirement, but he insisted it was. I asked him if his sponsor in Washington said, "I don't care what kind of targets this thing detects, as long as it is complicated and uses multiple levels of interrupts!" He assured me that's what the sponsor demanded. I couldn't convince him that the goal was to detect certain kinds of targets in a certain environment.

It may be that the problem can be solved using an interrupt-driven microprocessor, and there might be several levels of interrupts, and it might be complicated, but that shouldn't be a requirement. Suppose someone thinks of a simpler, cheaper, more accurate, more reliable solution that only uses a single-level interrupt. Do you want to exclude that solution because it doesn't meet the requirements? I don't!

The goal is absolute. It represents a need that must be satisfied. Requirements reflect the current thinking of what intermediate steps must be taken on the road to achieving the goal. Requirements can (and should) change if a better way to achieve the goal is discovered.

I believe the first step in software engineering is to document the goal. To the mainstream, respected software professionals, this means writing a software specification. Although I agree with this in principle, I've found that writing a software specification doesn't help much. Software specification tend to focus on requirements, not goals. This often locks you into a requirement that is counter-productive to the goal. Furthermore, the software specification tends to be written in legalese. In theory, it is so precise it can be interpreted only one way by a court of law. In practice, it is usually so complicated that nobody really understands it, and everybody thinks it means something different (especially the customer and programmers). Typically, the customer isn't happy with the final product, and the blame eventually falls on the party with the poorest lawyer.

I set design goals by writing a sales brochure and a user's manual. The sales brochure emphasizes the goals (what it does, why you need it, and what it costs). The user's manual explains how it works. Most people wait until the project is over before writing these documents. Then they realize too late that the product doesn't do what the customer needs, is too expensive to sell, or is too complicated to use.

Whenever I pick up the manual for my word processor, I ask myself, "Did someone write this user's manual before the product was designed? Did they maliciously intend it to be this difficult to use?" I suspect that some managers made a list of requirements consisting of every feature they could think of. Then a hoard of programmers did whatever they had to do, so they could claim they met all the requirements. Then some unfortunate soul got stuck with the job of trying to write a manual to explain how to use it. (Of course, the technical writer gets all the blame for the lousy manual.) Consider this: If you can't easily explain how to use your program, how can any user be expected to learn to use it?

The user's manual sets the requirements for the user interface. You have to write the user's manual first, or who knows what mess you will end up with.

4.6.4 Case Study

Using an example, let's show how the sales brochure and user's manual relate to Ada program development. This case study assumes that we want to get into the business of selling video card games. Our first product is going to be a video draw-poker gambling machine. (Later we could expand the product line to include blackjack, bridge, canasta, and maybe even old maid.) The first step is to imagine the product is done. We need a sales brochure describing it and a user's manual that tells how to play it.

4.6.5 Sales Brochure

What should the sales brochure have to say, for us to be able to sell our product? It should rave about the attractive graphics that encourage players to gamble because it is fascinating to watch the cards being shuffled and dealt. It would be a big selling point if we said that it accepted coins or paper money of any denomination, so players won't stop gambling just because they run out of quarters. That would also let players bet variable amounts, which encourages them to try a system they think will help them beat the house. The minimum bet the machine will accept should be $1, so penny players won't keep the machine busy while real gamblers are waiting to use the machine. The maximum bet should be $999 for safety. (You have to be suspicious of anyone willing to bet $1,000 or more on a coin-operated machine.) The machine should shuffle the cards before every hand to prevent players from gaining an advantage by counting cards.

Perhaps the most important section of the sales brochure is the cost analysis. It should tell prospective customers the average amount of money gambled per hour, the house advantage, and the resulting income per hour. When this income is compared with the cost of the machine, it shows how quickly the machine pays for itself. Then a comparison of the expected income to the anticipated monthly maintenance will show how much money the machine makes per day. Every day the customer delays in purchasing the machine, he loses that much money. He can't afford not to buy it!

The cost analysis is just as important to us as it is to the customer. It tells us the maximum amount we can sell the machine for. If an honest sales brochure says that it takes 10 years for the machine to pay for itself, no rational person will buy it. We will have limited the market to people who are too stupid to realize it is a bad investment. Knowing how much we can get for each machine, the number of machines we can produce per month, and the amount of profit we need to make each month, we can figure how much profit we must make on each machine. When we subtract the profit from the selling price, that gives us the production cost. If we can't produce the machine at that price (including nonrecurring engineering costs), then there isn't any point in even starting the project.

The sales brochure should also include hardware features (vandal resistant, won't accept slugs, silent alarm when theft attempts are detected, and so on) that we will ignore here, since this is a book on software. You can't ignore those aspects in the real world.

4.6.6 User's Manual

The user's manual tells how the machine will work. We have to remember that someone who has had too much to drink and has gotten discouraged playing the roulette wheel, isn't going to pick up a one hundred page manual and read it before playing a draw poker game. The user's manual has to be printed in a few large words on the face of the machine. It has to be short and sweet. Something like the following:

Put in as much money as you want to BET.
Press DEAL.
Press the button under each card you want to DISCARD.
Press DEAL again.
If you win, THE MACHINE PAYS YOU!
Play again. It's fun!

You also need pictures showing winning hands and how much they pay off.

4.6.7 Checking the Requirements

Periodically during the course of the design, you should check your design against the sales brochure and user's manual. Are they still accurate descriptions of your product? If not, try changing the documents to match the design and see if you still have a viable product. If so, continue with the product development. If not, don't continue on this path because you will just wind up spending more money to design a product you can't sell. Change the design to match the original descriptions. If you find it isn't possible to design what you originally described or something close enough to your original idea that is marketable, then quit now before you waste any more money.

I think this is a major cause of defense contract overruns. Checking a design against a software specification doesn't tell you much. It just tells if requirements are being satisfied. That doesn't tell you if you are meeting your goals or not. If you aren't meeting the requirements, the tendency is to lower them so you can meet them. That doesn't help. You just spend more money to build something that's inadequate.

4.6.8 Planning for Reuse

Of course, it isn't enough to just set goals and periodically check to make sure you are still heading toward them. You have to make progress at a fast enough rate that you achieve the goal in your lifetime. An important part of software engineering is learning how to cut a big project down to size, so it is possible to complete it on time and under budget. One way to do that is to reuse code you've previously written and tested before. If you are lucky, you might find something lying around that you can use, but that seldom happens. The best way to reuse software is to plan ahead and create components you are likely to be able to use in the future.

Let's return to the *Draw_Poker* example. If this is to be the first of a whole line of video card games, then it seems likely that some of the routines we develop for this game will be useful on other games. For example, routines that shuffle, deal, and display playing cards aren't limited to poker. These universal routines are in the *PLAYING_CARDS* package (Listing 66), so they can be reused in other card games.

If we were writing this project in FORTRAN or assembly language, we might recognize the utility of general-purpose routines that shuffle, deal, and otherwise manipulate playing cards. We would be wise to collect them in a file and compile (or assemble) them into object code modules that could be saved in a library. You might think that the *PLAYING_CARDS* package is just like one of these files of library routines. Well, in some ways it is, but it is really much more. What makes the *PLAYING_CARDS* package different from a FORTRAN or assembly language library is the fact that those libraries contain nothing more than executable routines. If you look in the *PLAYING_CARDS* package specification you will find routines, but you will also find abstract data types, constants, and error conditions. This makes it more complete (and therefore more useful) software component than a simple library of general-purpose routines.

4.6.9   Abstract Data Types

If I were going to write card playing programs in FORTRAN or assembly language, the first thing I would have to do is decide how to represent individual playing cards. In those languages, I would be limited to a few standard data types. The two logical choices are strings and integers. (I think I can safely rule out real numbers without too much consideration.) If I chose to use strings, I might represent the four of diamonds as "4D". If I chose to use integers, then I might use the numbers 1–52 to indicate the 52 cards in the deck, or I might let the numbers 102–114 represent two through ace of clubs, 202–214 represent two through ace of diamonds, and so on. How I choose to represent cards will greatly affect how easy it is to sort cards; shuffle them; check for a flush; check for two-, three-, or four-of-a-kind; or tell which card wins a trick. A poor choice of data representation will make solving the problem much more difficult. Human thought will be diverted from the main problem (how to play poker) and will be wasted on an artificially created problem (how to force an integer or string to have the properties of a playing card).

Furthermore, the decisions I make about data-type representations will greatly affect how I write my executable routines. If I change the representation of playing cards late in the program, then I'll probably have to throw away everything I've done already.

Ada's abstract data types take the burden from you and put it on the compiler. She lets you make the data types fit the problem, rather than trying to change the problem to fit the available data types. Then she lets you develop algorithms that don't depend on how the data is represented. This leaves you free to change the representation at any time without losing much (if any) of the work you've already done.

Your initial reaction to abstract data types might be influenced by your emotional reaction to the term "abstract." If your immediate reaction to the term "abstract art" is, "A confusing picture that's distorted and hard to understand," then you probably are a little afraid of abstract data types. You will expect them to be weird and hard to understand. Well, don't let a few bad artists scare you off.

A good abstract artist has the ability to separate the important features from meaningless ones. Certainly an abstract artist distorts reality, but a good one does so in a way that emphasizes the important points and makes the trivial points disappear. If this is properly done, it isn't confusing at all. In fact, it conveys meaning to the spectators with remarkable clarity because it shows just the objects of interest without the clutter of extraneous details.

The same thing is true of the abstract of a technical paper. The abstract describes the paper by concentrating the important facts in a small space, without cluttering the description with a lot of minute details.

An abstract data type does the same thing an abstract painting or the abstract of a paper does. It represents the important characteristics of the object without cluttering it up with the unimportant details (details like how many bits are used and how the bits are encoded).

If an abstract artist wanted to capture the essential details of a poker game on canvas, what would he do? He would watch the game and decide what was important to the fundamental activity. He would elim-inate the table from the picture because it isn't necessary to the game. Sure, it keeps the cards from falling on the floor, but it doesn't affect who wins, so it isn't an important part of the picture. The only important objects the artist would include in the picture are the cards that were dealt, the players' hands, and the deck. It doesn't matter what shape, size, or color the cards are, as long as you can tell what rank and suit they have. Ranks and suits are important abstract qualities of cards. The thickness of the card and design on the back aren't important. The artist is free to represent a card in any manner, just so long as you can tell what suit and rank it has.

The actions that are important are the shuffling of the cards, dealing of the cards, discarding the cards, and determining the value of a hand to see who the winner is. The skillful artist must figure out how to show these dynamic actions happening on a static piece of canvas.

The artist may or may not show the cards being sorted. Sorting the cards in a hand is an optional action. It makes it easier to see if a hand holds a winning combination, but you could figure that out without sorting the hand if you had to. Who knows, maybe there is a way to hash code the values in a hand, that allows you to tell a winning hand from a losing hand quicker than you could if you sorted it. You are probably wise to sort a hand, but it isn't a requirement.

The *PLAYING_CARDS* package specification (Listing 66) is just an abstract painting in words instead of oils. It describes important objects and actions, and it eliminates all the other details.

Look near the beginning of the package specification. I've told Ada to create a data type called *Suits*. Objects that are *Suits* can have values of *CLUBS*, *DIAMONDS*, *HEARTS*, or *SPADES*. I don't care how Ada represents these things internally. She can use 0, 1, 2, 3 or 1, 2, 3, 4 or 'C', 'D', 'H', 'S' or anything else she desires. It doesn't matter to me as long as she is consistent. I have, however, given her an implied precedence. *CLUBS* is the lowest value and *SPADES* is the highest. Similarly, I've defined an ordered set of values called *Ranks*.

Then I have defined three data types that are even more abstract. *Cards*, *Hands*, and *Decks* are private data types. We don't know what values they can have or how they are represented, but we really don't care about those details at this level of the program.

Skipping over the three exceptions for the moment, we see the things we can do with these abstract objects. We can find out the suit and rank of a card. We can open a new deck or shuffle it. We can open a new hand, sort it, peek at each individual card, play any card, tell if a card has been played, see if a hand is full, or deal a card to a particular hand.

Returning to the exceptions, I have defined three things that could go wrong. When you take the cellophane off a box of cards and inspect it, you might find an extra seven of hearts, or discover that the two of spades is missing. This shouldn't happen, but you should know about it if it does. You don't want to force every application program to check for it, so the *Open_New* action does it automatically. A more likely error is that an application program will get carried away and try to deal a 53d card from the deck. If the application program is careless enough to do that, it probably isn't doing any special error checking for that condition. The *Deal* action had better take responsibility for checking for that error. By the same reasoning, we can conclude that an application program may try to deal a card to a hand that is already full and not check for that error. That's why I included these exceptions in the package. They remind me that these are error conditions I must check for when I write the package body, and they tell whoever uses this package what error flags might be raised.

These are all the things we need to do to all the objects we need for a poker game. To be truly reusable, we should also include objects needed for other card games (tricks and trumps for bridge, melds for canasta, and so on), but I didn't want to complicate the package with unnecessary objects or operations.

4.6.10 *Private* Types

I chose to use *private* types to represent *Cards*, *Hands*, and *Decks*. I could have used visible records and arrays, or *limited private* types. I chose not to. There were good reasons to use *private* types, and those reasons are worth an explanation.

Suppose I had used visible records and arrays. (That is, suppose I had moved the type definitions from the private part to the place where the three "... *is private;*" declarations are. That would have eliminated the need for the *Suit_Of* and *Rank_Of* functions because application programs could simply use *CARD.SUIT* and *CARD.RANK*. That is exactly what I wanted to avoid. By making the definition of *Cards* private, I can be sure that I can change the definition from a record to a simple integer if I like, and it won't affect any other part of the program.

You say, "Why would you want to change the representation of *Cards* to an integer?" Well, suppose I discovered that my program wouldn't fit in memory. Looking at the code generated by the compiler, I see that a card is represented by a two-component record. The first component, the *SUIT*, is a number from 0 to 3 represented as a 32-bit integer. The second component, the *RANK*, is a number from 0 to 12, also represented by a 32-bit integer. Therefore it takes 64 bits (8 bytes) to represent a card. Since there are 52 cards in a deck, the representation of those 52 cards takes 416 bytes. If I represented a card as a number from 0 through 51, then I could use 1 byte per card and only 52 bytes per deck. That's a storage savings of 88%!

If I change to an integer representation, and I have used *private* types, all I have to do is rewrite the *Suit_Of* and *Rank_Of* functions. That's easy enough to do. I can use integer division by 13 and the *VAL* attribute to get the *SUIT*, and modulo 13 operator and *VAL* attribute to get the *RANK*. I can recompile any program that uses *PLAYING_CARDS* and I can be sure it will still work. (It will take less space, and may run slightly slower, but it will still work.)

If I change the representation of a card from a record to a 1-byte integer, and I have used visible types without the *Suit_Of* and *Rank_Of* functions, then I will have to find every line of every application program that contains *CARD.SUIT* or *CARD.RANK*. Granted this is easy to do with a text editor, and Ada will tell me if I missed any, but I still have to insert division and modulo operators all over the place. There is a good chance I will make a mistake doing that.

So visible types aren't a good choice. But if *private* is good, then *limited private* must be better. Isn't it? Well, the decision between *private* and *limited private* isn't always easy. If you immediately see a reason why you will want to assign values to an object or need to check to see if two objects are equal, then you can't use a *limited private* type. (*Limit private* types don't have assignment operators or equality tests.) If you don't need to do these things, it is better to use a *limited private* type.

Rather than spending a lot of time and effort figuring out if I need *private* or *limited private*, I usually just try *limited private* first and see if that leads me into trouble. I couldn't see any reason to assign a value to *Cards* (I wasn't going to put any cheating in the game), nor did I see a need to check two *Cards* for equality (there's only one deck and every card is unique), so I decided to use *limited private* for *Cards* at first. It didn't appear that I would need assignment or equality for *Hands* or *Decks* either, so I made them *limited private*, too.

I ran into trouble when I tried to make a copy of a hand and sort the copy. Then I realized that I did have a legitimate need to assign a value to a hand. I made *Hands private* instead of *limited private*. Then I realized I might want to make a copy of a deck for a duplicate bridge game, so I would need to assign values to decks, too. Then I realized I might not want to wait until I randomly dealt myself a royal flush to see if the royal-flush detection algorithm really works, and so I might want to assign particular values to *Cards* in my hand in a test routine. There went the last *limited private* type.

I think it is a good idea to use *limited private* types whenever possible, so I always try them first. If they don't work, it is a simple matter to strike the word *limited* with a text editor. If I start out with a *private* type first, I might not realize I don't need to assign a value to it or test it for equality, and I might leave it *private* when it should be *limited private*.

4.6.11 Keep I/O Routines Separate

Some of you may have read an article I wrote for the February 1986 issue of *Dr. Dobb's Journal of Software Tools*. It contained version 1 of the *PLAYING_CARDS* package. That version contained overloaded *put* procedures that I have removed from the version 2. That's because I now realize that it was a mistake to mix I/O routines with processing routines.

I used to believe I should always include I/O routines for new data types in the package that defines the data types. I thought, "There's not much point in creating things if you can't input or output them." Well, that's true, but it doesn't mean those I/O routines have to be in the same package. Version 1 used *TEXT_IO* to write phrases like "Three of Hearts" to the screen. If I ever write a book of advanced Ada examples, I will probably expand on this example by using a graphic interface to draw the cards on the screen. *TEXT_IO* wouldn't be of any use in that application. I shouldn't have to modify and recompile the *PLAYING_CARDS* package just because I'm using a graphics package instead of *TEXT_IO* to display *Cards*. If I change the output device or output method, I expect to have to rewrite I/O packages, but I shouldn't have to rewrite any processing packages. Routines that turn pixels on and off (or write messages to the screen) have nothing to do with routines that shuffle and deal cards. Therefore, they don't belong in the same package.

4.6.12   A Limit to Reuse

The *PLAYING_CARDS* package body is shown in Listing 67. It's simple enough that it doesn't require much explanation, but I do have to justify my *Sort* routine. People have spent years searching for the ultimate sort routine, and here I've used this simple bubble sort. Isn't this a golden opportunity to reuse a generic sort routine?

I'm all for reuse (the *Draw_Poker* program reuses *RANDOM_NUMBERS*, *STANDARD_INTEGERS*, *MONEY*, *DIM_INT_32*, *SCROLL_TERMINAL*, and *ASCII_UTILITIES*), but sometimes reuse is more trouble than its worth. It's true a more exotic sort routine might be faster, but how long can it take to sort five cards, even using the most inefficient routine? If I were sorting 5,000 cards and speed were important, then I might instantiate somebody else's super-optimized generic sort package. In this case, it was quicker to write thirteen lines of simple code than search for a reusable component that will do the job.

If I already had a generic *Sort* routine that was easy to instantiate and had established its reliability, of course I would have used it. If I expected to need to sort large collections often, then it would make sense to write (or buy) a generic sort routine, verify it, and use it in whenever I needed it. But this is the first time in 22 years of programming that I've ever needed a sort routine, and I don't anticipate needing one again in the next 22 years. A reusable sort routine isn't high on my priority list right now.

Writing a book is a lot like doing a real project. There is a deadline that has to be met, and you can't waste your time searching for the most elegant solution when you already have something that works perfectly well, especially when there are other things that aren't done yet. Taking the time to find a generic *Sort* routine would have been counterproductive.

4.6.13   Efficiency vs Verifiability

The *Sort* routine also brings up another issue. Which is more important, efficiency or verifiability? The answer depends on the situation. The *Draw_Poker* program runs so quickly I had to add some *delay* statements to slow it down (I like to keep the player in suspense while the cards are being dealt), and it fits easily in memory so I'm not concerned about size. In this situation I don't care at all about efficiency, but I want to be sure the program works correctly, so this time it is an easy question to answer. Verifiability is the only important feature. It would be a more difficult question to answer if I had to worry about speed and space.

I bring the issue up because schools tend to emphasize efficiency, and as a result, young programmers tend to do a bad job by optimizing too much. Suppose such a programmer is faced with the job of writing the *Sort* routine. First, he wastes time calculating logs and powers to determine which is the optimum sort routine to use. Sort routines work for numbers, not playing cards, so he has to modify it to sort cards. (If it is generic this may be as simple as defining the < operator.) Then he has to verify it to see if it works. This is probably going to take longer than coding and verifying a simple sort routine. Time is money. The optimized version costs more (because it took more time to develop), and doesn't do the job any better. That's bad engineering.

Furthermore, the optimized version may cost more again later in the life cycle. If the program fails to work (or needs to be modified to sort by suits as well as ranks), a maintenance programmer will have to look at the code and figure out what it is doing. A simple sort routine is easier to verify than a complicated one. Therefore it will take less time (that is, cost less) to maintain the simple version than the optimized one.

4.6.14   Hidden Dependencies

In a moment, you are about to see the *Draw_Poker* program listing. Before you look at the whole listing, let me tell you that the first line is **with PLAYING_ CARDS, MONEY;** . This makes it appear to depend only on two other software components, but you already know that *MONEY* depends on *DIM_INT_32*, *ASCII_UTILITIES*, and *STANDARD_INTEGERS*. *DIM_INT_32* depends on *STANDARD_INTEGERS* and *INTEGER_UNITS*. *ASCII_UTILITIES* depends on *STANDARD_INTEGERS*. *PLAYING_CARDS* depends on *RANDOM_NUMBERS* (which you will see in the next section) and *STANDARD_INTEGERS*. *RANDOM_NUMBERS* depends on *STANDARD_INTEGERS* and *CALENDAR*. Who knows what the *CALENDAR* package body needs.

That's just a list of the units you get from the context clause. Some of the subunits of *Draw_Poker* depend on *SCROLL_ TERMINAL* (to simulate hardware I/O), and it would depend on special interface packages if the product was ever built. *SCROLL_TERMINAL* depends on *VIRTUAL_TERMINAL*, which may depend on *DOS*, *VMS*, or *CURSOR* and *TTY*. There's no telling what the special interface packages might need.

Usually we try to avoid hidden dependencies because they might cause unexpected side effects. We don't want to be unpleasantly surprised if we make a change to one module and find out that an apparently unrelated module doesn't work anymore.

The really amazing thing about Ada is that all these dependencies exist, but you don't have to worry about them. The dependencies are hidden in the sense that they don't clutter the program listings, but they aren't undocumented. Ada keeps track of the dependencies, so tools can be written that tell you all the units that will be affected if you make a change to a particular unit. Even if you don't use such a tool, Ada always makes sure that everything is current and that all the interfaces match before she will link object code modules into an executable image.

Ada uses layers of abstraction to hide these dependencies so they don't confuse you. You can obtain the power of so many previously written components with so little effort and without cluttering your program with the details of how they work. The *Draw_Poker* program appears to be just a couple of pages, but it generates a sizable program because it takes such good advantage of reusable software components.

4.6.15 Building from the Bottom

I haven't said so, but the *PLAYING_CARDS* package is a bottom-up design. I tried to keep this a secret until now because bottom-up design is frowned upon in some circles. It earned a bad reputation because undisciplined programmers often start at the bottom of a design and keep building. When you start at multiple roots, you have to be incredibly lucky for all of these roots to grow together into a neat solid trunk. Normally there is burl where things that don't really fit together have been forced into place. A pure bottom-up design usually isn't very good.

That doesn't mean all bottom-up techniques are bad. I've shown how you can build a *SCROLL_TERMINAL* on top of a *VIRTUAL_TERMINAL* that is built on top of operating-system interface packages. That's a bottom-up design, and it's good. Bottom-up design helps you write basic utility programs that can be used as building blocks in many different programs.

You only get into trouble when you try to get these individual building blocks to continue to grow and somehow merge with each other to form one program. You just can't start from many places and expect to be able to join them all with one golden spike.[1] They probably aren't going to line up. The key to success is to recognize when you have built all the foundation modules you need, then stop working from the bottom-up.

4.6.16   Top-Down Design

When it comes time to establish the program flow, I think it is best to start from the top and work down. This means stating the solution to the problem in the most general terms, then defining those general terms with more specific terms until the solution is spelled out in complete detail. We saw an example of this in Chapter 3.5.9, and here is another example.

Listing 68 shows the top level of the *Draw_Poker* program. Don't think for a moment it was written sequentially. I used a screen-oriented editor and jumped all over that file. I started with a top-level skeleton and put flesh on it. That is, it began like this

```
procedure Draw_Poker is
begin
  loop
    (cursor)
  end loop;
end Draw_Poker;
```

I knew I wanted an infinite loop. I just had to decide what to put in the loop. I began with comments derived directly from the requirements.

```
-- Play as long as the user is willing to bet.
-- Shuffle before every deal.
-- Deal a hand to the player.
-- Show him what he has.
-- Let the player hold or draw each card.
-- Replace any cards he may have discarded.
-- Show him what he has now.
-- Pay him if he won.
```

Then under each comment, I wrote a few lines of code to do what the comment said. Usually I just invented a subprogram to do it. For example, under **- - Show him what he has.** I wrote **put(PLAYERS_HAND,**

---

[1] Note to international readers who might be unfamiliar with American history. Two companies were given the task of building the first transcontinental railroad. One started from the East, the other started from West. When they met in the middle, the last two sections of track were joined by a golden spike.

VALUE); . I knew I would need a routine that would display the cards in the hand and display the value of the hand (*NOTHING* through *ROYAL_FLUSH*). At that point in the program development I didn't really care how it worked, just so long as it did work.

I realized I would need a function called *Value_Of* that would look at a hand and tell me if it contained a winning combination of cards. I considered the merits of simply passing the *PLAYERS_HAND* to the *put* routine and letting *put* call *Value_Of*, instead of the main program calling *Value_Of* and passing the result to *put*. You can see I finally decided to do the latter. I did this partly because I wanted to avoid having both *put* and *Payout* call *Value_Of* (both need to know the value of the hand), and partly because I wanted to make it obvious at the top level that *put* was displaying the value of the hand. (If the procedure call was just **put(PLAYERS_HAND);** then it would not be obvious that *put* calls *Value_Of* and tells the player if he has a winning combination or not.)

This approach allowed me to partition the problem into five smaller problems. If I had five programmers working for me, I could have assigned one the job of writing a procedure to get the player's wager. I could let the second one write a function that determines the value of a hand. The other three programmers could work on procedures that display the hand and value, let the player discard, and drop the player's winnings loudly into a dish.

When I wrote the top level program, I didn't worry about any declarations. I just compiled the program and got lots of error messages. Then, based on the error messages, I declared objects (*STOCK, PLAYERS_HAND, WAGER, VALUE*), the data type *Values*, and two library packages (*PLAYING_CARDS, MONEY*). I find that easier than trying to guess what declarations I will need before writing the code.

4.6.17 Renaming Declarations

Time out now for a short comment on a technical point. Notice I have included the line **function "="(LEFT, RIGHT : MONEY.Cents) return boolean renames MONEY."=";** . I needed that because of the line **exit when WAGER = MONEY.Type_Convert(0);** . Let's talk about those two lines for a moment.

If I just wrote **exit when WAGER = 0;** I would get a type-mismatch error. *WAGER* is a dimensioned quantity. It is a value expressed in *Cents*. The number 0 is a pure number with no units attached to it. It could represent dollars, francs, guilders, or pounds sterling. It happens that 0 cents equals 0 francs regardless of the current rate of exchange, but that's just a coincidence. I have to convert 0 to 0 *Cents*, and I can do that using the *Type_Convert* function in the *MONEY* package.

Having done that, I now have a problem with the = sign. The visible meanings for the = sign include comparisons of integers, real numbers, and *Values*, but not *Cents*. The function that compares *Cents* is in the *MONEY* package (inherited from *DIM_INT_32*). It isn't directly visible. I have three choices. First I can *use MONEY*; , which makes everything in *MONEY* visible. Second, I can use this awkward expression: **exit when MONEY."=" (WAGER,MONEY.Type_Convert(0));** . (I'm sure you can see why I avoided that solution.) The third choice is to use a renaming declaration to make the operation visible. I used the third option partly because I wanted to include an example of renaming in this book. I have a slight preference for the first solution (especially if there are several operators that need to be seen), but if organizational programming guidelines prohibit *use* clauses, the renaming technique is a simple way to comply.

4.6.18 Prototyping

No amount of planning will ever anticipate all the problems you will encounter, and the sooner you find out where the problem areas are, the better. As soon as you have established a top-level design, it is a good idea to write a prototype of that design. You can take any shortcut you like. Use a different language on a different computer if it will help you get the job done quicker. The important thing is to practice solving the problem once, so you will learn things you need to learn to solve the problem for real.

If I was really going to build and sell the *Draw_Poker* machine, I would be looking at a significant hardware investment. I would pay engineers a lot of money to design an embedded computer, graphic displays, a mechanism that accepts coins and bills, the winnings dispenser, and the control panel containing the buttons the players push to deal and hold cards. Before I spend all that money, I want to be sure of the design.

What do I expect to learn from a prototype? If I knew that, I wouldn't have to build the prototype. I usually learn things I never would have thought of in a million years. The *Draw_Poker* prototype was no exception.

The *Draw_Poker* top-level design defined five separately compiled subunits. The prototype was built by writing the simplest possible bodies for those subunits.

The first subunit is the procedure *get* that gets the *WAGER* from some special hardware that recognizes the values of coins and paper money. I can easily simulate this using the *SCROLL_TERMINAL* to ask the user how much he wants to bet, converting the input string to a number of pennies, and returning the amount. When I wrote this module (Listing 69), I had to check for error conditions. Some of these error conditions couldn't happen in the real machine. The value of the U.S. dollar is less than it has been in the past, but it isn't negative yet. The real machine won't have to check for negative values of money, but it will have to check for the minimum and maximum bets. All of a sudden I realized, "I never specified what the machine should do if the player enters less than $1 or more than $999.99." I said it shouldn't accept those bets, but should it just spit the money back out without comment? Should it tell the user what he did wrong? If so, should I flash a light behind a red plastic lens that says, "BET WAS TOO SMALL", or should I display that message in big red letters on the screen? These are decisions that could affect the control panel or display screen, and I should make them now, before the hardware is designed and built.

The second subunit of *Draw_Poker* is *Value_Of*, shown in Listing 70. Unlike the other subunits, this one won't get thrown away when I build the real machine. Putting it in the prototype gives us an opportunity to start testing it early in the design phase. It turned out that version 1.0 of this subunit failed to recognize *ACE, TWO, THREE, FOUR, FIVE* is a *STRAIGHT*. I discovered that while playing with the prototype. A rigorous testing program may have discovered that flaw, but then again, it might not. It always pays to have all the experience you can with a product before you begin to sell it.

The third subunit is *put* (Listing 71). I was surprised to learn that it ran too fast. *Draw_Poker* shuffled and dealt all five cards before I got my fingers off the keyboard, and *put* displayed them before I was ready to see them. I can't explain why, but that made me feel uncomfortable when I was playing the game. I guess I missed the thrill of seeing the first three cards turn up hearts and wondering, "Will the last two also be hearts?" When I added a one-second delay in the display loop, it made it a much better game.

I also didn't like the fact that the cards I held were redealt to me. (If you compile and run the prototype, you will find that after you decide to hold or discard each card, all the cards disappear, and you are dealt a new hand. Some of the cards in that new hand are the cards you elected to hold.) I didn't fix that in the prototype because it was too much trouble, but I learned something important even though I didn't fix it. I now know that a graphic display of the playing cards will have to be able to erase individual cards and slowly move new cards into the empty holes. I can tell that to the person designing the graphic display before the design is started. If I hadn't done the prototype, I probably wouldn't have thought of that, and I would have been unhappy with a display that showed the whole hand all at once. It probably would have been difficult, time consuming, and expensive to go back and modify the display routine.

The fourth and fifth subunits, *Discard_From* (Listing 72) and *Payout* (Listing 73) aren't particularly interesting or informative, but you need them if you want to play the game.

I wrote this prototype on my IBM PC AT clone. That's much more power than I need to do the job. When building the production units, I want to put in the cheapest computer that will do the job. How do I know what size computer to use? Can I get by with a single-board 8086 computer with 640 KB memory, or will I need 80286 with 4 MB?

Without the prototype, I'd just have to make a wild guess. The prototype doesn't tell me all the answers, but it helps me make a reasonable estimate. The Alsys compiler will let me generate object code for the 8086 or 80286. I can compile the prototype both ways to see what difference it makes.

The size of the real program won't be exactly the same size as the prototype. There are major differences, especially in the display routines, but at least I can tell a little bit about the program size from the prototype. I know exactly how big the *Value_Of* function will be. I know how few bytes are needed for the top-level procedure. I'll have to put some serious thought into how much the other routines will take, but I can make some assumptions and do some experiments. I won't be able to estimate the program to within a few bytes, certainly, but I should be able to tell if I will need extended memory or not. As I work on each subunit I can revise my memory estimate and check to make sure I'm not getting into trouble. If I am in trouble, the sooner I find out about it, the better.

4.6.19 Validation and Verification

Before we sell the product we have to validate and verify the program. This two-step certification process (1) assures that the program contains modules or statements that satisfy every stated requirement (and no unstated ones) and (2) verifies that each module operates correctly. Early in the program development, it doesn't make sense to try to verify that each module operates correctly because most of them haven't even been written yet, but it is never too early to validate the design against the requirements.

If we validate the *Draw_Poker* program at this point in the development, we find some interesting things. It does everything it is required to do, but it also does some extra things. It has a default bet of $1. There isn't any requirement to do that. It also tells the player if he has a winning hand before he discards and draws. It lets the player end the program by entering a $0 bet. These are extra features not found in the requirements, and we have to address them somehow. We will have to

(1) change the requirements, (2) change the design, or (3) ignore the problem for now.

These discrepancies crept in because the requirements are for a coin-operated machine, but I built a prototype on a general-purpose computer. The coin-operated game should run forever, but I have to be able to stop the prototype program, so I can use the computer for other things. It's a real nuisance to have to reboot the system every time I want to stop the prototype. I added the zero bet to give me an easy way to quit. I don't want to change the requirements, nor do I want to change the design of the prototype, so I'll ignore the problem for the moment. If I was going to continue with this example, I would add some comments to the prototype code to remind me to change the design for the coin-operated version. (I'm ignoring the fact I could just as easily use *CONTROL-C* to quit, because I wanted an example of an instance when I might purposely violate the requirements in a prototype.)

The default bet makes no sense in a coin-operated game. The bet is whatever amount of money has been inserted. It was convenient for the prototype, but not really necessary, and it violates the requirements. I should take it out.

The early display of a winning hand was a side effect of using the same display routine before and after cards were discarded. In this case I decided to change the requirements because it makes the game more attractive (that is, easier to sell) to the player. (I could have also solved the problem by changing the design to match the requirements. This is easily done by assigning **VALUE := NOTHING;** before displaying the hand the first time.)

4.6.20   Integration

Things that work individually don't always work when you put them together. Or perhaps they work, but they don't work the way you expected them to. You never find these things out until you integrate the system. Many software development projects leave integration till the end. I believe in early integration. This is easy to do in Ada if you have written a prototype.

Suppose we have built the *Draw_Poker* prototype and done the validation on it. We've made the changes eliminating the default bet and the zero bet. We can integrate modules as soon as they are finished.

If I was actually going to build and market the machine, I imagine the *get* procedure would be done first. I've seen dollar bill changers and candy machines, so I know devices that recognize the value of money exist. A little investigation would probably turn up a list of vendors who sell something I could use. I'd pick one and figure out how to connect it to a parallel I/O port. There are probably two handshaking signals. The first lets the device tell the computer that money has been entered. The second lets the computer acknowledge that it has read the amount and is ready for the device to accept more money.

The *get* routine has to monitor the input handshaking line and read the I/O port every time some money is inserted in the device. Then it can add that amount to a running total and use the other handshaking line to indicate it is ready for more money. It also has to monitor the DEAL button. When the user presses the DEAL button on the control panel, it passes the *WAGER* up to *Draw_Poker* and clears the total.

The *get* routine could be tested using a breadboard circuit. The money input device and the DEAL button could be mounted on the breadboard and wired to a connector that plugs into the parallel I/O port. A simple test routine could be written to make sure it works. The body of the program might look something like this

```
SCROLL_TERMINAL.put_line("enter money");
get(WAGER); -- The routine under test.
SCROLL_TERMINAL.put_line(MONEY.Image(WAGER));
```

Just put in a known amount of money, press DEAL, and check the screen to see if it correctly tells you how much you entered. Do this as often as it takes you to convince yourself that it is working correctly.

After you are convinced it works, link this real *get* procedure in place of the simulated *get* procedure you used in the *Draw_Poker* prototype. When you put some money in the machine and press DEAL, the prototype does what it always used to do. (The terminal screen shows you some cards, asks you which you want to keep, and pays you if you won.)

The disturbing thing is that it doesn't do anything while it is waiting for you to enter money. It doesn't prompt you, flash lights, or anything. It just sits there until you put some money in it. Someone walking by the machine doesn't even know it is on! Now your prototype has told you something else. There is a flaw in the design.

You have to decide what to do. You could add something to the *get* routine to make it flash a light behind a lens that says, "What's your bet?" If so, you need to add that light to the control panel.

On the other hand, the machine has a nice color display monitor. You may want *get* to call a graphic cartoon routine that tells people to step up and put money in the machine. That change may involve turning *get* into a task, adding a *Come_On* task, and using a timed call in a *select* statement to call *Come_On* if the player hasn't entered any money lately. We're talking about major changes here!

Using the prototype to integrate pieces of the solution can warn you of problems when it is still early enough to do something about it.

You don't want to find out that you need a "What's your bet?" light after you have manufactured 20,000 control panels. You don't have time to start developing a lot of new graphic routines just before the final design review. I think it is vital to use a prototype program as an integration test bed early in development.

4.6.21 Maintenance Manual

In most cases, if you give a maintenance programmer a source-code listing and a pile of documentation relating to the program, the only thing the maintenance programmer will read is the source code. That's because the source code is the only thing that counts and the only thing you can trust. It doesn't matter what it says in the documentation, the computer is going to do what the source code tells it to do. People have great intentions of keeping the documentation correct and up-to-date, but they seldom do. Often it is poorly written and confusing. Maintenance programmers usually don't read it. You may not like it, but those are the facts of life.

Since the only thing you can be sure the maintenance programmer will read is the source code, that's where the bulk of the information has to be. Chapter 2.11.1 described in detail how to document specifications and bodies. Putting these important comments in the source code (instead of a separate document) increases the probability that someone will read them.

Even if you write good comments in the source code, there are still things that need to go in a maintenance manual. The problem is getting the maintenance programmer to read the maintenance manual. Most people want to put everything in the maintenance manual. They want structure charts and data flow diagrams for every module. They wind up with a massive, expensive document that's boring and hard to read. All the information is there, but nobody can find it in the clutter. Few people have the patience to even try. That's why I believe it is important to keep the maintenance manual short and well organized. If you give someone a small, helpful document, he might read it.

A good maintenance manual begins with the theory of operation. This is a brief overview of what the program is doing. A few carefully chosen diagrams (structure charts, state transition diagrams, or data flow diagrams) should be used, but there is no need for diagrams of every module. After giving an overview, you should list the modules and tell how each module fits in the general scheme.

Analysis and design decisions should be documented in the body of the maintenance manual. If there were several viable ways to do something, explain why one approach was taken and the others rejected. You should devote a subsection to each software component.

Section 3.1 of this book is a pretty good example of a maintenance manual for the *ASCII_UTILITIES* package. It gives general background for the subprograms in the package, and Section 3.1.4 explains why I used short-circuit control forms in some places but not others. These are the kinds of things that need to be documented but don't belong in the source code itself. Section 3.5.9 could be turned into a maintenance manual for the *Get_Response* subunit by adding structure chart and data flow diagram. Section 3.6 is *not* a very good example of a maintenance manual because it is too long and goes off on too many tangents. (It was written to be a tutorial of general concepts, not a maintenance manual for the *FORM_TERMINAL*. I was looking for excuses to digress and found lots of them.)

4.6.22 Other Software Engineering Concepts

There are three other things you need to consider when working on a big project that you don't need to worry about for small projects. They are (1) configuration management, (2) error reporting, and (3) cost and schedule. These things don't have a lot to do with Ada and probably don't belong in this book at all, but I just wanted to call your attention to them briefly.

4.6.22.1 Configuration Management. A big part of software engineering is configuration management. When you build a large software product, you have to break it down into modules. The side effect of modularization is that you now have a lot of little pieces to keep track of. You have to know which of the pieces you need to use when building a larger unit. The little pieces are often revised, and you need to make sure you are using the correct revision.

Ada takes care of some aspects of configuration management. She knows what units need to be linked to create a main program. She knows if any of the units are obsolete. This could lead you to believe there is no need for configuration management if you use Ada. Unfortunately, that's not true.

Ada doesn't relieve you of the responsibility of configuration management. I've been trying to keep current copies of all the listings in this book on an AT clone (with the Meridian compiler), a genuine AT (with the Alsys compiler), and a VAX (with the DEC compiler). Every time I make an improvement in a listing on one machine, I have to remember to make the same correction on the other two. It is a nightmare. Even if you use Ada, you still have to use some discipline and/or a configuration management tool to keep things straight.

4.6.22.2 Error Reporting. Another important part of the life cycle is error reporting. This is perhaps just another aspect of configuration management because you need to keep track of the software errors you discover during development and after delivery. This should include a description of the symptoms, the consequences of the failure, the revision it was found in, and the correction made to the software. I've never seen anything that makes me believe error reporting is any easier or more difficult in Ada than in any other language.

4.6.22.3 Cost and Schedule.

For a little program like *More*, it would take you longer to estimate how long it will take than it takes to do it. Planning isn't an issue in these cases. Big programs involve massive expenditures over long periods of time, and you need to have a good idea of how much time and money the project will involve.

I always use time and money in the same breath, because for software development they are practically the same thing. If you want to estimate how much a software project will cost, it really comes down to estimating how many man-hours it will take. There may be a few expenses that don't have anything to do with labor, but they are easy to estimate. You may have to buy a compiler or other software engineering tools, but you can pick up the telephone, call a few vendors, and you know what you will have to spend for them. The real trick is figuring out how many people you need and for how long, so you know how much you will have to spend in salaries and office expenses.

Other costs (such as testing, documentation, configuration management, and error reporting) will be related to the size of the project, which is related to how long it takes to develop it. So the problem really boils down to "how do you know how many man-hours will be required to complete the project?" If you know how many man-hours it takes to write the software, you can multiply by some factor (that you have determined from your previous experience with software projects) to determine the overhead and support costs.

I'm still searching for a method that reliably predicts the duration of a software project. Experience seems to indicate that software development lasts as long as there is money to fund it, so if you tell me how much money you will give me, I will tell you how long it will take. I know that's not the answer you want to hear, so let me try another one. My first estimate is usually a wild guess. You probably don't like that answer any better, but that's the only honest one I can give you.

Although I don't have a good way to get an initial schedule estimate, I do know a way to tell if I am on schedule. After a little while, I can revise the estimated schedule based on the progress made in the elapsed time.

How do you measure progress? When you've written 100 lines of code, are you 1% done or 10% done? You can't tell unless you know the program is going to be 1,000 or 10,000 lines, but you won't know that until the project is all over. Then it's too late. Counting lines of code doesn't tell you anything.

Fortunately it is a little easier to measure progress in Ada than other languages. That's because you can partition the work into modules and figure completion on the basis of number of modules completed. For example, take the *Draw_ Poker* program. At the beginning of the program, you know *Draw_ Poker* consists of the modules *PLAYING_ CARDS, MONEY, get, Value_ Of, put, Discard_ From*, and *Payout*. There are seven major modules, so if you'll settle for a crude estimate you can figure that each module is one-seventh (14%) of the job. Each time a module is completed, you know you are another seventh of the way home.

To be more accurate requires a little more effort, judgment and skill. Let's assume that *MONEY* is a completed reusable component and you don't need to figure it in the schedule. That leaves us with six modules. Let's rank them in order of difficulty. I think *put* will be hardest (it involves complicated graphics). The *get* and *Payout* modules will be moderately hard (because they interface with hardware I don't have yet). *PLAYING_ CARDS* is likely to be lengthy. *Value_ Of* and *Discard_ From* will be the easiest. If I let one unit of effort be the effort required to write the easiest module, I can estimate the relative difficulty of the others. *PLAYING_ CARDS*, I feel, will take five times as long as *Discard_ From*. *Payout* will probably take twice as long as *PLAYING_ CARDS*, and so on. Intuition (and that's all it is) tells me the effort to complete the whole program can be allocated in this way.

Units of Effort	Module Name
(50)	*put*
(10)	*get*
(10)	*Payout*
(5)	*PLAYING_ CARDS*
(1)	*Value_ Of*
(1)	*Discard_ From*

That all adds up to 77 units of work. Each unit of work is worth 1.3% of the total job. When *Payout* is done, then the project is 13% complete. When *put* is done, it is 65% complete. If *Payout* and *put* are both done, the job is 78% finished.

We don't have to wait for a module to be complete to estimate how far along we are. *PLAYING_ CARDS* consists of eleven subprograms, which are probably equally difficult. If any three of the eleven are done, then 27% of *PLAYING_ CARDS* is done. Since *PLAYING_ CARDS* represents five of the seventy-seven units of work (6.5%), then 27% of 6.5% of the job is done. (It is 1.76% done.)

Once a month, I can measure my progress. If each month shows 5% increase in the amount of completion, I can revise my estimate to 20 months, regardless of what the initial wild guess was. (Total project time = time spent so far / fraction complete. 20 months = 1 month / 0.05 = 2 months / 0.10.)

It probably won't be nice and linear because you probably didn't estimate the relative difficulties of the individual software components properly. When you discover some project is more difficult than expected, you can change the relative difficulty based on actual experience. As you get farther along in the project, the estimate should get better. If your initial wild guess was high, it will predict an early completion. If the wild guess was low, it will tell you that you are behind schedule in a few months.

4.7 CONCLUSION

We've taken the *Draw_Poker* program about as far as we can without buying some hardware and actually building it. In the process, we've talked about every aspect of writing large or small programs that I could think of, except one. The only thing we haven't talked about is how to test software. I've avoided that issue until now because it is a subject worthy of an entire chapter.

TESTING SOFTWARE
COMPONENTS AND PROGRAMS

Once you have written a program, how do you verify that it works as designed? The customary approach to verification is testing. Unfortunately, testing only shows the presence of errors, not the absence of them. If you test a program and don't find any errors, it doesn't necessarily mean there aren't any errors in it. It often means you didn't look hard enough. Testing can prove the absence of errors only when 100% of all possible conditions are tested. There are rare instances when 100% testing is feasible, but most of the time it isn't.

Generally, people test a program until they have confidence in it. This is a nebulous concept. Generally, you will find many errors when you begin testing your program. The error detection rate drops as you continue testing and fixing bugs. Finally, the error rate is low enough that you feel confident that you have caught all the major problems.

How you test your software depends on the situation. In this section, we will look at some of the code developed in previous sections and see some of the different things we can do to convince ourselves that it is correct.

5.1 SOFTWARE TEST PLANS

Large projects usually test their product in accordance with a software test plan. Or, at least they *say* they do. The test plan is filled with "motherhood" statements saying that each module will be thoroughly tested, with special emphasis on values just inside and outside the nominal input limits and values clearly outside the normal input range to stress it. It sounds great on paper, but it is usually impractical. I've never seen a software test plan that wasn't a waste of time.

Suppose you tried to test the *Write* program in accordance with such a software test plan. What file names are just inside or outside "nominal input limits?" Is C:\HERECOMES\JAWS.NOW more stressful than BAMBI.AAH? Suppose the file you try to write is an object-code file rather than an ASCII text file. What constitutes success or failure?

I don't care what the software test plan says; testing is an ad hoc procedure. The incredible amount of time it takes to write, debate, and approve the test plan (and especially the time it takes to explain why you didn't test in accordance with it) could be much better spent actually testing the software.

5.2 WHAT IS TRUTH?

We test algorithms to find out if they give the right answers. The problem is, how do we know what the right answers are? In this subsection we will look at several different ways of answering the question, "What is truth?"

5.2.1 Trust

Suppose you want to test the *Cos* function in the TRIG package. You ask it to compute the cosine of 23 degrees, and it tells you the answer is 0.92050. Is that right? Granted it probably isn't exact, because the true value almost certainly needs more than five decimal places for an exact expression; but is 0.92050 the closest value that can be represented by five decimal places? How do you know what the right answer is?

Perhaps you have a book containing trigonometric functions, and you compare the answer to the value in the table. How do you know the table is correct? It was probably generated by computer program. How do you know its computer program is more accurate than *TRIG.Cos*? You could check the result with your pocket calculator. Are you going to take the word of a $29 piece of plastic containing a 4-bit processor over an expensive 16- or 32-bit computer?

When it comes right down to it, it becomes a question of trust. You will accept the math tables in the handbook because it is published by John Wiley & Sons and therefore cannot contain any errors. Perhaps you trust the pocket calculator because it was made by a well-known manufacturer with a reputation you can trust. Your confidence may be boosted by the fact that the math tables and the calculator both agree. For one reason or another, you put your faith in something.

Listing 74 shows the program I used to test the *TRIG.Cos* function with input values from −5.0 degrees to +370.0 degrees in 1 degree steps. That's almost 400 values, but it only takes the computer a few seconds to generate them all. (You can easily test more values by changing the loop increment to 0.1 degree or 0.001 degree if you like.)

The program creates a data file listing the 376 input angles and the function result for each angle on the same line. At 50 lines per page, that's almost 8 pages of data. You can quickly scan the data, looking at angles that are multiples of 30 or 45 degrees and verify that those angles give the expected results. Then you can look for obviously wild values. If you don't find any, that gives you some confidence, but it doesn't prove all the values are correct. What are we going to do?

The trick is to try to obtain the result two different ways and compare the results. If they agree, the answer is almost certainly correct. If they disagree, you need to find a third method to independently check the answer.

One of the reasons for using the identity **Cos(THETA) = Sin(THETA + PI_OVER_TWO)** for the Meridian and Alsys versions of the *TRIG* package was to use a different way of computing the cosine than the one used by the DEC version of the *TRIG* package.

The DEC version is the one I trust. Digital Equipment Corporation has supplied scientific run-time libraries to FORTRAN programs for years, and I'm sure they have discovered an outstanding, accurate method for computing all the trigonometric functions. The *Cos* function in the DEC *TRIG* package calls *Cosd* function in the VAX/VMS math library.

The *THETA + PI_OVER_TWO* method I used in the Meridian and Alsys versions is mathematically inferior because it introduces round-off error. Suppose I want to find the cosine of an angle *THETA* near -90 degrees. Perhaps the angle *THETA* is exactly -1.57 radians. The cosine of that angle is 7.9632686×10^{-4} (according to my pocket calculator). Suppose the value I use to approximate *PI_OVER_TWO* is 1.5708 radians. When I compute *Sin(-1.57 + 1.5708)* I get 7.9999986×10^{-4}, an error of 3.6729994×10^{-6}! That bothers mathematicians. It only bothers engineers if they know the angle *THETA* was measured to an accuracy better than 3.673 microradians (about 0.00021 degrees).

I ran the *Cos_Test* program on Meridian, Alsys, and DEC machines, expecting to get slightly different results. I wanted to know the magnitude of the difference. I also wanted to know what input angle gives the poorest results.

Cos_Test always creates an output file called COS.DAT. I could have modified the source code every time I moved the *Cos_Test* from one computer to another, or I could have made the program ask the user what file to put the output data in, but I decided it is simpler to let it put the data in COS.DAT and use an operating-system command to rename COS.DAT to DECCOS.DAT, MERCOS.DAT, or ALSCOS.DAT after it was created.

Figure 40 shows some of the results I got with the Meridian version of the cosine routine. Eight pages of cosine data isn't very interesting reading, so I've shown a few segments of the output just to give you a sample of what it looks like. The DEC and Alsys results are almost identical, often differing by 1 in the least-significant digit.

If a person compares two eight-page printouts and doesn't notice any major errors, that gives you some measure of confidence. People get careless sometimes, so you can't really be sure the printouts match. You could have more confidence if a computer meticulously compared both listings, line by line.

MS-DOS has a file comparison utility that I hoped to use to compare them. When I tried it, I found it wasn't totally successful. So many lines differed by one digit that the utility program got discouraged and gave up. That meant I had to write a program to read two files and find the differences. I could have made the program compute the average difference and standard deviation, but I was more interested in the maximum error.

The *COS_DIF* program is shown in Listing 75. It asks the user for two file names and compares them, line by line. The first entry on each line (the angle tested) should be identical. If it isn't, then one of the files has been corrupted. The program ends with an error message telling where the error was detected. Otherwise, it goes through the whole file, keeping track of the maximum errors in the positive and negative directions. When it is finished it prints the maximum differences. When I used it to compare the Meridian results to the DEC "truth," I got the results shown in Figure 41. Results comparing Alsys to DEC outputs were similar.

Now I have confidence in the Meridian and Alsys versions of the *TRIG.COS* function, because I have compared them to a standard I can trust (a routine in the DEC math library).

5.2.2   Inverse Functions

Another way to discover What is truth? is to use inverse functions. I use this technique often. I tested the *TRIG.Log* function by taking the logarithm of a number, then taking the antilogarithm of the result to see if I got the same number back. I tested *TRIG.Sqrt* by squaring a number, taking the square root of the result, and comparing it to the original number. I tested the *Fixed_Image*, *Float_Image*, and *Value* functions by taking the image of a floating point number, then finding the value of the image, and comparing the result with the original number.

In a perfect world, you would always get exactly what you started with. Unfortunately, round-off errors give you a result that is nearly equal to the original value, which makes comparison more difficult. You can take two approaches when comparing the results: (1) You can establish an acceptable error and declare any difference between the original value and the reconstructed value smaller than this threshold value to be okay. (2) You can measure the difference between the original and reconstructed values and keep track of the maximum positive and negative errors.

The first method is most useful for situations where you know how accurate you need to be. For example, suppose the *COORDINATES* package is going to be used in a program that guides a missile to a target. If the missile warhead has a lethal radius of X feet, then the *COORDINATES* package must not introduce any inaccuracy resulting in a miss distance greater than X feet. It would probably be a good idea to be conservative, and set the threshold at $X/2$ feet, or $X/10$ feet or whatever is appropriate to the application.

The second method is better for situations where you want to know what is the best you can do. For example, you could use the second method to find the maximum error introduced by the *COORDINATES* package. If the calculations can be off by as much as Y feet, then you will have to design the warhead to have a lethal radius of at least Y feet. It would probably be a good idea to be conservative, and make it $2 \times Y$ feet or $10 \times Y$ feet.

Both methods have weaknesses, especially in situations where there there is one really wild point and many points that just barely fail. Suppose there is one input condition that gives absolutely crazy results (perhaps a location near the origin where a division by a value near zero occurs) and several other points that are moderately over threshold. The first method will tell you many points failed, but won't tell you the magnitude of the one spectacular failure. You might look at four or five points, see they are all just barely out of tolerance and decide it's close enough. The second method will tell you the magnitude of the failure at that one awful point, but will not tell you that there were a dozen other points that were 20% over the threshold. You might look at the one wild point, decide it is a pathological case that can't occur in normal operation, and think everything is okay.

The even functions, such as square root, are partially symmetrical. You can square 2 to get 4 and take the square root of 4 to get 2 again, but the method doesn't work when the original value is -2. This doesn't mean you can't use the method on even functions, you just have to be more careful. When testing the square root, for example, you could test it with positive values expecting to get the original value back. Then test a second time with all negative values, expecting to get the absolute value back. When testing trigonometric functions, you may want to test one quadrant at a time because inverse functions return mirror images of the input angle in certain quadrants. (The arcsine of the sine of 100 degrees is 80 degrees).

Inverse testing may leave some gaps in the test suite. The square-root test described above won't tell you what will happen if you try to take the square root of a negative number because all the input values were created by squaring a positive or negative number, the result of which can never be negative. Furthermore, if you are testing a 32-bit integer square root, the test cases will be sparse at the higher values. If you square 46,339 it will yield the test input 2,147,302,921. Squaring 46,340 results in 2,147,395,600. There are 92,679 values between 2,147,302,921 and 2,147,395,600 that can never be tested using this approach.

5.2.3 Manufactured Data

Embedded computers are often used in applications where the input signals are corrupted by noise. An algorithm must process the true signal and ignore the noise. Again the question is, What is truth?

This sort of situation doesn't lend itself to the inverse function testing we just discussed. You can put noisy data into the input of a filter and get clean data out, but you usually can't shove the clean data into the output of the filter to reproduce the same noisy input.

If you have an established algorithm that is believed to work, you can put faith in its results using the first method we discussed. You just record some noisy, real-world data, process it with both algorithms, and compare the results. But if you are developing an entirely new algorithm, then you don't have an old one to tell you what the right answer is. If you do have an old one, and it gives different results from the new one, then it might test your faith. Are you really sure the old algorithm gives the right answers? There is likely to be some doubt in your mind.

In situations like these, I like to use a different approach. I manufacture some realistic input data by starting with clean data and adding artificially generated, known noise. Then when I use an algorithm to separate the signal from the noise, I know exactly what the correct answer should be.

The description of a valid input signal for your algorithm depends entirely on the problem, but generally you can create a pure, valid input signal by adding several sine waves with various amplitudes, frequencies, and phase differences. You can compute the value of this input signal at the moments of interest and put them in a file called CLEAN.DAT. Use this as the input to your algorithm and store the resulting output in TRUTH.DAT.

The next step is to create some realistic corruption. Maybe the signal is corrupted by frequencies that are out of band or by periodic noise spikes. If the signal is likely to be corrupted by Gaussian noise, you can use the *RANDOM_NUMBERS.Noise* function to create a noise waveform. If appropriate you can add a bias and/or filter the noise waveform. You should have a good idea of the characteristics of the noise in your system (if you don't, you haven't done your homework), and should be able to model it. Simulate a representative noise waveform and store it in NOISE.DAT.

The third step is to add each element in CLEAN.DAT to the corresponding element in NOISE.DAT, and store the result in INPUT.DAT. You now have a realistic, noisy input signal for testing your algorithm.

Finally, process the noisy input and store the result in OUTPUT.DAT. You can compare OUTPUT.DAT to TRUTH.DAT to see how well the algorithm performed in the presence of noise. You can do this as often as you want with different kinds of input signals and different kinds of noise.

5.3 SELECTING INPUT CONDITIONS

Now that we know what truth is, we need to know how to select input values. The five methods generally used to do this are 100% testing, uniform sampling, Monte Carlo testing, good judgment, and dumb luck. I hesitated to include the last method, but let's be honest—that's how many errors are found!

5.3.1   Testing Every Case

Clearly the best thing you can do is to test every possible input. This usually isn't practical, but in some special cases it is. For example, all possible inputs to the *ASCII_UTILITIES.Upper_Case* function that returns a character can be easily be tested. Just write a program that loops through all 128 ASCII characters and compares the input character with the output character. If they are the same, do nothing. If they are different, then print the input character, the output character, and call *new_line*. You should get twenty-six lines of output that look like the following:

```
a A
b B
c C
```

(and so on)

```
x X
y Y
z Z
```

Here's another case where 100% testing is possible. Suppose we want to test the *COORDINATES* package, and the input values are given as one byte integers. That means the values can range from -128 to $+127$ feet. Figure 42 shows a short test program designed to check the *COORDINATES* package transformations with all possible inputs. It uses the inverse function technique to test both *Transform* functions, by transforming a rectangular point into a polar point and then transforming it back again. The program does this for all rectangular positions included in the area from 128 feet west to 127 feet east, and 128 feet south to 127 feet north. It keeps track of the largest errors and prints them when finished. It also tells us how long it took the test program to run.

The two previous examples are exceptions to the general rule. It is more likely that the *COORDINATES* package is expected to work for all locations within 100 miles from the origin. In theory, we could 100% test this package by simply changing the loop limits to $\pm$ 528,000 feet to get full 100-mile testing coverage. In practice we can't do this. It took 177 seconds for the test program shown in Figure 42 to run on a 10 MHz AT clone. The number of points tested was $256^2 = 65,536$ points. That's

370 points per second. To test $(2 \times 528,000 + 1)^2$ points would take 753,473,124 seconds. That's almost 24 years. By the time we finished testing it, the weapon it was being designed for would be obsolete.

5.3.2 Sparse Uniform Testing

Sparse uniform testing is often a viable alternative to 100% testing. We could start a test program running at 4 P.M. Friday afternoon and check the results at 7 A.M. Monday morning. That means the test program would run 63 hours. At 370 points per second, the *Coordinates_Test* program could check 83,916,000 points. That's about 9160 squared, so we could let the two loop indices go from -4580 feet to $+4580$ over the weekend. If we wanted to check the algorithm to make sure it works over a 100 mile range we could let *EAST* and *NORTH* be 115 times the loop index. The program could run over the weekend and we would have uniform test coverage over the whole area.

The coverage wouldn't be as dense as 100% testing because we would be checking it every 115 feet instead of every foot, but this kind of sparse uniform testing is good because it quickly covers the entire range of inputs and is likely to uncover overflow conditions. (In fact, 46,341 squared overflows on a 32-bit integer machine, so the transformations fail at 8.78 miles.)

We said it would take almost 24 years to test all the points in a square $\pm$ 100 miles from the origin (to 1 foot resolution), but if you add a third dimension and want to test all those points at all altitudes from 0 to 8 miles in 1 foot increments, the schedule stretches out to 971,520 years. Nobody is going to fund a project for that long!

We've already calculated that the test program can test 83,916,000 points over the weekend. If we uniformly distribute those test points over the volume 8 miles high and 100 miles in each direction from the origin, then the points fall on grid lines 825 feet apart. That's sparse, but it gives gives good, uniform coverage over the entire space.

The disadvantage of uniform testing is that the inputs are regular multiples of the index. Therefore, certain ratios of input conditions occur over and over, and other ratios never happen. Differences between two variables tend to be multiples of certain values. This nice, regular input pattern sometimes misses small differences of large numbers or division by numbers near zero.

Another problem with uniform testing is that it is too uniform. It spends just as much time testing the coordinate transformations of targets 90 miles away as it does testing coordinate transforms 90 feet away. If you are testing an early warning system, you want to test lots of cases at the outer boundary and don't care about short ranges. If you are testing a short-range gun system, you care more about the performance at short range than long range. In these cases you don't want a uniform distribution. Monte Carlo testing might be more appropriate.

5.3.3   Monte Carlo Testing

Real data often isn't regular and predictable, so it is sometimes a good idea to test algorithms with pseudorandom data. This is especially true when there are more than just two variables and when sparse uniform testing is awfully sparse. Monte Carlo testing is an important part of software engineering.

Let's suppose we decided to test the *COORDINATES* package using Monte Carlo techniques for picking the *X* and *Y* coordinates. We still have all weekend, so we want to generate about 84 million coordinate pairs and test them. If we try to do that, we will be in for several surprises.

First, we will find the program is still running Monday morning when we get to work. That's because it takes more time to generate a random number than it does to simply bump the index in a loop. You won't be able to test as many points in a given time period as you will if you use a uniform distribution.

Second, you may not be testing as much as you think. Suppose you generated X and Y by doing this

```
X := integer(RANDOM_NUMBERS.Rnd *
     (2.0 * 528000.0) - 528000.0);
Y := integer(RANDOM_NUMBERS.Rnd *
     (2.0 * 528000.0) - 528000.0);
```

It appears that you are generating a random distance from 0 to 200 miles (in feet) and subtracting 100 miles (in feet) to get a random distance from −100 to +100 miles (expressed as a number of feet). Well, you are, but the distances aren't as random as you expect.

5.3.3.1   *RANDOM_NUMBERS* Package. You've read a little bit about the *RANDOM_NUMBERS* package already. It was used in the *PLAYING_CARDS* package to deal the cards. It was also used to create noise for manufactured data. I didn't say much about it then because it wasn't important to know how it works. Now we need to understand its limitations, so let's look at Listings 76 and 77.

If you read the fine print in the *RANDOM_NUMBERS* package specification, you will see the *Rnd* function generates a random sequence that repeats after 2048 numbers. After you have generated 1024 *X,Y* pairs, you will begin to repeat the same pairs. So the algorithm above doesn't really test 84 million random positions. It tests 1024 random positions 82,000 times. The last 81,999 times don't tell you anything you didn't already learn the first time.

Furthermore, every random number generated by *Rnd* can be expressed as N/2048 where *N* is 0 through 2047. If you multiply by 2*528000, then every value can be expressed as 515.63 * *N*, where *N* is an integer from 0 through 2047. So even though it appeared to be testing 84 million different points where *X* and *Y* could take on any integer value of feet, it was really only testing 1024 sparsely distributed points.

The moral of the story is, "You better know the characteristics of your random distribution, or you could badly mislead yourself."

If you read the whole *RANDOM_NUMBERS* package specification, you will see a procedure called *Random_Digit*. It returns a random integer in the range from 0 to 9. The comments in the package body describe how it works. I don't think the sequence repeats, but I haven't proved it. (Proving that a random sequence doesn't repeat and is completely uncorrelated is quite a job.) If you need a sequence longer than 2048 numbers or need a very dense sequence, then use the *Random_Digit* function to build random numbers one digit at a time. Be patient, though. The *Random_Digit* function is slow.

Let me be the first to admit this isn't a very good random-number package. Remember, this is a book about how to write Ada programs, not about how to design the ultimate random-number generator. I didn't want to waste a lot of time confusing readers with things that don't really have anything to do with Ada. There must be people who have made it their life's work to figure out the fastest, longest, densest random sequence. If you need a really good random-number generator, it would be a good idea for you to search the literature and rewrite the package body of *RANDOM_NUMBERS* using a better technique. I just needed something that would generate a random sequence of 52 numbers so I could shuffle the poker deck, so I used this simple, well-known random-number generator.

Despite the limitations of the simple random-number generator, it teaches a valuable lesson: "Simple approaches can be taken in a package body when you need to do a quick feasibility study, then upgraded later." Maybe the *RANDOM_NUMBERS* package isn't good enough for a real *Draw_Poker* program. That doesn't matter when I'm first testing the logic of the program. Who cares if somebody notices the 157th card after the three of clubs is always the eight of hearts? Before I start selling the machine, I can fix that sort of thing by giving the *RANDOM_NUMBERS* package specification to somebody who really enjoys writing random-number generators. When they come back with an improved body, I can just compile it and link it, and I will not have to worry about making any other changes in the *Draw_Poker* program. The important thing is that I can test the *Draw_Poker* concept now, using a mediocre random-number generator.

Starting with the simplest approach helps me define the requirements for the final solution. For example, I learned that I have to throw in 1 second delays just to slow the *Draw_Poker* program down. This means I can tell a designer to come up with a random-number generator without any detectable correlation (that would give a gambler an edge) and no speed constraints. On the other hand, if I need the random number generator for testing the *COORDINATES* package and find out the simple package body only lets me test 10 points a second, speed will be important to me. I'd accept something that quickly generates a long string of dense random numbers derived from the CPU clock, even though it has a mild (but noticeable) 60 Hertz correlation in it.

5.3.4   Good Judgment

When you do Monte Carlo testing, you have to know what you are doing. Let's accept that fact. When I hear people promoting their software development methodologies, they tend to claim their way is so simple it doesn't even require thought. They say you could train monkeys to follow the rules, and they could do it for you. This line is attractive to managers who want to hire hoards of people at the minimum wage. The truth is there is no substitute for intelligence and good judgment.

Testing the *ASCII_UTILITIES.Upper_Case* function that works on a whole string is an example of a situation where all you can use is good judgment when selecting test cases. You can't test 100% of all possible input strings, simply because you can't even list 100% of all possible input strings. Even a sparse uniform distribution of all possible input strings boggles my mind. It would be possible to use Monte Carlo techniques for generating random input strings, but how many would I need to generate to assure myself it works? If there are thousands of these strings generated, how do I check to see if they were properly converted by the *Upper_Case* function? This is a case where, like it or not, there is no substitute for intelligence. You have to use some good judgment and come up with a few, well-chosen test cases.

It's hard to teach good judgment. Techniques that work one time don't make any sense at other times. I'll just give you an example, and then I'm afraid you're pretty much on your own.

The string *Upper_Case* function has three basic parts: (1) There is a loop that indexes through all the characters in the string, (2) the assignment statement that gives values to each character in the string, and (3) the return statement. If I can convince myself that each of these three parts works, then I have some assurance that the whole thing works.

To test the loop index, I will need to try the function on strings of different lengths. I certainly want to try one-character strings, and some moderate length strings, but what do I do about bizarre string lengths? How do I test it for a string -2 characters long? How do I declare the input test string? Will Ada let me declare **TEST : string(2. .1);** ? What value will she let me assign to *TEST*? What exception do I expect *Upper_Case* to raise if I do succeed in giving it an invalid string? What do I define the proper response to be?

Of course, I have to ask the same questions about strings that are longer than the maximum length. Those questions are a little more plausible because it isn't unreasonable to anticipate a line like **X := Upper_Case(Y & Z);** where the lengths of *Y* and *Z* exceed the maximum string length. But even in that case, I have to declare *X* to be longer than the maximum length, and Ada probably won't let me compile my test case. If she does, she should raise *CONSTRAINT_ERROR* when she tries to elaborate *X*, and the program will terminate before I get to my test case.

So, here is my stand: Despite all my best efforts, I can't consciously create a situation that tries to process an illegal string, so I probably won't create one by accident. If I do create one by accident, it is the result of an error, and I should detect that error before I call the *Upper_Case* function. If I fail to detect the error, the part of the program I should fix is the part that caused the error or failed to detect it, not the innocent *Upper_Case* function. Judgment tells me that I don't need to test strings less than one character long, or longer than the maximum allowed by the implementation.

Therefore, to assure myself that the loop in the *Upper_Case* function works, I will test it with some minimum length strings, some maximum length strings, and a few intermediate length strings, and I will be satisfied if all those cases work.

Testing the assignment statement is relatively easy. I've already done 100% testing on the character *Upper_Case* function, so I know it works. Therefore, the few tests cases that checked the loop will also suffice to check the assignment. I'll want some of those cases to include lower-case letters and some to include upper-case letters, numbers, and punctuation marks, to show they aren't changed.

It isn't hard to convince myself that the return statement works. The few test cases I've already planned won't work unless the return statement works, so they provide valuable information about the return statement. The only feature I need to test that hasn't already been tested is to see what happens when I try to *Upper_Case* a string *N* characters long and assign it to a string M characters long, when N is not equal to M. It should raise *CONSTRAINT_ERROR*. If N and M are known at compiler time, Ada may warn me about the *CONSTRAINT_ERROR* before I run the test.

Therefore, good judgment tells me that a few test cases satisfying the requirements in the preceding paragraphs are sufficient to test the string *Upper_Case* function.

5.3.5 Dumb Luck

Most people won't admit it, but a lot of errors are found by dumb luck. That's how I found a bug in *Fixed_Image* function.

The *Fixed_Image* function is one of those routines that is impossible to test for all possible inputs. There are an infinite number of floating-point values. The computer can only represent a finite number of them, but even so, that finite number is far too large to test. Besides, the *Fixed_Image* function has three independent options (the number of digits before the decimal point, number after the decimal point, and leading characters). You can't test all input values for all combinations of options.

I had no choice but to use good judgment when selecting the test cases. I tested *Fixed_Image* with a bunch of different values. I used big values, small values, positive values, negative values, fixed length, variable length, and so on. It passed.

Then I wrote some routines to test the logarithm functions in the *TRIG* package using the inverse function method. I was taking logs of powers of two and then taking the antilog of the result to see if I got the original value back again. For example, $Ln(0.5)$ should be -0.69315, and $Exp(-0.69315)$ should be 0.5 (or very close to it). $Ln(2.0)$ should be $+0.69315$, and $Exp(+0.69315)$ should be 2.0. The test program was automatically checking the results, so there really wasn't any need to print them out, but I did anyway.

My test routine told me everything was fine, but I happened to notice on the printout that $Ln(0.5)$ was $+0.69315$, and $Exp(+0.69315)$ was 0.5. That's clearly an error in both the *Ln* and *Exp* functions. I thought they didn't work for values less than one. But then I noticed $Ln(0.25)$ was -1.38629, and $Exp(-1.38629)$ was 0.25, so the functions appeared to work for numbers less than one after all. Then I noticed $Ln(2.0)$ was also $+0.69315$, and $Exp(+0.69315)$ was 2.0! How could $Exp(+0.69315)$ evaluate to two different answers and always the right one? It was very confusing.

It turned out that the bug was in *Fixed_Image*. Numbers in the interval from -1.0 to 0.0 were printed as positive values. Even though I had tested *Fixed_Image* with many different values, I didn't happen to pick a value in that small interval. I just discovered it through dumb luck.

After you have tried one or more of the previous input selection methods, dumb luck will finish the job. Just put a fully-debugged, error-free module to normal use and you will almost always find errors you didn't find before, no matter how much you tested it.

Don't think that dumb luck is a substitute for the other kinds of testing. It is the final line of defense and should just find minor coding errors that can be fixed without changing any documentation. If normal usage finds an error that requires a major program revision, it is too late in the development cycle for that. You have to do everything you can to find major errors early.

Routines that involve user interfaces are very difficult to test, because it is so difficult to predict what a user will do. These routines need lots of operational testing, because dumb luck is the only way of finding strange responses to illegal inputs.

5.4 TESTING MECHANISMS

After you have decided what method you are going to use to select the inputs for your test cases and what outputs are correct, you are still faced with the problem of writing the code that will actually test your software. There are several ways to do this.

5.4.1 Test Drivers

A common way to test lower-level modules is to use a test driver program. You've already seen the technique used in the *Cos_ Test* program (Listing 74) and the *Coordinates_ Test* program (Figure 42).

The approach is to write a program that passes input data to the unit under test and compares the output to truth. The input comes from a loop index for 100% or uniform testing, from a random number generator for Monte Carlo testing, from carefully selected input conditions coded directly in the program, or from a file of manufactured data. The output is determined to be good or bad by comparing it to some trusted results, using an inverse function, or comparing it to a file containing data that is defined to be correct.

5.4.1.1 White-Box Testing.
Test drivers are good for testing a single unit in isolation, but can also be used to test several modules at once to save time if you do "white-box" testing. White-box testing takes advantage of things you know about the internal workings of the module under test.

You may have wondered why I tested the cosine function that uses degrees instead of the sine function that uses radians. I did that simply because it tests several features of the Meridian *TRIG* package at once. The *Sin* and *Units_Convert* functions are nested in the *Cos* function. As the index goes from −5.0 degrees to 370.0 degrees, it uses the *Units_Convert* function to convert from degrees to radians at each of those angles, so there is no need for me to waste time seperately testing the *Units_Convert* function. I know the *Cos* function in the Meridian *TRIG* body calls the *Sin* function, so the *Sin* function is tested at the same time.

White-box testing saves time, but it has its disadvantages, too. If you are testing several things at once and you get the right answer, it is a pretty good indication that everything works. If you don't get the right answer, then you can't be sure what went wrong. If the *Cos_Test* results are wrong, it could be because there is an error in the *Cos* function, the *Sin* function, or the *Units_Convert* function. Then you will have to test *Sin* and *Units_Convert* separately, using a similar test driver program to isolate the error.

5.4.1.2 Black-Box Testing.
You have to know all about the internal workings of the module under test to do white-box testing. Since I know the Meridian *Cos* function calls *Units_Convert* and *Sin*, I took advantage of that fact to reduce the number of tests. The DEC trig functions, on the other hand, are black boxes. I don't have any idea what is inside them. Since I don't know how the DEC *Cosd* function works, I can't assume that *Cosd* calls *Sind*, *Sin* or *Cos*. (It probably doesn't.) If *Cosd* passes its test, it is still necessary to test *Sin*.

5.4.1.3 Which Color is Better?
Is black-box testing better than white-box testing? That's hard to say. Both methods have their advantages and disadvantages. You could argue that black-box testing is more reliable because you make fewer assumptions. For example, the white-box test of *TRIG.Cos* assumes that *Cos* always calls *Sin*. If the *TRIG* body is changed to call *Cos* directly, then *Sin* never gets tested.

On the other hand, you could argue that white-box testing is more reliable because you know more about the thing you are testing and will be more alert to potential problems. For example, if you are white-box testing a *Tan* function and know that it computes *Sin/Cos*, you may be more likely to remember to check for conditions that may cause a division by zero than you would if it was just a black box.

It really comes down to the person doing the testing, rather than the method used. Either method, consciously applied, will do the job. Either method, poorly done, will fail to catch errors.

5.4.2   Test Stubs

Since test drivers are higher-level routines that call lower-level subprograms, that makes it nearly impossible to use them for testing the top level of a program. (I say "nearly impossible" because there are situations where you can create a super-level driver that is one level higher than the top level.) In general, it is easier to test the higher levels of your program using a test stub instead.

A stub is a simple routine that takes the place of the real routine. It may be a null procedure, or it may simply write a message to the screen that says, "I was called!" These stubs let you check the interfaces and higher levels of the program.

When I was working on the *Show* program, I wanted to test the concept of adding the command-line input to the main program before I had figured out how to make the command line work. I did this using the test stubs shown in Figures 43 and 44. Figure 43 just returned a constant string. When I verified that it worked, then I used Figure 44 to see what happened with various inputs. If I had just leaped into trying to implement the *Get_Command_Line* procedure and found that *Show* didn't work, I wouldn't have been able to tell if the error was in *Show* or *Get_Command_Line*. The two test stubs were so simple, I could have more confidence that they were correct and could focus my attention on *Show*, where the problem probably was.

Test stubs don't need to be limited to fixed data or user-supplied data. You can write test stubs that take input data from a file. Test stubs need not be just input simulators. They can also display or record data sent to them. Sometimes stubs count how many times they are called or record the maximum or minimum values they receive. They can set a flag after they have been called a certain number of times. What you can do with a stub is limited only by your imagination.

5.4.3   Using Stubs and Drivers

Let's use an example to show how drivers and stubs can be used to check a program. Suppose you are writing a program that replays data from a test flight. The user enters the number of the flight he wants to replay. A procedure then searches a data base to see which reel of tape contains the data for that flight and tells the computer operator to mount that reel. Suppose the wrong reel is consistently mounted. Where is the problem?

If you think the problem is in the routine that looks up the reel number for a given flight, you can use a test driver. The test driver could be as simple as the one shown in Figure 45. It asks you for a flight number and tells you what reel it is on. It will tell you if the *Lookup* routine works or not.

If there are symptoms that suggest the *Lookup* routine is working correctly, is getting wrong data, or maybe isn't being called at all, you can replace it with a stub like the one shown in Figure 46. Whenever it is called, it writes, "What reel contains flight number XXX?" where *XXX* is the parameter that was passed to the stub. You enter *YYY* and press RETURN. Then you can isolate the problem. Was *XXX* the correct flight number, or was the wrong parameter passed to the stub? Did the operator get a message to mount reel *YYY*, or was he told to mount a different reel?

5.4.4   Test and Demo Programs

The disks containing the source code for the listings also include some test and demo programs. There is a subtle difference between the two. A test program is thorough and usually doesn't involve much operator intervention. The *Coordinates_ Test* program in Figure 42 is called a test program because it thoroughly tests the *COORDINATES* package and prints the results.

A demo program is just a quick confidence check. It may not check every part of the package, and it usually involves a user interface. For example, a demo program might ask the user to enter an angle in degrees and then print the sine, cosine, and tangent of the angle. The user can run this program a couple of times and observe the results, just to see if the program compiles and runs.

5.5   THE COST OF TESTING

It is well known that most of an iceberg is hidden under water. The same is true of software. The size of a software project is often described by the number of lines of code in the product, but that's just the tip of the iceberg. The amount of software that needs to be written to test the product can be staggering. Often the number of lines of code of test software will exceed the lines of code in the product software.

Test software can get out of hand in a hurry. Suppose you have to write three lines of test software for every new line of software you deliver. (That's probably what I average.) Then suppose management says that all your test software must be formally tested. (You've got to know your test suite works, don't you?) So for every line of test software you write, you need to write 3 lines of software that tests the software that tests your product. If X is the number of lines in your product, you will have to write $3X$ lines of test software, and $9X$ lines of code that tests the test software. Your job has just increased by a factor of 12! If management then insists you fully test the software that tests the software that tests your product, your job (and cost and schedule) has increased by a factor of 39. Sooner or later, you have to call an end to the madness. (Fortunately, the managers I've worked for have required formally testing the test software, and no more.)

What generally happens is that people write as much test software as they can in the time left over at the end of the project. (Is there ever time left over at the end of a project?) The test software is inadequate, so the product gets shipped with some bugs in it.

Maybe you don't believe you have to write more test software than product software. Well, just look at size of the *Cos_Test* (Listing 74) and *Cos_Dif* (Listing 75) compared to the fraction of the *TRIG* package they are testing. I wanted to include complete test programs for all the source code in this book, but there's just not enough room for it all. That's why I've only described the *Cos_Test*.

Testing is a big job. You have to plan money, people, and most of all, *time* for it. If you write three lines of test code for every line of product code, it will take you three times as long to write the test code. Don't expect to write and debug all your test code in the last month before the critical design review. Even if you could, it wouldn't do you much good. By that time the design is cast in concrete (and probably behind schedule), so nobody is going to change anything unless your test programs find catastrophic errors. If you find moderate errors, people will just say, "That's a shame, but we can't do anything about it now. Why didn't you catch these errors sooner?" You have to code and test early in the development cycle while there is still time to take corrective action. Some people believe it is possible to do such good planning during the design phase that flawless code can be written in a few weeks at the end of the project. They think testing is a mere formality to show that the design is correct. That's nonsense.

CONCLUSION

I've tried to give you the benefit of years of experience in a few pages. You can use it, ignore it, or build on it. It's up to you.

If you only learn one lesson from this whole book, I hope it is this: You can make your job much easier by filling your bag-of-tricks with reusable software components. Then most of your work reduces to simply putting those building blocks together to make whatever you want. It becomes child's play, like building something out of Tinkertoys.

If you do this, your job becomes more fun because you eliminate a lot of the drudgery. You don't keep solving the same old problems over and over. You use solutions you've already found for those problems and devote most of your time to solving newer, more challenging problems. You cut down on the time you spend testing and documenting your software because many of the components have been tested and documented already.

The only way you can make this work is by learning to write independent modules. You have to hide special operational details inside a black box where they can't be seen. Start with modules that are small and simple, then build the smaller modules into bigger ones. Control the flow of information between modules by using parameter lists whenever possible.

This method works. I've used it in FORTRAN, assembly, and HPL. It works especially well in Ada because Ada was designed to support this way of writing software. Let it work for you.

FIGURES

Figure 1
POOR_COORDINATES package specification.

```
package POOR_COORDINATES is

  type Rectangular_points is
    record
      NORTH : integer; -- feet;
      EAST  : integer; -- feet;
    end record;

  type Polar_points is
    record
      R     : integer; -- feet;
      THETA : float;   -- degrees;
    end record;

  function Transform(RP : Rectangular_points)
    return Polar_points;

  function Transform(PP : Polar_points)
    return Rectangular_points;

end POOR_COORDINATES;
```

Figure 2
Distinct types.

```
-- Each declared type is distinct, even if they
-- have the same name and definition as another
-- integer type and are in the same file.

-- In the example below, the two packages X and
-- Y, and the procedure P, are in a file called
-- XYP.ada.

--    XYP.ada

package X is

   type Whole_numbers is range -32768..32767;

   procedure Fool_With(
                   N : in out Whole_numbers);

end X;

package Y is

   type Whole_numbers is range -32768..32767;

   procedure Produce(Z : out Whole_numbers);

end Y;

with X, Y; use X, Y;
procedure P is

   type Whole_numbers is range -32768..32767;

   W : Whole_numbers;

begin
   Produce(W);    -- this is line 28
   Fool_With(W); -- this is line 29
end P;

-----------------------------------------------
When you compile the file XYP.ada above, you
get the error message shown on the next page.
```

Figure 2
Distinct types. (Cont'd.)

```
Meridian AdaVantage(tm) Compiler
[v1.5 Apr  3, 1987] Target 8086

Package x added to library.
Package y added to library.
"XYP.ada", line 28: <<error>> identifier has
                                wrong type "w"
"XYP.ada", line 29: <<error>> identifier has
                                wrong type "w"
31 lines compiled.
2 errors detected.
```

Figure 3
SLIGHTLY_ BETTER_COORDINATES package specification.

```
-- This package is better because it will always
-- use integers with 32 bit range, regardless of
-- the computer.

with STANDARD_INTEGERS; use STANDARD_INTEGERS;
package SLIGHTLY_BETTER_COORDINATES is

   type Rectangular_points is
     record
       NORTH : Integer_32; -- feet;
       EAST  : Integer_32; -- feet;
     end record;

   type Polar_points is
     record
       R     : Integer_32; -- feet;
       THETA : float;      -- degrees;
     end record;

   function Transform(RP : Rectangular_points)
     return Polar_points;

   function Transform(PP : Polar_points)
     return Rectangular_points;

end SLIGHTLY_BETTER_COORDINATES;
```

Figure 4
Shared types.

```
-- The units X, Y, and P in file XYP2.ada can
-- all declare objects of type Integer_16
-- because they can share the declaration of
-- that type in STANDARD_INTEGERS.

--   XYP2.ada

with STANDARD_INTEGERS; use STANDARD_INTEGERS;
package X is

  procedure Fool_With(N : in out Integer_16);

end X;

with STANDARD_INTEGERS; use STANDARD_INTEGERS;
package Y is

  procedure Produce(Z : out Integer_16);

end Y;

with X, Y, STANDARD_INTEGERS;
use  X, Y, STANDARD_INTEGERS;
procedure P is

  W : Integer_16;

begin
  Produce(W);
  Fool_With(W);
end P;
```

Figure 5
Dimensional units example.

```
-- Ada can spot equations that are
-- dimensionally incorrect and add correct
-- conversion factors at compile time.

--    D_U_EX.ada

with STANDARD_INTEGERS, DIM_INT_32;
procedure Dimensional_Units_Example is

   type Feet is new DIM_INT_32.Units;
   type Meters is new DIM_INT_32.Units;

   A, B, C : Feet;
   X, Y, Z : Meters;

   function Units_Convert(M : Meters)
       return Feet is
     use STANDARD_INTEGERS; -- for multiply
     DISTANCE : Integer_32;
   begin
     -- 1 meter is approximately 3 feet.
     DISTANCE := 3 * Dimensionless(M);
     return Type_Convert(DISTANCE);
   end Units_Convert;

begin
   A := B + C;
   X := Y + Z;
   A := B + Y; -- this line (25) is wrong
   A := B + Units_Convert(Y);
end Dimensional_Units_Example;
-------------------------------------------
The above code is in a file called D_U_EX.ada.
When you compile it, here's what you get:

C:>ada D_U_EX.ada
Meridian AdaVantage(tm) Compiler
[v2.1 Feb 29, 1988] Target 8086

"D_U_EX.ada", 25: type of function
does not match context "+" [LRM 6.4]

28 lines compiled.
1 error detected.
```

Figure 6
Range checking example.

```
-- Ada knows that objects of type Celsius can
-- never be colder than absolute zero, and will
-- raise CONSTRAINT_ERROR if an attempt is made
-- to assign a value that is out of range.

with FLOAT_UNITS;
with TEXT_IO; use TEXT_IO;
procedure Range_Checking_Example is

  package TEMPERATURE is new FLOAT_UNITS
    (Float_type => float,
     MIN => -273.16,
     MAX => 32000.0,
     Integer_type => integer);
  type Celsius is new TEMPERATURE.Units;
  LAB_TEMPERATURE : Celsius;

begin
  begin
    LAB_TEMPERATURE := Type_Convert(25.0);
      put_line("Ada will let you assign"
               & " reasonable values.");
  exception
    when others =>
      put_line("Ada FAILED to assign"
               & " a correct value.");
  end;
  begin
    LAB_TEMPERATURE := Type_Convert(-300.0);
    put_line("FAILED to detect too cold.");
  exception
    when CONSTRAINT_ERROR =>
      put_line("Ada won't let you assign");
      put_line("values that are too cold.");
  end;
  begin
    LAB_TEMPERATURE := Type_Convert(32100.0);
    put_line("FAILED to detect too hot.");
   exception
    when CONSTRAINT_ERROR =>
      put_line("Ada won't let you assign");
      put_line("values that are too hot.");
  end;
```

Figure 6
Range checking example. (Cont'd).

```
end Range_Checking_Example;

--- When you run it, here's what you get: ---

C:>RANGE_CHECKING_EXAMPLE
Ada will let you assign reasonable values.
Ada won't let you assign
values that are too cold.
Ada won't let you assign
values that are too hot.
```

Figure 7
Dimensional division.

```
-- The Dimensionless function can be used in
-- special operators which convert units
-- automatically.

with DIM_INT_32, STANDARD_INTEGERS;
procedure Program_Fragment is

  -- create some dimensional data types
  type Feet        is new DIM_INT_32.Units;
  type Feet_per_sec is new DIM_INT_32.Units;
  type Milliseconds is new DIM_INT_32.Units;

  -- define some dimensioned objects
  MOVEMENT, PRESENT_POSITION,
  PAST_POSITION : Feet;
  SPEED         : Feet_per_sec;
  DELTA_T       : Milliseconds;

  -- Tell Ada how to divide Feet by
  -- Milliseconds to get an answer in
  -- Feet_per_sec (including the scale
  -- factor of 1000.)
  function "/"(LEFT : Feet;
               RIGHT : Milliseconds)
     return Feet_per_sec is
    use STANDARD_INTEGERS;
    X, Y, Z : Integer_32;
  begin
    X := Dimensionless(LEFT);
    Y := Dimensionless(RIGHT);
    Z := Integer_32(1000.0 * float(X)
       / float(Y));
    return Type_Convert(Z);
  end "/";

begin
  loop

    -- Missing statements here have assigned
    -- values to PRESENT_POSITION, PAST_POSITION,
    -- and DELTA_T.
```

Figure 7
Dimensional division. (Cont'd).

```
      -- Ada checks the next two lines for
      -- dimensional consistency, and they
      -- are OK.
      MOVEMENT := PRESENT_POSITION
                 - PAST_POSITION;
      SPEED := MOVEMENT / DELTA_T;

    -- Do something with SPEED and
    -- PRESENT_POSITION and exit the
    -- loop if appropriate.

      PAST_POSITION := PRESENT_POSITION;
    end loop;
end Program_Fragment;
```

Figure 8
Precise division.

```
-- The Dimensionless function can be used to
-- obtain a ridiculously precise ratio.

with DIM_INT_32; use DIM_INT_32;
procedure Program_Fragment is

   type Feet     is new DIM_INT_32.Units;
   type Float_15 is digits 15;

   PRESENT_POSITION, PAST_POSITION : Feet;
   PRECISE_RATIO : Float_15;

begin

   -- Missing statements here have assigned
   -- values to PRESENT_POSITION and
   -- PAST_POSITION.

   PRECISE_RATIO := Float_15(
    Dimensionless(PRESENT_POSITION))
    / Float_15(Dimensionless(PAST_POSITION)));

end Program_Fragment;
```

Figure 9
Simple output.

```
--The Dimensionless function can be used to
-- output a value.

with DIM_INT_32; use DIM_INT_32;
with STANDARD_INTEGERS; use STANDARD_INTEGERS;
with TEXT_IO; use TEXT_IO;
procedure Program_Fragment is

   type Feet is new DIM_INT_32.Units;

   PRESENT_POSITION : Feet;

begin

   PRESENT_POSITION := Type_Convert(10);
   put("The present position is");
   put(Integer_32'IMAGE(Dimensionless(
     PRESENT_POSITION)));
   put_line(" feet.");

end Program_Fragment;
```

Figure 10
Better output.

```
-- If there are many places in your program
-- where dimensional data types will be printed,
-- it might be worth while to write a function
-- to do it.

with DIM_INT_32; use DIM_INT_32;
with STANDARD_INTEGERS; use STANDARD_INTEGERS;
with TEXT_IO; use TEXT_IO;
procedure Program_Fragment is

  type Feet is new DIM_INT_32.Units;

  PRESENT_POSITION : Feet;

  procedure put(X : Feet) is
  begin
    put(Integer_32'IMAGE(Dimensionless(X)));
    put(" feet");
  end put;

begin

  PRESENT_POSITION := Type_Convert(10);
  put("The present position is");
  put(PRESENT_POSITION);
  put_line(".");

end Program_Fragment;
```

Figure 11
NUMERIC_ UNITS example.

```
-- Sometimes trying to make a generic unit too
-- universal is more trouble than it is worth.
-- Here's what happens if you try to combine
-- the integer and floating dimensional
-- packages. (This is just the beginning of
-- trouble.)

with STANDARD_INTEGERS;
generic
  type Numeric_type is private;
  with function "-"(RIGHT : Numeric_type)
    return Numeric_type is <>;
  with function "+"(LEFT, RIGHT : Numeric_type)
    return Numeric_type is <>;
  with function "-"(LEFT, RIGHT : Numeric_type)
    return Numeric_type is <>;
  with function "*"(LEFT, RIGHT : Numeric_type)
    return Numeric_type is <>;
  with function "/"(LEFT, RIGHT : Numeric_type)
    return Numeric_type is <>;
  with function "/"(LEFT, RIGHT : Numeric_type)
    return STANDARD_INTEGERS.Integer_32;
  with function "/"(LEFT, RIGHT : Numeric_type)
    return float;
  with function "abs"(RIGHT : Numeric_type)
    return Numeric_type is <>;
  with function "rem"
    (LEFT, RIGHT : Numeric_type)
      return Numeric_type is <>;
  with function "mod"
    (LEFT, RIGHT : Numeric_type)
      return Numeric_type is <>;
  with function ">"(LEFT, RIGHT : Numeric_type)
    return boolean is <>;
  with function ">="
    (LEFT, RIGHT : Numeric_type)
      return boolean is <>;
  with function "<"(LEFT, RIGHT : Numeric_type)
    return boolean is <>;
  with function "<="
    (LEFT, RIGHT : Numeric_type)
      return boolean is <>;
```

Figure 11
NUMERIC_UNITS example. (Cont'd)

```
package NUMERIC_UNITS is
 type Units is new Numeric_type;

  -- These functions convert pure numbers into
  -- dimensioned quantities, and vice versa.

  function Type_Convert(X : Numeric_type)
    return Units;
  function "+"(X : Numeric_type) return Units;
  function "-"(X : Numeric_type) return Units;

  -- These are all the arithmetic functions you
  -- need.

  function "+"(RIGHT : Units)
    return Units;
  function "-"(RIGHT : Units)
    return Units;

-- and so on

end NUMERIC_UNITS;
```

Figure 12
Polar Coordinates: Mathematicians measure angles counterclockwise from the horizontal axis.

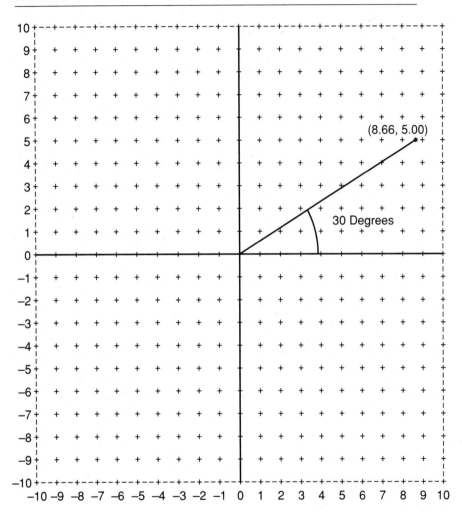

Figure 13
Directions: Pilots measure angles clockwise from North.

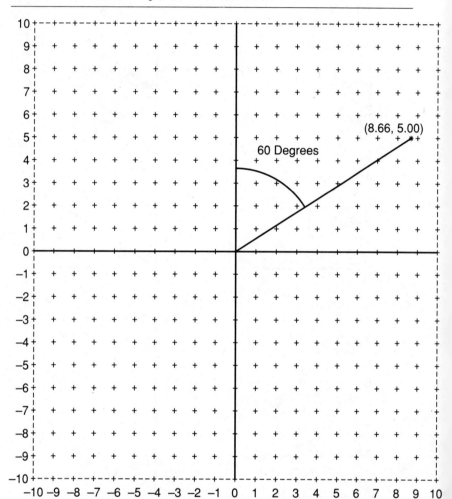

Figure 14
COORDINATES package specification.

```
-- This is an improved version of the
-- POOR_COORDINATES package given in figure 1.

with DIM_INT_32, TRIG;
package COORDINATES is

  type Feet is new DIM_INT_32.Units;

  type Rectangular_points is
    record
      NORTH : Feet;
      EAST  : Feet;
    end record;

  type Polar_points is
    record
      R     : Feet;
      THETA : TRIG.Deg;
    end record;

  function Transform(RP : Rectangular_points)
    return Polar_points;

  function Transform(PP : Polar_points)
    return Rectangular_points;

end COORDINATES;
```

Figure 15
POOR_COORDINATES body.

```
-- The body of the much-maligned package in
-- figure 1.

with MATH_LIB; -- Meridian Ada utility package
package body POOR_COORDINATES is

  PI : constant float := MATH_LIB.PI;

  function Transform(RP : Rectangular_points)
    return Polar_points is
    RADIANS_TO_DEGREES : constant float
      := 180.0 / PI;
    X : Polar_points;
    R_SQUARED : integer;
    ANGLE, NORTH, EAST : float;
  begin
    R_SQUARED := RP.NORTH * RP.NORTH
               + RP.EAST * RP.EAST;
    X.R := integer(MATH_LIB.Sqrt(
           float(R_SQUARED)));
    if RP.NORTH = 0 then
      if RP.EAST >= 0 then
        X.THETA := 90.0;
      else
        X.THETA := 270.0;
      end if;
      return X;
    end if;
    NORTH := float(RP.NORTH);
    EAST  := float(RP.EAST);
    if NORTH > 0.0 and EAST >= 0.0 then
      -- 0 to 90 degrees
      ANGLE := MATH_LIB.Atan(EAST/NORTH);
    elsif NORTH < 0.0 and EAST >= 0.0 then
      -- 90 to 180 deg
      ANGLE := PI - MATH_LIB.Atan(
               EAST/(-NORTH));
    elsif NORTH < 0.0 and EAST < 0.0 then
      -- 180 to 270 deg
      ANGLE := PI + MATH_LIB.Atan(EAST/NORTH);
    elsif NORTH > 0.0 and EAST < 0.0 then
      -- 270 to 360 deg
```

```
      ANGLE := 2.0 * PI - MATH_LIB.Atan(
             -EAST/NORTH);
   end if;
   X.THETA := ANGLE * RADIANS_TO_DEGREES;
   return X;
exception
   when NUMERIC_ERROR =>
      if EAST >= 0.0 then
        X.THETA := 90.0;
      else
        X.THETA := 270.0;
      end if;
      return X;
end Transform;

function Transform(PP : Polar_points)
   return Rectangular_points is
   DEGREES_TO_RADIANS : constant float
     := PI / 180.0;
   ANGLE : float;
   X : Rectangular_points;
begin
   ANGLE := PP.THETA * DEGREES_TO_RADIANS;
   X.NORTH := integer(float(PP.R)
            * MATH_LIB.Cos(ANGLE));
   X.EAST  := integer(float(PP.R)
            * MATH_LIB.Sin(ANGLE));
   return X;
end Transform;

end POOR_COORDINATES;
```

Figure 16
COORDINATES body.

```
-- A better way to write the package body.

with STANDARD_INTEGERS; use STANDARD_INTEGERS;
package body COORDINATES is

   function Transform(RP : Rectangular_points)
     return Polar_points is
     X : Polar_points;
     R_SQUARED, NORTH, EAST : float;
   begin
     -- begin dimensionless processing
     NORTH := float(Dimensionless(RP.NORTH));
     EAST  := float(Dimensionless(RP.EAST));
     R_SQUARED := NORTH * NORTH + EAST * EAST;
     X.R := Type_Convert(
             Integer_32(TRIG.Sqrt(R_SQUARED)));
     -- end dimensionless processing
     X.THETA := TRIG.Atan(EAST,NORTH);
     return X;
   end Transform;

   function Transform(PP : Polar_points)
     return Rectangular_points is
     X : Rectangular_points;
     DISTANCE : float;
   begin
     -- begin partially dimensionless processing
     DISTANCE := float(Dimensionless(PP.R));
     X.NORTH := Type_Convert(Integer_32(DISTANCE
             * TRIG.Cos(PP.THETA)));
     X.EAST := Type_Convert(Integer_32(DISTANCE
             * TRIG.Sin(PP.THETA)));
     -- end partially dimensionless processing
     return X;
   end Transform;

end COORDINATES;
```

Figure 17
The *IMAGE* attribute is awkward to use.

```
procedure Move_Cursor_To(LINE : Line_numbers;
                         COL  : Column_numbers)
     is
  L, C : string(1..3);
begin
  put(ESC & '[');
  if LINE < 10 then
    L(2..3) := integer'IMAGE(LINE);
    put(L(3..3));
  else
    L(1..3) := integer'IMAGE(LINE);
    put(L(2..3));
  end if;
  put(';');
  if COL < 10 then
    C(2..3) := integer'IMAGE(COL);
    put(C(3..3));
  else
    C(1..3) := integer'IMAGE(COL);
    put(C(2..3));
  end if;
  put('H');
end Move_Cursor_To;
```

Figure 18
The *Image* function is easy to use.

```
procedure Move_Cursor_To(LINE : Line_numbers;
                         COL  : Column_numbers)
    is
  L, C : string(1..3);
begin
  put(ASCII.ESC & '[');
  put(string'(ASCII_UTILITIES.Image(LINE)));
  put(';');
  put(string'(ASCII_UTILITIES.Image(COL)));
  put('H');
end Move_Cursor_To;
```

Figure 19
ASCII_UTILITIES demo.

```
with ASCII_UTILITIES, TEXT_IO;
procedure ASCII_UTILITIES_Demo is

   type Values is (NOTHING, A_PAIR, TWO_PAIR,
     THREE_OF_A_KIND, A_STRAIGHT, A_FLUSH,
     A_FULL_HOUSE, FOUR_OF_A_KIND,
     A_STRAIGHT_FLUSH, A_ROYAL_FLUSH);

   S : string(1..16);

begin
   TEXT_IO.put_line("Possible poker hands are:");
   for i in Values loop
      -- Make all values 16 character strings,
      -- padding with nulls if necessary.
      ASCII_UTILITIES.String_Copy
        (FROM => Values'IMAGE(i),
         TO   => S,
         FILL => ASCII.NUL);
      -- Convert all character to lower case.
      S := ASCII_UTILITIES.Lower_Case(S);
      -- Change underlines to spaces.
      S := ASCII_UTILITIES.Change(S);
      -- Capitalize the first letter.
      S(1) := ASCII_UTILITIES.Upper_Case(S(1));
      -- indent and print it
      TEXT_IO.put_line("    " & S & ',');
   end loop;
end ASCII_UTILITIES_Demo;
```

```
----------------------------------
```

```
When directed to a printer, the output looks
like this:

Possible poker hands are:
   Nothing,
   A pair,
   Two pair,
   Three of a kind,
   A straight,
```

Figure 19
ASCII_ UTILITIES demo. (Cont'd.)

```
A flush,
A full house,
Four of a kind,
A straight flush,
A royal flush,
```

Figure 20
Sales Tax.

```
-- This program shows how to use the MONEY
-- package.

with MONEY, ASCII_UTILITIES, STANDARD_INTEGERS;
with TEXT_IO; use TEXT_IO;
procedure Sales_Tax is

  PRICE, TAX, COST : MONEY.Cents;
  RATE             : float;
  TEXT             : string(1..79);
  LENGTH           : natural;

  function "*"(
    LEFT : MONEY.Cents; RIGHT : float)
      return MONEY.Cents is
    use STANDARD_INTEGERS;
    X      : float;
    RESULT : Integer_32;
  begin
    -- Compute exact amount
    X := float(MONEY.Dimensionless(LEFT))
       * RIGHT;
    -- Round to the nearest cent
    RESULT := Integer_32(X);
    -- Convert the answer to Cents
    return MONEY.Type_Convert(RESULT);
  end "*";

  use MONEY;  -- for "+" operator in
              -- COST := PRICE + TAX;

begin
  put("What is the cost of the item? ");
  get_line(TEXT,LENGTH); new_line;
  PRICE := MONEY.Value(TEXT(1..LENGTH));
  put("What is the sales tax rate? " );
  get_line(TEXT,LENGTH); new_line;
  RATE := ASCII_UTILITIES.Value(
          TEXT(1..LENGTH));
  -- if RATE > 1, the user must have entered
  -- a percentage (i.e. 6%) instead of 0.06.
```

Figure 20
Sales Tax. (Cont'd.)

```
   if RATE > 1.0 then
     RATE := RATE / 100.0;
   end if;
   TAX := PRICE * RATE;
   declare
     TAX_STRING : string(1..MONEY.Width(TAX));

   begin
     TAX_STRING := MONEY.Image(TAX);
     put_line("The tax on that item is "
               & TAX_STRING);
   end;
   COST := PRICE + TAX;
   put("Your total cost is ");
   put(MONEY.Image(COST));
   put_line(".");
end Sales_Tax;
```

Figure 21
Usual_Dilemma.

```
-- A beginning Ada programmer sometimes finds
-- himself in this dilemma.

with SCROLL_TERMINAL; use SCROLL_TERMINAL;
procedure Usual_Dilemma is

   NAME            : string(1..30);
   ADDRESS         : string(1..40);
   CITY_STATE_ZIP  : string(1..40);

begin

   get("What is your Name? ", NAME);
   get("What is your Address? ",ADDRESS);
   get("Where do you Live? ",CITY_STATE_ZIP);

   SCROLL_TERMINAL.new_line(10);
   SCROLL_TERMINAL.put_line
     ("NAME = " & NAME);
   SCROLL_TERMINAL.put_line
     ("ADDRESS = " & ADDRESS);
   SCROLL_TERMINAL.put_line
     ("CITY = " & CITY_STATE_ZIP);

exception
   when NEEDS_HELP =>
     null; -- nothing you can do now!
end Usual_Dilemma;
```

Figure 22
Usual_Solution.

```
-- The usual solution is to avoid the problem
-- by handling the exception where it occurs.

with SCROLL_TERMINAL; use SCROLL_TERMINAL;
procedure Usual_Solution is

  NAME            : string(1..30);
  ADDRESS         : string(1..40);
  CITY_STATE_ZIP  : string(1..40);

  procedure Get_Name(NAME : out string) is
  begin
    get("What is your Name? ", NAME);
  exception
    when NEEDS_HELP =>
      put_line(
        "Don't you even know your own name?");
      Get_Name(NAME);
  end Get_Name;

  procedure Get_Address(ADDRESS : out string)
    is
  begin
    get("What is your Address? ", ADDRESS);
  exception
    when NEEDS_HELP =>
      put_line(
        "What is your street or P.O Box?");
      Get_Address(ADDRESS);
  end Get_Address;

  procedure Get_City(CITY : out string) is
  begin
    get("Where do you Live? ", CITY);
  exception
    when NEEDS_HELP =>
      put_line("Please enter City, State,"
            & " and Zip code.");
      Get_City(CITY);
  end Get_City;
```

Figure 22
Usual_Solution. (Cont'd.)

```
begin

  Get_Name(NAME);
  Get_Address(ADDRESS);
  Get_City(CITY_STATE_ZIP);

  SCROLL_TERMINAL.new_line(10);
  SCROLL_TERMINAL.put_line
    ("NAME = " & NAME);
  SCROLL_TERMINAL.put_line
    ("ADDRESS = " & ADDRESS);
  SCROLL_TERMINAL.put_line
    ("CITY = " & CITY_STATE_ZIP);

end Usual_Solution;
```

Figure 23
Form_Dilemma.

```
-- In this case it wouldn't do any good to try
-- to give Update a local exception handler
-- because you don't know what field the user
-- was updating when he requested help.

with SCROLL_TERMINAL;
with FORM_TERMINAL; use FORM_TERMINAL;
procedure Form_Dilemma is

   NAME            : string(1..30);
   ADDRESS         : string(1..40);
   CITY_STATE_ZIP  : string(1..40);
   DOESNT_MATTER   : boolean;

begin

   Read("ADDRESS.DAT");
   Update(CURSOR_AT => "Name field
               NEXT => DOESNT_MATTER);

   get("Name field        ", NAME);
   get("Address field     ", ADDRESS);
   get("City field        ", CITY_STATE_ZIP);

   SCROLL_TERMINAL.New_Line(10);
   SCROLL_TERMINAL.put_line("NAME = " & NAME);
   SCROLL_TERMINAL.put_line("ADDRESS = "
     & ADDRESS);
   SCROLL_TERMINAL.put_line("CITY = "
     & CITY_STATE_ZIP);

exception
   when NEEDS_HELP =>
     null; -- nothing you can do now!
end Form_Dilemma;
```

Figure 24
FORTRAN_ Mentality_ Solution.

```
-- This is the wrong way to solve the problem.

with SCROLL_TERMINAL;
with FORM_TERMINAL; use FORM_TERMINAL;
procedure FORTRAN_Mentality_Solution is

   NAME             : string(1..30);
   ADDRESS          : string(1..40);
   CITY_STATE_ZIP   : string(1..40);
   DOESNT_MATTER    : boolean;
   HELP_REQUEST     : integer;
   CURSOR_POSITION  : Field_names;

begin
   Read("ADDRESS.DAT");
   CURSOR_POSITION := "Name field

   << ASK_NAME_AND_ADDRESS >>
   Update(CURSOR_AT => CURSOR_POSITION,
              NEXT => DOESNT_MATTER,
            STATUS => HELP_REQUEST);
   if HELP_REQUEST = 0 then
     null; -- no help needed
   elsif HELP_REQUEST = 1 then
     SCROLL_TERMINAL.new_line(10);
     SCROLL_TERMINAL.put_line
       ("Don't you even know your own name?");
     SCROLL_TERMINAL.Wait_For_User;
     CURSOR_POSITION := "Name field
     goto ASK_NAME_AND_ADDRESS;
   elsif HELP_REQUEST = 2 then
     SCROLL_TERMINAL.new_line(10);
     SCROLL_TERMINAL.put_line
       ("What is your street or P.O. Box?");
     SCROLL_TERMINAL.Wait_For_User;
     CURSOR_POSITION := "Address field        ";
     goto ASK_NAME_AND_ADDRESS;
   elsif HELP_REQUEST = 3 then
     SCROLL_TERMINAL.new_line(10);
     SCROLL_TERMINAL.put_line
       ("Where do you live?");
     SCROLL_TERMINAL.Wait_For_User;
```

Figure 24
FORTRAN_ Mentality_ Solution. (Cont'd.)

```
      CURSOR_POSITION := "City field              ";
      goto ASK_NAME_AND_ADDRESS;
   end if;

   get("Name field          ", NAME);
   get("Address field       ", ADDRESS);
   get("City field          ", CITY_STATE_ZIP);

   SCROLL_TERMINAL.new_line(10);
   SCROLL_TERMINAL.put_line("NAME = " & NAME);
   SCROLL_TERMINAL.put_line("ADDRESS = "
      & ADDRESS);
   SCROLL_TERMINAL.put_line("CITY = "
      & CITY_STATE_ZIP);
end FORTRAN_Mentality_Solution;
```

Figure 25
Form_Solution.

```
-- The right way to solve the problem, using a
-- local exception handler and a function that
-- returns additional error information.

with SCROLL_TERMINAL;
with FORM_TERMINAL; use FORM_TERMINAL;
procedure Form_Solution is

  NAME            : string(1..30);
  ADDRESS         : string(1..40);
  CITY_STATE_ZIP  : string(1..40);

  procedure get(FIRST_FIELD : Field_names;
        NAME, ADDRESS, CITY : out string) is
    DOESNT_MATTER : boolean;
  begin
    Update(CURSOR_AT => FIRST_FIELD,
                NEXT => DOESNT_MATTER);
    get("Name field       ", NAME);
    get("Address field    ", ADDRESS);
    get("City field       ",
      CITY_STATE_ZIP);
  exception
    when NEEDS_HELP =>
      SCROLL_TERMINAL.new_line(10);
      if Confusing_Field =
         "NAME FIELD           " then
        SCROLL_TERMINAL.put_line
          ("Don't you even know"
         & " your own name?");
      elsif Confusing_Field =
        "ADDRESS FIELD        " then
        SCROLL_TERMINAL.put_line
          ("What is your street or P.O Box?");
      elsif Confusing_Field =
        "CITY FIELD           " then
        SCROLL_TERMINAL.put_line
          ("Please enter City, State,"
         & " and Zip code.");
      end if;
      SCROLL_TERMINAL.Wait_for_User;
      get(Confusing_Field, NAME, ADDRESS,
        CITY_STATE_ZIP);
    end get;
```

Figure 25
Form_Solution. (Cont'd.)

```
begin

  Read("ADDRESS.DAT");
  get("Name field          ",NAME, ADDRESS,
    CITY_STATE_ZIP);

  SCROLL_TERMINAL.New_Line(10);
  SCROLL_TERMINAL.put_line("NAME = " & NAME);
  SCROLL_TERMINAL.put_line("ADDRESS = "
    & ADDRESS);
  SCROLL_TERMINAL.put_line("CITY = "
    & CITY_STATE_ZIP);
end Form_Solution;
```

Figure 26
Objects need a constraint.

```
-- This procedure illustrates the consequences
-- of LRM Section 3.7.2 paragraph 8.

procedure Objects_Need_A_Constraint is

   type No_default (LENGTH : natural) is
     record
       TEXT : string(1..LENGTH);
     end record;

   type Default (LENGTH : natural := 0) is
     record
       TEXT : string(1..LENGTH);
     end record;

   FIRST_NAME : No_default(8);
   MY_NAME    : No_default;      -- illegal
   WHOLE_NAME : Default(14);
   LAST_NAME  : Default;

   -- MY_NAME is illegal because no constraint
   -- was supplied (as it was for FIRST_NAME).

   -- LAST_NAME doesn't need a constraint because
   -- there is a default value for it.

   -- WHOLE_NAME shows that you can give a
   -- constraint that is different from the
   -- default value if you like.

begin
   null;
end Objects_Need_A_Constraint;
```

Figure 27
Constrained objects can't change constraints.

```
-- This procedure illustrates thee consequences
-- of LRM Section 3.2.1 paragraph 12.

procedure
  Constrained_Objects_Cant_Change_Constraints
    is

  type No_default (LENGTH : natural) is
    record
      TEXT : string(1..LENGTH);
    end record;

  type Default (LENGTH : natural := 0) is
    record
      TEXT : string(1..LENGTH);
    end record;

  FIRST_NAME : No_default(8);
  WHOLE_NAME : Default(14);
  LAST_NAME  : Default;

begin

  -- I can let LAST_NAME hold a 5 character
  -- name.
  LAST_NAME := (LENGTH => 5, TEXT => "Jones");

  -- Then I can stretch it to hold a 10
  -- character name.
  LAST_NAME := (10, "Washington");

  -- FIRST_NAME can hold an 8 character name.
  FIRST_NAME := (8, "Do-While");

  -- But it can't shrink to hold a shorter one
  -- because it was constrained to be 8
  -- characters when it was declared.
  FIRST_NAME := (4, "Dave"); -- ILLEGAL

  -- You might think WHOLE_NAME can be changed
  -- because it has a default length, but the
  -- fact is it was constrained to be 14
```

Figure 27
Constrained objects can't change constraints. (Cont'd.)

```
   -- characters when it was declared, so it
   -- can't be changed either.
   WHOLE_NAME := (17, "George Washington");
      -- ILLEGAL

end
   Constrained_Objects_Cant_Change_Constraints;
```

Figure 28
You can't change the constraint alone.

```
-- This procedure illustrates the consequences
-- of LRM Section 3.7.1 paragraph 9.

procedure Cant_Change_Constraint_Alone is

   type Default (LENGTH : natural := 0) is
      record
         TEXT : string(1..LENGTH);
      end record;

   WHOLE_NAME : Default(14);
   LAST_NAME  : Default;

begin

   -- I can let LAST_NAME hold a 5 character name.
   LAST_NAME := (LENGTH => 5, TEXT => "Jones");

   -- Then I can change those five characters
   -- alone.
   LAST_NAME.TEXT := "Smith";

   -- But I can't change the discriminant alone.
   LAST_NAME.LENGTH := 10; -- ILLEGAL

   -- WHOLE_NAME was constrained to be 14
   -- characters, so I can do this:
   WHOLE_NAME.TEXT := "Do-While Jones";

   -- And I can expand LAST_NAME by changing both
   -- the LENGTH and TEXT in one shot by an
   -- assignment statement.
   LAST_NAME := WHOLE_NAME;
   -- (LAST_NAME now contains (14,"Do-While
   -- Jones").)

   -- Or I can assign the whole record using an
   -- aggregate, like this:
   LAST_NAME := (5, "Jones");

end Cant_Change_Constraint_Alone;
```

Figure 29
ADDRESS.DAT

```
 7
-- data --
FORM TITLE
 4
 3
 23
P
Name and Address Form
-- data --
NAME PROMPT
 7
 1
 20
P
Name
-- data --
NAME FIELD
 7
 22
 51
U

-- data --
ADDRESS PROMPT
 8
 1
 20
P
Address
-- data --
ADDRESS FIELD
 8
 22
 61
U

-- data --
CITY PROMPT
 9
 1
 20
```

Figure 29
ADDRESS.DAT. (Cont'd.)

```
P
City, State, & ZIP :
-- data --
CITY FIELD
 9
 22
 61
U

[end of file]
```

Figure 30
Erroneous FORTRAN *SPLIT* subroutine.

```
SUBROUTINE SPLIT(TIME,HOURS,MIN,SEC)
IMPLICIT NONE
INTEGER*4 TIME, HOURS, MIN
REAL*4 SEC

HOURS = TIME / 3600000
TIME  = MOD (TIME,3600000)
MIN   = TIME / 60000
TIME  = MOD (TIME,60000)
SEC   = TIME / 1000.0

RETURN
END
```

Figure 31
Erroneous *Split* procedure.

```
with STANDARD_INTEGERS; use STANDARD_INTEGERS;
procedure Split(TIME  :     Integer_32;
                HOURS : out Integer_32;
                MIN   : out Integer_32;
                SEC   : out float) is
begin
  HOURS := TIME / 3600_000;
  TIME  := TIME mod 3600_000;        -- line 10
  MIN   := TIME / 60_000;
  TIME  := TIME mod 60_000;          -- line 12
  SEC   := float(TIME) / 1000.0;
end Split;

Meridian AdaVantage(tm) Compiler
[v2.1 Feb 29, 1988] Target 8086
"split.ada", 10: assignment to read-only object
                                        [LRM 6.2/5]
"split.ada", 12: assignment to read-only object
                                        [LRM 6.2/5]
15 lines compiled.
2 errors detected.
```

Figure 32
Correct *Split* procedure.

```
with STANDARD_INTEGERS; use STANDARD_INTEGERS;
procedure Split(TIME  :     Integer_32;
                HOURS : out Integer_32;
                MIN   : out Integer_32;
                SEC   : out float) is
  T : Integer_32;
begin
  T     := TIME;
  HOURS := T / 3600_000;
  T     := T mod 3600_000;
  MIN   := T / 60_000;
  T     := T mod 60_000;
  SEC   := float(T) / 1000.0;
end Split;

Meridian AdaVantage(tm) Compiler
[v2.1 Feb 29, 1988] Target 8086
Subprogram body split added to library.
17 lines compiled.
No errors detected.
Meridian 8086 Code Generator
[v1.8 Jan 20, 1988] Target 8086 object
Generating code for split
```

Figure 33
VIRTUAL_PRINTER body for COM2 port.

```
--                  VPBCOM2.ada
--                  20 October 1987
--                  Version 2.0

--                  Do-While Jones
--                  324 Traci Lane
--                  Ridgecrest, CA 93555
--                  (619) 375-4607

-- This version works for Alsys & Meridian Ada
-- on an IBM with the printer connected to the
-- COM2 serial output port.

-- The printer connected to COM2 is an ancient
-- Microline 83, which seems to be a little
-- slow to tell the PC that it can't accept
-- another character because it is printing a
-- line. Consequently, the first character of a
-- line sometimes gets lost. The solution is to
-- send an ASCII.NUL after every CR and LF. If
-- the NUL gets lost, no harm is done.

with TEXT_IO;
package body VIRTUAL_PRINTER is

  PRINTER : TEXT_IO.File_type;

  PRINTER_NAME : string(1..80);
  LENGTH       : natural;

  procedure put(C : character) is
  begin
    TEXT_IO.put(PRINTER,C);
    -- the following is required by the
    -- Microline 83 printer
    if C = ASCII.CR or C = ASCII.LF then
      TEXT_IO.put(PRINTER,ASCII.NUL);
    end if;
  end put;

  procedure put(S : string) is
  begin
```

Figure 33
VIRTUAL_ PRINTER body for COM2 port. (Cont'd.)

```
   for i in S'RANGE loop
     put(S(i));
   end loop;
end put;

procedure Set_Output(DEVICE : string) is
begin
  TEXT_IO.Close(PRINTER);
  TEXT_IO.Create(
    PRINTER,TEXT_IO.OUT_FILE,DEVICE);
  LENGTH := DEVICE'LENGTH;
  PRINTER_NAME(1..LENGTH) := DEVICE;
exception
  when TEXT_IO.NAME_ERROR =>
    raise NAME_ERROR;
  when TEXT_IO.USE_ERROR =>
    raise USE_ERROR;
end Set_Output;

function Current_Output return string is
begin
  return PRINTER_NAME(1..LENGTH);
end Current_Output;

function Standard_Output return string is
begin
  return "COM2";
end Standard_Output;

begin
  TEXT_IO.Create(
    PRINTER,TEXT_IO.OUT_FILE,Standard_Output);
  LENGTH := 4;
  PRINTER_NAME(1..LENGTH) := Standard_Output;
end VIRTUAL_PRINTER;
```

Figure 34
The first version of *Show*.

```
--                 SHOW.ada
--                 9 June 1987
--                 Do-While Jones

with TEXT_IO; use TEXT_IO;
procedure Show is
   TEXT   : string(1..200);
   LENGTH : natural;
   FILE   : File_type;
begin
   put("What file? ");
   get_line(TEXT,LENGTH);
   Open(FILE, IN_FILE, TEXT(1..LENGTH));
   MAIN:
   loop
     for i in 1..22 loop
       exit MAIN when End_Of_File(FILE);
       get_line(FILE, TEXT, LENGTH);
       put_line(TEXT(1..LENGTH));
     end loop;
     put_line(
       "Press RETURN for the next screen");
     get_line(TEXT,LENGTH);
   end loop MAIN;
exception
   when NAME_ERROR =>
     put("File """);put(TEXT(1..LENGTH));
     put_line(""" could not be found.");
end Show;
```

Figure 35
The first *Get_Command_Line* procedure.

```
--                    GCLBAIBM.ada
--                    19 October 1987

--                    Do-While Jones
--                    324 Traci Lane
--                    Ridgecrest, CA 93555
--                    (619) 375-4607

-- This version works with Alsys Ada on the IBM
-- PC. The Alsys DOS package contains a
-- function Get_Parms which returns a string
-- with a length depending upon the number of
-- characters entered by the user. Since this
-- probably isn't the exact number of
-- characters requested by the calling program,
-- a little bit of data massaging has to be
-- done to put the command line in the first
-- part of the longer output string.

with DOS;
procedure Get_Command_Line(S : out string;
                           L : out natural) is

  procedure Extract(S_IN :     string;
                    S_OUT : out string;
                       L : out natural) is
  begin
    L := S_IN'LENGTH;
    S_OUT(1..S_IN'LENGTH) := S_IN;
  end Extract;

begin
  Extract(DOS.Get_Parms, S, L);
end Get_Command_Line;
```

Figure 36
Improved version of *Show*.

```
--                    SHOW.ada
--                    9 June 1987
--                    Do-While Jones

with Get_Command_Line;
with TEXT_IO; use TEXT_IO;
procedure Show is
  TEXT    : string(1..200);
  LENGTH  : natural;
  FILE    : File_type;
begin
  Get_Command_Line(TEXT,LENGTH);
  if LENGTH = 0 then
    put("What file? ");
    get_line(TEXT,LENGTH);
  end if;
  Open(FILE, IN_FILE, TEXT(1..LENGTH));
  MAIN:
  loop
    for i in 1..22 loop
      exit MAIN when End_Of_File(FILE);
      get_line(FILE, TEXT, LENGTH);
      put_line(TEXT(1..LENGTH));
    end loop;
    put_line(
      "Press RETURN for the next screen");
    get_line(TEXT,LENGTH);
  end loop MAIN;
exception
  when NAME_ERROR =>
    put("File """);put(TEXT(1..LENGTH));
    put_line(""" could not be found.");
end Show;
```

Figure 37
The original *Get_ Command_ Line* body for Meridian.

```
--                    GCLBMIBM.ada
--                    9 June 1987
--                    Do-While Jones

--   Meridian command line interface for IBM PC.

--   This procedure is NOT PORTABLE because it
--   uses some utility packages available from
--   Meridian Software Systems, Inc. These
--   packages are compatible with the Meridian
--   AdaVantage compiler, but are not included
--   with the compiler. (They must be purchased
--   separately.)

with TEXT_HANDLER, ARG;
 -- Meridian Utility packages.
procedure Get_Command_Line
    (TAIL   : out string;
     LENGTH : out natural) is
  BUFFER : TEXT_HANDLER.Text(127);
  LEN    : natural;
begin
  if ARG.Count < 2 then
    LENGTH := 0;
    return;
  end if;
  TEXT_HANDLER.Set(BUFFER, ARG.Data(2));
  LEN := TEXT_HANDLER.Length(BUFFER);
  LENGTH := LEN;
  TAIL(1..LEN) := TEXT_HANDLER.Value(BUFFER);
end Get_Command_Line;
```

Figure 38
Get_Command_Line body for Gould Aplex Ada.

```
--                  GCLBG.ada
--                  9 June 1987
--                  Do-While Jones

--   Command line interface for Gould APLEX Ada
--   running under MPX-32.

--   This procedure is NOT PORTABLE because it
--   uses a utility package supplied by Gould
--   with their APLEX Ada compiler.

with HOST_LCD_IF;
-- HOST Lowest Common Denominator InterFace.
procedure Get_Command_Line
    (TAIL   : out string;
     LENGTH : out natural) is
  TEXT : string(1..80);
  N    : natural;
begin
  HOST_LCD_IF.Get_Param_String(TEXT,N);
  LENGTH := N-1;
  S(1..N-1) := TEXT(1..N-1);
end Get_Command_Line;
```

Figure 39
Write without help and error recovery.

```
with Get_Command_Line;
with SCROLL_TERMINAL, SCROLL_PRINTER, TEXT_IO;
procedure No_Help_Write is
   TITLE               : string(1..79);
   FILENAME            : string(1..68);
   LENGTH              : natural;
   FILE                : TEXT_IO.File_type;
   PAGE                : positive;
   DOUBLE_SPACED       : boolean;
   LINES_LEFT_TO_PRINT : natural;
   TEXT                : string(1..250);
   RESPONSE            : character;
   PAGE_NO             : string(1..4);

begin
   Get_Command_Line(FILENAME,LENGTH);
   TEXT_IO.Open(FILE, TEXT_IO.IN_FILE,
     FILENAME(1..LENGTH));
   TITLE := (others => ' ');
   TITLE(1..LENGTH) := FILENAME(1..LENGTH);
   SCROLL_TERMINAL.put_line(
     "Enter page TITLE, please.");
   SCROLL_TERMINAL.get("", TITLE, TITLE);
   SCROLL_TERMINAL.get(
     "Start numbering pages at page ",
     "1",PAGE_NO);
   PAGE := integer'VALUE(PAGE_NO);
   SCROLL_TERMINAL.get(
     "SINGLE or DOUBLE spaced? (S/D) ",
     'S', RESPONSE);
   case RESPONSE is
     when 'D' | 'd' =>
       DOUBLE_SPACED := TRUE;
     when others =>
       DOUBLE_SPACED := FALSE;
   end case;
   loop
     exit when TEXT_IO.End_Of_File(FILE);
     SCROLL_PRINTER.new_line(4);
     SCROLL_PRINTER.put_line(TITLE);
     SCROLL_PRINTER.new_line(3);
     LINES_LEFT_TO_PRINT := 50;
```

Figure 39
Write without help and error recovery. (Cont'd.)

```
loop
  exit when TEXT_IO.End_Of_File(FILE);
  TEXT_IO.get_line(FILE,TEXT,LENGTH);
  SCROLL_PRINTER.put_line(TEXT(1..LENGTH));
  LINES_LEFT_TO_PRINT :=
    LINES_LEFT_TO_PRINT-1;
  if DOUBLE_SPACED then
    SCROLL_PRINTER.new_line;
    LINES_LEFT_TO_PRINT :=
      LINES_LEFT_TO_PRINT-1;
  end if;
  exit when LINES_LEFT_TO_PRINT < 1;
end loop;
SCROLL_PRINTER.new_line(
  LINES_LEFT_TO_PRINT+3);
SCROLL_PRINTER.Set_Col(30);
SCROLL_PRINTER.put_line(
  integer'IMAGE(PAGE));
PAGE := PAGE+1;
SCROLL_PRINTER.new_page;
  end loop;
  TEXT_IO.Close(FILE);
  SCROLL_TERMINAL.put_line("Done.");
end No_Help_Write;
```

Figure 40
Portions of Meridian COS.DAT.

−5.00	0.996195
−4.00	0.997564
−3.00	0.998630
−2.00	0.999391
−1.00	0.999848
0.00	1.000000
1.00	0.999848
2.00	0.999391
29.00	0.874620
30.00	0.866026
31.00	0.857168
44.00	0.719340
45.00	0.707107
46.00	0.694659
59.00	0.515039
60.00	0.500000
61.00	0.484810
88.00	0.034900
89.00	0.017453
90.00	0.000001
91.00	−0.017452
92.00	−0.034899
134.00	−0.694658
135.00	−0.707106
136.00	−0.719339
178.00	−0.999391
179.00	−0.999848
180.00	−1.000000
181.00	−0.999848
182.00	−0.999391
268.00	−0.034901
269.00	−0.017454
270.00	−0.000001
271.00	0.017451
272.00	0.034898

Figure 40
Portions of Meridian COS.DAT. (Cont'd.)

358.00	0.999391
359.00	0.999848
360.00	1.000000
361.00	0.999848
362.00	0.999391
363.00	0.998630
364.00	0.997564
365.00	0.996195
366.00	0.994522
367.00	0.992546
368.00	0.990268
369.00	0.987689

Figure 41
Accuracy of Meridian *TRIG.Cos* function.

```
C:>cos_dif
What is the name of the REFERENCE file?
                                        deccos.dat
What is the name of the TEST file? mercos.dat
The maximum positive error was 0.000001 at 21.00
                                        degrees.
The maximum negative error was -0.000002 at
                                308.00 degrees.
```

Figure 42
Coordinates_ Test program.

```
with COORDINATES, CALENDAR;
with STANDARD_INTEGERS; use STANDARD_INTEGERS;
with TEXT_IO; use TEXT_IO;
procedure Coordinates_Test is
use COORDINATES; -- for Type_Convert and "+"
  R, WORST_MAX_NORTH, WORST_MIN_NORTH,
  WORST_MAX_EAST, WORST_MIN_EAST
    : COORDINATES.Rectangular_points;
  P : COORDINATES.Polar_points;
  EAST, NORTH, ERROR : COORDINATES.Feet;
  MAX_NORTH_ERROR, MAX_EAST_ERROR
    : COORDINATES.Feet := +(Integer_32'FIRST);
  MIN_NORTH_ERROR, MIN_EAST_ERROR
    : COORDINATES.Feet := +(Integer_32'LAST);
  START_TIME, STOP_TIME
    : CALENDAR.Day_Duration;
begin
  put_line("Starting COORDINATES Test");
  START_TIME :=
    CALENDAR.Seconds(CALENDAR.Clock);
  for i in Integer_32 range -128..127 loop
    EAST := Type_Convert(i);
    for j in Integer_32 range -128..127 loop
      NORTH := Type_Convert(j);
      R.NORTH := NORTH;
      R.EAST  := EAST;
      P := COORDINATES.Transform(R);
      R := COORDINATES.Transform(P);
      ERROR := R.NORTH-NORTH;
      if ERROR > MAX_NORTH_ERROR then
        MAX_NORTH_ERROR := ERROR;
        WORST_MAX_NORTH.NORTH := NORTH;
        WORST_MAX_NORTH.EAST  := EAST;
      end if;
      if ERROR < MIN_NORTH_ERROR then
        MIN_NORTH_ERROR := ERROR;
        WORST_MIN_NORTH.NORTH := NORTH;
        WORST_MIN_NORTH.EAST  := EAST;
      end if;
      ERROR := R.EAST-EAST;
      if ERROR > MAX_EAST_ERROR then
        MAX_EAST_ERROR := ERROR;
```

Figure 42
Coordinates_Test program. (Cont'd.)

```
          WORST_MAX_EAST.NORTH := NORTH;
          WORST_MAX_EAST.EAST  := EAST;
       end if;
       if ERROR < MIN_EAST_ERROR then
          MIN_EAST_ERROR := ERROR;
          WORST_MIN_EAST.NORTH := NORTH;
          WORST_MIN_EAST.EAST  := EAST;
       end if;
     end loop;
  end loop;
  STOP_TIME :=
     CALENDAR.Seconds(CALENDAR.Clock);
  put("The computed value for NORTH was");
  put(Integer_32'IMAGE(
     Dimensionless(MAX_NORTH_ERROR)));
  put(" HIGH at");
  put("(" & Integer_32'IMAGE(
     Dimensionless(WORST_MAX_NORTH.NORTH)));
  put("," & Integer_32'IMAGE(
     Dimensionless(WORST_MAX_NORTH.EAST)));
  put_line(").");
  put("The computed value for NORTH was");
  put(Integer_32'IMAGE(
     Dimensionless(MIN_NORTH_ERROR)));
  put(" LOW  at");
  put("(" & Integer_32'IMAGE(
     Dimensionless(WORST_MIN_NORTH.NORTH)));
  put("," & Integer_32'IMAGE(
     Dimensionless(WORST_MIN_NORTH.EAST)));
  put_line(").");
  put("The computed value for EAST was");
  put(Integer_32'IMAGE(
     Dimensionless(MAX_EAST_ERROR)));
  put(" HIGH at");
  put("(" & Integer_32'IMAGE(
     Dimensionless(WORST_MAX_EAST.NORTH)));
  put("," & Integer_32'IMAGE(
     Dimensionless(WORST_MAX_EAST.EAST)));
  put_line(").");
  put("The computed value for EAST was");
  put(Integer_32'IMAGE(
     Dimensionless(MIN_EAST_ERROR)));
```

Figure 42
Coordinates_Test program. (Cont'd.)

```
   put(" LOW   at");
   put("(" & Integer_32'IMAGE(
     Dimensionless(WORST_MIN_EAST.NORTH)));
   put("," & Integer_32'IMAGE(
     Dimensionless(WORST_MIN_EAST.EAST)));
   put_line(").");
   new_line;
   put("The test took");
   put(integer'IMAGE(integer(
     STOP_TIME-START_TIME)));
   put_line(" seconds to run.");
   new_line;
   put_line("Done.");
end Coordinates_Test;

C> coordinates_test
Starting COORDINATES Test
The computed value for NORTH was 0 HIGH
 at(-128,-128).
The computed value for NORTH was 0 LOW
 at(-128,-128).
The computed value for EAST was 0 HIGH
 at(-128,-128).
The computed value for EAST was 0 LOW
 at(-128,-128).

The test took 177 seconds to run.

Done.
```

Figure 43
Get_Command_Line stub 1.

```
--                      GCLS1.ada
--                      9 June 1987

--                      Do-While Jones
--                      324 Traci Lane
--                      Ridgecrest, CA 93555
--                      (619) 375-4607

-- Get_Command_Line, Stub 1


procedure Get_Command_Line(
   TAIL    : out string;
   LENGTH : out natural) is
begin
   TAIL(1..8) := "SHOW.ADA";
   LENGTH := 8;
end Get_Command_Line;
```

Figure 44
Get_Command_Line stub 2.

```
--              GCLS2.ada
--              9 June 1987

--              Do-While Jones
--              324 Traci Lane
--              Ridgecrest, CA 93555
--              (619) 375-4607

-- Get_Command_Line, Stub 2


with TEXT_IO;
procedure Get_Command_Line(
    TAIL   : out string;
    LENGTH : out natural) is
  TEXT : string(1..80);
  L    : natural;
begin
  TEXT_IO.put("What's on the command line? ");
  TEXT_IO.get_line(TEXT,L);
  TAIL(1..L) := TEXT(1..L);
  LENGTH := L;
end Get_Command_Line;
```

Figure 45
Lookup driver.

```
with SCROLL_TERMINAL; use SCROLL_TERMINAL;
with Lookup;
procedure Lookup_Driver is
   FLIGHT_NUMBER, REEL : integer;
   FLIGHT : string(1..5);
begin
   put_line("Lookup Driver");
   loop
      new_line;
      get("What flight? (0 to quit) ",FLIGHT);
      FLIGHT_NUMBER := integer'VALUE(FLIGHT);
      exit when FLIGHT_NUMBER = 0;
      Lookup(FLIGHT_NUMBER, REEL);
      put_line("Flight"
         & integer'IMAGE(FLIGHT_NUMBER)
         & " is on reel" & integer'IMAGE(REEL));
   end loop;
   put_line("Done.");
exception
   when PANIC =>
      put_line("Done.");
end Lookup_Driver;
```

Figure 46
Lookup Stub.

```
with SCROLL_TERMINAL; use SCROLL_TERMINAL;
procedure Lookup(FLIGHT : integer;
                 REEL   : out integer) is
  REEL_NAME : string(1..6);
begin
  put("What reel contains flight");
  put(integer'IMAGE(FLIGHT));
  get(" ? ",REEL_NAME);
  REEL := integer'VALUE(REEL_NAME);
end Lookup;
```

PROGRAM LISTINGS

```
-- Listing 1.

--              SIS.ada
--              Version 1
--              25 October 1987

--              Do-While Jones
--              324 Traci Lane
--              Ridgecrest, CA 93555
--              (619) 375-4607

-- Copyright 1989 by John Wiley & Sons, Inc.
--          All Rights Reserved.

package STANDARD_INTEGERS is

  type Integer_8 is range -2**7..2**7-1;
    subtype Natural_8  is Integer_8
      range 0..Integer_8'LAST;
    subtype Positive_8 is Integer_8
      range 1..Integer_8'LAST;

  type Integer_16 is range -2**15..2**15-1;
    subtype Natural_16  is Integer_16
      range 0..Integer_16'LAST;
    subtype Positive_16 is Integer_16
      range 1..Integer_16'LAST;

  type Integer_32 is range -2**31..2**31-1;
    subtype Natural_32  is Integer_32
      range 0..Integer_32'LAST;
    subtype Positive_32 is Integer_32
      range 1..Integer_32'LAST;

end STANDARD_INTEGERS;
```

```
-- Listing 2.

--              GIU.ada
--              Version 1
--              21 August 1988

--              Do-While Jones
--              324 Traci Lane
--              Ridgecrest, CA 93555
--              (619) 375-4607

-- Copyright 1989 by John Wiley & Sons, Inc.
--         All Rights Reserved.

generic
  type Integer_type is range <>;
  MIN : Integer_type := Integer_type'FIRST;
  MAX : Integer_type := Integer_type'LAST;
package INTEGER_UNITS is

  -- This package provides useful parent types
  -- for derived dimensional units. That is, it
  -- makes it possible to do this:

  -- package DIMENSIONAL_INTEGER is new
  --   INTEGER_UNITS(integer);
  -- type Feet is
  --   new DIMENSIONAL_INTEGER.Units;

  -- package TEMPERATURE is new INTEGER_UNITS
  --   (Integer_type =>
  --       STANDARD_INTEGERS.Integer_16;
  --   MIN => -273;
  --   MAX =>
  --       STANDARD_INTEGERS.Integer_16'LAST);
  --   -- Use 16 bit integers (defined in
  --   -- STANDARD_INTEGERS).
  --   -- Absolute Zero is -273 degrees C.
  -- type Celsius is new TEMPERATURE.Units;

  -- Objects of type Feet can be added to other
  -- objects of type Feet to produce a result
  -- in Feet, but Ada will not allow you to
  -- erroneously multiply objects of type Feet
```

```
-- together and assign the result to another
-- object of type Feet. Ada will raise
-- CONSTRAINT_ERROR if you try to assign a
-- value colder than absolute zero to an
-- object of type Celsius.

type Units is private;

-- Because Units are PRIVATE types, Ada can't
-- be sure they are integers. Therefore, she
-- will not let you do this:

   -- TARGET_RANGE : Feet := 587;

-- Since you have to be able to assign
-- numeric values to objects of type Feet, I
-- have given you three type conversion
-- routines.

-- The preferred way is to do this:

   -- TARGET_RANGE : Feet :=
   --    Type_Convert(587);

-- This makes it obvious to other programmers
-- that you have converted a numeric literal
-- to a special kind of data type.

-- But if you do this a lot, your program
-- will be filled with so many Type_Convert()
-- statements that people will get so used to
-- them that they will ignore them. They
-- loose their value, so you might as well
-- use an operator which is 11 characters
-- shorter.


   -- TARGET_RANGE : Feet := +587; -- or -587;

function Type_Convert(X : Integer_type)
   return Units;
function "+"(X : Integer_type) return Units;
function "-"(X : Integer_type) return Units;

-- The derived data types will inherit all
```

```
-- the operations in the package below. These
-- are all the operations that make sense for
-- dimensional quantities.

function "+"(RIGHT : Units)
  return Units;
function "-"(RIGHT : Units)
  return Units;
function "abs"(RIGHT : Units)
  return Units;
function "+"(LEFT, RIGHT : Units)
  return Units;
function "-"(LEFT, RIGHT : Units)
  return Units;
function "*"(LEFT : Integer_type;
            RIGHT : Units) return Units;
function "*"(LEFT : Units;
            RIGHT : Integer_type)
  return Units;
function "/"(LEFT : Units;
            RIGHT : Integer_type)
  return Units;
function "/"(LEFT, RIGHT : Units)
  return Integer_type;
function "/"(LEFT, RIGHT : Units)
  return float;
function "rem"(LEFT, RIGHT : Units)
  return Units;
function "mod"(LEFT, RIGHT : Units)
  return Units;
-- "=" and "/=" are already defined for
-- private types
function "<"(LEFT, RIGHT : Units)
  return boolean;
function "<="(LEFT, RIGHT : Units)
  return boolean;
function ">"(LEFT, RIGHT : Units)
  return boolean;
function ">="(LEFT, RIGHT : Units)
  return boolean;

-- Suppose you want to multiply two objects
-- of type Feet together to get an answer in
-- Square_feet. You need to write your own
-- multiplication routine which converts
```

```
-- the objects to dimensionless integers,
-- multiplies them, and converts them to type
-- Square_feet. You are given the
-- Dimensionless function to do this.

    -- function "*"(LEFT,RIGHT : Feet)
    --    return Square_feet is
    --    L, R : integer; -- or Integer_32,
    --                    -- or whatever
    --                    -- type you used to
    --                    -- instantiate
    --                    -- this package.
    -- begin
    --    L := Dimensionless(LEFT);
    --    R := Dimensionless(RIGHT);
    --    return Type_Convert(L * R);
    -- end "*";

-- The Dimensionless function is also handy
-- for printing values. If you instantiated
-- this package for type Integer_X, (where X
-- is 8, 16, or 32) you can do this:


    -- put(Integer_X'IMAGE(
    --    Dimensionless(TARGET_RANGE)));

function Dimensionless(LEFT : Units)
  return Integer_type;

-- Since private types don't have 'FIRST and
-- 'LAST attributes, I have given you
-- functions that will act like those
-- attributes.

function First return Integer_type;
function Last return Integer_type;
  -- For example,
  --    ABSOLUTE_ZERO : constant Celsius
  --       := Type_Convert(TEMPERATURE.First);

private

  type Units is new Integer_type
```

```
      range MIN..MAX;
end INTEGER_UNITS;

package body INTEGER_UNITS is

  function Type_Convert(X : Integer_type)
     return Units is
  begin
    return Units(X);
  end Type_Convert;

  function "+"(X : Integer_type)
    return Units is
  begin
    return Units(X);
  end "+";

  function "-"(X : Integer_type)
     return Units is
    NEG : Integer_type;
  begin
    NEG := -1 * X;
    return Units(NEG);
  end "-";

  function "+"(RIGHT : Units)
    return Units is
  begin
    return RIGHT;
  end "+";

  function "-"(RIGHT : Units)
    return Units is
      NEG : Integer_type;
  begin
    NEG := -1 * Integer_type(RIGHT);
    return Units(NEG);
  end "-";

  function "abs"(RIGHT : Units)
    return Units is
  begin
    return Units(abs(Integer_type(RIGHT)));
  end "abs";
```

```
function "+"(LEFT, RIGHT : Units)
  return Units is
begin
  return Units(Integer_type(LEFT)
           + Integer_type(RIGHT));
end "+";

function "-"(LEFT, RIGHT : Units)
  return Units is
begin
  return Units(Integer_type(LEFT)
           - Integer_type(RIGHT));
end "-";

function "*"(LEFT : Integer_type;
           RIGHT : Units) return Units is
begin
  return Units(LEFT * Integer_type(RIGHT));
end "*";

function "*"(LEFT : Units;
           RIGHT : Integer_type)
  return Units is
begin
  return Units(Integer_type(LEFT) * RIGHT);
end "*";

function "/"(LEFT : Units;
           RIGHT : Integer_type)
  return Units is
begin
  return Units(Integer_type(LEFT) / RIGHT);
end "/";

function "/"(LEFT, RIGHT : Units)
  return Integer_type is
begin
  return Integer_type(LEFT)
       / Integer_type(RIGHT);
end "/";

function "/"(LEFT, RIGHT : Units)
  return float is
    EXACT_QUOTIENT : float;
```

```
begin
  EXACT_QUOTIENT := float(LEFT)
                    / float(RIGHT);
  return EXACT_QUOTIENT;
end "/";

function "rem"(LEFT, RIGHT : Units)
  return Units is
begin
  return Units (Integer_type(LEFT)
          rem Integer_type(RIGHT));
end "rem";

function "mod"(LEFT, RIGHT : Units)
  return Units is
begin
  return Units (Integer_type(LEFT)
          mod Integer_type(RIGHT));
end "mod";

function Dimensionless(LEFT : Units)
  return Integer_type is
begin
  return Integer_type(LEFT);
end Dimensionless;

function "<"(LEFT, RIGHT : Units)
  return boolean is
begin
  return Integer_type(LEFT)
       < Integer_type(RIGHT);
end "<";

function "<="(LEFT, RIGHT : Units)
  return boolean is
begin
  return Integer_type(LEFT)
       <= Integer_type(RIGHT);
end "<=";

function ">"(LEFT, RIGHT : Units)
  return boolean is
begin
  return Integer_type(LEFT)
```

```
            > Integer_type(RIGHT);
   end ">";


   function ">="(LEFT, RIGHT : Units)
     return boolean is
   begin
     return Integer_type(LEFT)
          >= Integer_type(RIGHT);
   end ">=";

   function First return Integer_type is
   begin
     return MIN;
   end First;

   function Last return Integer_type is
   begin
     return MAX;
   end Last;

end INTEGER_UNITS;
```

```
-- Listing 3.

--                DI32.ada
--                Version 1
--                11 November 1987

--                Do-While Jones
--                324 Traci Lane
--                Ridgecrest, CA 93555
--                (619) 375-4607

--  Copyright 1989 by John Wiley & Sons, Inc.
--          All Rights Reserved.

--          Dimensioned 32-bit Integers

-- This package is an instantiation of the
-- generic INTEGER_UNITS for
-- STANDARD_INTEGERS.Integer_32.

with STANDARD_INTEGERS, INTEGER_UNITS;
use STANDARD_INTEGERS;
package DIM_INT_32 is
   new INTEGER_UNITS(Integer_32);
```

```
-- Listing 4.

--              GFU.ada
--              Version 1
--              1 September 1988

--              Do-While Jones
--              324 Traci Lane
--              Ridgecrest, CA 93555
--              (619) 375-4607

-- Copyright 1989 by John Wiley & Sons, Inc.
--          All Rights Reserved.

generic
  type Float_type is digits <>;
  MIN : Float_type := -1.0e25;
  MAX : Float_type :=  1.0e25;
  type Integer_type is range <>;
package FLOAT_UNITS is

  -- This package provides useful parent types
  -- for derived dimensional units. That is, it
  -- makes it possible to do this:

  -- package DIMENSIONAL_FLOAT is
  --   new FLOAT_UNITS(float,Integer_type =>
  --     STANDARD_INTEGERS.Integer_32);
  -- type Feet is new DIMENSIONAL_FLOAT.Units;

  -- package TEMPERATURE is new FLOAT_UNITS
  --   (Float_type => float, MIN => -273.16,
  --     MAX => 32000.0, Integer_type =>
  --       integer);
  -- type Celsius is new TEMPERATURE.Units;

  -- Objects of type Feet can be added to other
  -- objects of type feet to produce a result
  -- in Feet, but Ada will not allow you to
  -- erroneously multiply objects of type Feet
  -- together and assign the result to another
  -- object of type Feet. Ada will raise
  -- CONSTRAINT_ERROR if you try to assign a
  -- value colder than absolute zero to an
  -- object of type Celsius.
```

```
type Units is private;

-- Because Units are PRIVATE types, Ada can't
-- be sure they are real numbers. Therefore,
-- she will not let you do this:

  -- TARGET_RANGE : Feet := 587.0;

-- Since you have to be able to assign
-- numeric values to objects of type Feet, I
-- have given you three type conversion
-- routines.

-- The preferred way is to do this:

  -- TARGET_RANGE := Feet :=
  --    Type_Convert(587.0);

-- This makes it obvious to other programmers
-- that you have converted a numeric literal
-- to a special kind of data type.

-- But if you do this a lot, your program
-- will be filled with so many Type_Convert()
-- statements that people will get so used to
-- them that they will ignore them. They
-- lose their value, so you might as well use
-- an operator which is 11 characters
-- shorter.

  -- TARGET_RANGE : Feet := +587.0;
  --                        -- or -587.0;

function Type_Convert(X : Float_type)
   return Units;
function "+"(X : Float_type) return Units;
function "-"(X : Float_type) return Units;

function "+"(RIGHT : Units)
   return Units;
function "-"(RIGHT : Units)
   return Units;
function "abs"(RIGHT : Units)
   return Units;
function "+"(LEFT, RIGHT : Units)
```

```ada
    return Units;
function "-"(LEFT, RIGHT : Units)
  return Units;
function "*"(LEFT : Float_type;
             RIGHT : Units) return Units;
function "*"(LEFT : Units;
             RIGHT : Float_type) return Units;
function "/"(LEFT : Units;
             RIGHT : Float_type) return Units;
function "/"(LEFT, RIGHT : Units)
  return Float_type;
-- "=" and "/=" are already defined for
-- private types.
function "<"(LEFT, RIGHT : Units)
  return boolean;
function "<="(LEFT, RIGHT : Units)
  return boolean;
function ">"(LEFT, RIGHT : Units)
  return boolean;
function ">="(LEFT, RIGHT : Units)
  return boolean;


-- The modulo operation for Units is provided
-- to make it easy to normalize angular
-- measurements. The division operator for
-- Units which returns integers truncates
-- toward zero (rather than rounding) to make
-- it consistent with integer division, and
-- it lets you do this:

-- type Radians is
--    new DIMENSIONAL_FLOAT.Units;

-- PI          : constant Radians
--    := +3.14159;
-- ANGLE       : Radians;
-- REVOLUTIONS : integer;
--    -- (if Integer_type is integer)

-- ANGLE := ANGLE mod (2.0 * PI);
-- REVOLUTIONS := ANGLE / (2.0 * PI);

function "/"(LEFT, RIGHT : Units)
  return Integer_type;
    -- truncates toward zero
```

```
function "rem"(LEFT, RIGHT : Units)
  return Units;
function "mod"(LEFT, RIGHT : Units)
  return Units;

-- Suppose you want to multiply two objects
-- of type Feet together to get an answer in
-- Square_feet. You need to write your own
-- multiplication routine which converts
-- the objects to dimensionless numbers,
-- multiplies them, and converts them to type
-- Square_feet. You are given the
-- Dimensionless function to do this.

  -- function "*"(LEFT,RIGHT : Feet)
  --      return Square_feet is
  --    L, R : float; -- or whatever
  --                  -- Float_type is
  -- begin
  --    L := Dimensionless(LEFT);
  --    R := Dimensionless(RIGHT);
  --    return Type_Convert(L * R);
  -- end "*";

-- The Dimensionless function is also handy
-- for printing values. Assuming you have
-- instantiated FLOAT_IO for Float_type and
-- called it FLOAT_TYPE_IO, you can do this:

  -- FLOAT_TYPE_IO.put(
  --    Dimensionless(TARGET_RANGE));

function Dimensionless(LEFT : Units)
  return Float_type;

-- Since private types (and the underlying
-- real type) don't have 'FIRST and 'LAST
-- attributes, I have given you functions
-- that will act like those attributes.

function First return Float_type;
function Last return Float_type;
  -- For example:
  --     ABSOLUTE_ZERO : constant Celsius
  --       := Type_Convert(TEMPERATURE.First);
```

```ada
private

   type Units is new Float_type range MIN..MAX;

end FLOAT_UNITS;

package body FLOAT_UNITS is

   function Type_Convert(X : Float_type)
     return Units is
   begin
     return Units(X);
   end Type_Convert;

   function "+"(X : Float_type) return Units is
   begin
     return Units(X);
   end "+";

   function "-"(X : Float_type) return Units is
     NEG : Float_type;
   begin
     NEG := -X;
     return Units(NEG);
   end "-";

   function "+"(RIGHT : Units)
     return Units is
   begin
     return RIGHT;
   end "+";

   function "-"(RIGHT : Units)
     return Units is
       NEG : Float_type;
   begin
     NEG := -1.0 * Float_type(RIGHT);
     return Units(NEG);
   end "-";

   function "abs"(RIGHT : Units)
     return Units is
   begin
     return Units(abs(Float_type(RIGHT)));
   end "abs";
```

```
function "+"(LEFT, RIGHT : Units)
  return Units is
begin
  return Units(Float_type(LEFT)
            + Float_type(RIGHT));
end "+";

function "-"(LEFT, RIGHT : Units)
  return Units is
begin
  return Units(Float_type(LEFT)
            - Float_type(RIGHT));
end "-";

function "*"(LEFT : Float_type;
             RIGHT : Units)
  return Units is
begin
  return Units(LEFT * Float_type(RIGHT));
end "*";

function "*"(LEFT : Units;
             RIGHT : Float_type)
  return Units is
begin
  return Units(Float_type(LEFT) * RIGHT);
end "*";

function "/"(LEFT : Units;
             RIGHT : Float_type)
  return Units is
begin
  return Units(Float_type(LEFT) / RIGHT);
end "/";

function "/"(LEFT, RIGHT : Units)
  return Float_type is
begin
  return Float_type(LEFT)
       / Float_type(RIGHT);
end "/";

function "<"(LEFT, RIGHT : Units)
  return boolean is
```

```
begin
  return Float_type(LEFT)
       < Float_type(RIGHT);
end "<";

function "<="(LEFT, RIGHT : Units)
  return boolean is
begin
  return Float_type(LEFT)
      <= Float_type(RIGHT);
end "<=";

function ">"(LEFT, RIGHT : Units)
  return boolean is
begin
  return Float_type(LEFT)
       > Float_type(RIGHT);
end ">";

function ">="(LEFT, RIGHT : Units)
  return boolean is
begin
  return Float_type(LEFT)
      >= Float_type(RIGHT);
end ">=";

function "/"(LEFT, RIGHT : Units)
  return Integer_type is
  -- divide and truncate toward zero
  EXACT : Float_type;
  ROUNDED, TRUNCATED : Integer_type;
begin
  EXACT := LEFT / RIGHT;
  ROUNDED := Integer_type(EXACT);
  if Float_type(abs(ROUNDED))
     > abs(EXACT) then
    if ROUNDED > 0 then
      TRUNCATED := ROUNDED-1;
    else
      TRUNCATED := ROUNDED+1;
    end if;
  else
    TRUNCATED := ROUNDED;
  end if;
```

```
      return TRUNCATED;
   end "/";

   function "rem"(LEFT, RIGHT : Units)
       return Units is
     COMPLETE_CYCLES : Integer_type;
     REMAINDER       : Units;
   begin
     COMPLETE_CYCLES := LEFT / RIGHT;
     REMAINDER := LEFT
       - Float_type(COMPLETE_CYCLES) * RIGHT;
     return REMAINDER;
   end "rem";

   function "mod"(LEFT, RIGHT : Units)
       return Units is
     REMAINDER : Units;
   begin
     REMAINDER := LEFT rem RIGHT;
     if LEFT * RIGHT > 0.0 then
       return REMAINDER;
     elsif REMAINDER = 0.0 then
       return REMAINDER;
     else
       return REMAINDER + RIGHT;
     end if;
   end "mod";

   function Dimensionless(LEFT : Units)
     return Float_type is
   begin
     return Float_type(LEFT);
   end Dimensionless;

   function First return Float_type is
   begin
     return MIN;
   end First;

   function Last return Float_type is
   begin
     return MAX;
   end Last;

end FLOAT_UNITS;
```

```
-- Listing 5.

--              DFU.ada
--              Version 1.0
--              1 September 1988

--              Do-While Jones
--              324 Traci Lane
--              Ridgecrest, CA 93555
--              (619) 375-4607

-- Copyright 1989 by John Wiley & Sons, Inc.
--          All Rights Reserved.

--      Dimensioned Floating Point Numbers

-- This package is an instantiation of the
-- generic FLOAT_UNITS for the predefined
-- floating point type and 32 bit integers.

with FLOAT_UNITS, STANDARD_INTEGERS;
package DIM_FLOAT is new FLOAT_UNITS(
  Float_type => float,
  Integer_type => STANDARD_INTEGERS.Integer_32);
```

```
-- Listing 6.

--                  DFU.ada
--                  Version 1.1
--                  1 September 1988

--                  Do-While Jones
--                  324 Traci Lane
--                  Ridgecrest, CA 93555
--                  (619) 375-4607

-- Copyright 1989 by John Wiley & Sons, Inc.
--          All Rights Reserved.

--          Dimensioned Floating Point Numbers

-- Revision 1.1 instantiates FLOAT_UNITS for the
-- predefined integer type, and avoids a bug in
-- the Meridian AdaVantage 2.1 compiler.

with FLOAT_UNITS;
package DIM_FLOAT is new FLOAT_UNITS(
  Float_type => float,
  Integer_type => integer);
```

```ada
-- Listing 7.

--              TS.ada
--              Version 1
--              19 August 1988

--              Do-While Jones
--              324 Traci Lane
--              Ridgecrest CA, 93555
--              (619) 375-4607

-- Copyright 1989 by John Wiley & Sons, Inc.
--          All Rights Reserved.

with DIM_FLOAT;
package TRIG is

  type Rad is new DIM_FLOAT.Units;
  type Deg is new DIM_FLOAT.Units;

  PI           : constant Rad := +3.141592;
  TWO_PI       : constant Rad := 2.0 * PI;
  PI_OVER_TWO  : constant Rad := PI / 2.0;

  INVALID_ARGUMENT : exception;
    -- Raised for undefined input values.

  function Units_Convert(X : Rad) return Deg;
  function Units_Convert(X : Deg) return Rad;

  function Sin(X : Rad) return float;
  function Sin(X : Deg) return float;

  function Cos(X : Rad) return float;
  function Cos(X : Deg) return float;

  function Tan(X : Rad) return float;
  function Tan(X : Deg) return float;

  function Asin(X : float) return Rad;
  function Asin(X : float) return Deg;
    -- Raises INVALID_ARGUMENT if abs(X) > 1.0;

  function Acos(X : float) return Rad;
  function Acos(X : float) return Deg;
```

```
   -- Raises INVALID_ARGUMENT if abs(X) > 1.0;

function Atan(X : float) return Rad;
function Atan(X : float) return Deg;

function Atan(EAST_OR_Y, NORTH_OR_X : float)
  return Rad;
function Atan(EAST_OR_Y, NORTH_OR_X : float)
  return Deg;
  -- Raises INVALID_ARGUMENT if you try to
  -- compute Atan(0.0,0.0).

-- Natural log (base e)
function Ln(X : float) return float;
 -- Raises INVALID_ARGUMENT if X <= 0.0;
function Exp(X : float) return float;

-- Common log (base 10)
function Log(X : float) return float;
 -- Raises INVALID_ARGUMENT if X <= 0.0;
function Alog(X : float) return float;

function "**"(LEFT, RIGHT : float)
  return float;

function Sqrt(X : float) return float;
 -- Raises INVALID_ARGUMENT if X < 0.0;

end TRIG;
```

```
-- Listing 8.

--                TBDEC.ada
--                Version 1.0
--                1 September 1988

--                Do-While Jones
--                324 Traci Lane
--                Ridgecrest CA, 93555
--                (619) 375-4607

-- Copyright 1989 by John Wiley & Sons, Inc.
--          All Rights Reserved.


-- This package uses the FLOAT_MATH_LIB package
-- supplied by Digital Equipment Corporation
-- with the DEC Ada compiler. Therefore, this
-- package body is NOT PORTABLE.

with FLOAT_MATH_LIB;
package body TRIG is

  HALF_CIRCLE : constant Deg := +180.0;
  SCALE : constant float := 2.302585; -- Ln(10)

  function Units_Convert(X : Rad) return Deg is
  begin
    return HALF_CIRCLE * (X / PI);
  end Units_Convert;

  function Units_Convert(X : Deg) return Rad is
  begin
    return PI * (X / HALF_CIRCLE);
  end Units_Convert;

  function Sin(X : Rad) return float is
  begin
    return FLOAT_MATH_LIB.Sin(
      Dimensionless(X));
  end Sin;

  function Sin(X : Deg) return float is
  begin
    return FLOAT_MATH_LIB.Sind(
```

```
      Dimensionless(X));
end Sin;

function Cos(X : Rad) return float is
begin
  return FLOAT_MATH_LIB.Cos(
    Dimensionless(X));
end Cos;

function Cos(X : Deg) return float is
begin
  return FLOAT_MATH_LIB.Cosd(
    Dimensionless(X));
end Cos;

function Tan(X : Rad) return float is
begin
  return FLOAT_MATH_LIB.Tan(
    Dimensionless(X));
exception
  when FLOAT_MATH_LIB.FLOOVEMAT =>
    if (X mod TWO_PI) - PI > +0.0 then
      -- Tan(3*pi/4) is most negative value
      return DIM_FLOAT.First;
    else
      -- Tan(pi/4) is largest positive
      return DIM_FLOAT.Last;
    end if;
end Tan;

function Tan(X : Deg) return float is
begin
  return FLOAT_MATH_LIB.Tand(
    Dimensionless(X));
exception
  when FLOAT_MATH_LIB.FLOOVEMAT =>
    if (X mod (+360.0)) -(+180.0) > +0.0 then
      -- Tan(270) is most negative value
      return DIM_FLOAT.First;
    else
      -- Tan(90) is largest positive
      return DIM_FLOAT.Last;
    end if;
end Tan;
```

```
function Asin(X : float) return Rad is
begin
  return Type_Convert(
    FLOAT_MATH_LIB.Asin(X));
exception
  when FLOAT_MATH_LIB.INVARGMAT =>
    raise INVALID_ARGUMENT;
end Asin;

function Asin(X : float) return Deg is
begin
  return Type_Convert(
    FLOAT_MATH_LIB.Asind(X));
exception
  when FLOAT_MATH_LIB.INVARGMAT =>
    raise INVALID_ARGUMENT;
end Asin;

function Acos(X : float) return Rad is
begin
  return Type_Convert(
    FLOAT_MATH_LIB.Acos(X));
exception
  when FLOAT_MATH_LIB.INVARGMAT =>
    raise INVALID_ARGUMENT;
end Acos;

function Acos(X : float) return Deg is
begin
  return Type_Convert(
    FLOAT_MATH_LIB.Acosd(X));
exception
  when FLOAT_MATH_LIB.INVARGMAT =>
    raise INVALID_ARGUMENT;
end Acos;

function Atan(X : float) return Rad is
begin
  return Type_Convert(
    FLOAT_MATH_LIB.Atan(X));
end Atan;

function Atan(X : float) return Deg is
begin
```

```
      return Type_Convert(
        FLOAT_MATH_LIB.Atand(X));
  end Atan;

  function Atan(EAST_OR_Y, NORTH_OR_X : float)
    return Rad is
  begin
    return Type_Convert
      (FLOAT_MATH_LIB.Atan2(
         EAST_OR_Y, NORTH_OR_X));
  exception
    when FLOAT_MATH_LIB.INVARGMAT =>
      raise INVALID_ARGUMENT;
  end Atan;

  function Atan(EAST_OR_Y, NORTH_OR_X : float)
    return Deg is
  begin
    return Type_Convert
      (FLOAT_MATH_LIB.Atan2d(
         EAST_OR_Y, NORTH_OR_X));
  exception
    when FLOAT_MATH_LIB.INVARGMAT =>
      raise INVALID_ARGUMENT;
  end Atan;

  function Ln(X : float) return float is
  begin
    return FLOAT_MATH_LIB.Log(X);
  exception
    when FLOAT_MATH_LIB.LOGZERNEG =>
      raise INVALID_ARGUMENT;
  end Ln;

  function Exp(X : float) return float is
  begin
    return FLOAT_MATH_LIB.Exp(X);
  end Exp;

  function Log(X : float) return float is
  begin
    return FLOAT_MATH_LIB.Log10(X);
  exception
    when FLOAT_MATH_LIB.LOGZERNEG =>
```

```
      raise INVALID_ARGUMENT;
  end Log;

  function Alog(X : float) return float is
  begin
    return FLOAT_MATH_LIB.Exp(X * SCALE);
  end Alog;

  function "**" (LEFT, RIGHT : float)
    return float is
  begin
    return Exp(RIGHT * Ln(LEFT));
  end "**";

  function Sqrt(X : float) return float is
  begin
    return FLOAT_MATH_LIB.Sqrt(X);
  exception
    when FLOAT_MATH_LIB.SQUROONEG =>
      raise INVALID_ARGUMENT;
  end Sqrt;

end TRIG;
```

```
-- Listing 9.

--                 TBMIBM.ada
--                 Version 1.1
--                 2 November 1988

--                 Do-While Jones
--                 324 Traci Lane
--                 Ridgecrest CA, 93555
--                 (619) 375-4607

--   Copyright 1989 by John Wiley & Sons, Inc.
--           All Rights Reserved.

-- This package works with the MATH_LIB package
-- purchased as an option with the Meridian Ada
-- compiler for the IBM PC. Therefore, this
-- package body is NOT PORTABLE.

with MATH_LIB;
package body TRIG is

   SCALE : constant float := 2.302585; -- Ln(10)
   HALF_CIRCLE : constant Deg
     := Type_Convert(180.0);

   function Units_Convert(X : Rad) return Deg is
   begin
      return HALF_CIRCLE * (X / PI);
   end Units_Convert;

   function Units_Convert(X : Deg) return Rad is
   begin
      return PI * (X / HALF_CIRCLE);
   end Units_Convert;

   function Sin(X : Rad) return float is
   begin
      return MATH_LIB.Sin(Dimensionless(X));
   end Sin;

   function Sin(X : Deg) return float is
   begin
      return Sin(Units_Convert(X));
   end Sin;
```

```
function Cos(X : Rad) return float is
begin
  return Sin(X+PI_OVER_TWO);
end Cos;

function Cos(X : Deg) return float is
begin
  return Cos(Units_Convert(X));
end Cos;

function Tan(X : Rad) return float is
begin
  return Sin(X)/Cos(X);
exception
  when CONSTRAINT_ERROR | NUMERIC_ERROR =>
    if (X mod TWO_PI) - PI
        > Type_Convert(0.0) then
      -- Tan(3*pi/4) is most negative value
      return DIM_FLOAT.First;
    else
      -- Tan(pi/4) is largest positive
      return DIM_FLOAT.Last;
    end if;
end Tan;

function Tan(X : Deg) return float is
begin
  return Tan(Units_Convert(X));
end Tan;

function Asin(X : float) return Rad is
begin
  -- Division will raise NUMERIC_ERROR
  -- or CONSTRAINT_ERROR if abs(X) = 0.0
  -- Sqrt will raise INVALID_ARGUMENT if
  -- abs(X) > 1.0
  return Type_Convert
    (MATH_LIB.Atan(X/MATH_LIB.Sqrt(
      -X*X+1.0)));
exception
  when NUMERIC_ERROR | CONSTRAINT_ERROR =>
    if X > 0.0 then
      return PI_OVER_TWO;
    else
      return -PI_OVER_TWO;
```

```
      end if;
end Asin;

function Asin(X : float) return Deg is
begin
  -- INVALID_ARGUMENT may be propagated.
  return Units_Convert(Asin(X));
end Asin;

function Acos(X : float) return Rad is
begin
  -- INVALID_ARGUMENT may be propagated.
  return -Asin(X) + PI_OVER_TWO;
end Acos;

function Acos(X : float) return Deg is
begin
  -- INVALID_ARGUMENT may be propagated.
  return Units_Convert(Acos(X));
end Acos;

function Atan(X : float) return Rad is
begin
  return Type_Convert(MATH_LIB.Atan(X));
end Atan;

function Atan(X : float) return Deg is
begin
  return Units_Convert(Atan(X));
end Atan;

function Atan(EAST_OR_Y, NORTH_OR_X : float)
    return Rad is
  ANGLE : Rad;
begin
  if EAST_OR_Y > 0.0
     and NORTH_OR_X >= 0.0 then
    -- first quadrant
    ANGLE := Atan(EAST_OR_Y/NORTH_OR_X);
    -- may raise NUMERIC_ERROR or
    -- CONSTRAINT_ERROR
  elsif EAST_OR_Y >= 0.0
     and NORTH_OR_X < 0.0 then
    -- second quadrant
    ANGLE := PI - Atan(EAST_OR_Y/(
```

```
            -NORTH_OR_X));
    elsif EAST_OR_Y < 0.0
        and NORTH_OR_X < 0.0 then
      -- third quadrant
      ANGLE := PI + Atan(EAST_OR_Y/NORTH_OR_X);
    elsif EAST_OR_Y < 0.0
        and NORTH_OR_X >= 0.0 then
      -- fourth quadrant
      ANGLE := TWO_PI - Atan(
        (-EAST_OR_Y)/NORTH_OR_X);
      -- may raise NUMERIC_ERROR or
      -- CONSTRAINT_ERROR
    else -- Both are 0.0
      raise INVALID_ARGUMENT;
    end if;
    return ANGLE;
exception -- when NORTH_OR_X is near zero
  when NUMERIC_ERROR | CONSTRAINT_ERROR =>
    if EAST_OR_Y > 0.0 then
      return PI_OVER_TWO;
    else
      return TWO_PI - PI_OVER_TWO;
    end if;
end Atan;

function Atan(EAST_OR_Y, NORTH_OR_X : float)
  return Deg is
begin
  return Units_Convert(
    Atan(EAST_OR_Y,NORTH_OR_X));
end Atan;

function Ln(X : float) return float is
begin
  if X <= 0.0 then
    raise INVALID_ARGUMENT;
  end if;
  return MATH_LIB.Ln(X);
end Ln;

function Exp(X : float) return float is
begin
  return MATH_LIB.Exp(X);
end Exp;
```

```
function Log(X : float) return float is
begin
  -- May propagate INVALID_ARGUMENT.
  return Ln(X) / SCALE;
end Log;

function Alog(X : float) return float is
begin
  return Exp(X * SCALE);
end Alog;

function "**"(LEFT, RIGHT : float)
  return float is
begin
  return Exp(RIGHT * Ln(LEFT));
end "**";

function Sqrt(X : float) return float is
begin
  if X < 0.0 then
    raise INVALID_ARGUMENT;
  end if;
  return MATH_LIB.Sqrt(X);
end Sqrt;

end TRIG;
```

```
-- Listing 10.

--                 TBAIBM.ada
--                 Version 1.1
--                 2 November 1988

--                 Do-While Jones
--                 324 Traci Lane
--                 Ridgecrest CA, 93555
--                 (619) 375-4607

--  Copyright 1989 by John Wiley & Sons, Inc.
--             All Rights Reserved.

-- This package works with the user contributed
-- MATH_LIB package that comes with Alsys
-- version 3.2 compiler. Since this isn't
-- really an Alsys product, Alsys doesn't
-- guarantee it or support it.

-- To use this package you must copy MATHL.ADS,
-- MATHL.ADB, and MATH.LIB into your working
-- directory. Compile MATHL.ADS and MATHL.ADB
-- as usual.

-- Presumably you have a file of defaults that
-- you invoke before compiling or linking. You
-- should add the following line to that file,
-- so the linker will find the assembly
-- language routines in MATH.LIB.

--     def.bind interface = (search = math)

-- For more information, see the READ.ME file
-- in \ALSYS\MATH.

with MATH_LIB;
package body TRIG is

  package FLOAT_MATH is new MATH_LIB(float);

  SCALE : constant float := 2.302585; -- Ln(10)
  HALF_CIRCLE : constant Deg
    := Type_Convert(180.0);
```

```ada
function Units_Convert(X : Rad) return Deg is
begin
  return HALF_CIRCLE * (X / PI);
end Units_Convert;

function Units_Convert(X : Deg) return Rad is
begin
  return PI * (X / HALF_CIRCLE);
end Units_Convert;

function Sin(X : Rad) return float is
begin
  return FLOAT_MATH.Sin(Dimensionless(X));
end Sin;

function Sin(X : Deg) return float is
begin
  return Sin(Units_Convert(X));
end Sin;

function Cos(X : Rad) return float is
begin
  return Sin(X+PI_OVER_TWO);
end Cos;

function Cos(X : Deg) return float is
begin
  return Cos(Units_Convert(X));
end Cos;

function Tan(X : Rad) return float is
begin
  return Sin(X)/Cos(X);
exception
  when CONSTRAINT_ERROR | NUMERIC_ERROR =>
    if (X mod TWO_PI) - PI >
        Type_Convert(0.0) then
      -- Tan(3*pi/4) is most negative value
      return DIM_FLOAT.First;
    else
      -- Tan(pi/4) is largest positive
      return DIM_FLOAT.Last;
    end if;
end Tan;
```

```
function Tan(X : Deg) return float is
begin
  return Tan(Units_Convert(X));
end Tan;

function Asin(X : float) return Rad is
begin
  -- Division will raise NUMERIC_ERROR
  -- or CONSTRAINT_ERROR if abs(X) = 0.0.
  -- Sqrt will raise INVALID_ARGUMENT if
  -- abs(X) > 1.0.
  return Type_Convert
    (FLOAT_MATH.Atan(X/FLOAT_MATH.Sqrt(
       -X*X+1.0)));
exception
  when NUMERIC_ERROR | CONSTRAINT_ERROR =>
    if X > 0.0 then
      return PI_OVER_TWO;
    else
      return -PI_OVER_TWO;
    end if;
end Asin;

function Asin(X : float) return Deg is
begin
  -- INVALID_ARGUMENT may be propagated.
  return Units_Convert(Asin(X));
end Asin;

function Acos(X : float) return Rad is
begin
  -- INVALID_ARGUMENT may be propagated.
  return -Asin(X) + PI_OVER_TWO;
end Acos;

function Acos(X : float) return Deg is
begin
  -- INVALID_ARGUMENT may be propagated.
  return Units_Convert(Acos(X));
end Acos;

function Atan(X : float) return Rad is
begin
```

```
      return Type_Convert(FLOAT_MATH.Atan(X));
   end Atan;

   function Atan(X : float) return Deg is
   begin
      return Units_Convert(Atan(X));
   end Atan;

   function Atan(EAST_OR_Y, NORTH_OR_X : float)
      return Rad is
      ANGLE : Rad;
   begin
      if EAST_OR_Y > 0.0
         and NORTH_OR_X >= 0.0 then
        -- first quadrant
        ANGLE := Atan(EAST_OR_Y/NORTH_OR_X);
        -- may raise NUMERIC_ERROR or
        -- CONSTRAINT_ERROR.
      elsif EAST_OR_Y >= 0.0
         and NORTH_OR_X < 0.0 then
        -- second quadrant
        ANGLE := PI - Atan(EAST_OR_Y/(
          -NORTH_OR_X));
      elsif EAST_OR_Y < 0.0
         and NORTH_OR_X < 0.0 then
        -- third quadrant
        ANGLE := PI + Atan(EAST_OR_Y/NORTH_OR_X);
      elsif EAST_OR_Y < 0.0
         and NORTH_OR_X >= 0.0 then
        -- fourth quadrant
        ANGLE := TWO_PI - Atan(
          (-EAST_OR_Y)/NORTH_OR_X);
        -- may raise NUMERIC_ERROR or
        -- CONSTRAINT_ERROR.
      else -- Both are 0.0
        raise INVALID_ARGUMENT;
      end if;
      return ANGLE;
   exception -- when NORTH_OR_X is near zero
      when NUMERIC_ERROR | CONSTRAINT_ERROR =>
        if EAST_OR_Y > 0.0 then
          return PI_OVER_TWO;
        else
```

```
        return TWO_PI - PI_OVER_TWO;
    end if;
end Atan;
function Atan(EAST_OR_Y, NORTH_OR_X : float)
  return Deg is
begin
  return Units_Convert(
    Atan(EAST_OR_Y,NORTH_OR_X));
end Atan;

function Ln(X : float) return float is
begin
  if X <= 0.0 then
    raise INVALID_ARGUMENT;
  end if;
  return FLOAT_MATH.Log(X);
end Ln;

function Exp(X : float) return float is
begin
  return FLOAT_MATH.Exp(X);
end Exp;

function Log(X : float) return float is
begin
  -- May propagate INVALID_ARGUMENT.
  return Ln(X) / SCALE;
end Log;

function Alog(X : float) return float is
begin
  return Exp(X * SCALE);
end Alog;

function "**"(LEFT, RIGHT : float)
  return float is
begin
  return Exp(RIGHT * Ln(LEFT));
end "**";

function Sqrt(X : float) return float is
begin
  if X < 0.0 then
    raise INVALID_ARGUMENT;
```

```
        end if;
        return FLOAT_MATH.Sqrt(X);
     end Sqrt;

  end TRIG;
```

```
-- Listing 11.

--              AUS.ada
--              Version 1.0
--              19 May 1988

--              Do-While Jones
--              324 Traci Lane
--              Ridgecrest, CA 93555
--              (619) 375-4607

-- Copyright 1989 by John Wiley & Sons, Inc.
--          All Rights Reserved.

with STANDARD_INTEGERS;
package ASCII_UTILITIES is

   -- Value and Image Functions.

   -- The attributes VALUE and IMAGE are defined
   -- for discrete types (integers & enumeration
   -- types), but not for type float. That's a
   -- shame, because it would be handy to be
   -- able to do string conversions for
   -- floating-point numbers just as easily as
   -- integers.

   -- The integer IMAGE attribute has the
   -- sometimes annoying characteristic of
   -- returning a variable length string.
   -- That is, the length of the string depends
   -- upon the number of digits. This makes it
   -- difficult to declare a string of the
   -- proper length.

   -- There aren't any Value or Image attributes
   -- for individual characters, either.

   -- The following Value and Image functions
   -- are designed to fill those gaps. They
   -- raise CONSTRAINT_ERROR if they can't do
   -- what you want them to, because that's what
   -- you've come to expect from VALUE and IMAGE
   -- attributes.

   function Value(S : string) return float;
```

```
        -- This is a very forgiving function. The
        -- string can be in almost any common human
        -- format. For example it will accept
        -- strings like "12.3", "12.", "12", "e5",
        -- and so on, and convert them to floating-
        -- point numbers. The only representation
        -- it doesn't accept is a based number. (It
        -- can't handle "2#1100_0001#".) I decided
        -- it would be so rare that anyone would
        -- ever enter a floating point number in
        -- based format that it wasn't worth
        -- complicating the code to handle that
        -- implausible situation. (If you really
        -- need to do it, instantiate FLOAT_IO and
        -- use the "get" procedure.)

        -- CONSTRAINT_ERROR will be raised if the
        -- string does not represent a floating-
        -- point number.

    function Fixed_Image(ITEM : float;
                         FORE : natural := 0;
                         AFT  : natural := 2)
        return string;
        -- This function converts the floating
        -- point item into a string using fixed-
        -- point form. (That is, -XXX.XXXX).
        -- Normally you will know how many places
        -- you want beFORE and AFTer the decimal
        -- point. You specify those numbers, and
        -- the function will produce a string one
        -- character longer than the sum of those
        -- two values. (The decimal point adds one
        -- character to the length.) If that size
        -- doesn't match the destination string
        -- size, CONSTRAINT_ERROR will be raised.

        -- A nice feature of the IMAGE attribute
        -- for integers is that it will use only as
        -- many characters as necessary to
        -- represent the significant digits. You
        -- can achieve the same effect with this
        -- function by letting FORE = 0. Unlike the
        -- integer IMAGE attribute, it will not add
        -- an extra space in front of positive
        -- numbers.
```

```
-- If you want the floating-point number
-- printed as the nearest integer, then let
-- AFT = 0.

function Float_Image(ITEM : float;
                     AFT  : positive := 5)
   return string;

   -- This function converts the floating-
   -- point ITEM intoa string in exponential
   -- form (-X.XXXXXe-XX). The length of the
   -- returned string will be 7 longer than
   -- the number of digits specified by AFT.
   -- (One sign character, one mantissa
   -- character, a decimal point, and a 4
   -- character exponent field adds up to 7
   -- more characters.)

   -- AFT specifies the number of digits after
   -- the decimal point, and must be at least
   -- 1.

   -- CONSTRAINT_ERROR is raised if the
   -- returned string does not match the
   -- length of the target string.

function Image(ITEM    : integer;
               FORE    : natural := 0;
               LEADING : character := ' ')
   return string;
function Image(
   ITEM    : STANDARD_INTEGERS.Integer_32;
   FORE    : natural := 0;
   LEADING : character := ' ') return string;
   -- These functions return a string of the
   -- desired length. The string is right-
   -- justified, and the characters used to
   -- pad the beginning of the string can be
   -- specified. (That is you can request
   -- leading zeros, dollar signs, stars, or
   -- whatever.) If FORE = 0 then the minimum
   -- length string is returned, and there
   -- are no leading characters.

-- The following are useful in converting
```

```
    -- characters to and from digits in any
    -- number base from 2 through 16.

subtype Number_bases is integer range 2..16;

function Value(C    : character;
               BASE : Number_bases := 10)
   return natural;
    -- If C is a character than can represent a
    -- digit in the specified number BASE, this
    -- function will return the numeric value
    -- of that digit.
    -- Raises CONSTRAINT_ERROR if C does not
    -- represent a legal digit.

function Image(N    : natural;
               BASE : Number_bases := 10)
   return character;
    -- If N is a number that can be represented
    -- by a single "digit" in the specified
    -- number BASE, this function will return
    -- the ASCII character that represents
    -- that number.
    -- Raises CONSTRAINT_ERROR if N is not a
    -- legal number in that number system.

-- Note: Name overloading can result in
-- ambiguous statements. For example,
-- "TEXT_IO.put(Image(X,8));" will raise a
-- compile-time error because Ada doesn't
-- know if you want to convert X to an 8
-- character string and put the string, or
-- convert X to an octal character and put
-- the character. She refuses to guess which
-- pair of put/image subprograms to use. Use
-- a qualified expression to help her out.
--    TEXT_IO.put(string'(Image(X,8)));
-- or
--    TEXT_IO.put(character'Image(X,8)));
-- Normally it will be clear from the context
-- which Image function to use, so you won't
-- need the qualified expression. You only
-- need the qualified expression in those
-- rare cases where multiple overloaded names
-- are used in the same statement.
```

```
-- The following four functions are useful
-- for text processing whenever differences
-- in upper or lower case are insignificant.

function Upper_Case(C : character)
  return character;
    -- This function converts a single lower
    -- case letter to an upper case letter. It
    -- has no effect on other ASCII characters.

function Upper_Case(S : string)
  return string;
    -- This function converts all the lower
    -- case letters in the string to upper case
    -- letters. It has no effect on any other
    -- ASCII characters that may be in the
    -- string.

function Lower_Case(C : character)
  return character;
    -- This function converts a single upper
    -- case letter to a lower case letter. It
    -- has no effect on other ASCII characters.

function Lower_Case(S : string)
  return string;
    -- This function converts all the upper
    -- case letters in the string to lower case
    -- letters. It has no effect on any other
    -- ASCII characters that may be in the
    -- string.

function Change(C    : character;
                FROM : character;
                TO   : character)
  return character;
    -- If character C matches the FROM
    -- character then this function will return
    -- the TO character. If character C does
    -- not match FROM, the function returns
    -- character C. The primary use of this
    -- function is in the function below.

function Change(S    : string;
                FROM : character := '_';
                TO   : character := ' ')
```

```
      return string;

      -- This checks all the characters in the
      -- string S, and whenever it finds a
      -- character matching the FROM character it
      -- changes it to the TO character. For
      -- example, if the string S was
      -- "QUEEN_OF_HEARTS" and the change
      -- function was called with the default
      -- values for FROM and TO, the resulting
      -- string would be "QUEEN OF HEARTS". This
      -- function could also be used to replace
      -- trailing blank characters with null
      -- characters.

   procedure Left_Justify(S : in out string);
      -- This procedure shifts characters in the
      -- string left until the first character is
      -- not a blank.

   procedure Right_Justify(S : in out string);
      -- This procedure shifts characters in the
      -- string right until the last character is
      -- not a blank.

   procedure String_Copy(
      FROM : string;
      TO   : out string;
      FILL : character := ' ');
      -- This procedure copies from one string to
      -- another, even if they have different
      -- lengths or different bounds. If the
      -- destination string is longer than the
      -- source string, then extra characters are
      -- added on the end to fill the
      -- destination. The default fill character
      -- is a blank space, but NUL might be
      -- another good choice. If the destination
      -- string is shorter than the source, then
      -- the source string is truncated to make
      -- it fit.

end ASCII_UTILITIES;
```

```
-- Listing 12.

--                    AUB.ada
--                    Version 1.0
--                    9 September 1988

--                    Do-While Jones
--                    324 Traci Lane
--                    Ridgecrest, CA 93555
--                    (619) 375-4607

-- Copyright 1989 by John Wiley & Sons, Inc.
--          All Rights Reserved.

package body ASCII_UTILITIES is

  SHIFT_KEY : constant integer
   := character'POS('A') - character'POS('a');

  ZERO : constant integer
   := character'POS('0');

  BIG_A : constant integer
   := character'POS('A');

  LITTLE_A : constant integer
   := character'POS('a');

  function Value(S : string) return float
    is separate;
    -- file AUBV.ada

  function Fixed_Image(ITEM : float;
                       FORE : natural := 0;
                       AFT  : natural := 2)
    return string is separate;
    -- file AUBFXI.ada

  function Float_Image(ITEM : float;
                       AFT  : positive := 5)
    return string is separate;
    -- file AUBFLI.ada

  function Image(ITEM    : integer;
```

```
                          FORE    : natural := 0;
                          LEADING : character := ' ')
      return string is
        use STANDARD_INTEGERS;
        X : Integer_32;
  begin
    X := Integer_32(ITEM);
    return Image(X,FORE,LEADING);
  end Image;

  function Image(
    ITEM    : STANDARD_INTEGERS.Integer_32;
    FORE    : natural := 0;
    LEADING : character := ' ') return string
    is separate;
    -- file AUBII.ada

  function Value(C    : character;
                 BASE : Number_bases := 10)
      return natural is
        VALUE : integer;
  begin
    case C is
      when '0'..'9' =>
        VALUE := character'POS(C) - ZERO;
      when 'A'..'F' =>
        VALUE := character'POS(C) - BIG_A + 10;
      when 'a'..'f' =>
        VALUE := character'POS(C)
           - LITTLE_A + 10;
      when others =>
        raise CONSTRAINT_ERROR;
    end case;
    if VALUE in 0..BASE-1 then
      return VALUE;
    else
      raise CONSTRAINT_ERROR;
    end if;
  end Value;

  function Image(N    : natural;
                 BASE : Number_bases := 10)
      return character is
  begin
```

```
      if N not in 0..BASE-1 then
        raise CONSTRAINT_ERROR;
      end if;
      case N is
        when 0..9 =>
          return character'VAL(N + ZERO);
        when 10..15 =>
          return character'VAL(N - 10 + BIG_A);
        when others =>
          raise CONSTRAINT_ERROR;
      end case;
    end Image;


    function Upper_Case(C : character)
      return character is
    begin
      if C in 'a'..'z' then
        return character'VAL(character'POS(C)
          + SHIFT_KEY);
      else
        return C;
      end if;
    end Upper_Case;


    function Upper_Case(S : string)
        return string is
      X : string(S'RANGE) := S;
    begin
      for i in S'RANGE loop
        X(i) := Upper_Case(S(i));
      end loop;
      return X;
    end Upper_Case;


    function Lower_Case(C : character)
      return character is
    begin
      if C in 'A'..'Z' then
        return character'VAL(character'POS(C)
          - SHIFT_KEY);
      else
        return C;
      end if;
    end Lower_Case;
```

```
function Lower_Case(S : string)
    return string is
  X : string(S'RANGE) := S;
begin
  for i in S'RANGE loop
    X(i) := Lower_Case(S(i));
  end loop;
  return X;
end Lower_Case;

function Change(C    : character;
                FROM : character;
                TO   : character)
  return character is
begin
  if C = FROM then
    return TO;
  else
    return C;
  end if;
end Change;

function Change(S    : string;
                FROM : character := '_';
                TO   : character := ' ')
    return string is
  X : string(S'RANGE) := S;
begin
  for i in S'RANGE loop
    X(i) := Change(S(i),FROM,TO);
  end loop;
  return X;
end Change;

procedure Left_Justify(S : in out string) is
  BLANKS : natural;
  ALL_BLANKS : string(S'RANGE)
    := (others => ' ');
begin
  if S(S'FIRST) /= ' ' or
     S = ALL_BLANKS then
    return; -- without doing anything
  else
    -- Left justify by counting the number of
    -- leading blanks. Then shift the last
```

```ada
    -- portion of the string to the left that
    -- many characters, and add that number
    -- of blanks to the end.

    -- Count the number of blanks.
    BLANKS := 0;
    for i in S'RANGE loop
      exit when S(i) /= ' ';
      BLANKS := BLANKS + 1;
    end loop;

    -- Shift non-blank characters left.
    for i in S'FIRST..S'LAST-BLANKS loop
      S(i) := S(i+BLANKS);
    end loop;

    -- Put the blanks at the end.
    for i in S'LAST-BLANKS+1..S'LAST loop
      S(i) := ' ';
    end loop;
  end if;
end Left_Justify;

procedure Right_Justify(S : in out string) is
  BLANKS : natural;
  ALL_BLANKS : string(S'RANGE)
    := (others => ' ');
begin
  if S(S'LAST) /= ' ' or
     S = ALL_BLANKS then
    return; -- without doing anything
  else
    -- Right justify by counting the number
    -- of trailing blanks. Then shift the
    -- first portion of the string to the
    -- right that many characters, and add
    -- that number of blanks to the
    -- beginning.

    -- Count the number of blanks (from the
    -- right).
    BLANKS := 0;
    for i in reverse S'RANGE loop
      exit when S(i) /= ' ';
      BLANKS := BLANKS + 1;
    end loop;
```

```
                  -- Shift non-blank characters right.
                  for i in reverse
                      S'FIRST+BLANKS..S'LAST loop
                    S(i) := S(i-BLANKS);
                  end loop;

                  -- Put the blanks at the beginning.
                  for i in S'FIRST..S'FIRST+BLANKS-1 loop
                    S(i) := ' ';
                  end loop;
                end if;
              end Right_Justify;

            procedure String_Copy(
              FROM : string;
              TO   : out string;
              FILL : character := ' ') is
            begin
              if FROM'LENGTH < TO'LENGTH then
                TO(TO'FIRST..TO'FIRST+FROM'LENGTH-1)
                  := FROM;
                for i in
                    TO'FIRST+FROM'LENGTH..TO'LAST loop
                  TO(i) := FILL;
                end loop;
              else
                TO(TO'RANGE) := FROM(FROM'FIRST..
                  FROM'FIRST+TO'LENGTH-1);
              end if;
            end String_Copy;

          end ASCII_UTILITIES;
```

```
-- Listing 13.

--                 AUBFXI.ada
--                 Version 1.0
--                 22 August 1988

--                 Do-While Jones
--                 324 Traci Lane
--                 Ridgecrest, CA 93555
--                 (619) 375-4607

-- Copyright 1989 by John Wiley & Sons, Inc.
--            All Rights Reserved.

separate(ASCII_UTILITIES)
function Fixed_Image(ITEM : float;
                     FORE : natural := 0;
                     AFT  : natural := 2)
    return string is
  use STANDARD_INTEGERS;
  X, WHOLE, TEMP : Integer_32;
  FRACTION : Natural_32;
  POWER, MIN_LENGTH, FORE_LENGTH : natural;

begin
  -- Let X be ITEM rounded to the desired
  -- precision.
  X := Integer_32(ITEM * float(10**AFT));

  if AFT = 0 then -- the job is done
    return Image(X,FORE);
  else

    -- Break X into a whole part and a
    -- fractional part.
    WHOLE := X / 10**AFT;
    FRACTION := abs(X) rem 10**AFT;

    -- The number of characters required to
    -- represent the whole part depends on its
    -- power of 10. It isn't worth dragging in
    -- a big math library to take a common log
    -- when we can easily find it by seeing how
    -- many times we can divide by 10;
```

```
POWER := 0;
TEMP := abs(WHOLE);
while TEMP >= 10 loop
  POWER := POWER+1;
  TEMP := TEMP/10;
end loop;

-- The number of whole digits is one more
-- than the power of 10 of the input
-- number. (For example, 100 is the second
-- power of 10, and has 3 digits.) The
-- image of a negative number needs an
-- extra character for a sign bit.
if ITEM < 0.0 then
  MIN_LENGTH := POWER + 2;
else
  MIN_LENGTH := POWER + 1;
end if;

-- Now see how that agrees with the user's
-- request.
if FORE = 0 then
  -- user wants minimum length
  FORE_LENGTH := MIN_LENGTH;
elsif MIN_LENGTH <= FORE then
  -- user wants more
  FORE_LENGTH := FORE;
else -- MIN_LENGTH > FORE, so it won't fit
  raise CONSTRAINT_ERROR;
end if;

-- The returned image is the image of the
-- whole part, followed by a decimal point,
-- followed by the image of the fractional
-- part.
declare
  S : string(1..FORE_LENGTH+1+AFT);
begin
  S := Image(WHOLE,FORE_LENGTH)
    & '.' & Image(FRACTION,AFT,'0');
  if X < 0 then
    -- Check for a special case. If X is in
    -- -0.9..-0.0, then the image of the
    -- whole part (-0) is returned as 0, so
```

```
           -- the - sign gets lost. If that is the
           -- case, we have to put it in.
           for i in reverse S'RANGE loop
             if S(i) = '-' then exit; end if;
             if S(i) = ' ' then
               S(i) := '-';
               exit;
             end if;
           end loop;
         end if;
         return S;
       end;
    end if;
 end Fixed_Image;
```

```
-- Listing 14.

--              AUBFLI.ada
--              Version 1.1
--              17 July 1988

--              Do-While Jones
--              324 Traci Lane
--              Ridgecrest, CA 93555
--              (619) 375-4607

-- Copyright 1989 by John Wiley & Sons, Inc.
--       All Rights Reserved.


-- Version 1.0 ran into trouble when ITEM was
-- very close to a power of 10. Instead of
-- 9.99999 to some power, it would be 10.00000
-- to some power, which caused a constraint
-- error because the mantissa was too long.

separate(ASCII_UTILITIES)
function Float_Image(ITEM : float;
                     AFT  : positive := 5)
   return string is
  EXPONENT : string(1..3);
  X : float;
  POWER : integer;
  MANTISSA_LENGTH, LENGTH : positive;
begin
  -- The plan is to adjust the power of 10 of
  -- ITEM until we get a number that can be
  -- expressed using Fixed_Image with FORE = 2
  -- and the requested value of AFT. Then we
  -- will add the exponent field.

  -- ITEM needs to be normalized
  -- to -9.999 .. +9.999.
  X := abs(ITEM);
  POWER := 0;
  if X > 0.0 then
    while X < 1.0 loop
      POWER := POWER - 1;
      X := X * 10.0;
    end loop;
```

```
end if;
while X >= 10.0 loop
  POWER := POWER + 1;
  X := X / 10.0;
end loop;
if ITEM < 0.0 then
  X := -X;
end if;

-- Compute the number of characters in the
-- mantissa. It will consist of a sign, one
-- whole digit, a decimal point, and AFT
-- digits after the decimal point.
MANTISSA_LENGTH := 3 + AFT;

-- The entire string will be the mantissa
-- plus the letter e, plus the 3 character
-- exponent.
LENGTH := MANTISSA_LENGTH + 4;
declare
  MANTISSA : string(1..MANTISSA_LENGTH);
  S : string(1..LENGTH);
begin

  -- convert Mantissa to a string
  begin
    MANTISSA := Fixed_Image(X,2,AFT);
    if MANTISSA(1) = '1' then
      -- X was rounded to 10
      X := X / 10.0;
      POWER := POWER + 1;
      MANTISSA := Fixed_Image(X,2,AFT);
    end if;
  exception -- when X is rounded to -10
    when CONSTRAINT_ERROR =>
      X := X / 10.0;
      POWER := POWER + 1;
      MANTISSA := Fixed_Image(X,2,AFT);
  end;

  -- Convert the power to a string.
  EXPONENT := Image(POWER,3,'0');
  if EXPONENT(1) = '0' then
    EXPONENT(1) := '+';
  end if;
```

```
      -- put the two pieces together
      S(1..MANTISSA_LENGTH) := MANTISSA;
      S(MANTISSA_LENGTH+1) := 'e';
      S(MANTISSA_LENGTH+2..LENGTH) := EXPONENT;
      return S;
   end;
end Float_Image;
```

```
-- Listing 15.

--              AUBII.ada
--              Version 1.0
--              14 February 1988

--              Do-While Jones
--              324 Traci Lane
--              Ridgecrest, CA 93555
--              (619) 375-4607

-- Copyright 1989 by John Wiley & Sons, Inc.
--          All Rights Reserved.

separate(ASCII_UTILITIES)
function Image(ITEM    : STANDARD_INTEGERS.Integer_3
              FORE    : natural := 0;
              LEADING : character := ' ')
   return string is
  use STANDARD_INTEGERS;
  X : Natural_32;
  LENGTH, S_LENGTH : positive;
  POWER : natural;

begin
  -- We need to know the power of 10 of the
  -- input ITEM so we know how many characters
  -- it will take to represent it. It isn't
  -- worth dragging in a big math library to
  -- take a common log. Let's do it by seeing
  -- how many times we can divide by 10.
  X := Abs(ITEM);
  POWER := 0;
  while X >= 10 loop
    POWER := POWER + 1;
    X := X / 10;
  end loop;

  -- The number of digits is one more than the
  -- power of ten of the input number. (For
  -- example, 100 is the second power of ten
  -- and has 3 digits.) The ITEM_IMAGE also
  -- needs a sign character.
```

```
LENGTH := POWER + 2;
-- If FORE is 0 it means that the string
-- returned should be minimum size. If FORE
-- is any positive number, then the returned
-- string must be exactly that long.
if FORE = 0 then
   -- S_LENGTH is minimum length
  if ITEM < 0 then
    S_LENGTH := LENGTH;
    -- need room for minus sign
  else
    S_LENGTH := LENGTH-1; -- no leading space
  end if;
elsif FORE < LENGTH then
   -- there may be a problem
  if FORE = LENGTH - 1 and ITEM >= 0 then
    S_LENGTH := FORE;
    -- drop the leading space
  else
    raise CONSTRAINT_ERROR; -- it won't fit
  end if;
else -- FORE is longer than necessary
  S_LENGTH := FORE;
end if;

declare
  ITEM_IMAGE : string(1..LENGTH);
  S : string(1..S_LENGTH)
   := (others => LEADING);
begin
  -- Since this string will be right-
  -- justified, we have to build the string
  -- from the back to the front.
  ITEM_IMAGE := Integer_32'IMAGE(ITEM);
  if ITEM < 0 then
    -- Copy ITEM_IMAGE to the right side of
    -- the string.
    S(S'LAST-ITEM_IMAGE'LENGTH+1..S'LAST)
     := ITEM_IMAGE;
    -- There is a special case when the
    -- number is negative and the leading
    -- characters are 0. We don't want
    -- something like 000-123, we want
```

```
            -- -000123 instead. (We do, however, want
            -- ***-123, not -***123.)
            if LEADING = '0' then
              if S(1) /= '-' then
                S(1) := '-';
                for i in
                 2..S'LAST-ITEM_IMAGE'LENGTH+1 loop
                  S(i) := '0';
                end loop;
              end if;
            end if;
          else -- don't copy the leading space
            S(S'LAST-ITEM_IMAGE'LENGTH+2..S'LAST)
              := ITEM_IMAGE(2..ITEM_IMAGE'LAST);
          end if;
          return S;
        end;
      end Image;
```

```
-- Listing 16.

--                    AUBV.ada
--                    Version 1.2
--                    21 August 1988

--                    Do-While Jones
--                    324 Traci Lane
--                    Ridgecrest, CA 93555
--                    (619) 375-4607

--   Copyright 1989 by John Wiley & Sons, Inc.
--          All Rights Reserved.

-- Revision 1.1 recognizes inputs such as "e5"
-- and rejects pathological inputs like ".e6"
-- and ".".

-- Revision 1.2 permits trailing blanks.

separate(ASCII_UTILITIES)
function Value(S : string) return float is

  use STANDARD_INTEGERS;

  PLUS : boolean;
  WHOLE, FRACTION, POWER, X : float;
  I, FIRST, LAST, SIGN, S_LAST : integer;
begin
  -- null string returns 0.0
  if S'LAST < S'FIRST then return 0.0; end if;

  -- find the real end of the string
  S_LAST := S'FIRST; -- if string is all
                     -- blanks, else
  for i in reverse S'FIRST..S'LAST loop
    if S(i) /= ' ' then
      S_LAST := i;
      exit;
    end if;
  end loop;

  -- find the real beginning of the string
  I := S'FIRST;
  -- skip leading blanks
```

```
while I <= S_LAST and then S(I) = ' ' loop
  I := I+1;
end loop;

-- blank string returns 0.0
if I > S_LAST then return 0.0; end if;

-- reject special cases
if I < S_LAST then
  if S(I..I+1) = "-."
      or S(I..I+1) = "+." then
    case S(I+2) is
      when '0'..'9' =>
        null;
      when others =>
        raise CONSTRAINT_ERROR;
    end case;
  end if;
  if S(I) = '.' then
    case S(I+1) is
      when '0'..'9' =>
        null;
      when others =>
        raise CONSTRAINT_ERROR;
    end case;
  end if;
end if;
if I = S_LAST and then S(I) = '.' then
  raise CONSTRAINT_ERROR;
end if;

-- check sign
if S(I) = '-' then
  PLUS := FALSE;
  I := I+1;
elsif S(I) = '+' then
  PLUS := TRUE;
  I := I+1;
else
  PLUS := TRUE;
end if;

-- check for exponent only
if S(I) = 'e' or S(I) = 'E' then
```

```
    WHOLE := 1.0;
    FRACTION := 0.0;
else

  -- compute whole part
  if S(I) = '.' then
    WHOLE := 0.0;
  else
    FIRST := I;
    while I <= S_LAST
        and then S(I) in '0'..'9' loop
      I := I+1;
    end loop;
    LAST := I-1;
    WHOLE := float(
      Integer_32'VALUE(S(FIRST..LAST)));
  end if;

  -- compute fractional part
  if I < S_LAST then
    if S(I) = '.' then
      I := I+1;
      if S(I) in '0'..'9' then
        FIRST := I;
        while I <= S_LAST
            and then S(I) in '0'..'9' loop
          I := I+1;
        end loop;
        LAST := I-1;
        FRACTION :=
         float(
           Integer_32'VALUE(S(FIRST..LAST)))
           / 10.0**(I-FIRST);
      else
        FRACTION := 0.0;
      end if;
    elsif S(I) = 'e' or S(I) = 'E' then
      FRACTION := 0.0;
    end if;
  else -- last character is a '.'
    FRACTION := 0.0;
    I := I+1;
  end if;
end if;
```

```
    -- compute power
  if I <= S_LAST then
    if S(I) = 'e' or S(I) = 'E' then
      I := I+1;
      if S(I) = '-' then
        SIGN := -1;
        I := I+1;
      elsif S(I) = '+' then
        SIGN := 1;
        I := I+1;
      else
        SIGN := 1;
      end if;
      FIRST := I;
      while I <= S_LAST
          and then S(I) in '0'..'9' loop
        I := I+1;
      end loop;
      LAST := I-1;
      POWER := 10.0**(SIGN
        * integer'VALUE(S(FIRST..LAST)));
    else
      POWER := 1.0;
    end if;

  else
    POWER := 1.0;
  end if;

  -- check to make sure there aren't any more
  -- characters
  if I <= S_LAST then raise CONSTRAINT_ERROR; end if;

  -- put it all together
  X := (WHOLE + FRACTION) * POWER;
  if PLUS then
    return X;
  else
    return -X;
  end if;
end Value;
```

```
-- Listing 17.

--              MS.ada
--              Version 1.0
--              2 September 1988

--              Do-While Jones
--              324 Traci Lane
--              Ridgecrest, CA 93555
--              (619) 375-4607

-- Copyright 1989 by John Wiley & Sons, Inc.
--         All Rights Reserved.

with DIM_INT_32;
package MONEY is

   type Cents is new DIM_INT_32.Units;
      -- can represent -$21,474,836.48
      -- to $21,474,836.47.

   function Value(S : string) return Cents;
      -- Convert a text string of the form
      -- $X,XXX.XX into the data type Cents.
      -- Raises CONSTRAINT_ERROR if the string
      -- does not represent a dollar value.
      -- The dollar sign and commas are optional
      -- and are ignored. (Underlines may also be
      -- used to separate digits, and are
      -- ignored.) Integer amounts are considered
      -- to represent dollars, not cents.

   function Image(C       : Cents;
                  LENGTH  : natural := 0;
                  PENNIES : boolean := TRUE)
      return string;
      -- Convert an object of type cents into a
      -- string including a $ sign and perhaps
      -- commas and a leading minus sign. The
      -- length of the string is exactly LENGTH
      -- characters long, unless LENGTH = 0.
      -- If LENGTH = 0, then the string is the
      -- minimum number of characters necessary
      -- to represent the string (without an
```

```
     -- annoying leading space on positive
     -- values). If PENNIES is TRUE, the string
     -- representing an amount in the tens of
     -- thousands of dollars takes the form
     -- "$XX,XXX.XX". If FALSE, it is rounded
     -- and displayed as "$XX,XXX".

  function Width(C       : Cents;
                 PENNIES : boolean := TRUE)
     return positive;
     -- Tells how many characters are required
     -- to hold the Image of the amount. If
     -- PENNIES is FALSE, the number returned is
     -- 3 less than when PENNIES is TRUE,
     -- because the final ".XX" is not used.

  -- Type_Convert and Dimensionless are
  -- available for converting between
  -- Integer_32 and Cents, of course.

end MONEY;
```

```
--  Listing 18.

--                  MB.ada
--                  Version 1.0
--                  13 September 1988

--                  Do-While Jones
--                  324 Traci Lane
--                  Ridgecrest, CA 93555
--                  (619) 375-4607

--  Copyright 1989 by John Wiley & Sons, Inc.
--          All Rights Reserved.

with ASCII_UTILITIES;
with STANDARD_INTEGERS; use STANDARD_INTEGERS;
package body MONEY is

  function Value(S : string) return Cents is
    PLUS : boolean;
    WHOLE, FRACTION : Natural_32;
    I, FIRST, LAST : integer;
    X : string(S'RANGE);
  begin
    -- copy S to X, discarding '$', ',',
    -- and '_'
    X(X'RANGE) := (others => ' ');
    I := X'FIRST;
    for j in S'RANGE loop
      case S(j) is
        when '$' | ',' | '_' =>
          null; -- ignore '$', ',', and '_'
        when others =>
          X(I) := S(j);
          I := I+1;
      end case;
    end loop;

    -- skip over leading blanks
    I := X'FIRST;
    while I <= X'LAST and then X(I) = ' ' loop
      I := I+1;
    end loop;

    -- null string or blank string returns
```

```
-- $0.00
if I > X'LAST then
  return Type_Convert(0);
end if;

-- check sign
if X(I) = '-' then
  PLUS := FALSE;
  I := I+1;
elsif X(I) = '+' then
  PLUS := TRUE;
  I := I+1;
else
  PLUS := TRUE;
end if;

-- compute whole part
if X(I) = '.' then
  WHOLE := 0;
else
  FIRST := I;
  while I <= X'LAST
      and then X(I) in '0'..'9' loop
    I := I+1;
  end loop;
  LAST := I-1;
  WHOLE := 100 * Integer_32'VALUE(
    X(FIRST..LAST));
end if;

-- compute fractional part
if I < X'LAST then
  if X(I) = '.' then
    -- find bounds of pennies field
    I := I+1;
    if X(I) in '0'..'9' then
      FIRST := I;
      while I <= X'LAST
          and then X(I) in '0'..'9' loop
        I := I+1;
      end loop;
      LAST := I-1;
      -- convert pennies field
      if LAST = FIRST then
        -- only 1 digit was entered
```

```
              FRACTION :=
                10 * Integer_32'VALUE(
                  X(FIRST..FIRST));
            elsif LAST = FIRST+1 then
               -- 2 digits entered
              FRACTION := Integer_32'VALUE(
                X(FIRST..LAST));
            else -- more than 2 digits entered
              raise CONSTRAINT_ERROR;
            end if;
            -- remaining characters, if any,
            -- should be blank
            for j in I..X'LAST loop
              if X(I) /= ' ' then
                raise CONSTRAINT_ERROR;
              end if;
            end loop;
          else
            raise CONSTRAINT_ERROR;
          end if;
        elsif X(I) = ' ' then
          FRACTION := 0;
        else
          raise CONSTRAINT_ERROR;
        end if;
      elsif I = X'LAST then
        if X(I) = '.' or X(I) = ' ' then
          FRACTION := 0;
        else
          raise CONSTRAINT_ERROR;
        end if;
      else
        FRACTION := 0;
      end if;

      if PLUS then
        return +(WHOLE + FRACTION);
      else
        return -(WHOLE + FRACTION);
      end if;
    end Value;

    -- The Image and Width functions both need to
    -- know how many digits are in the number.
    -- Here's a function they can both use.
```

```
function Digits_In(C : Cents)
     return positive is
  X : Natural_32;
  POWER : natural;
begin
  -- The number of digits is one more than
  -- the power of ten of the input number.
  -- (For example, 100 is the second power of
  -- ten and has 3 digits.) It isn't worth
  -- dragging in a 32 bit math library to
  -- take a common log. Let's do it by seeing
  -- how many times we can divide by 10.
  POWER := 0;
  X := Abs(Dimensionless(C));
  while X >= 10 loop
    POWER := POWER+1;
    X := X/10;
  end loop;
  return POWER+1;
end Digits_In;


function Image(C        : Cents;
              LENGTH   : natural := 0;
              PENNIES : boolean := TRUE)
     return string is
  X    : Cents;
  SIZE : integer;
begin
  -- if PENNIES is FALSE, then round to the
  -- nearest dollar
  if PENNIES then
    X := C;
  else
    if C < Type_Convert(0) then
      X := C - Type_Convert(50);
    else
      X := C + Type_Convert(50);
    end if;
  end if;

  -- see how big to make the string
  SIZE := Width(X);
  if PENNIES then
    if LENGTH >= SIZE then
      -- make it the requested length
```

```
      SIZE := LENGTH;
   elsif LENGTH = 0 then
    null; -- SIZE is OK
   else -- it won't fit
     raise CONSTRAINT_ERROR;
   end if;
else -- no spaces needed for pennies
   if LENGTH >= SIZE-3 then
     -- make it the requested length + 3
     -- because it will return a string
     -- SIZE-3 characters long
     SIZE := LENGTH+3;
   elsif LENGTH = 0 then
     null; -- SIZE is OK
   else -- it won't fit
     raise CONSTRAINT_ERROR;
   end if;
end if;

-- create output strings the right size
declare
   S1, S2 : string(1..SIZE);
   NUMBER_OF_DIGITS : positive;
begin
   -- S1 is the integer image of the amount
   -- (with leading 0s)
   S1 := ASCII_UTILITIES.Image(
         Dimensionless(X),SIZE,'0');

   -- S2 is the formatted image (with $ and
   -- commas). Initially S2 is all blanks.
   S2 := (others => ' ');

   -- always copy last 3 digits from S1
   -- to S2
   S2(S2'LAST-1..S2'LAST)
      := S1(S1'LAST-1..S1'LAST);
   S2(S2'LAST-2) := '.';
   S2(S2'LAST-3) := S1(S1'LAST-2);

   -- copy other digits if they are
   -- significant
   NUMBER_OF_DIGITS := Digits_In(X);
   case NUMBER_OF_DIGITS is
     when 1..3 =>
```

```
              -- all digits have been copied
              null;
          when 4 => -- copy tens of dollars
            S2(S2'LAST-4) := S1(S1'LAST-3);
          when 5 => -- copy tens and hundreds
            S2(S2'LAST-5..S2'LAST-4) :=
              S1(S1'LAST-4..S1'LAST-3);
          when 6 =>
            -- copy tens, hundreds, & thousands
            S2(S2'LAST-5..S2'LAST-4) :=
              S1(S1'LAST-4..S1'LAST-3);
            S2(S2'LAST-6) := ',';
            S2(S2'LAST-7) := S1(S1'LAST-5);
          when 7 =>
            -- copy tens through ten thousands
            S2(S2'LAST-5..S2'LAST-4) :=
              S1(S1'LAST-4..S1'LAST-3);
            S2(S2'LAST-6) := ',';
            S2(S2'LAST-8..S2'LAST-7) :=
              S1(S1'LAST-6..S1'LAST-5);
          when 8 => -- copy tens through
                    -- hundred thousands
            S2(S2'LAST-5..S2'LAST-4) :=
              S1(S1'LAST-4..S1'LAST-3);
            S2(S2'LAST-6) := ',';
            S2(S2'LAST-9..S2'LAST-7) :=
              S1(S1'LAST-7..S1'LAST-5);
          when 9 => -- copy tens through millions
            S2(S2'LAST-5..S2'LAST-4) :=
              S1(S1'LAST-4..S1'LAST-3);
            S2(S2'LAST-6) := ',';
            S2(S2'LAST-9..S2'LAST-7) :=
              S1(S1'LAST-7..S1'LAST-5);
            S2(S2'LAST-10) := ',';
            S2(S2'LAST-11) := S1(S1'LAST-8);
          when 10 => -- copy tens through
                     -- ten millions
            S2(S2'LAST-5..S2'LAST-4) :=
              S1(S1'LAST-4..S1'LAST-3);
            S2(S2'LAST-6) := ',';
            S2(S2'LAST-9..S2'LAST-7) :=
              S1(S1'LAST-7..S1'LAST-5);
            S2(S2'LAST-10) := ',';
            S2(S2'LAST-12..S2'LAST-11) :=
              S1(S1'LAST-9..S1'LAST-8);
```

```
         when others =>
           raise PROGRAM_ERROR; -- can't happen
      end case;

      -- place $ sign
      for i in reverse S2'RANGE loop
        if S2(i) = ' ' then
          S2(i) := '$';
          exit;
        end if;
      end loop;

      -- insert minus sign if necessary
      if X < Type_Convert(0) then
        for i in reverse S2'RANGE loop
          if S2(i) = ' ' then
            S2(i) := '-';
            exit;
          end if;
        end loop;
      end if;

      -- return the formatted string
      if PENNIES then
        -- return the whole string
        return S2;
      else -- don't return last 3 characters
        return S2(1..S2'LAST-3);
      end if;
    end;
  end Image;

function Width(C        : Cents;
              PENNIES : boolean := TRUE)
     return positive is
  NUMBER_OF_DIGITS, NUMBER_OF_CHARACTERS
     : positive;
begin
  NUMBER_OF_DIGITS := Digits_In(C);

  case NUMBER_OF_DIGITS is
    when 1..2 => -- represent it as $0.XX
      NUMBER_OF_CHARACTERS := 5;
    when 3..5 => -- add '$' and '.'
      NUMBER_OF_CHARACTERS
```

```
              := NUMBER_OF_DIGITS + 2;
      when 6..8 => -- add '$', '.', and ','
        NUMBER_OF_CHARACTERS
          := NUMBER_OF_DIGITS + 3;
      when 9..11 =>
        -- add '$', '.', and 2 commas
        NUMBER_OF_CHARACTERS
          := NUMBER_OF_DIGITS + 4;
      when others =>
        raise PROGRAM_ERROR; -- can't happen
    end case;

    if C < Type_Convert(0) then
      -- add a minus sign
      NUMBER_OF_CHARACTERS
        := NUMBER_OF_CHARACTERS + 1;
    end if;

    if not PENNIES then
      -- throw away '.' and 2 digits
      NUMBER_OF_CHARACTERS
        := NUMBER_OF_CHARACTERS - 3;
    end if;

    return NUMBER_OF_CHARACTERS;
  end Width;

end MONEY;
```

```
-- Listing 19.

--                    VTS.ada
--                    17 May 1988
--                    Version 1.0

--                    Do-While Jones
--                    324 Traci Lane
--                    Ridgecrest, CA 93555
--                    (619) 375-4607

--  Copyright 1989 by John Wiley & Sons, Inc.
--          All Rights Reserved.

-- This package hides individual terminal
-- characteristics and converts them into a
-- standard form. This VIRTUAL_TERMINAL package
-- can be used as the foundation for the
-- SCROLL_TERMINAL, FORM_TERMINAL, or a user-
-- designed custom terminal.

package VIRTUAL_TERMINAL is

   subtype Line_numbers is integer range 1..23;
   subtype Column_numbers is
     integer range 1..79;
       -- Note Line_numbers and Column_numbers are
       -- limited to avoid terminal dependent
       -- quirks (auto wrap and auto scroll) that
       -- may happen at screen boundaries.

   -- ASCII characters

   CTRL_A : constant character
     := ASCII.SOH; -- Add (Insert)
   CTRL_B : constant character
     := ASCII.STX; -- Back Tab
   CTRL_C : constant character
     := ASCII.ETX; -- Panic
   CTRL_D : constant character
     := ASCII.EOT; -- Down Arrow
   CTRL_E : constant character
     := ASCII.ENQ; -- Erase
   CTRL_F : constant character
     := ASCII.ACK; -- Function Key
```

```
      CTRL_G : constant character
        := ASCII.BEL; -- Bell
      CTRL_H : constant character
        := ASCII.BS;  -- Backspace
      CTRL_I : constant character
        := ASCII.HT;  -- Tab
      CTRL_J : constant character
        := ASCII.LF;  -- Line Feed
      CTRL_L : constant character
        := ASCII.FF;  -- Left Arrow
      CTRL_M : constant character
        := ASCII.CR;  -- Return
      CTRL_R : constant character
        := ASCII.DC2; -- Right Arrow
      CTRL_U : constant character
        := ASCII.NAK; -- Up Arrow


      TAB      : constant character := CTRL_I;
      BACK_TAB : constant character := CTRL_B;
      RIGHT    : constant character := CTRL_R;
      LEFT     : constant character := CTRL_L;
      UP       : constant character := CTRL_U;
      DOWN     : constant character := CTRL_D;
      INSERT   : constant character := CTRL_A;
      DELETE   : constant character := ASCII.DEL;
      FUN_KEY  : constant character := CTRL_F;
        -- Note: It is unfortunate that INSERT
        -- can't be CRTL_I, but that has been
        -- assigned to TAB by a higher power.
        -- CTRL_A was selected because it can be
        -- considered to ADD characters to the
        -- middle of a text string.
        -- CTRL_E can be used as an erase key on
        -- terminals lacking a delete/rub out key.

      PANIC : exception;
        -- Raised whenever the User presses the
        -- Panic Button (CTRL_C).

      INVALID_FUNCTION_KEY : exception;
        -- Raised if the function key is out of
        -- range.

      -- Screen control
```

```
procedure Clear_Screen;
  -- Erase the entire screen and move the
  -- cursor to the upper left corner of the
  -- screen.

-- Cursor control

procedure Move_Cursor_Right;
procedure Move_Cursor_Left;
procedure Move_Cursor_Up;
procedure Move_Cursor_Down;
procedure Move_Cursor_To(
  LINE : Line_numbers;
  COL : Column_Numbers);

-- Output services

procedure put(C : character);
  -- Sends a character to the screen without
  -- filtering.

procedure put(S : string);
  -- Sends a string to the screen without
  -- filtering.

-- Input services

procedure get(C : out character);
  -- Get a character without echo. Special
  -- control keys are automatically converted
  -- into standard control keys.
  --    RIGHT arrow => CTRL_R
  --    LEFT arrow =>  CTRL_L
  --    UP arrow =>    CTRL_U
  --    DOWN arrow =>  CTRL_D
  --    TAB =>         CTRL_I
  --    BACK_TAB =>    CTRL_B
  --    INSERT =>      CTRL_A
  --    DELETE =>      DELETE
  --    CTRL_E =>      DELETE
  --    FUN_KEY =>     CTRL_F
  --    CTRL_C =>      raises PANIC exception
  -- Note that terminals without cursor
  -- control keys or function keys can
```

```
        -- achieve the desired effect using
        -- control characters.

    function Function_Key return natural;

        -- 20 function keys are supported.

        -- If the Get function detects a function
        -- key it will return CTRL_F and decode the
        -- function key number. The main program
        -- can then call Function_Key to find out
        -- which one it was. Function_Key will
        -- return a number 1 through 20
        -- representing the function key pressed.
        -- (Some keyboards may used SHIFTED
        -- function keys 1 through 10 to get
        -- functions 11 through 20.)

        -- If the user presses CTRL_F when using
        -- the Get function, the Get function will
        -- interpret the next character as a
        -- function key. If the next key pressed
        -- is 1 through 9 then Function_Key  will
        -- return 1 through 9. Characters A through
        -- K return values of 10 through 20. (Both
        -- 'A' and 'a' return 10 because
        -- Function_Key is not case sensitive.)

        -- A function key outside the range 1..20
        -- raises INVALID_FUNCTION_KEY.

    function Keyboard_Data_Available
        return boolean;
        -- Tells if any key has been pressed,
        -- without reading the character.

end VIRTUAL_TERMINAL;
```

```
-- Listing 20.

--                 VTBAIBM.ada
--                 Version 1.1
--                 2 May 1988

--                 Do-While Jones
--                 324 Traci Lane
--                 Ridgecrest, CA 93555
--                 (619) 375-4607

--   Copyright 1989 by John Wiley & Sons, Inc.
--           All Rights Reserved.

-- Revision 1.1 is the Alsys IBM PC AT Version.

-- IMPORTANT! You must use the "Extended Screen
-- and Keyboard Control" features provided by
-- the ANSI.SYS driver. If you don't,
-- Clear_Screen will write [2J on the screen,
-- and the right arrow will echo as [C, and so
-- on. If this happens, add the following line
-- to your CONFIG.SYS file in your root
-- directory:

--    device = ANSI.SYS

--   Then REBOOT the system, and it should work.

with DOS, ASCII_UTILITIES;
package body VIRTUAL_TERMINAL is

  F_KEY : natural;

  -- The following are special IBM PC AT
  -- keyboard codes

  SPECIAL : constant character
    := character'VAL(16#00#);
  L       : constant := 75;
  R       : constant := 77;
  U       : constant := 72;
  D       : constant := 80;
  INS     : constant := 82;
  DEL     : constant := 83;
```

```
BK_TAB  : constant := 15;
PG_UP   : constant := 73;  -- unused
PG_DN   : constant := 81;  -- unused
HOME    : constant := 71;  -- unused
END_KEY : constant := 79;  -- unused
subtype Base_Functions is
  integer range 59..68;
subtype Shifted_Functions is
  integer range 84..93;

procedure Clear_Screen is
begin
  put(ASCII.ESC & "[2J");
end Clear_Screen;

procedure Move_Cursor_Right is
begin
  put(ASCII.ESC & "[C");
end Move_Cursor_Right;

procedure Move_Cursor_Left is
begin
  put(ASCII.ESC & "[D");
end Move_Cursor_Left;

procedure Move_Cursor_Up is
begin
  put(ASCII.ESC & "[A");
end Move_Cursor_Up;

procedure Move_Cursor_Down is
begin
  put(ASCII.ESC & "[B");
end Move_Cursor_Down;

procedure Move_Cursor_To(
    LINE : Line_numbers;
    COL  : Column_numbers) is
  L, C : string(1..3);
begin
  put(ASCII.ESC & '[');
  put(string'(ASCII_UTILITIES.Image(LINE)));
  put(';');
  put(string'(ASCII_UTILITIES.Image(COL)));
```

```
      put('H');
   end Move_Cursor_To;

   procedure put(C : character) is
   begin
     DOS.Display_Char(C);
   end put;

   procedure put(S : string) is
   begin
     for i in S'RANGE loop
       put(S(i));
     end loop;
   end put;

   procedure get(C : out character) is
     X : character;
   begin
     X := DOS.Read_Kbd_Direct_No_Echo;
     case X is
       when SPECIAL =>
         X := DOS.Read_Kbd_Direct_No_Echo;
         case character'POS(X) is
           when INS =>
             X := INSERT;
           when DEL =>
             X := DELETE;
           when L =>
             X := LEFT;
           when R =>
             X := RIGHT;
           when U =>
             X := UP;
           when D =>
             X := DOWN;
           when BK_TAB =>
             X := BACK_TAB;
           when 59..68 =>
             F_KEY := character'POS(X)
               - Base_functions'FIRST + 1;
             if F_KEY not in 1..20 then
               raise INVALID_FUNCTION_KEY;
             end if;
             X := CTRL_F;
```

```
            when 84..93 =>
              F_KEY := character'POS(X)
               - Shifted_functions'FIRST + 11;
              if F_KEY not in 1..20 then
                raise INVALID_FUNCTION_KEY;
              end if;
              X := CTRL_F;
            when others =>
              -- null for invalid special key
              X := ASCII.NUL;
          end case;
      when CTRL_E =>
        X := DELETE;
      when CTRL_C =>
        raise PANIC;
      when others =>
        null; -- don't mess with X
    end case;
    C := X;
end get;

function Function_Key return natural is
  X : natural;
  C : character;
begin
  if F_KEY = 0 then
    C := DOS.Read_Kbd_Direct_No_Echo;
    case C is
      when '1'..'9' =>
        F_KEY := character'POS(C)
           - character'POS('0');
      when 'A'..'K' =>
        F_KEY := character'POS(C)
                - character'POS('A') + 10;
      when 'a'..'k' =>
        F_KEY := character'POS(C)
                - character'POS('a') + 10;
      when others =>
        raise INVALID_FUNCTION_KEY;
    end case;
  end if;
  X := F_KEY;
  F_KEY := 0;
  return X;
end Function_Key;
```

```
function Keyboard_Data_Available
  return boolean is
begin
  return DOS.Kbd_Data_Available;
end Keyboard_Data_Available;

end VIRTUAL_TERMINAL;
```

```
-- Listing 21.

--                 VTBMIBM.ada
--                 Version 1.0
--                 28 April 1988

--                 Do-While Jones
--                 324 Traci Lane
--                 Ridgecrest, CA 93555
--                 (619) 375-4607

-- Copyright 1989 by John Wiley & Sons, Inc.
--          All Rights Reserved.

-- Revision 1.0 is the IBM PC AT (Meridian)
-- Version.

with TTY, CURSOR; -- Meridian Dos Environment package
package body VIRTUAL_TERMINAL is

  F_KEY : natural;

  -- The following are IBM PC AT keyboard
  -- codes.

  SPECIAL : constant character
    := character'VAL(16#00#);
  L        : constant := 75;
  R        : constant := 77;
  U        : constant := 72;
  D        : constant := 80;
  INS      : constant := 82;
  DEL      : constant := 83;
  BK_TAB   : constant := 15;
  PG_UP    : constant := 73; -- unused
  PG_DN    : constant := 81; -- unused
  HOME     : constant := 71; -- unused
  END_KEY  : constant := 79; -- unused
  subtype Base_Functions is
    integer range 59..68;
  subtype Shifted_Functions is
    integer range 84..93;

  procedure Clear_Screen is
  begin
```

```
      TTY.Clear_Screen;
      CURSOR.Move(0,0);
   end Clear_Screen;

   procedure Move_Cursor_Right is
   begin
      CURSOR.Right;
   end Move_Cursor_Right;

   procedure Move_Cursor_Left is
   begin
      CURSOR.Left;
   end Move_Cursor_Left;

   procedure Move_Cursor_Up is
   begin
      CURSOR.Up;
   end Move_Cursor_Up;

   procedure Move_Cursor_Down is
   begin
      CURSOR.Down;
   end Move_Cursor_Down;

   procedure Move_Cursor_To(
      LINE : Line_numbers;
      COL  : Column_numbers) is
   begin
      CURSOR.Move(LINE-1,COL-1);
      -- Meridian CURSOR package counts
      -- from 0, not 1
   end Move_Cursor_To;

   procedure put(C : character) is
   begin
      TTY.Put(C);
   end put;

   procedure put(S : string) is
   begin
      for i in S'RANGE loop
         put(S(i));
      end loop;
   end put;
```

```
procedure get(C : out character) is
  X : character;
begin
  X := TTY.Get(No_Echo => TRUE,
               Direct  => TRUE);
  case X is
    when SPECIAL =>
      X := TTY.Get(No_Echo => TRUE,
                   Direct  => TRUE);
      case character'POS(X) is
        when INS =>
          X := INSERT;
        when DEL =>
          X := DELETE;
        when L =>
          X := LEFT;
        when R =>
          X := RIGHT;
        when U =>
          X := UP;
        when D =>
          X := DOWN;
        when BK_TAB =>
          X := BACK_TAB;
        when Base_functions =>
          F_KEY := character'POS(X)
            - Base_functions'FIRST + 1;
          if F_KEY not in 1..20 then
            raise INVALID_FUNCTION_KEY;
          end if;
          X := CTRL_F;
        when Shifted_functions =>
          F_KEY := character'POS(X)
            - Shifted_functions'FIRST + 11;
          if F_KEY not in 1..20 then
            raise INVALID_FUNCTION_KEY;
          end if;
          X := CTRL_F;
        when others =>
          -- null for invalid special key
          X := ASCII.NUL;
      end case;
    when CTRL_C =>
      raise PANIC;
```

```
      when CTRL_E =>
        X := DELETE;
      when others =>
        null; -- don't mess with X
    end case;
    C := X;
  end get;

  function Function_Key return natural is
    X : natural;
    C : character;
  begin
    if F_KEY = 0 then
      C := TTY.Get(No_Echo => TRUE,
                   Direct  => TRUE);
      case C is
        when '1'..'9' =>
          F_KEY := character'POS(C)
            - character'POS('0');
        when 'A'..'K' =>
          F_KEY := character'POS(C)
            - character'POS('A')+10;
        when 'a'..'k' =>
          F_KEY := character'POS(C)
            - character'POS('a')+10;
        when others =>
          raise INVALID_FUNCTION_KEY;
      end case;
    end if;
    X := F_KEY;
    F_KEY := 0;
    return X;
  end Function_Key;

  function Keyboard_Data_Available
    return boolean is
  begin
    return TTY.Char_Ready;
  end Keyboard_Data_Available;

end VIRTUAL_TERMINAL;
```

```ada
-- Listing 22.

--                  STS.ada
--                  Version 1
--                  10 October 1988

--                  Do-While Jones
--                  324 Traci Lane
--                  Ridgecrest, CA 93555
--                  (619) 375-4607

-- Copyright 1989 by John Wiley & Sons, Inc.
--          All Rights Reserved.

with VIRTUAL_TERMINAL;
package SCROLL_TERMINAL is

  subtype Column_numbers is
    VIRTUAL_TERMINAL.Column_numbers;

  PANIC : exception renames
    VIRTUAL_TERMINAL.PANIC;
  -- Raised when the user presses the Panic
  -- Button (CTRL_C). Can be raised by
  -- Wait_For_User and all forms of Get.

  NEEDS_HELP : exception; -- raised when user
  -- presses ? key. Can be raised by all forms
  -- of Get and Get_Line.

  ------------ OUTPUT SUBPROGRAMS ------------

  -- All the output routines are compatible
  -- with TEXT_IO.

  procedure put(C : character);
  -- The put procedure automatically expands
  -- tabs, keeps track of columns, and knows
  -- that certain characters (like ASCII.LF and
  -- ASCII.BEL) should not affect the column
  -- counter. Non-printable characters are
  -- converted to an ASCII.BEL.

  procedure put(S : string);
  -- Call the character put routine until all
```

```
-- the characters in the string have been
-- sent.

procedure new_line(LINES : positive := 1);
-- Use the string put routine to send a
-- <CR><LF> sequence the desired number of
-- times.

procedure put_line(S : string);
-- Use the string put procedure to send the
-- string, then follow it immediately with a
-- call of new_line;

procedure New_Page;
-- Clear the CRT screen.

procedure Set_Col(N : Column_numbers);
-- Use the character put routine to print
-- spaces until the cursor is at column N.
-- (If the cursor is already at column N,
-- then nothing is done. If the cursor is
-- past column N, then new_line is called and
-- the cursor spaces over to column N.)

procedure Set_Tabs(
  STOPS : Column_numbers := 8);
-- This procedure gives the character put
-- routine the information it needs to expand
-- TAB characters.

function Column return Column_numbers;
-- Tells the main program which column is
-- about to be printed.

------------ INPUT SUBPROGRAMS -------------


-- All forms of string input allow the user
-- to enter data using the following line
-- editing functions:

--    LEFT and RIGHT Arrow Keys (Move the
--       cursor without changing characters
--       underneath.)
--    CTRL_L (Same as the LEFT Arrow Key.)
```

```
--    CTRL_R (Same as the RIGHT Arrow Key.)
--    BACKSPACE (Delete the character just
--      entered.)
--    CTRL_H (Same as BACKSPACE.)
--    DELETE (Delete character under cursor
--      and move characters from the right to
--      fill in the gap. Acts like BACKSPACE
--      if the cursor is past the last
--      character entered.)
--    CTRL_E (Same as DELETE.)
--    INSERT (Change from replace to insert
--      mode until another command, except
--      BACKSPACE, is entered.)
--    CTRL_A (Same as INSERT.)
--    ? (Ask for help and restore DEFAULT
--      response.)

-- If the user's first keystroke is a
-- carriage return, then take the DEFAULT as
-- the RESPONSE.

-- If the user's first keystroke is not an
-- editing key, then erase the DEFAULT and
-- allow the use to enter a completely new
-- RESPONSE.

-- If the user's first keystroke is an
-- editing key, then let the user edit the
-- DEFAULT until the user presses the return
-- key. At that point take the entire visible
-- edited DEFAULT as the RESPONSE.

-- Raises NEEDS_HELP immediately if the user
-- presses '?'.

-- Raises PANIC immediately if the
-- PANIC_CHARACTER is entered.

function Any_Key_Pressed return boolean;
-- Are there any unprocessed keyboard
-- entries?

procedure Flush_Input;
-- Ignore any characters which may be in the
```

```
-- type-ahead buffer at the moment (including
-- the PANIC_CHARACTER).

procedure Wait_For_User;
-- Prompt the user with "Press Any Key To
-- Continue." Do a "busy wait" until the user
-- presses a key. Get the user's response
-- (without echo), throw it away, and call
-- new_line. (It is the responsibility of
-- the application program to call New_Page
-- if appropriate.)

-- Raises PANIC if the key is the
-- PANIC_CHARACTER.

procedure Echo_On;
-- Echo all subsequent keyboard entries
-- (until Echo_Off). Echo_On is the default.

procedure Echo_Off;
-- Do not echo subsequent keyboard entries
-- (until Echo_On).

procedure get_line(TEXT   : out string;
                   LENGTH : out natural);
  -- Just like TEXT_IO, for compatibility
  -- only. Not recommended for new programs.
  -- (It is better behaved than TEXT_IO
  -- because character positions past LENGTH
  -- are always blanks.)

procedure get(TEXT : out string);
  -- A lot like TEXT_IO, for compatibility
  -- only. Not recommended for new programs.
  -- (It differs from TEXT_IO because it lets
  -- you use INSERT and DELETE, and doesn't
  -- immediately return when the last
  -- character is entered. All unentered
  -- characters are returned as blanks.)

procedure get_line(PROMPT : string;
                   TEXT   : out string;
                   LENGTH : out natural);
-- Put the PROMPT and use get_line (above) to
```

```
-- let the user enter a response.

procedure get_line(PROMPT  : string;
                    DEFAULT : string;
                    TEXT    : out string;
                    LENGTH  : out natural);
-- Put the PROMPT and DEFAULT response and
-- let the user enter data.

procedure get(PROMPT : string;
              TEXT   : out string;
              FILL   : character := ' ');
-- Put the PROMPT and let the user enter
-- data. Add FILL characters to the end of
-- the string to make it the right length.
-- ASCII.NUL is the other obvious choice for
-- FILL.

-- When called with two parameters it works
-- like TEXT_IO.get, except the characters at
-- the end of the string are blank spaces
-- instead of random characters.)

procedure get(PROMPT  : string;
              DEFAULT : string;
              TEXT    : out string;
              FILL    : character := ' ');
-- Put the PROMPT and DEFAULT response and
-- let the user enter data. Add FILL
-- characters to make the TEXT the
-- correct length.

procedure get(RESPONSE : out character);
-- This works the way you probably expect
-- TEXT_IO to work. It gets one character at
-- a time, immediately (without waiting for a
-- carriage return). It is included for
-- compatibility with old programs that used
-- TEXT_IO. New programs should use the next
-- procedure to get a single character
-- response (because it includes a prompt) or
-- VIRTUAL_TERMINAL to process individual
-- keystrokes (for special screen-oriented
-- applications).
```

```
procedure get(PROMPT   : string;
              RESPONSE : out character);
-- Put the PROMPT and wait for the user to
-- respond with a single character (usually Y
-- or N). No editing is allowed because the
-- user's response is processed immediately.

-- Raises PANIC immediately if the
-- PANIC_CHARACTER is entered.

procedure get(PROMPT   : string;
              DEFAULT  : character;
              RESPONSE : out character);
-- Put the PROMPT and DEFAULT, then wait for
-- the user to respond with a single
-- character (usually Y or N). No editing is
-- allowed.

-- If the user presses the carriage return
-- the DEFAULT response is taken.

-- Raises PANIC immediately if the
-- PANIC_CHARACTER is entered.

end SCROLL_TERMINAL;
```

```ada
-- Listing 23.

--              STB.ada
--              Version 1.0
--              10 October 1988

--              Do-While Jones
--              324 Traci Lane
--              Ridgecrest, CA 93555
--              (619) 375-4607

-- Copyright 1989 by John Wiley & Sons, Inc.
--          All Rights Reserved.

package body SCROLL_TERMINAL is

   subtype Cursor_positions is integer
      range 1..Column_numbers'LAST+1;

   COLUMN_NUMBER : Cursor_positions;
   TAB_STOPS     : Column_numbers;
   ECHO          : boolean;

   CR  : constant character := ASCII.CR;
   LF  : constant character := ASCII.LF;
   BEL : constant character := ASCII.BEL;
   TAB : constant character := ASCII.HT;
   BS  : constant character := ASCII.BS;

   procedure Get_Response(DEFAULT : string;
                          TEXT    : out string;
                          LENGTH  : out natural)
   is separate; -- file STBGR.ada

   procedure put(C : character) is
   begin
      case C is
         when ' ' .. '~' =>
            if COLUMN_NUMBER
               <= Column_numbers'LAST then
              COLUMN_NUMBER := COLUMN_NUMBER + 1;
            else
              New_Line;
            end if;
```

```
            VIRTUAL_TERMINAL.put(C);
         when BS =>
            if COLUMN_NUMBER > 1 then
               COLUMN_NUMBER := COLUMN_NUMBER - 1;
               VIRTUAL_TERMINAL.Move_Cursor_Left;
            else
               VIRTUAL_TERMINAL.put(BEL);
            end if;
         when CR =>
            COLUMN_NUMBER := 1;
            VIRTUAL_TERMINAL.put(C);
         when LF | BEL =>
            VIRTUAL_TERMINAL.put(C);
         when TAB =>
            -- TAB is worth at least one space
            put(' ');
            while COLUMN_NUMBER
                  mod TAB_STOPS /= 0 loop
               -- use recursion to control
               -- COLUMN_NUMBER
               put(' ');
            end loop;
         when others =>
            -- (non-printable characters)
            VIRTUAL_TERMINAL.put(BEL);
      end case;
   end put;

   procedure put(S : string) is
   begin
      for i in S'RANGE loop
         put(S(i));
      end loop;
   end put;

   procedure new_line(LINES : positive := 1) is
   begin
      for i in 1..LINES loop
         put(CR); put(LF);
      end loop;
   end new_line;

   procedure put_line(S : string) is
   begin
```

```
   put(S); new_line;
end put_line;

procedure New_Page is
begin
  VIRTUAL_TERMINAL.Clear_Screen;
  COLUMN_NUMBER := 1;
end New_Page;

procedure Set_Col(N : Column_numbers) is
begin
  if N < COLUMN_NUMBER then new_line; end if;
  for i in COLUMN_NUMBER+1..N loop
    put(' ');
  end loop;
end Set_Col;

procedure Set_Tabs(
   STOPS : Column_numbers := 8) is
begin
  TAB_STOPS := STOPS;
end Set_Tabs;

function Column return Column_numbers is
begin
  return COLUMN_NUMBER;
end Column;

function Any_Key_Pressed return boolean is
begin
  return VIRTUAL_TERMINAL.
    Keyboard_Data_Available;
end Any_Key_Pressed;

procedure Flush_Input is
  IGNORED_CHARACTER : character;
begin
  while Any_Key_Pressed loop
    VIRTUAL_TERMINAL.get(IGNORED_CHARACTER);
  end loop;
end Flush_Input;

procedure Wait_For_User is
  IGNORED_CHARACTER : character;
```

```
begin
  Flush_Input;
  new_line;
  put("Press Any Key To Continue");
  VIRTUAL_TERMINAL.get(IGNORED_CHARACTER);
  Flush_Input;
  new_line;
end Wait_For_User;

procedure Echo_On is
begin
  ECHO := TRUE;
end Echo_On;

procedure Echo_Off is
begin
  ECHO := FALSE;
end Echo_Off;

procedure get_line(TEXT   : out string;
                   LENGTH : out natural) is
begin
  Get_Response("", TEXT, LENGTH);
end get_line;

procedure get(TEXT : out string) is
  TEMP   : string(1..TEXT'LENGTH);
  LENGTH : natural;
begin
  Get_Response("", TEMP, LENGTH);
  TEXT(TEXT'RANGE) := (others => ' ');
  TEXT(TEXT'FIRST..TEXT'FIRST+LENGTH-1)
    := TEMP(1..LENGTH);
end get;

procedure get_line(PROMPT : string;
                   TEXT   : out string;
                   LENGTH : out natural) is
begin
  put(PROMPT);
  Get_Response("", TEXT, LENGTH);
end get_line;

procedure get_line(PROMPT  : string;
```

```
                    DEFAULT : string;
                    TEXT    : out string;
                    LENGTH  : out natural) is
begin
  put(PROMPT);
  Get_Response(DEFAULT, TEXT, LENGTH);
end get_line;

procedure get(PROMPT : string;
              TEXT    : out string;
              FILL    : character := ' ') is
  TEMP   : string(1..TEXT'LENGTH);
  LENGTH : natural;
begin
  put(PROMPT);
  Get_Response("", TEMP, LENGTH);
  TEXT(TEXT'RANGE) := (others => FILL);
  TEXT(TEXT'FIRST..TEXT'FIRST+LENGTH-1)
    := TEMP(1..LENGTH);
end get;

procedure get(PROMPT  : string;
              DEFAULT : string;
              TEXT    : out string;
              FILL    : character := ' ') is
  TEMP   : string(1..TEXT'LENGTH);
  LENGTH : natural;
begin
  put(PROMPT);
  Get_Response(DEFAULT, TEMP, LENGTH);
  TEXT(TEXT'RANGE) := (others => FILL);
  TEXT(TEXT'FIRST..TEXT'FIRST+LENGTH-1)
    := TEMP(1..LENGTH);
end get;

procedure get(RESPONSE : out character) is
  C : character;
begin
  VIRTUAL_TERMINAL.get(C);
  if C = '?' then raise NEEDS_HELP; end if;
  RESPONSE := C;
  if ECHO then
    put(C);
  end if;
end get;
```

```
      procedure get(PROMPT   : string;
                    RESPONSE : out character) is
        C : character;
      begin
        put(PROMPT);
        VIRTUAL_TERMINAL.get(C);
        if C = '?' then raise NEEDS_HELP; end if;
        RESPONSE := C;
        if ECHO then
          put(C);
        end if;
      end get;

      procedure get(PROMPT   : string;
                    DEFAULT  : character;
                    RESPONSE : out character) is
        C : character;
      begin
        put(PROMPT);
        put(DEFAULT);
        -- backspace to put cursor over DEFAULT
        put(BS);
        VIRTUAL_TERMINAL.get(C);
        if C = '?' then raise NEEDS_HELP; end if;
        if C = CR then C := DEFAULT; end if;
        RESPONSE := C;
        if ECHO then
          put(C);
        end if;
      end get;

    begin
      COLUMN_NUMBER := 1;
      Set_Tabs;
      Echo_On;
    end SCROLL_TERMINAL;
```

```ada
-- Listing 24.

--              STBGR.ada
--              Version 1.1
--              2 September 1988

--              Do-While Jones
--              324 Traci Lane
--              Ridgecrest, CA 93555
--              (619) 375-4607

-- Copyright 1989 by John Wiley & Sons, Inc.
--        All Rights Reserved.

  separate(SCROLL_TERMINAL)
  procedure Get_Response(DEFAULT : string;
                         TEXT    : out string;
                         LENGTH  : out natural)
     is
   X       : natural; -- position of character
                      -- just entered
   C       : character; -- temporary storage
   FIRST : Column_numbers := COLUMN_NUMBER;
   LAST  : Column_numbers
     := FIRST + TEXT'LENGTH-1;
   SIZE  : natural range 0..TEXT'LENGTH;
   -- SIZE tells the number of valid
   -- characters in the buffer
   BUFFER : string(FIRST..LAST);
   INSERT_MODE : boolean;
   DONE        : boolean;

   procedure Beep is
   begin
     VIRTUAL_TERMINAL.put(ASCII.BEL);
   end Beep;

   procedure Forward is
   begin
     if X < BUFFER'LAST then
       X := X+1;
       if ECHO then
         put(BUFFER(X));
       else
         put(' ');
```

```
        end if;
    else
      Beep;
    end if;
end Forward;


procedure Backup is
begin
    if X >= FIRST then
      COLUMN_NUMBER := COLUMN_NUMBER - 1;
      X := X - 1;
      VIRTUAL_TERMINAL.Move_Cursor_Left;
    else
      Beep;
    end if;
end Backup;


procedure Remove is
    P : positive;
begin
    if SIZE > 0 then
      SIZE := SIZE-1;
      P := X; -- number of characters left of
              -- the cursor
      for i in P+1..BUFFER'LAST loop
        BUFFER(i-1) := BUFFER(i);
      end loop;
      BUFFER(BUFFER'LAST) := ' ';
      Backup;
      if ECHO then
        put(BUFFER(P..BUFFER'LAST));
      else
        for i in P..BUFFER'LAST loop
          put(' ');
        end loop;
      end if;
      X := BUFFER'LAST;
      for i in P..BUFFER'LAST loop
        Backup;
      end loop;
    else
      Beep;
    end if;
end Remove;
```

```ada
procedure Process_Character(
   C    : character;
   DONE : out boolean) is

  procedure Add is
    P : natural;
  begin
    if X < BUFFER'LAST then
      P := X+1; -- cursor position
      -- shove all the characters back
      -- one position
      for i in
          reverse P..BUFFER'LAST-1 loop
        BUFFER(i+1) := BUFFER(i);
      end loop;
      -- add the new character
      BUFFER(P) := C;
      if SIZE = BUFFER'LENGTH then
        -- buffer was full
        -- one character fell out the end
        SIZE := SIZE-1;
      end if;
      -- one more valid character now
      SIZE := SIZE+1;
      if ECHO then
        -- show what's in the buffer now
        put(BUFFER(P..BUFFER'LAST));
      else
        for i in P..BUFFER'LAST loop
          put(' ');
        end loop;
      end if;
      -- the pointer is at the end of
      -- the buffer
      X := BUFFER'LAST;
      -- move the pointer back to where
      -- it was
      for i in P..BUFFER'LAST-1 loop
        Backup;
      end loop;
    else
      Beep;
    end if;
  end Add;
```

```
procedure Rubout is
begin
  if X >= FIRST then
    Remove;
  else
    Beep;
  end if;
end Rubout;

procedure Replace is
begin
  if X < BUFFER'LAST then
    -- Note: C must be written to the
    -- BUFFER before X is incremented to
    -- avoid a bug in the Meridian
    -- Version 2.1 compiler.
    BUFFER(X+1) := C;
    X := X+1;
    if ECHO then
      put(C);
    else
      put(' ');
    end if;
    if SIZE < X-FIRST+1 then
      SIZE := X-FIRST+1;
    end if;
  else
    Beep;
  end if;
end Replace;

begin -- Process_Character
  DONE := FALSE;
  case C is
    when CR =>
      DONE := TRUE;
    when BS =>
      Rubout;
    when VIRTUAL_TERMINAL.INSERT =>
      INSERT_MODE := TRUE;
    when VIRTUAL_TERMINAL.DELETE =>
      INSERT_MODE := FALSE;
      if X < FIRST+SIZE-1 then
        Forward;
```

```
                  end if;
                  if X > FIRST+SIZE-1 then
                    Beep;
                  else
                    Remove;
                  end if;
              when VIRTUAL_TERMINAL.LEFT =>
                  INSERT_MODE := FALSE;
                  Backup;
              when VIRTUAL_TERMINAL.RIGHT =>
                  INSERT_MODE := FALSE;
                  Forward;
              when ' '..'~' =>
                  if C = '?' then
                    raise NEEDS_HELP;
                  elsif INSERT_MODE then
                    Add;
                  else
                    Replace;
                  end if;
              when others =>
                  Beep;
            end case;
        end Process_Character;

    begin -- Get_Response

        INSERT_MODE := FALSE;

        -- fill the BUFFER with the DEFAULT
        -- response
        BUFFER := (others => ' ');
        BUFFER(FIRST..FIRST+DEFAULT'LENGTH-1)
          := DEFAULT;
        SIZE := DEFAULT'LENGTH;

        -- show the user the default
        if ECHO then
          put(BUFFER);
        else
          for i in BUFFER'RANGE loop
            put(' ');
          end loop;
        end if;

        -- move the cursor to the beginning of the
        -- BUFFER
```

```
   X := BUFFER'LAST;
   for i in BUFFER'RANGE loop
     Backup;
   end loop;

   -- get and process the first keystroke
   DONE := FALSE;
   VIRTUAL_TERMINAL.get(C);
   case C is
     when VIRTUAL_TERMINAL.INSERT =>
       INSERT_MODE := TRUE;
     when VIRTUAL_TERMINAL.DELETE =>
       Forward;
       Remove;
     when VIRTUAL_TERMINAL.RIGHT =>
       Forward;
     when CR =>
       TEXT := BUFFER;
       LENGTH := SIZE;
       new_line;
       return;
     when others =>
       -- erase the default
       BUFFER := (others => ' ');
       put(BUFFER);
       X := BUFFER'LAST;
       for i in BUFFER'RANGE loop
         Backup;
       end loop;
       SIZE := 0;
       -- process the first character
       Process_Character(C,DONE);
   end case;

   -- let the user enter more characters
   while not DONE loop
     VIRTUAL_TERMINAL.get(C);
     Process_Character(C, DONE);
   end loop;

   -- return the data to the application
   -- program
   TEXT := BUFFER;
   LENGTH := SIZE;
   new_line;
end Get_Response;
```

```
-- Listing 25.

--                  FTS.ada
--                  Version 2.1
--                  19 September 1988

--                  Do-While Jones
--                  324 Traci Lane
--                  Ridgecrest, CA 93555
--                  (619) 374-4607

--   Copyright 1989 by John Wiley & Sons, Inc.
--           All Rights Reserved.

-- The FORM_TERMINAL is a user interface
-- appropriate for applications where the user
-- is likely to want to enter data in a non-
-- deterministic order. That is, instead of
-- presenting the user with a step-by-step
-- series of questions to answer (as
-- SCROLL_TERMINAL does), this interface
-- presents the user with a blank (or perhaps
-- partially complete) form. The user fills in
-- the blanks in any order.

-- The form consists of up to 200 fields. Some
-- of the fields are prompts for the user and
-- cannot be changed. These fields are called
-- "protected" fields. The other fields
-- (unprotected fields) are places where the
-- user can enter data.

with VIRTUAL_TERMINAL;
package FORM_TERMINAL is

  MAX_FIELDS : constant integer := 200;

  subtype Line_numbers is integer range
    VIRTUAL_TERMINAL.Line_numbers'FIRST
    ..VIRTUAL_TERMINAL.Line_numbers'LAST-1;
    -- Reserve the bottom line for
    -- STATUS/INSTRUCTIONS.

  subtype Column_numbers is
    VIRTUAL_TERMINAL.Column_numbers;
```

```
subtype Field_names is string(1..20);
   -- Fields can have 20 character names with
   -- significant embedded blanks and
   -- underscores. Names are not case
   -- sensitive.

PANIC : exception renames
   VIRTUAL_TERMINAL.PANIC;
   -- Raised when the user presses CONTROL_C.
   -- Can be raised by Update, Display,
   -- Create, or Edit.

LAYOUT_ERROR : exception;
   -- Raised by Read if an attempt is made to
   -- improperly place a field on the form.
   -- This may happen if the new field
   -- overlaps an existing field, if LAST_COL
   -- is less than FIRST_COL, or if an invalid
   -- line number or column number is entered.

ASSIGNMENT_ERROR : exception;
   -- Raised by Get, Put, and Update if an
   -- attempt is made to read or write data
   -- to/from a nonexistent field.

NEEDS_HELP : exception;
   -- Raised by Update if the user presses the
   -- ? key. The function Confusing_Field can
   -- be used to tell which field on the form
   -- confused the user.

READ_ERROR : exception;
   -- Raised by Read if it is unable to open
   -- or read the file containing the form.
   -- This could happen if the input file
   -- doesn't exist, doesn't contain a form,
   -- or contains an erroneous form.

WRITE_ERROR : exception;
   -- Raised by Write if it is unable to open
   -- or write to the specified file. This
   -- could happen if the disk is full, or a
   -- read-only file of the same name already
   -- exists.
```

```
  --CONSTRAINT_ERROR : exception;
      -- Raised by Get and Put if the name of the
      -- field, or the length of the text string
      -- is not exactly correct.

   procedure Read(FILENAME : string);
      -- Fill the form with the data found in
      -- file named FILENAME.

      -- Raises READ_ERROR if it can't find,
      -- open, or read the file.

      -- Raises LAYOUT_ERROR if the data in the
      -- file is invalid.

   procedure Write(FILENAME : string);
      -- Store the data on the form in the file
      -- named FILENAME.

      -- Raises WRITE_ERROR if it can't write the
      -- data to the file.

   procedure Display(WAIT : boolean := FALSE);
      -- This procedure clears the screen and
      -- then displays the form on it. If WAIT is
      -- true it displays the message "Press Any
      -- Key To Continue" at the bottom of the
      -- screen and waits for the user to press
      -- any key before proceeding.

   procedure Update(CURSOR_AT : Field_names;
                    NEXT      : out boolean);
      -- This procedure clears the screen and
      -- then displays the form on it. It gives
      -- the user an opportunity to modify all
      -- unprotected fields. The editing keys
      -- work just like they do in the
      -- SCROLL_TERMINAL package. In addition,
      -- the UP and DOWN arrows, TAB and BACK_TAB
      -- keys also work.

      -- The cursor is initially placed at the
      -- field designated by CURSOR_AT. This is
      -- just a default starting point. The user
```

```
      -- can put data into unprotected fields in
      -- any order.

      -- Pressing CR or TAB causes the cursor to
      -- move to the next unprotected field.
      -- BACK_TAB causes the cursor to move to
      -- the previous unprotected field.

      -- If the user presses CR or TAB in the
      -- last field, or uses the DOWN arrow in
      -- any field, the procedure returns control
      -- to the main program with the NEXT
      -- variable set to TRUE, indicating that
      -- the user wants to go to the next form.

      -- If the user presses BACK_TAB in the
      -- first field, or uses the the UP arrow in
      -- any field, the procedure returns control
      -- to the main program with the NEXT
      -- variable set to FALSE, indicating that
      -- the user wants to go to the previous
      -- form.

   procedure get(NAME : Field_names;
                 TEXT : out string);
      -- After the user has Updated a FORM, this
      -- procedure can be used to extract the
      -- data from any individual field.

      -- Raises ASSIGNMENT_ERROR if the field
      -- does not exist.

      -- Raises CONSTRAINT_ERROR if NAME or TEXT
      -- is not exactly the right length.

   procedure put(NAME : Field_names;
                 TEXT : string);
      -- After a form has been read from a disk
      -- file, this procedure can be used to put
      -- data in any field (even protected
      -- fields).

      -- Raises ASSIGNMENT_ERROR if the field
      -- does not exist.
```

```
          -- Raises CONSTRAINT_ERROR if NAME or TEXT
          -- is not exactly the right length.

       function Confusing_Field return Field_names;
          -- This function is used only with the
          -- NEEDS_HELP exception. It tells the main
          -- program which field the user was editing
          -- when he pressed the ? key.

       -- The following can be major components of
       -- utility programs that make or modify a
       -- form.

       procedure Create;
          -- This procedure allows you to
          -- interactively create a new form.

       procedure Edit;
          -- This procedure allows you to inspect and
          -- modify the parameters that shape the
          -- form.

    end FORM_TERMINAL;
```

```
-- Listing 26.

--              FTB.ada
--              Version 2.1
--              19 September 1988

--              Do-While Jones
--              324 Traci Lane
--              Ridgecrest, CA 93555
--              (619) 375-4607

--  Copyright 1989 by John Wiley & Sons, Inc.
--          All Rights Reserved.

with ASCII_UTILITIES;
package body FORM_TERMINAL is

   subtype Lines is string(Column_numbers);

   type Screens is array(Line_numbers) of Lines;

   type Field_specs is
     record
       NAME       : Field_names;
       LINE       : Line_numbers;
       FIRST_COL  : Column_numbers;
       LAST_COL   : Column_numbers;
       PROTECTED  : boolean;
     end record;

   type Field_arrays is
     array (integer range <>) of Field_specs;

   subtype Field_numbers is
     positive range 1..MAX_FIELDS;

   type Forms(FIELDS : Field_numbers := 1) is
     record
       FIELD  : Field_arrays(1..FIELDS);
       SCREEN : screens;
     end record;

   FORM : Forms;
```

332   PROGRAM LISTINGS

```
type Actions is (NEXT_FIELD, PREVIOUS_FIELD,
                 NEXT_FORM, PREVIOUS_FORM);

WORKING_FIELD : positive := 1;
  -- Set by Update before raising NEEDS_HELP.
  -- Read by Confusing_Field.

type Errors is
  (TEXT_FIELD, NAME_CONFLICT, OVERLAP);
ERROR : Errors;
  -- Set by Check_Form before raising
  -- LAYOUT_ERROR.

CURRENT_FIELD, CONFLICTING_FIELD : natural
  := 0;
  -- Set by Check_Form before raising
  -- LAYOUT_ERROR.

procedure Check_Form is
  -- Called by Read, Edit, and Create, to
  -- make sure the FORM is valid. It raises
  -- LAYOUT_ERROR if it is not.
  NAME  : Field_names;
  LINE  : Line_numbers;
  FIRST : Column_numbers;
  LAST  : Column_numbers;
begin
  for i in 1..FORM.FIELDS loop
    -- Get the characteristics of this field
    CURRENT_FIELD := i;
    NAME  := FORM.FIELD(i).NAME;
    LINE  := FORM.FIELD(i).LINE;
    FIRST := FORM.FIELD(i).FIRST_COL;
    LAST  := FORM.FIELD(i).LAST_COL;

    -- Check it for internal consistency.
    if LAST < FIRST then
      -- it is a null string
      ERROR := TEXT_FIELD;
      raise LAYOUT_ERROR;
    end if;

    -- Check to make sure it doesn't conflict
```

```
            -- with any previously defined field,
            -- FORM.FIELD(j).
            for j in 1..i-1 loop
              CONFLICTING_FIELD := j;
              -- The name must be unique.
              if FORM.FIELD(j).NAME = NAME then
                ERROR := NAME_CONFLICT;
                raise LAYOUT_ERROR;
              end if;

              if FORM.FIELD(j).LINE = LINE then
                -- check for overlap.
                if FIRST in FORM.FIELD(j).FIRST_COL
                    .. FORM.FIELD(j).LAST_COL then
                  ERROR := OVERLAP;
                  raise LAYOUT_ERROR;
                end if;
                if LAST in FORM.FIELD(j).FIRST_COL
                    .. FORM.FIELD(j).LAST_COL then
                  ERROR := OVERLAP;
                  raise LAYOUT_ERROR;
                end if;
                if FORM.FIELD(j).FIRST_COL
                    in FIRST..LAST then
                  ERROR := OVERLAP;
                  raise LAYOUT_ERROR;
                end if;
                if FORM.FIELD(j).LAST_COL
                    in FIRST..LAST then
                  ERROR := OVERLAP;
                  raise LAYOUT_ERROR;
                end if;
              end if;
            end loop;
          end loop;
        end Check_Form;

        procedure Get_Form(A : out Actions)
          is separate;
          -- file FTBGF.ada

        procedure Read(FILENAME : string)
          is separate;
```

```
-- file FTBRW.ada

procedure Write(FILENAME : string)
  is separate;
  -- file FTBRW.ada

procedure Display(WAIT : boolean := FALSE)
  is separate;
  -- file FTBD.ada

function Field_Number(NAME : Field_names)
  return positive is
    CAP_NAME : Field_names;
begin
  CAP_NAME
    := ASCII_UTILITIES.Upper_Case(NAME);
  for i in 1..FORM.FIELDS loop
    if FORM.FIELD(i).NAME = CAP_NAME then
      return i;
    end if;
  end loop;
  -- if the name doesn't match an assigned
  -- field, then
  raise ASSIGNMENT_ERROR;
end Field_Number;

procedure Update(CURSOR_AT : Field_names;
                 NEXT      : out boolean)
  is separate;
  -- file FTBU.ada

procedure get(NAME : Field_names;
              TEXT : out string) is
  FIRST, LAST : Column_numbers;
  LINE : Line_numbers;
  I : positive;
begin
  I := Field_Number(NAME);
  -- may raise ASSIGNMENT_ERROR
  FIRST := FORM.FIELD(I).FIRST_COL;
  LAST  := FORM.FIELD(I).LAST_COL;
  LINE := FORM.FIELD(I).LINE;
  TEXT(TEXT'RANGE)
    := FORM.SCREEN(LINE)(FIRST..LAST);
```

```
      -- may raise CONSTRAINT_ERROR
   end get;

   procedure put(NAME : Field_names;
                 TEXT : string) is
     FIRST, LAST : Column_numbers;
     LINE : Line_numbers;
     I : positive;
   begin
     I := Field_Number(NAME);
     -- may raise ASSIGNMENT_ERROR
     FIRST := FORM.FIELD(I).FIRST_COL;
     LAST  := FORM.FIELD(I).LAST_COL;
     LINE := FORM.FIELD(I).LINE;
     FORM.SCREEN(LINE)(FIRST..LAST) := TEXT;
     -- may raise CONSTRAINT_ERROR
   end put;

   function Confusing_Field
     return Field_names is
   begin
     return FORM.FIELD(WORKING_FIELD).NAME;
   end Confusing_Field;

   procedure Error_Recovery is separate;
      -- file FTBER.ada
      -- Helps you out if you have created/edited
      -- a form that contains a LAYOUT_ERROR.

   procedure Create is separate;
      -- file FTBC.ada

   procedure Edit is separate;
      -- file FTBE.ada

end FORM_TERMINAL;
```

```
-- Listing 27.

--                FTBGF.ada
--                Version 2.0
--                4 July 1988

--                Do-While Jones
--                324 Traci Lane
--                Ridgecrest, CA 93555
--                (619) 375-4607

-- Copyright 1989 by John Wiley & Sons, Inc.
--           All Rights Reserved.

  separate(FORM_TERMINAL)
  procedure Get_Form(A : out Actions) is
     X        : natural; -- position of character
                         -- just entered
     C        : character; -- temporary storage
     FIRST  : Column_numbers
       := FORM.FIELD(WORKING_FIELD).FIRST_COL;
     LAST   : Column_numbers
       := FORM.FIELD(WORKING_FIELD).LAST_COL;
     LINE    : Line_numbers
       := FORM.FIELD(WORKING_FIELD).LINE;
     SIZE   : constant positive
       := (LAST-FIRST)+1;
     BUFFER : string(FIRST..LAST);
     INSERT_MODE : boolean;
     DONE       : boolean;

     procedure Beep is
     begin
       VIRTUAL_TERMINAL.put(ASCII.BEL);
     end Beep;

     procedure Forward is
     begin
       if X < BUFFER'LAST then
         X := X+1;
         VIRTUAL_TERMINAL.put(BUFFER(X));
       else
         Beep;
       end if;
     end Forward;
```

```
procedure Backup is
begin
  if X >= FIRST then
    X := X - 1;
    VIRTUAL_TERMINAL.Move_Cursor_Left;
  else
    Beep;
  end if;
end Backup;

procedure Remove is
  P : positive;
begin
  P := X; -- number of characters left of
          -- the cursor
  for i in P+1..BUFFER'LAST loop
    BUFFER(i-1) := BUFFER(i);
  end loop;
  BUFFER(BUFFER'LAST) := ' ';
  Backup;
  VIRTUAL_TERMINAL.put(
    BUFFER(P..BUFFER'LAST));
  X := BUFFER'LAST;
  for i in P..BUFFER'LAST loop
    Backup;
  end loop;
end Remove;

procedure Process_Character(
    C    : character;
    DONE : out boolean) is

  procedure Add is
    P : natural;
  begin
    if X < BUFFER'LAST then
      P := X+1; -- cursor position
      for i in
          reverse P..BUFFER'LAST-1 loop
        BUFFER(i+1) := BUFFER(i);
      end loop;
      BUFFER(P) := C;
      VIRTUAL_TERMINAL.put(
        BUFFER(P..BUFFER'LAST));
      X := BUFFER'LAST;
```

```
            for i in P..BUFFER'LAST-1 loop
              Backup;
            end loop;
          else
            Beep;
          end if;
        end Add;

        procedure Rubout is
        begin
          if X >= FIRST then
            Remove;
          else
            Beep;
          end if;
        end Rubout;

        procedure Replace is
        begin
          if X < BUFFER'LAST then
            -- Note: X must be used before being
            -- incremented to avoid a bug in the
            -- Meridian version 2 code generator.
            BUFFER(X+1) := C;
            X := X+1;
            VIRTUAL_TERMINAL.put(C);
          else
            Beep;
          end if;
        end Replace;

        use VIRTUAL_TERMINAL;
          -- for INSERT, DELETE, etc.

    begin -- Process_Character
      case C is
        when ASCII.CR | TAB =>
          A := NEXT_FIELD;
          DONE := TRUE;
        when ASCII.BS =>
          Rubout;
        when INSERT =>
          INSERT_MODE := TRUE;
        when DELETE =>
```

```
            INSERT_MODE := FALSE;
            if X < BUFFER'LAST then
              Forward;
            end if;
            Remove;
          when LEFT =>
            INSERT_MODE := FALSE;
            Backup;
          when RIGHT =>
            INSERT_MODE := FALSE;
            Forward;
          when UP =>
            A := PREVIOUS_FORM;
            DONE := TRUE;
          when DOWN =>
            A := NEXT_FORM;
            DONE := TRUE;
          when BACK_TAB =>
            A := PREVIOUS_FIELD;
            DONE := TRUE;
          when ' '..'~' =>
            if C = '?' then
              raise NEEDS_HELP;
            elsif INSERT_MODE then
              Add;
            else
              Replace;
            end if;
          when others =>
            Beep;
      end case;
   end Process_Character;

   use VIRTUAL_TERMINAL;
      -- for INSERT, DELETE, etc.

begin -- Get_Form
   INSERT_MODE := FALSE;
   -- Copy the default to the BUFFER
   BUFFER := FORM.SCREEN(LINE)(FIRST..LAST);
   -- put the cursor at the beginning of the
   -- WORKING_FIELD
   VIRTUAL_TERMINAL.Move_Cursor_To(
     LINE,FIRST);
```

```
      X := FIRST-1;
      VIRTUAL_TERMINAL.get(C);
      case C is
        when INSERT | DELETE | UP | DOWN | RIGHT
           | '?' | ASCII.CR | TAB | BACK_TAB =>
          Process_Character(C, DONE);
        when others =>
          -- erase the default
          BUFFER := (others => ' ');
          VIRTUAL_TERMINAL.put(BUFFER);
          X := BUFFER'LAST;
          for i in BUFFER'RANGE loop
            Backup;
          end loop;
          Process_Character(C, DONE);
      end case;
      while not DONE loop
        VIRTUAL_TERMINAL.get(C);
        Process_Character(C, DONE);
      end loop;
      FORM.SCREEN(LINE)(FIRST..LAST) := BUFFER;
   end Get_Form;
```

```
-- Listing 28.

--              FTBRW.ada
--              Version 2.0
--              19 September 1988

--              Do-While Jones
--              324 Traci Lane
--              Ridgecrest, CA 93555
--              (619) 375-4607

--  Copyright 1989 by John Wiley & Sons, Inc.
--         All Rights Reserved.

-- This file contains two subunits. The first
-- one Reads a FORM from a file and puts it in
-- the FORM_TERMINAL. The second subunit Writes
-- the current FORM in the FORM_TERMINAL to an
-- external file.

-------------------------------------------------

--              READ a FORM

with TEXT_IO, ASCII_UTILITIES;
separate (FORM_TERMINAL)
procedure Read(FILENAME : string) is
  INPUT          : TEXT_IO.File_type;
  TEXT           : Lines;
  LENGTH         : natural;
  FIELDS_STORED  : natural;

    function Stored_Form(SIZE : positive)
        return Forms is
      TEMP         : Forms(SIZE);
      LINE         : Line_numbers;
      FIRST, LAST  : Column_numbers;
    begin
      -- Start with a blank form.
      TEMP.SCREEN
        := (others => (others => ' '));

      for i in 1..SIZE loop

        -- Read header.
```

```
        TEXT_IO.get_line(INPUT,TEXT,LENGTH);
        if TEXT(1..10) /= "-- data --" then
          raise READ_ERROR;
        end if;

        -- Read the next field name.
        TEXT_IO.get_line(INPUT,TEXT,LENGTH);
        TEMP.FIELD(i).NAME
          := ASCII_UTILITIES.Upper_Case(
             TEXT(1..LENGTH));

        -- Find out what line it goes on.
        TEXT_IO.get_line(INPUT,TEXT,LENGTH);
        LINE := integer'VALUE(TEXT(1..LENGTH));
        TEMP.FIELD(i).LINE := LINE;

        -- Find out where it starts.
        TEXT_IO.get_line(INPUT,TEXT,LENGTH);
        FIRST := integer'VALUE(
          TEXT(1..LENGTH));
        TEMP.FIELD(i).FIRST_COL := FIRST;

        -- Find out where it stops.
        TEXT_IO.get_line(INPUT,TEXT,LENGTH);
        LAST := integer'VALUE(TEXT(1..LENGTH));
        TEMP.FIELD(i).LAST_COL := LAST;

        -- Is it protected?
        TEXT_IO.get_line(INPUT,TEXT,LENGTH);
        TEMP.FIELD(i).PROTECTED
          := 'P' = TEXT(1);

        -- Fill it with data from the file.
        -- (Maybe all blanks.)
        TEXT_IO.get_line(INPUT,TEXT,LENGTH);
        TEMP.SCREEN(LINE)(FIRST..LAST)
          := TEXT(1..LENGTH);
      end loop;
      return TEMP;
    end Stored_Form;

  begin
    -- Open the input file.
    TEXT_IO.Open(INPUT,TEXT_IO.IN_FILE,FILENAME);
    -- Find out how many fields are in the form.
```

```
      TEXT_IO.get_line(INPUT,TEXT,LENGTH);
      FIELDS_STORED := integer'VALUE(
        TEXT(1..LENGTH));
      -- Read a form that size from the file.
      FORM := Stored_Form(SIZE => FIELDS_STORED);
      -- Close the input file.
      TEXT_IO.Close(INPUT);
      Check_Form; -- May raise LAYOUT_ERROR
   exception
      when LAYOUT_ERROR =>
        raise; -- propagate it
      when TEXT_IO.END_ERROR | CONSTRAINT_ERROR =>
        -- END_ERROR could be generated by
        -- get_line. CONSTRAINT_ERROR could be
        -- raised by get_line, integer'VALUE, or
        -- assignment to NAME or TEXT.
        TEXT_IO.Close(INPUT);
        raise READ_ERROR;
      when others =>
        -- NAME_ERROR, USE_ERROR, STATUS_ERROR
        -- on Open.
        raise READ_ERROR;
   end Read;


   -------------------------------------------------


   --                  WRITE a FORM

   with TEXT_IO, ASCII_UTILITIES;
   separate (FORM_TERMINAL)
   procedure Write(FILENAME : string) is
      OUTPUT       : TEXT_IO.File_type;
      TEXT         : Lines;
      LENGTH       : natural;
      LINE         : Line_numbers;
      FIRST, LAST : Column_numbers;
   begin
      TEXT_IO.Create(
        OUTPUT,TEXT_IO.OUT_FILE,FILENAME);
      -- Write the number of fields in the form.
      TEXT_IO.put_line(OUTPUT,
        integer'IMAGE(FORM.FIELDS));
      -- Write each field to the file.
      for i in 1..FORM.FIELDS loop
        -- (LINE, FIRST, and LAST just rename
```

```
       -- components to make the put_line
       -- statements shorter.)
       LINE  := FORM.FIELD(i).LINE;
       FIRST := FORM.FIELD(i).FIRST_COL;
       LAST  := FORM.FIELD(i).LAST_COL;

       TEXT_IO.put_line(OUTPUT,
         "-- data --");
       TEXT_IO.put_line(OUTPUT,
         ASCII_UTILITIES.Upper_Case
           (FORM.FIELD(i).NAME));
       TEXT_IO.put_line(OUTPUT,
         integer'IMAGE(LINE));
       TEXT_IO.put_line(OUTPUT,
          integer'IMAGE(FIRST));
       TEXT_IO.put_line(OUTPUT,
         integer'IMAGE(LAST));
       if FORM.FIELD(i).PROTECTED then
         TEXT_IO.put_line(OUTPUT,"P");
       else
         TEXT_IO.put_line(OUTPUT,"U");
       end if;
       -- Write data in the field.
       TEXT_IO.put_line(OUTPUT,
         FORM.SCREEN(LINE)(FIRST..LAST));
     end loop;
     -- Close the output file.
     TEXT_IO.Close(OUTPUT);
exception
  when others =>
     raise WRITE_ERROR;
end Write;
```

```
-- Listing 29.

--              FTBD.ada
--              Version 2.0
--              3 July 1988

--              Do-While Jones
--              324 Traci Lane
--              Ridgecrest, CA 93555
--              (619) 375-4607

-- Copyright 1989 by John Wiley & Sons, Inc.
--         All Rights Reserved.

separate(FORM_TERMINAL)
procedure Display(WAIT : boolean := FALSE) is
  CRLF : constant string
    := ASCII.CR & ASCII.LF;

  procedure Wait_For_User is
    IGNORED_CHARACTER : character;

    procedure Flush_Input is
      IGNORED_CHARACTER : character;
    begin
      while VIRTUAL_TERMINAL.
          Keyboard_Data_Available loop
        VIRTUAL_TERMINAL.get(
          IGNORED_CHARACTER);
      end loop;
    end Flush_Input;

  begin
    VIRTUAL_TERMINAL.Move_Cursor_To(
      LINE => Line_numbers'LAST,
      COL  => Column_numbers'FIRST);
    VIRTUAL_TERMINAL.Move_Cursor_Down;
    VIRTUAL_TERMINAL.put(
      "Press Any Key To Continue");
    Flush_Input;
    VIRTUAL_TERMINAL.get(IGNORED_CHARACTER);
  end Wait_For_User;

begin
  VIRTUAL_TERMINAL.Clear_Screen;
```

```
      for i in Line_numbers loop
        VIRTUAL_TERMINAL.put(FORM.SCREEN(i)
          & CRLF);
      end loop;
      if WAIT then
        Wait_For_User;
      end if;
   end Display;
```

```
-- Listing 30.

--                    FTBU.ada
--                    Version 2.0
--                    19 September 1988

--                    Do-While Jones
--                    324 Traci Lane
--                    Ridgecrest, CA 93555
--                    (619) 375-4607

--  Copyright 1989 by John Wiley & Sons, Inc.
--          All Rights Reserved.

separate(FORM_TERMINAL)
procedure Update(CURSOR_AT : Field_names;
                 NEXT       : out boolean) is
  ACTION : Actions;
  DONE : boolean;

  procedure Next_Unprotected_Field(
    DONE : out boolean) is
  begin
    if WORKING_FIELD < FORM.FIELDS then
      WORKING_FIELD := WORKING_FIELD + 1;
      if FORM.FIELD(WORKING_FIELD).PROTECTED
          then
        Next_Unprotected_Field(DONE);
      else
        DONE := FALSE;
      end if;
    else
      NEXT := TRUE;
      DONE := TRUE;
    end if;
  end Next_Unprotected_Field;

  procedure Previous_Unprotected_Field(
    DONE : out boolean) is
  begin
    if WORKING_FIELD > 1 then
      WORKING_FIELD := WORKING_FIELD - 1;
      if FORM.FIELD(WORKING_FIELD).PROTECTED
          then
```

```
          Previous_Unprotected_Field(DONE);
        else
          DONE := FALSE;
        end if;
      else
        NEXT := FALSE;
        DONE := TRUE;
     end if;
   end Previous_Unprotected_Field;

begin
  Display(FALSE);
  DONE := FALSE;
  WORKING_FIELD := Field_Number(CURSOR_AT);
  if FORM.FIELD(WORKING_FIELD).PROTECTED then
    Next_Unprotected_Field(DONE);
  end if;
  while not DONE loop
    Get_Form(ACTION);
    case ACTION is
      when NEXT_FIELD =>
        Next_Unprotected_Field(DONE);
      when PREVIOUS_FIELD =>
        Previous_Unprotected_Field(DONE);
      when NEXT_FORM =>
        NEXT := TRUE;
        DONE := TRUE;
      when PREVIOUS_FORM =>
        NEXT := FALSE;
        DONE := TRUE;
    end case;
  end loop;
end Update;
```

```
-- Listing 31.

--                FTBC.ada
--                Version 2.1
--                19 September 1988

--                Do-While Jones
--                324 Traci Lane
--                Ridgecrest, CA 93555
--                (619) 375-4607

-- Copyright 1989 by John Wiley & Sons, Inc.
--         All Rights Reserved.

with SCROLL_TERMINAL;
separate(FORM_TERMINAL)
procedure Create is

  TEXT   : string(1..80);
  LENGTH : natural;

  type Form_specs is
    record
      SIZE   : positive;
      SCREEN : Screens;
      FIELD  : Field_arrays(1..MAX_FIELDS);
    end record;

  DATA : Form_specs;

  function User_Wants_Instructions
      return boolean is
    use SCROLL_TERMINAL;
    RESPONSE : character;
  begin
    get("Do you need instructions? (Y/N) ",
      'N', RESPONSE);
    case RESPONSE is
      when 'Y' | 'y' =>
        return TRUE;
      when 'N' | 'n' =>
        return FALSE;
      when others =>
        raise NEEDS_HELP;
```

```
      end case;
   exception
     when NEEDS_HELP =>
       put_line("Do you want me to tell you"
             & " how to create a form?");
       put_line("Please answer Yes or No.");
       new_line;
       return User_Wants_Instructions;
   end User_Wants_Instructions;

   procedure Instructions is separate;
   -- file FTBCI.ada

   procedure Get_Field(DATA : in out Form_specs)
     is separate;
     -- file FTBCGF.ada

   function New_Form(DATA : Form_specs)
       return Forms is
     FORM : Forms(DATA.SIZE);
   begin
     FORM.SCREEN := DATA.SCREEN;
     for i in 1..DATA.SIZE loop
       FORM.FIELD(i) := DATA.FIELD(i);
     end loop;
     return FORM;
   end New_Form;

begin
  -- Sign-on message.
  SCROLL_TERMINAL.new_line;
  SCROLL_TERMINAL.put_line(
    "Ready for you to create a new form.");
  SCROLL_TERMINAL.new_line;

  if User_Wants_Instructions then
    Instructions;
    SCROLL_TERMINAL.Wait_For_User;
  end if;

  -- Let the user enter the new form.
  Get_Field(DATA);
  FORM := New_Form(DATA);
```

```
   Check_Form;  -- may raise LAYOUT_ERROR

   SCROLL_TERMINAL.put_line("Form Created.");
exception
  when LAYOUT_ERROR =>
    Error_Recovery;
end Create;
```

```
-- Listing 32.

--                  FTBCI.ada
--                  Version 2.1
--                  8 July 1988

--                  Do-While Jones
--                  324 Traci Lane
--                  Ridgecrest, CA 93555
--                  (619) 375-4607

-- Copyright 1989 by John Wiley & Sons, Inc.
--         All Rights Reserved.

separate(FORM_TERMINAL.Create)
procedure Instructions is
  use SCROLL_TERMINAL;
begin
  New_Page;
  put_line("You will be shown a screen filled"
          & " with ""~"" characters.");
  put_line("(The ""~"" characters are just" &
         " there to help you count spaces.)");
  put_line("Use the cursor keys to place" &
          " prompts and default responses");
  put_line("wherever you want them.");
  new_line;
  put_line("When the form looks right, place" &
          " the cursor on the first");
  put_line("character of the first field. If" &
          " this is to be a protected");
  put_line("field (that is, a prompt which the"
         & " user can't modify), then");
  put_line("press F1. If this is to be an" &
          " unprotected field (a default or");
  put_line("blank field which the user is" &
          " expected to modify), then");
  put_line("press F2. Use the RIGHT ARROW" &
          " key to move the cursor to the");
  put_line("last character in the first field."
        & " Mark the end of the field");
  put_line("with F3.");
  new_line;
  put_line("You will then be asked to give" &
          " this field a unique name.");
```

```
      put_line("This name is required for the" &
              " application program to get");
      put_line("and put data to this field.");
      new_line;
      put_line("Repeat this process until all the"
            & " fields have been defined.");
      put_line("Then press F10 to store the form" &
              " in a disk file.");
      Wait_For_User;

      New_Page;
      put_line("If you need HELP at any time," &
              " press the '?' key.");
      new_line;
      put_line("If you want to enter the '?'" &
              " character, use the ESC key.");
      new_line;
      put_line(
        "Press CONTROL-C to abort an operation.");
   end Instructions;
```

```
-- Listing 33.

--              FTBCGF.ada
--              Version 2.1
--              10 July 1988

--              Do-While Jones
--              324 Traci Lane
--              Ridgecrest, CA 93555
--              (619) 375-4607

-- Copyright 1989 by John Wiley & Sons, Inc.
--          All Rights Reserved.

  separate(FORM_TERMINAL.Create)
  procedure Get_Field(DATA : in out Form_specs)
       is

    ROW  : FORM_TERMINAL.Line_numbers;
    COL  : FORM_TERMINAL.Column_numbers;
    i    : natural;
    DONE : boolean;

    procedure Refresh_Screen is
    begin
      VIRTUAL_TERMINAL.Clear_Screen;
      for i in FORM_TERMINAL.Line_numbers loop
        VIRTUAL_TERMINAL.put(DATA.SCREEN(i)
          & ASCII.CR & ASCII.LF);
      end loop;
    end Refresh_Screen;

    function Name_Of_Field
     return FORM_TERMINAL.Field_Names is
      NAME : FORM_TERMINAL.Field_names;
    begin
      VIRTUAL_TERMINAL.Move_Cursor_TO(
        FORM_TERMINAL.Line_numbers'LAST+1,1);
      NAME := (others => ' '); -- blank default
      SCROLL_TERMINAL.get("Field Name: ",
        NAME,NAME);
      VIRTUAL_TERMINAL.Move_Cursor_To(ROW,COL);
      return ASCII_UTILITIES.Upper_Case(NAME);
    exception
```

```
      when SCROLL_TERMINAL.NEEDS_HELP =>
        SCROLL_TERMINAL.New_Page;
        SCROLL_TERMINAL.put_line(
            "You need to give every field"
          & " a unique name.");
        SCROLL_TERMINAL.put_line(
            "The name can be 20 characters"
          & " long, and may");
        SCROLL_TERMINAL.put_line(
            "include significant blanks and"
          & " underscores,");
        SCROLL_TERMINAL.put_line(
            "but may not include non-printable"
          & " characters.");
        SCROLL_TERMINAL.new_line;
        SCROLL_TERMINAL.Wait_For_User;
        Refresh_Screen;
        return Name_Of_Field;
   end Name_Of_Field;


   -- find the end of the field
   function End_Of_Field
        return FORM_TERMINAL.Column_numbers is
     X   : FORM_TERMINAL.Column_numbers;
     C   : character;
     KEY : positive;
     use VIRTUAL_TERMINAL;
   begin
     -- Let the user move the cursor left or
     -- right until it is on top of the last
     -- character in the field. When the
     -- cursor is in the correct place, the
     -- user presses function key F3. Return
     -- the column number of the cursor when
     -- that happens.
     loop
       get(C);
       case C is
         when CTRL_R | ' ' =>
           if COL < FORM_TERMINAL.
               Column_numbers'LAST then
             COL := COL + 1;
             Move_Cursor_Right;
           else
```

```
               put(ASCII.BEL);
             end if;
         when CTRL_L | ASCII.BS =>
           if COL > FORM_TERMINAL.
               Column_numbers'FIRST then
               COL := COL - 1;
               Move_Cursor_Left;
             else
               put(ASCII.BEL);
             end if;
         when FUN_KEY =>
           if Function_Key = 3 then
               X := COL;
               exit;
             else
               put(ASCII.BEL);
             end if;
         when '?' =>
           raise NEEDS_HELP;
         when others =>
           put(ASCII.BEL);
       end case;
    end loop;
    return X;
end End_Of_Field;

procedure Protect_Field(
  PROTECTION : boolean) is separate;
  -- file FTBCGFP.ada
  -- This procedure saves the name,
  -- location, and protection of the
  -- designated field in DATA.FIELD(i).

procedure Process_Keystrokes(
    DONE : out boolean) is
  C   : character;
  KEY : positive;
  use VIRTUAL_TERMINAL;
begin
  -- Let the user doodle on the screen
  -- until the form looks right. When the
  -- user presses function key F1 or F2, it
  -- marks the beginning of a protected or
  -- unprotected field. When the user
  -- presses F10 it means he is done.
```

```
DONE := FALSE;
get(C);
case C is
  when CTRL_R =>
    if COL < FORM_TERMINAL.
        Column_numbers'LAST then
      COL := COL + 1;
      Move_Cursor_Right;
    else
      put(ASCII.BEL);
    end if;
  when CTRL_L | ASCII.BS =>
    if COL > FORM_TERMINAL.
        Column_numbers'FIRST then
      COL := COL - 1;
      Move_Cursor_Left;
    else
      put(ASCII.BEL);
    end if;
  when CTRL_D | ASCII.LF =>
    if ROW < FORM_TERMINAL.
        Line_numbers'LAST then
      ROW := ROW + 1;
      Move_Cursor_Down;
    else
      put(ASCII.BEL);
    end if;
  when CTRL_U =>
    if ROW > FORM_TERMINAL.
        Line_numbers'FIRST then
      ROW := ROW - 1;
      Move_Cursor_Up;
    else
      put(ASCII.BEL);
    end if;
  when ASCII.CR =>
    while
     COL > FORM_TERMINAL.
        Column_numbers'FIRST loop
      Move_Cursor_Left;
      COL := COL - 1;
    end loop;
  when FUN_KEY =>
    KEY := Function_Key;
    case KEY is
```

```
            when 1 =>
              Protect_Field(TRUE);
            when 2 =>
              Protect_Field(FALSE);
            when 10 =>
              DONE := TRUE;
            when others =>
              put(ASCII.BEL);
          end case;
        when ' '..'~' =>
          if C = '?' then
            Instructions;
            SCROLL_TERMINAL.Wait_For_User;
            Refresh_Screen;
            Move_Cursor_To(ROW,COL);
          else
            put(C);
            DATA.SCREEN(ROW)(COL) := C;
            if COL < FORM_TERMINAL.
                Column_numbers'LAST then
              COL := COL + 1;
            else -- stick in last column
              Move_Cursor_Left;
            end if;
          end if;
        when ASCII.ESC =>
          -- ESCAPE is used as question mark
          put('?');
          DATA.SCREEN(ROW)(COL) := '?';
          if COL < FORM_TERMINAL.
              Column_numbers'LAST then
            COL := COL + 1;
          else
            Move_Cursor_Left;
          end if;
        when others =>
          put(ASCII.BEL);
      end case;
  end Process_Keystrokes;

begin
  -- Put wiggles all over the screen.
  DATA.SCREEN := (others => (others => '~'));
  Refresh_Screen;
```

```
      i := 0; -- an index used to keep track
              -- of the field number

      -- Move the cursor to the top left corner.
      ROW := 1;
      COL := 1;
      VIRTUAL_TERMINAL.Move_Cursor_To(ROW,COL);

      -- Let the user draw the form.
      DONE := FALSE;
      while not DONE loop
        -- Put data in DATA.FIELD(i).
        Process_Keystrokes(DONE);
      end loop;

      DATA.SIZE := i;

      -- Move the cursor out of the way.
      VIRTUAL_TERMINAL.Move_Cursor_To
        (FORM_TERMINAL.Line_numbers'LAST+1,1);
      SCROLL_TERMINAL.new_line;
  end Get_Field;
```

```
-- Listing 34.

--                 FTBCGFP.ada
--                 Version 2.1
--                 10 July 1988

--                 Do-While Jones
--                 324 Traci Lane
--                 Ridgecrest, CA 93555
--                 (619) 375-4607

--  Copyright 1989 by John Wiley & Sons, Inc.
--         All Rights Reserved.

separate(FORM_TERMINAL.Create.Get_Field)
procedure Protect_Field(PROTECTION : boolean)
    is
  FIELD_NAME   : Field_names;
  FIRST, LAST : Column_numbers;
begin
  FIRST := COL;
  LAST := End_Of_Field;
  i := i+1;
  FIELD_NAME := Name_Of_Field;
  DATA.FIELD(i) := (
    NAME => FIELD_NAME,
    LINE => ROW,
    FIRST_COL => FIRST,
    LAST_COL => LAST,
    PROTECTED => PROTECTION);
exception
  when VIRTUAL_TERMINAL.PANIC =>
    SCROLL_TERMINAL.New_Page;
    SCROLL_TERMINAL.put_line(
        "All the data you have entered about"
      & " this field");
    SCROLL_TERMINAL.put_line(
        "has been IGNORED at your request.");
    SCROLL_TERMINAL.new_line;
    if i > 0 then
      SCROLL_TERMINAL.put_line(
        "The fields that have been defined so"
      & " far are:");
      for j in 1..i loop
        SCROLL_TERMINAL.put_line
```

```
                (DATA.FIELD(j).NAME);
        end loop;
        SCROLL_TERMINAL.new_line;
      end if;
      SCROLL_TERMINAL.Wait_For_User;
      Refresh_Screen;
      VIRTUAL_TERMINAL.Move_Cursor_To(ROW,COL);
    when NEEDS_HELP =>
      Instructions;
      if i > 0 then
        SCROLL_TERMINAL.put_line(
            "We need to start over with this"
          & " field.");
        SCROLL_TERMINAL.put_line(
            "The fields that have been defined"
          & " so far are:");
        for j in 1..i loop
          SCROLL_TERMINAL.put_line
            (DATA.FIELD(j).NAME);
        end loop;
        SCROLL_TERMINAL.new_line;
      end if;
      SCROLL_TERMINAL.Wait_For_User;
      Refresh_Screen;
      VIRTUAL_TERMINAL.Move_Cursor_To(ROW,FIRST);
      Protect_Field(PROTECTION);
  end Protect_Field;
```

```
-- Listing 35.

--                FTBE.ada
--                Version 2.1
--                19 September 1988

--                Do-While Jones
--                324 Traci Lane
--                Ridgecrest, CA 93555
--                (619) 375-4607

-- Copyright 1989 by John Wiley & Sons, Inc.
--            All Rights Reserved.

with SCROLL_TERMINAL;
separate(FORM_TERMINAL)
procedure Edit is

  type Commands is (PREVIOUS_20, NEXT_20,
    CHANGE, INSERT, DELETE, MOVE, QUIT);

  COMMAND   : Commands;
  POINTER   : positive;
  TOP_FIELD : integer;

  type Form_specs is
    record
      SIZE   : positive;
      SCREEN : Screens;
      FIELD  : Field_arrays(1..MAX_FIELDS);
    end record;

  DATA : Form_specs;

  function User_Wants_Instructions
      return boolean is
    use SCROLL_TERMINAL;
    RESPONSE : character;
  begin
    get("Do you need instructions? (Y/N) ",
      'N', RESPONSE);
    case RESPONSE is
      when 'Y' | 'y' =>
        return TRUE;
```

```
            when 'N' | 'n' =>
              return FALSE;
        ,   when others =>
              raise NEEDS_HELP;
        end case;
exception
  when NEEDS_HELP =>
    put_line(
        "Do you want me to tell you how to"
      & " edit a form?");
    put_line("Please answer Yes or No.");
    new_line;
    return User_Wants_Instructions;
end User_Wants_Instructions;

procedure Edit_Instructions is separate;
  -- file FTBEI.ada

procedure Edit_Fields(INDEX   : positive;
                      COMMAND : out Commands;
                      POINTER : out positive)
  is separate;
  -- file FTBEF.ada

procedure Change_Field(POINTER : positive)
  is separate;
  -- file FTBECF.ada

procedure Insert_Field(POINTER : positive)
  is separate;
  -- file FTBEIF.ada

procedure Delete_Field(POINTER : positive)
  is separate;
  -- file FTBEDF.ada

procedure Move_Field(POINTER : positive)
  is separate;
  -- file FTBEMF.ada

procedure Edit_At(TOP_FIELD : in out integer)
  is
begin
  loop
```

```
      Edit_Fields(TOP_FIELD,COMMAND,POINTER);
      case COMMAND is
        when PREVIOUS_20 =>
          TOP_FIELD := TOP_FIELD - 20;
          If TOP_FIELD < 1 then
            TOP_FIELD := 1;
          end if;
        when NEXT_20 =>
          TOP_FIELD := TOP_FIELD + 20;
          if TOP_FIELD > DATA.SIZE - 19 then
            TOP_FIELD := DATA.SIZE - 19;
            if TOP_FIELD < 1 then
              TOP_FIELD := 1;
            end if;
          end if;
        when CHANGE =>
          Change_Field(POINTER);
        when INSERT =>
          Insert_Field(POINTER);
        when DELETE =>
          Delete_Field(POINTER);
        when MOVE =>
          Move_Field(POINTER);
        when QUIT =>
          exit;
      end case;
    end loop;
exception
  when NEEDS_HELP =>
    Edit_Instructions;
    SCROLL_TERMINAL.Wait_For_User;
    Edit_At(TOP_FIELD);
end Edit_At;

function New_Form(DATA : Form_specs)
    return Forms is
  FORM : Forms(DATA.SIZE);
begin
  FORM.SCREEN := DATA.SCREEN;
  for i in 1..DATA.SIZE loop
    FORM.FIELD(i) := DATA.FIELD(i);
  end loop;
  return FORM;
end New_Form;
```

```
begin
  -- Sign-on message.
  Display;
  SCROLL_TERMINAL.new_line;

  if User_Wants_Instructions then
    Edit_Instructions;
    SCROLL_TERMINAL.Wait_For_User;
  end if;

  -- copy form to DATA workspace
  DATA.SIZE := FORM.FIELDS;
  DATA.SCREEN := FORM.SCREEN;
  for i in 1..FORM.FIELDS loop
    DATA.FIELD(i) := FORM.FIELD(i);
  end loop;
  -- set index to first field and edit it
  TOP_FIELD := 1;
  Edit_At(TOP_FIELD);
  -- copy workspace DATA to the FORM
  FORM := New_Form(DATA);

  Check_Form; -- may raise LAYOUT_ERROR

exception
  when LAYOUT_ERROR =>
    Error_Recovery;
end Edit;
```

```
-- Listing 36.

--                  FTBEI.ada
--                  Version 2.1
--                  16 September 1988

--                  Do-While Jones
--                  324 Traci Lane
--                  Ridgecrest, CA 93555
--                  (619) 375-4607

--  Copyright 1989 by John Wiley & Sons, Inc.
--          All Rights Reserved.

separate(FORM_TERMINAL.Edit)
procedure Edit_Instructions is
  use SCROLL_TERMINAL;
begin
  New_Page;
  put_line("You will be shown a list" &
          " of fields in this form:");
  new_line;
  put_line("Beginning of text in the field"
          & " ------------+");
  put_line("Last Column Number -----------"
          & "------+        |");
  put_line("First Column Number ----------"
          & "---+   |        |");
  put_line("Line Number-------------------"
          & "+  |   |        |");
  put_line("Protected/Unprotected -----+  "
          & "|  |   |        |");
  put_line("Field Name ---+            |  "
          & "|  |   |        |");
  put_line("              |            |  "
          & "|  |   |        |");
  put_line("     +--------+--------+" &
          "  |  |   |  | +-----+-----+");
  put_line("     |                 |" &
          "  |  |  |  | |            |");
  put_line("    xx 20  characters xx" &
          "   x NN NN NN xx 44 char xx");
  new_line(2);
```

```
      put_line("Use the UP and DOWN arrow" &
              " keys to move the cursor next to");
      put_line("the field you want to edit." &
              " (If there are more than 20");
      put_line("fields on the form, you can "
              & "scroll off the bottom or top");
      put_line("of the list to get to the"
              & " one you want.)");
      new_line;
      Wait_For_User;
      New_Page;
      put_line("Your choices are:");
      new_line;
      put_line("      A        =     Insert a" &
              " new field AFTER this one.");
      put_line("      B        =     Insert a" &
              " new field BEFORE this one.");
      put_line("      C        =     CHANGE" &
              " something in this field.");
      put_line("      D        =     DELETE" &
              " this field.");
      put_line("      M        =     MOVE this" &
              " field someplace else.");
      new_line;
      put_line("    UP         =     Move the cursor"
              & " UP to the previous field.");
      put_line("    DOWN       =     Move the cursor"
              & " DOWN to the next field.");
      put_line("    F10        =     Done editing.");
      new_line;
   end Edit_Instructions;
```

```
-- Listing 37.

--              FTBEF.ada
--              Version 2.1
--              19 September 1988

--              Do-While Jones
--              324 Traci Lane
--              Ridgecrest, CA 93555
--              (619) 375-4607

-- Copyright 1989 by John Wiley & Sons, Inc.
--          All Rights Reserved.

separate(FORM_TERMINAL.Edit)
procedure Edit_Fields(INDEX   : positive;
                      COMMAND : out Commands;
                      POINTER : out positive)
    is
  LINE         : FORM_TERMINAL.Line_numbers;
  FIRST, LAST  : FORM_TERMINAL.Column_numbers;
  TEXT         : string(1..44);

  procedure Get_Changes(COMMAND : out Commands;
                        POINTER : out positive)
    is separate;
    -- file FTBEFG.ada

  use ASCII_UTILITIES;
begin
  SCROLL_TERMINAL.New_Page;
  for i in INDEX..INDEX+19 loop
    exit when i > DATA.SIZE;
    -- if SIZE < INDEX+19

    -- rename LINE, FIRST, and LAST
    -- to keep statements short
    LINE  := DATA.FIELD(i).LINE;
    FIRST := DATA.FIELD(i).FIRST_COL;
    LAST  := DATA.FIELD(i).LAST_COL;
    -- show field name
    SCROLL_TERMINAL.Set_Col(3);
    SCROLL_TERMINAL.put(DATA.FIELD(i).NAME);
    -- show protection
```

```
      SCROLL_TERMINAL.Set_Col(24);
      if DATA.FIELD(i).PROTECTED then
        SCROLL_TERMINAL.put('P');
      else
        SCROLL_TERMINAL.put('U');
      end if;
      -- show line
      SCROLL_TERMINAL.Set_Col(26);
      SCROLL_TERMINAL.put
        (string'(Image(LINE,2)));
      -- show first column
      SCROLL_TERMINAL.Set_Col(29);
      SCROLL_TERMINAL.put
        (string'(Image(FIRST,2)));
      -- show last column
      SCROLL_TERMINAL.Set_Col(32);
      SCROLL_TERMINAL.put
        (string'(Image(LAST,2)));
      -- show first 44 characters of TEXT
      SCROLL_TERMINAL.Set_Col(35);
      String_Copy(
        FROM => DATA.SCREEN(LINE)(FIRST..LAST),
        TO => TEXT);
      SCROLL_TERMINAL.put_line(TEXT);
    end loop;
    VIRTUAL_TERMINAL.Move_Cursor_To(1,1);
    Get_Changes(COMMAND,POINTER);
  end Edit_Fields;
```

```
-- Listing 38.

--              FTBEFG.ada
--              Version 2.1
--              16 September 1988

--              Do-While Jones
--              324 Traci Lane
--              Ridgecrest, CA 93555
--              (619) 375-4607


--   Copyright 1989 by John Wiley & Sons, Inc.
--            All Rights Reserved.

separate(FORM_TERMINAL.Edit.Edit_Fields)
procedure Get_Changes(COMMAND : out Commands;
                      POINTER : out positive)
    is
  ROW : FORM_TERMINAL.Line_numbers;
  C : character;
begin
  ROW := 1;
  POINTER := 1; -- to avoid random
                -- CONSTRAINT_ERRORs
  loop
    VIRTUAL_TERMINAL.get(C);
    case C is
      when VIRTUAL_TERMINAL.UP =>
        if ROW > 1 then
          VIRTUAL_TERMINAL.Move_Cursor_Up;
          ROW := ROW - 1;
        else
          if INDEX = 1 then
            VIRTUAL_TERMINAL.put(ASCII.BEL);
          else
            COMMAND := PREVIOUS_20;
            return;
          end if;
        end if;
      when VIRTUAL_TERMINAL.DOWN =>
        if INDEX + ROW - 1 < DATA.SIZE then
          if ROW < 20 then
            VIRTUAL_TERMINAL.Move_Cursor_Down;
            ROW := ROW + 1;
          else
```

```
                   COMMAND := NEXT_20;
                   return;
                 end if;
               else
                 VIRTUAL_TERMINAL.put(ASCII.BEL);
               end if;
           when VIRTUAL_TERMINAL.FUN_KEY =>
               if VIRTUAL_TERMINAL.Function_Key
                   = 10 then
                 COMMAND := QUIT;
                 return;
               else
                 VIRTUAL_TERMINAL.put(ASCII.BEL);
               end if;
           when 'C' | 'c' =>
               POINTER := INDEX + ROW - 1;
               COMMAND := CHANGE;
               return;
           when 'B' | 'b' =>
               -- insert BEFORE this field
               POINTER := INDEX + ROW - 1;
               COMMAND := INSERT;
               return;
           when 'A' | 'a' =>
               -- insert AFTER this field
               POINTER := INDEX + ROW;
               COMMAND := INSERT;
               return;
           when 'D' | 'd' =>
               POINTER := INDEX + ROW - 1;
               COMMAND := DELETE;
               return;
           when 'M' | 'm' =>
               POINTER := INDEX + ROW - 1;
               COMMAND := MOVE;
               return;
           when '?' =>
               raise NEEDS_HELP;
           when others =>
               VIRTUAL_TERMINAL.put(ASCII.BEL);
       end case;
   end loop;
end Get_Changes;
```

```ada
-- Listing 39.

--              FTBECF.ada
--              Version 2.1
--              2 November 1988

--              Do-While Jones
--              324 Traci Lane
--              Ridgecrest, CA 93555
--              (619) 375-4607

-- Copyright 1989 by John Wiley & Sons, Inc.
--         All Rights Reserved.

separate(FORM_TERMINAL.Edit)
procedure Change_Field(POINTER : positive) is

  use SCROLL_TERMINAL, ASCII_UTILITIES;

  procedure Change_Name is
  begin
    get("Field Name: ",
        DATA.FIELD(POINTER).NAME,
        DATA.FIELD(POINTER).NAME);
  end Change_Name;

  procedure Change_Line is
    X : string(1..2);
  begin
    X := Image(DATA.FIELD(POINTER).LINE,2);
    get("Line: ", X, X);
    DATA.FIELD(POINTER).LINE
      := integer'VALUE(X);
  end Change_Line;

  procedure Change_First is
    X : string(1..2);
  begin
    X := Image(
      DATA.FIELD(POINTER).FIRST_COL,2);
    get("First Column: ", X, X);
    DATA.FIELD(POINTER).FIRST_COL
      := integer'VALUE(X);
  end Change_First;
```

```
procedure Change_Last is
  X : string(1..2);
begin
  X := Image(DATA.FIELD(POINTER).LAST_COL,2);
  get("Last Column: ", X, X);
  DATA.FIELD(POINTER).LAST_COL
    := integer'VALUE(X);
end Change_Last;

procedure Change_Protection is
  C : character;
begin
  if DATA.FIELD(POINTER).PROTECTED then
    C := 'Y';
  else
    C := 'N';
  end if;
  get("Is this field protected? (Y/N) ",
    C, C);
  new_line;
  case C is
    when 'Y' | 'y' =>
      DATA.FIELD(POINTER).PROTECTED := TRUE;
    when 'N' | 'n' =>
      DATA.FIELD(POINTER).PROTECTED := FALSE;
    when others =>
      raise NEEDS_HELP;
  end case;
end Change_Protection;

procedure Change_Text(
    LINE, FIRST, LAST : positive) is
  TEXT : string(FIRST..LAST);
begin
  TEXT(FIRST..LAST) :=
    DATA.SCREEN(LINE)(FIRST..LAST);
  put_line("Text:");
  get("",TEXT,TEXT);
  DATA.SCREEN(LINE)(FIRST..LAST) := TEXT;
end Change_Text;

begin
  New_Page;
```

```
    Change_Name;
    Change_Line;
    Change_First;
    Change_Last;
    Change_Protection;
    Change_Text(
      DATA.FIELD(POINTER).LINE,
      DATA.FIELD(POINTER).FIRST_COL,
      DATA.FIELD(POINTER).LAST_COL);

  end Change_Field;
```

```
-- Listing 40.

--                FTBEIF.ada
--                Version 2.1
--                12 August 1988

--                Do-While Jones
--                324 Traci Lane
--                Ridgecrest, CA 93555
--                (619) 375-4607

-- Copyright 1989 by John Wiley & Sons, Inc.
--          All Rights Reserved.

separate(FORM_TERMINAL.Edit)
procedure Insert_Field(POINTER : positive) is

   use SCROLL_TERMINAL, ASCII_UTILITIES;

   procedure Insert_Name is
   begin
      SCROLL_TERMINAL.get("Field Name: ",
          DATA.FIELD(POINTER).NAME);
   end Insert_Name;

   procedure Insert_Line is
      X : string(1..2);
   begin
      SCROLL_TERMINAL.get("Line: ", X);
      DATA.FIELD(POINTER).LINE
         := integer'VALUE(X);
   end Insert_Line;

   procedure Insert_First is
      X : string(1..2);
   begin
      SCROLL_TERMINAL.get("First Column: ", X);
      DATA.FIELD(POINTER).FIRST_COL
         := integer'VALUE(X);
   end Insert_First;

   procedure Insert_Last is
      X : string(1..2);
   begin
      SCROLL_TERMINAL.get("Last Column: ", X);
```

```
            DATA.FIELD(POINTER).LAST_COL
              := integer'VALUE(X);
        end Insert_Last;

        procedure Insert_Protection is
          C : character;
        begin
          get("Is this field protected? (Y/N) ", C);
          case C is
            when 'Y' | 'y' =>
              DATA.FIELD(POINTER).PROTECTED := TRUE;
            when 'N' | 'n' =>
              DATA.FIELD(POINTER).PROTECTED := FALSE;
            when others =>
              raise NEEDS_HELP;
          end case;
        end Insert_Protection;

        procedure Insert_Text(
            LINE, FIRST, LAST : positive) is
          TEXT : string(FIRST..LAST);
        begin
          put_line("Text:");
          SCROLL_TERMINAL.get("",TEXT);
          DATA.SCREEN(LINE)(FIRST..LAST) := TEXT;
        end Insert_Text;

      begin
        -- Move all existing fields back to make
        -- room.
        for i in reverse POINTER..DATA.SIZE loop
          DATA.FIELD(i+1) := DATA.FIELD(i);
        end loop;

        -- There is one more field now.
        DATA.SIZE := DATA.SIZE + 1;

        New_Page;

        Insert_Name;
        Insert_Line;
        Insert_First;
        Insert_Last;
        Insert_Protection;
```

```
Insert_Text(
  DATA.FIELD(POINTER).LINE,
  DATA.FIELD(POINTER).FIRST_COL,
  DATA.FIELD(POINTER).LAST_COL);

end Insert_Field;
```

```
-- Listing 41.

--                    FTBEDF.ada
--                    Version 2.1
--                    19 September 1988

--                    Do-While Jones
--                    324 Traci Lane
--                    Ridgecrest, CA 93555
--                    (619) 375-4607

-- Copyright 1989 by John Wiley & Sons, Inc.
--          All Rights Reserved.

separate(FORM_TERMINAL.Edit)
procedure Delete_Field(POINTER : positive) is
begin

  -- There is 1 less field now.
  DATA.SIZE := DATA.SIZE - 1;

  -- Move all the later fields up one space.
  for i in POINTER..DATA.SIZE loop
    DATA.FIELD(i) := DATA.FIELD(i+1);
  end loop;

end Delete_Field;
```

```
-- Listing 42.

--                FTBEMF.ada
--                Version 2.1
--                19 September 1988

--                Do-While Jones
--                324 Traci Lane
--                Ridgecrest, CA 93555
--                (619) 375-4607

-- Copyright 1989 by John Wiley & Sons, Inc.
--          All Rights Reserved.

separate(FORM_TERMINAL.Edit)
procedure Move_Field(POINTER : positive) is
  TEMP : Field_specs;
  POSITION : positive;
begin
  -- Save the field to be moved in TEMP.
  TEMP := DATA.FIELD(POINTER);

  -- Then delete it.
  Delete_Field(POINTER);

  -- Ask the user where to put it.
  SCROLL_TERMINAL.New_Page;
  SCROLL_TERMINAL.put_line(
      "Move cursor to correct position"
    & " and press");
  SCROLL_TERMINAL.put(
      "B or A to put " & TEMP.NAME);
  SCROLL_TERMINAL.put_line(
      " Before or After that field.");
  SCROLL_TERMINAL.Wait_For_User;
  TOP_FIELD := 1;
  loop
    Edit_Fields(TOP_FIELD,COMMAND,POSITION);
    case COMMAND is
      when PREVIOUS_20 =>
        TOP_FIELD := TOP_FIELD - 20;
        If TOP_FIELD < 1 then
          TOP_FIELD := 1;
        end if;
      when NEXT_20 =>
```

```
            TOP_FIELD := TOP_FIELD + 20;
            If TOP_FIELD > DATA.SIZE - 19 then
               TOP_FIELD := DATA.SIZE - 19;
               If TOP_FIELD < 1 then
                  TOP_FIELD := 1;
               end if;
            end if;
         when INSERT =>
            exit;
         when others =>
            SCROLL_TERMINAL.put(ASCII.BEL);
      end case;
   end loop;

   -- Insert TEMP at position designated by
   -- POSITION.

   -- Move all existing fields back to make
   -- room.
   for i in reverse POSITION..DATA.SIZE loop
      DATA.FIELD(i+1) := DATA.FIELD(i);
   end loop;

   -- Put TEMP in the right place
   DATA.FIELD(POSITION) := TEMP;

   -- There is one more field now.
   DATA.SIZE := DATA.SIZE + 1;

end Move_Field;
```

```
-- Listing 43.

--                    FTBER.ada
--                    Version 2.1
--                    12 August 1988

--                    Do-While Jones
--                    324 Traci Lane
--                    Ridgecrest, CA 93555
--                    (619) 375-4607

--  Copyright 1989 by John Wiley & Sons, Inc.
--          All Rights Reserved.

with SCROLL_TERMINAL;
separate(FORM_TERMINAL)
procedure Error_Recovery is
  use SCROLL_TERMINAL;
begin
  -- Tell the user what went wrong.
  put(ASCII.BEL);
  put_line("WARNING! You have created" &
           " a form containing a LAYOUT ERROR!");
  case ERROR is
    when TEXT_FIELD =>
      put(FORM.FIELD(CURRENT_FIELD).NAME);
      put_line(" contains a NULL STRING.");
    when NAME_CONFLICT =>
      put("TWO FIELDS are called ");
      put(FORM.FIELD(CURRENT_FIELD).NAME);
      put_line(".");
    when OVERLAP =>
      put(FORM.FIELD(CURRENT_FIELD).NAME
        & " and ");
      put(FORM.FIELD(CONFLICTING_FIELD).NAME);
      put(" OVERLAP on line");
      put(integer'IMAGE(
        FORM.FIELD(CURRENT_FIELD).LINE));
      put_line(".");
  end case;
  Wait_For_User;

  -- Give the user a chance to fix it.
  Edit;
end Error_Recovery;
```

```
-- Listing 44.

--              MF.ada
--              Version 2.1
--              19 September 1988

--              Do-While Jones
--              324 Traci Lane
--              Ridgecrest, CA 93555
--              (619) 375-4607

-- Copyright 1989 by John Wiley & Sons, Inc.
--          All Rights Reserved.

with SCROLL_TERMINAL, FORM_TERMINAL;
procedure Make_Form is
  FILE : string(1..40);

  procedure Get_Name_Of(FILE : out string) is
    DEFAULT : string(1..40);
  begin
    DEFAULT := (others => ' ');
    SCROLL_TERMINAL.get(
      "What file should I store it in? ",
      DEFAULT, FILE);
  exception
    when SCROLL_TERMINAL.NEEDS_HELP =>
      SCROLL_TERMINAL.put_line
        ("Enter a file name or path name.");
      Get_Name_Of(FILE);
  end Get_Name_Of;

begin
  SCROLL_TERMINAL.New_Page;
  SCROLL_TERMINAL.put_line("Make Form");
  SCROLL_TERMINAL.new_line;
  FORM_TERMINAL.Create;
  SCROLL_TERMINAL.New_Page;
  Get_Name_Of(FILE);
  FORM_TERMINAL.Write(FILE);
  -- Read it back to check it.
  FORM_TERMINAL.Read(FILE);
  FORM_TERMINAL.Display;
  SCROLL_TERMINAL.put_line("Is in " & FILE & ".");
```

```
exception
  when FORM_TERMINAL.PANIC =>
    SCROLL_TERMINAL.put_line
      ("Program aborted at your request.");
end Make_Form;
```

```ada
-- Listing 45.


--              EF.ada
--              Version 1
--              16 September 1988

--              Do-While Jones
--              324 Traci Lane
--              Ridgecrest, CA 93555
--              (619) 375-4607

--   Copyright 1989 by John Wiley & Sons, Inc.
--           All Rights Reserved.

with FORM_TERMINAL,SCROLL_TERMINAL;
procedure Edit_Form is

  FILE    : string(1..40);
  DEFAULT : string(1..40) := (others => ' ');

  procedure Get_Name_Of(FILE : out string) is
  begin
    SCROLL_TERMINAL.get("",DEFAULT,FILE);
  exception
    when SCROLL_TERMINAL.NEEDS_HELP =>
      SCROLL_TERMINAL.put_line
        ("Enter a file name or path name.");
      Get_Name_Of(FILE);
  end Get_Name_Of;

begin
  SCROLL_TERMINAL.put_line(
     "What file contains the form you want"
   & " to edit?");
  Get_Name_Of(FILE);
  begin
    FORM_TERMINAL.Read(FILE);
  exception
    when FORM_TERMINAL.LAYOUT_ERROR =>
      null; -- ignore error so we can fix it
  end;
  FORM_TERMINAL.Edit;
  SCROLL_TERMINAL.New_Page;
```

```
      SCROLL_TERMINAL.put_line(
        "What file do you want to store it in?");
      DEFAULT := FILE;
      Get_Name_Of(FILE);
      FORM_TERMINAL.Write(FILE);
      -- Read it back to check it.
      FORM_TERMINAL.Read(FILE);
      FORM_TERMINAL.Display;
      SCROLL_TERMINAL.put_line(
        "Is in " & FILE & ".");
   exception
     when FORM_TERMINAL.READ_ERROR =>
       SCROLL_TERMINAL.put_line
          ("I could not read the form in " & FILE);
     when FORM_TERMINAL.PANIC =>
       SCROLL_TERMINAL.put_line
          ("Program aborted at your request.");
   end Edit_Form;
```

```
-- Listing 46.

--              xFTBC.ada

--              Do-While Jones
--              324 Traci Lane
--              Ridgecrest, CA 93555
--              (619) 375-4607

--  Copyright 1989 by John Wiley & Sons, Inc.
--          All Rights Reserved.

-- This stub reduces the size of the
-- FORM_TERMINAL package by replacing a lot of
-- dead code associated with the Create
-- procedure by this relatively small amount of
-- dead code.

with SCROLL_TERMINAL; use SCROLL_TERMINAL;
separate(FORM_TERMINAL)
procedure Create is
begin
  put_line("Sorry, CREATE is not implemented"
        & " in this version.");
  put_line("Just a stub in file xFTBC.ada.");
end Create;
```

```
-- Listing 47.

--              xFTBE.ada

--              Do-While Jones
--              324 Traci Lane
--              Ridgecrest, CA 93555
--              (619) 375-4607

--  Copyright 1989 by John Wiley & Sons, Inc.
--          All Rights Reserved.

-- This stub reduces the size of the
-- FORM_TERMINAL package by replacing a lot of
-- dead code associated with the Edit procedure
-- by this relatively small amount of dead
-- code.

with SCROLL_TERMINAL; use SCROLL_TERMINAL;
separate(FORM_TERMINAL)
procedure Edit is
begin
  put_line("Sorry, EDIT is not implemented"
        & " in this version.");
  put_line("Just a stub in file xFTBE.ada.");
end Edit;
```

```
-- Listing 48.


--                    VMSS.ada
--                    Version 1
--                    2 March 1988

--                    Do-While Jones
--                    324 Traci Lane
--                    Ridgecrest, CA 93555
--                    (619) 375-4607

--   Copyright 1989 by John Wiley & Sons, Inc.
--          All Rights Reserved.

-- WARNING: The VMS operating system insists
-- on intercepting CONTROL_C, CONTROL_Y, and
-- CONTROL_Z, before passing them to this
-- package. If the user presses any of these
-- three keys, bad things happen, and there
-- isn't much you can do about it (except
-- try to log off and log in again).

package VMS is

  VMS_IO_ERROR : exception;
    -- This exception should never occur. It
    -- only happens when a VMS system service
    -- fails. I suggest you not handle this
    -- exception and let it terminate your
    -- program with an unhandled exception. The
    -- operating system will tell you which
    -- line in the package body caused the
    -- failure. (But if this package couldn't
    -- get access to the terminal it is likely
    -- that the error reporting routine won't
    -- be able to, either.)

  procedure Display_Char(C : character);
    -- Send an ASCII character to the screen,
    -- including escape sequences and control
    -- codes.

  function Kbd_Data_Available return boolean;
```

```
            -- Returns TRUE if any key has been pressed
            -- but not yet read.

        procedure Read_Keyboard_Direct(
            C : out character);
            -- Get a character from the keyboard
            -- without echoing it to the screen or
            -- interpreting it.

    end VMS;
```

```ada
-- Listing 49.

--                        VMSB.ada
--                        Version 1.0
--                        15 April 1988

--                        Do-While Jones
--                        324 Traci Lane
--                        Ridgecrest, CA 93555
--                        (619) 375-4607

-- Copyright 1989 by John Wiley & Sons, Inc.
--          All Rights Reserved.

package body VMS is

  task INPUT is
    entry Keypush;
    pragma AST_Entry(Keypush);
      -- Asynchronous System Trap from the
      -- operating system tells the INPUT task
      -- a character has been entered.
    entry Ready(STATUS : out boolean);
      -- Tells if a character has been received
      -- or not.
    entry get(C : out character);
      -- Waits for a character to be entered
      -- and returns it.
  end INPUT;

  package OUTPUT is
    procedure put(C : character);
      -- Send a character to the screen.
  end OUTPUT;

  task body INPUT is separate;
  -- file VMSBI.ada

  package body OUTPUT is separate;
  -- file VMSBO.ada

  procedure Display_Char(C : character) is
  begin
    OUTPUT.put(C);
  end Display_Char;
```

```ada
      function Kbd_Data_Available return boolean is
        STATUS : boolean;
      begin
        INPUT.Ready(STATUS);
        return STATUS;
      end Kbd_Data_Available;

      procedure Read_Keyboard_Direct(
        C : out character) is
      begin
        INPUT.get(C);
      end Read_Keyboard_Direct;

   end VMS;
```

```
-- Listing 50.

--                      VMSBI.ada
--                      Version 1.0
--                      3 March 1988

--                      Do-While Jones
--                      324 Traci Lane
--                      Ridgecrest CA, 93555
--                      (619) 375-4607

--  Copyright 1989 by John Wiley & Sons, Inc.
--          All Rights Reserved.


-- Thanks to Lee Lucas and Dave Dent for
-- helping me figure out how to interface with
-- the VMS system calls. This task body is
-- based on an example program by Dee
-- DeCristofaro.

with CONDITION_HANDLING,STARLET,SYSTEM;
use SYSTEM; -- for bit-set function "or"
            -- in STARLET.Qio
separate(VMS)
task body INPUT is
  ASG_STATUS : CONDITION_HANDLING.Cond_value_type;
  CHANNEL    : STARLET.Channel_type;
  QIO_STATUS : CONDITION_HANDLING.Cond_value_type;
  QIO_IOSB   : STARLET.IOSB_type;
               -- IO Status Block
  pragma Volatile(QIO_IOSB);
  KEYINPUT   : string(1..1);
  NEW_DATA   : boolean;
begin

  -- Assign the input channel
  STARLET.Assign(STATUS => ASG_STATUS,
                 DEVNAM => "SYS$COMMAND",
                 CHAN   => CHANNEL);
  if not CONDITION_HANDLING.Success(ASG_STATUS)
     then
    raise VMS_IO_ERROR; -- should never happen
  end if;
```

```
loop
  -- Ask VMS to get an input character from
  -- the keyboard.
  NEW_DATA := FALSE;
  STARLET.Qio(
    STATUS => QIO_STATUS,
    CHAN   => CHANNEL,
    FUNC   => (STARLET.IO_READVBLK
              -- read virtual block
              or STARLET.IO_M_NOECHO
              -- don't echo
              or STARLET.IO_M_NOFILTR),
              -- don't edit
    IOSB   => QIO_IOSB,
    ASTADR => Keypush'AST_Entry,
    P1     => SYSTEM.To_Unsigned_Longword(
              KEYINPUT'ADDRESS),
    P2     => SYSTEM.Unsigned_Longword(
              KEYINPUT'LENGTH));
  if not CONDITION_HANDLING.Success(
     QIO_STATUS) then
    raise VMS_IO_ERROR;
  end if;

  -- Wait for the user to press a key, or for
  -- the program to ask if any key has been
  -- pressed. Don't accept a  "get" because
  -- there isn't anything to get. (Accepting
  -- a get would suspend you in a rendezvous,
  -- so you couldn't accept a keypush.)
  loop
    select
      accept Keypush;
      if not CONDITION_HANDLING.Success(
         QIO_IOSB.STATUS)
       then
         raise VMS_IO_ERROR;
      end if;
      NEW_DATA := TRUE;
    or
      accept Ready(STATUS : out boolean) do
        STATUS := FALSE;
      end;
```

```
      or
        terminate;
      end select;
      exit when NEW_DATA;
   end loop;

   -- Now a key has been pressed, you we can
   -- accept a "get" or a status request. We
   -- can't accept another key because it
   -- would erase the last key pressed before
   -- it was processed.
   loop
     select
       accept get(C : out character) do
         C := KEYINPUT(1);
       end;
       NEW_DATA := FALSE;
     or
       accept Ready(STATUS : out boolean) do
         STATUS := TRUE;
       end;
     or
       terminate;
     end select;
     exit when not NEW_DATA;
   end loop;

   -- They key has been processed. We can
   -- accept another one now.
  end loop;

end INPUT;
```

```ada
-- Listing 51.

--                    VMSBO.ada
--                    Version 1.0
--                    15 April 1988

--                    Do-While Jones
--                    324 Traci Lane
--                    Ridgecrest CA, 93555
--                    (619) 375-4607

-- Copyright 1989 by John Wiley & Sons, Inc.
--          All Rights Reserved.

with CONDITION_HANDLING,STARLET,SYSTEM;
separate(VMS)
package body OUTPUT is

  ASG_STATUS :
    CONDITION_HANDLING.Cond_value_type;
  CHANNEL     : STARLET.Channel_type;

  procedure put(C : character) is
    QIO_STATUS :
      CONDITION_HANDLING.Cond_value_type;
    QIO_IOSB   : STARLET.IOSB_type;
                 -- IO Status Block
    pragma Volatile(QIO_IOSB);
    CHAROUT    : string(1..1);
  begin
    CHAROUT(1) := C;
    STARLET.Qiow(
      STATUS => QIO_STATUS,
      CHAN   => CHANNEL,
      FUNC   => STARLET.IO_WRITEVBLK,
      IOSB   => QIO_IOSB,
      P1     => SYSTEM.To_Unsigned_Longword(
                CHAROUT'ADDRESS),
      P2     => SYSTEM.Unsigned_Longword(
                CHAROUT'LENGTH));
    if not CONDITION_HANDLING.Success(
        QIO_STATUS) then
      raise VMS_IO_ERROR;
```

```
      end if;
   end put;

begin
   -- Assign the output channel
   STARLET.Assign(STATUS  => ASG_STATUS,
                  DEVNAM  => "SYS$COMMAND",
                  CHAN    => CHANNEL);
   if not CONDITION_HANDLING.Success(
      ASG_STATUS) then
     raise VMS_IO_ERROR; -- should never happen
   end if;
end OUTPUT;
```

```
-- Listing 52.

--                      VTSDEC.ada
--                      2 September 1988
--                      Version 1.1

--                      Do-While Jones
--                      324 Traci Lane
--                      Ridgecrest, CA 93555
--                      (619) 375-4607

--   Copyright 1989 by John Wiley & Sons, Inc.
--            All Rights Reserved.

-- This package hides individual terminal
-- characteristics and converts them into a
-- standard form. This VIRTUAL_TERMINAL package
-- can be used as the foundation for the
-- SCROLL_TERMINAL, FORM_TERMINAL, or a user-
-- designed custom terminal.

-- Version 1.1 is a special version for
-- VAX/VMS. VMS intercepts the CONTROL_C
-- character before any Ada routine can process
-- it. This is a "powder keg", because a
-- careless user can mess things up badly by
-- pressing CONTROL_C, CONTROL_Y, or CONTROL_Z.
-- I need to find a good solution for this
-- problem, but for the time being the
-- workaround is to use ! as the panic button,
-- and hope the user never presses one of the
-- VMS forbidden keys.

-- This specification is different from the
-- other VIRTUAL_TERMINAL specifications
-- because it propagates the special
-- VMS_IO_ERROR exception.

with VMS;
package VIRTUAL_TERMINAL is

  VMS_IO_ERROR : exception
    renames VMS.VMS_IO_ERROR;
      -- Raised if VMS detects an IO error.
```

```
subtype Line_numbers is integer range 1..23;
subtype Column_numbers is
   integer range 1..79;
   -- Note Line_numbers and Column_numbers are
   -- limited to avoid terminal dependent
   -- quirks (auto wrap and auto scroll) that
   -- may happen at screen boundaries.

-- ASCII characters

CTRL_A : constant character
   := ASCII.SOH; -- Add (Insert)
CTRL_B : constant character
   := ASCII.STX; -- Back Tab
CTRL_C : constant character
   := '!'; -- Panic Button, VMS ONLY
CTRL_D : constant character
   := ASCII.EOT; -- Down Arrow
CTRL_E : constant character
   := ASCII.ENQ; -- Erase/Delete
CTRL_F : constant character
   := ASCII.ACK; -- Function Key
CTRL_G : constant character
   := ASCII.BEL; -- Bell
CTRL_H : constant character
   := ASCII.BS;  -- Backspace
CTRL_I : constant character
   := ASCII.HT;  -- Tab
CTRL_J : constant character
   := ASCII.LF;  -- Line Feed
CTRL_L : constant character
   := ASCII.FF;  -- Left Arrow
CTRL_M : constant character
   := ASCII.CR;  -- Return
CTRL_R : constant character
   := ASCII.DC2; -- Right Arrow
CTRL_U : constant character
   := ASCII.NAK; -- Up Arrow

TAB      : constant character := CTRL_I;
BACK_TAB : constant character := CTRL_B;
RIGHT    : constant character := CTRL_R;
LEFT     : constant character := CTRL_L;
UP       : constant character := CTRL_U;
```

```
DOWN     : constant character := CTRL_D;
INSERT   : constant character := CTRL_A;
DELETE   : constant character := ASCII.DEL;
FUN_KEY  : constant character := CTRL_F;
   -- Note: It is unfortunate that INSERT
   -- can't be CRTL_I, but that has been
   -- assigned to TAB by a higher power.
   -- CTRL_A was selected because it can be
   -- considered to ADD characters to the
   -- middle of a text string. CTRL_E can be
   -- used as an erase key on terminals
   -- lacking a delete/rub out key.

PANIC : exception;
   -- Raised whenever the User presses the
   -- Panic Button (! key).

INVALID_FUNCTION_KEY : exception;
   -- Raised if the function key is out of
   -- range.

-- Screen control

procedure Clear_Screen;
   -- Erase the entire screen and move the
   -- cursor to the upper left corner of the
   -- screen.

-- Cursor control

procedure Move_Cursor_Right;
procedure Move_Cursor_Left;
procedure Move_Cursor_Up;
procedure Move_Cursor_Down;
procedure Move_Cursor_To(
  LINE : Line_numbers;
  COL  : Column_Numbers);

-- Output services

procedure put(C : character);
   -- Sends a character to the screen without
   -- filtering.
```

```
procedure put(S : string);
    -- Sends a string to the screen without
    -- filtering.

-- Input services
procedure get(C : out character);
    -- Get a character without echo. Special
    -- control keys are automatically converted
    -- into standard escape sequences.
    --    RIGHT arrow => CTRL_R
    --    LEFT arrow => CTRL_L
    --    UP arrow =>    CTRL_U
    --    DOWN arrow => CTRL_D
    --    TAB =>        CTRL_I
    --    BACK_TAB =>   CTRL_B
    --    INSERT =>     CTRL_A
    --    DELETE =>     DELETE
    --    CTRL_E =>     DELETE
    --    FUN_KEY =>    CTRL_F
    --    ! =>     raises PANIC exception
    -- Note that terminals without cursor
    -- control keys or function keys can
    -- achieve the desired effect using
    -- control characters.

function Function_Key return natural;

    -- 20 function keys are supported.

    -- If the Get function detects a function
    -- key it will return CTRL_F and decode the
    -- function key number. The main program
    -- can then call Function_Key to find out
    -- which one it was.

    -- Function_Key will return a number 1
    -- through 20 representing the function key
    -- pressed. (Some keyboards may use
    -- SHIFTED function keys 1 through 10
    -- to get functions 11 through 20.)

    -- If the user presses CTRL_F when using
    -- the Get function, the Get function will
```

```
                    -- interpret the next character as a
                    -- function key. If the next key pressed
                    -- is 1 through 9 then Function_Key will
                    -- return 1 through 9. Characters A through
                    -- K return values of 10 through 20. (Both
                    -- 'A' and 'a' return 10 because
                    -- Function_Key is not case sensitive.)
                    -- A function key outside the range 1..20
                    -- raises INVALID_FUNCTION_KEY.

             function Keyboard_Data_Available
                return boolean;
                    -- Tells if any key has been pressed,
                    -- without reading the character.

          end VIRTUAL_TERMINAL;
```

```
-- Listing 53.

--              VTBDEC.ada
--              Version 1.1
--              2 September 1988

--              Do-While Jones
--              324 Traci Lane
--              Ridgecrest, CA 93555
--              (619) 375-4607

-- Copyright 1989 by John Wiley & Sons, Inc.
--          All Rights Reserved.

--              DEC VAX/VMS Version
--      for DEC VT100 or VT200 series terminals

with ASCII_UTILITIES;
package body VIRTUAL_TERMINAL is

  F_KEY : natural;

  procedure Clear_Screen is
  begin
    put(ASCII.ESC & "[2J");
    Move_Cursor_To(1,1);
  end Clear_Screen;

  procedure Move_Cursor_Right is
  begin
    put(ASCII.ESC & "[C");
  end Move_Cursor_Right;

  procedure Move_Cursor_Left is
  begin
    put(ASCII.ESC & "[D");
  end Move_Cursor_Left;

  procedure Move_Cursor_Up is
  begin
    put(ASCII.ESC & "[A");
  end Move_Cursor_Up;

  procedure Move_Cursor_Down is
  begin
```

```
      put(ASCII.ESC & "[B");
   end Move_Cursor_Down;

   procedure Move_Cursor_To(
      LINE : Line_numbers;
      COL  : Column_numbers) is
     L, C : string(1..3);
   begin
     put(ASCII.ESC & '[');
     put(string'(ASCII_UTILITIES.Image(LINE)));
     put(';');
     put(string'(ASCII_UTILITIES.Image(COL)));
     put('H');
   end Move_Cursor_To;

   procedure put(C : character) is
   begin
     VMS.Display_Char(C);
   end put;

   procedure put(S : string) is
   begin
     for i in S'RANGE loop
       put(S(i));
     end loop;
   end put;

   procedure get(C : out character) is
     X : character;
   begin
     VMS.Read_Keyboard_Direct(X);
     case X is
       when ASCII.ESC =>
         VMS.Read_Keyboard_Direct(X);
         if X = '[' then
           VMS.Read_Keyboard_Direct(X);
           case X is
             when 'A' =>
               X := UP;
             when 'B' =>
               X := DOWN;
             when 'C' =>
               X := RIGHT;
             when 'D' =>
               X := LEFT;
```

```
            when others =>
              -- invalid special key
              X := ASCII.NUL;
          end case;
        else
          -- invalid special key
          X := ASCII.NUL;
        end if;
    when CTRL_E =>
      X := DELETE;
    when CTRL_C =>
      raise PANIC;
    when others =>
      null; -- don't mess with X
  end case;
  C := X;
end get;

function Function_Key return natural is
  X : natural;
  C : character;
begin
  if F_KEY = 0 then
    VMS.Read_Keyboard_Direct(C);
    case C is
      when '1'..'9' =>
        F_KEY := character'POS(C)
                 - character'POS('0');
      when 'A'..'K' =>
        F_KEY := character'POS(C)
                 - character'POS('A') + 10;
      when 'a'..'k' =>
        F_KEY := character'POS(C)
                 - character'POS('a') + 10;
      when others =>
        raise INVALID_FUNCTION_KEY;
    end case;
  end if;
  X := F_KEY;
  F_KEY := 0;
  return X;
end Function_Key;

function Keyboard_Data_Available
  return boolean is
```

```
   begin
     return VMS.Kbd_Data_Available;
   end Keyboard_Data_Available;

 end VIRTUAL_TERMINAL;
```

```
-- Listing 54.

--              VPS.ada
--              19 October 1987
--              Version 2

--              Do-While Jones
--              324 Traci Lane
--              Ridgecrest, CA 93555
--              (619) 375-4607

--  Copyright 1989 by John Wiley & Sons, Inc.
--              All Rights Reserved.


-- This package hides the operating system
-- device name of the system printer and turns
-- it into a standard form.

-- Version 2 allows you to direct the output to
-- another printer, or to a file.

package VIRTUAL_PRINTER is

  NAME_ERROR : exception;
    -- Raised if the output device doesn't
    -- exist.

  USE_ERROR : exception;
    -- Raised if you try to output to a Read
    -- Only file.

  procedure put(C : character);
    -- Sends a character to the printer. If the
    -- physical printer does not use ASCII.FF
    -- for a form feed, the body substitutes
    -- the escape sequence whenever it receives
    -- an ASCII.FF.

  procedure put(S : string);
    -- Sends a string to the printer,
    -- substituting for ASCII.FF if necessary.

  procedure Set_Output(DEVICE : string);
    -- Stop sending the output to the current
```

```
                    -- printer and start sending it to the new
                    -- printer.

             function Current_Output return string;
                    -- Tells you the name of the current
                    -- printer.

             function Standard_Output return string;
                    -- Tells you the name of the default
                    -- printer.

        end VIRTUAL_PRINTER;
```

```ada
-- Listing 55.

--              VPBLPT1.ada
--              19 October 1987
--              Version 2.0

--              Do-While Jones
--              324 Traci Lane
--              Ridgecrest, CA 93555
--              (619) 375-4607

--   Copyright 1989 by John Wiley & Sons, Inc.
--           All Rights Reserved.

-- This version works for Alsys & Meridian Ada
-- on an IBM with the printer connected to the
-- LPT1 parallel output port.

with TEXT_IO;
package body VIRTUAL_PRINTER is

  PRINTER : TEXT_IO.File_type;

  PRINTER_NAME : string(1..80);
  LENGTH       : natural;

  procedure put(C : character) is
  begin
    TEXT_IO.put(PRINTER,C);
  end put;

  procedure put(S : string) is
  begin
    for i in S'RANGE loop
      put(S(i));
    end loop;
  end put;

  procedure Set_Output(DEVICE : string) is
  begin
    TEXT_IO.Close(PRINTER);
    TEXT_IO.Create(
      PRINTER,TEXT_IO.OUT_FILE,DEVICE);
    LENGTH := DEVICE'LENGTH;
    PRINTER_NAME(1..LENGTH) := DEVICE;
```

```ada
      exception
        when TEXT_IO.NAME_ERROR =>
          raise NAME_ERROR;
        when TEXT_IO.USE_ERROR =>
          raise USE_ERROR;
      end Set_Output;

      function Current_Output return string is
      begin
        return PRINTER_NAME(1..LENGTH);
      end Current_Output;

      function Standard_Output return string is
      begin
        return "LPT1";
      end Standard_Output;

    begin
      TEXT_IO.Create(
        PRINTER,TEXT_IO.OUT_FILE,Standard_Output);
      LENGTH := 4;
      PRINTER_NAME(1..LENGTH) := Standard_Output;
    end VIRTUAL_PRINTER;
```

```
-- Listing 56.

--                    SPS.ada
--                    Version 1
--                    16 October 1987

--                    Do-While Jones
--                    324 Traci Lane
--                    Ridgecrest, CA 93555
--                    (619) 375-4607

--  Copyright 1989 by John Wiley & Sons, Inc.
--            All Rights Reserved.

with VIRTUAL_PRINTER;
package SCROLL_PRINTER is

  PAGE_WIDTH : constant integer := 80;

  subtype Column_numbers is
    integer range 1..PAGE_WIDTH;

  procedure put(C : character);
  -- The put procedure automatically expands
  -- TABS, keeps track of columns, and knows
  -- that certain characters (like ASCII.LF and
  -- ASCII.BEL) should not affect the column
  -- counter. Non-printable characters are
  -- printed as an ASCII.BEL.

  procedure put(S : string);
  -- Call the character put routine until all
  -- the characters in the string have been
  -- sent.

  procedure new_line(LINES : positive := 1);
  -- Use the string put routine to send a
  -- <CR><LF> sequence the desired number of
  -- times.

  procedure put_line(S : string);
  -- Use the string put procedure to send the
  -- string, then follow it immediately with a
  -- call of new_line;
```

```
procedure New_Page;
-- Send a Page Eject command to the printer.

procedure Set_Col(N : Column_numbers);
-- Use the character put routine to print
-- spaces until the print head is at column
-- N. (If the print head is already at column
-- N, then nothing is done. If the print head
-- is past column N, then new_line is called
-- and the printer spaces over to column N.)

procedure Set_Tabs(
  STOPS : Column_numbers := 8);
-- This procedure gives the character put
-- routine the information it needs to expand
-- TAB characters.

function Column return Column_numbers;
-- Tells the main program which column is
-- about to be printed.

end SCROLL_PRINTER;
```

```ada
-- Listing 57.

--              SPB.ada
--              Version 1.0
--              18 October 1987

--              Do-While Jones
--              324 Traci Lane
--              Ridgecrest, CA 93555
--              (619) 375-4607

--  Copyright 1989 by John Wiley & Sons, Inc.
--          All Rights Reserved.

with VIRTUAL_PRINTER;
package body SCROLL_PRINTER is

  COLUMN_NUMBER, TAB_STOPS : Column_numbers;

  TAB : constant character := ASCII.HT;
  use ASCII; -- CR, LF, and FF

  procedure put(C : character) is
  begin
    case C is
      when ' ' .. '≠' =>
        if COLUMN_NUMBER <
            Column_numbers'LAST then
          COLUMN_NUMBER := COLUMN_NUMBER + 1;
        else
          New_Line;
        end if;
        VIRTUAL_PRINTER.put(C);
      when CR =>
        COLUMN_NUMBER := 1;
        VIRTUAL_PRINTER.put(C);
      when LF =>
        VIRTUAL_PRINTER.put(C);
      when FF =>
        VIRTUAL_PRINTER.put(C);
        put(CR);
```

```
      when TAB =>
        -- TAB is worth at least 1 space
        put(' ');
        while COLUMN_NUMBER
            mod TAB_STOPS /= 0 loop
            -- use recursion to control
            -- COLUMN_NUMBER
          put(' ');
        end loop;
      when others =>
        -- (non-printable characters)
        put(ASCII.BEL);
    end case;
  end put;

  procedure put(S : string) is
  begin
    for i in S'RANGE loop
      put(S(i));
    end loop;
  end put;

  procedure new_line(LINES : positive := 1) is
  begin
    for i in 1..LINES loop
      put(CR); put(LF);
    end loop;
  end new_line;

  procedure put_line(S : string) is
  begin
    put(S); new_line;
  end put_line;

  procedure New_Page is
  begin
    put(FF);
  end New_Page;

  procedure Set_Col(N : Column_numbers) is
  begin
```

```
      if N < COLUMN_NUMBER then new_line; end if;
      for i in COLUMN_NUMBER+1..N loop
        put(' ');
      end loop;
   end Set_Col;

   procedure Set_Tabs(
      STOPS : Column_numbers := 8) is
   begin
      TAB_STOPS := STOPS;
   end Set_Tabs;

   function Column return Column_numbers is
   begin
      return COLUMN_NUMBER;
   end Column;

begin
   COLUMN_NUMBER := 1;
   Set_Tabs;
end SCROLL_PRINTER;
```

```
-- Listing 58.

--                    GCLBAIBM.ada
--                    Version 2
--                    15 August 1988

--                    Do-While Jones
--                    324 Traci Lane
--                    Ridgecrest, CA 93555
--                    (619) 375-4607

--   Copyright 1989 by John Wiley & Sons, Inc.
--           All Rights Reserved.

-- This version works with Alsys Ada on the IBM
-- PC. The Alsys DOS package contains a
-- function Get_Parms which returns a string
-- with a length depending upon the number
-- of characters entered by the user. Since
-- this probably isn't the exact number of
-- characters requested by the calling program,
-- a little bit of data massaging has to be
-- done to put the command line in the first
-- part of the longer output string.

-- This version uses a trick found in AlsyNews,
-- Volume 2, Number 2, June 1988. The clever
-- trick is found in Ben Brosgol's AlsyHints
-- column.

with DOS;
procedure Get_Command_Line(
    TAIL   : out string;
    LENGTH : out natural) is

  COMMAND : constant string := DOS.Get_Parms;

begin
  TAIL(1..COMMAND'LENGTH) := COMMAND;
  LENGTH := COMMAND'LENGTH;
end Get_Command_Line;
```

```
-- Listing 59.

--                      GCLS.ada
--                      Version 1
--                      9 June 1987

--                      Do-While Jones
--                      324 Traci Lane
--                      Ridgecrest, CA 93555
--                      (619) 375-4607

-- Copyright 1989 by John Wiley & Sons, Inc.
--           All Rights Reserved.

-- This procedure gets the command line tail.
-- That is, if the user enters "SOME_COMMAND
-- FILE.EXT" at the system prompt, then this
-- procedure contains the string "FILE.EXT" and
-- tells you that it is 8 characters long.

procedure Get_Command_Line(
    TAIL    : out string;
    LENGTH  : out natural);
```

```
-- Listing 60.

--              GCLBDEC.ada
--              Version 1.0
--              2 October 1988

--              Do-While Jones
--              324 Traci Lane
--              Ridgecrest, CA 93555
--              (619) 375-4607

-- Copyright 1989 by John Wiley & Sons, Inc.
--         All Rights Reserved.

-- Get_Command_Line body for DEC Ada running
-- under VAX/VMS.

-- Thanks to Dave Dent for discovering
-- Get_Foreign for me, and showing me how to
-- use it.

-- Note: If you try to $RUN SOME_COMMAND
-- FILE.EXT you will get an error because RUN
-- doesn't expect multiple parameters. You need
-- to redefine SOME_COMMAND by adding this line
-- to your login file:

-- $ SOME_COMMAND
--    :== $DISKn:[YOUR_DIR]SOME_COMMAND.EXE

-- Then you can SOME_COMMAND FILE.EXT and it
-- should work.

with Condition_Handling;
procedure Get_Command_Line(
    TAIL   : out string;
    LENGTH : out natural) is
  STATUS : Condition_Handling.cond_value_type;
```

```
-- Get_Foreign is a routine in the system
-- library.

procedure Get_Foreign(
  STATUS        : out
    Condition_Handling.cond_value_type;
  GET_STR       : out string;
  USER_PROMPT   : in string
    := string'null_parameter;
  OUT_LEN       : out integer;
  FORCE_PROMPT  : in integer
    := integer'null_parameter);

  pragma Interface(SYS_LIB, GET_FOREIGN);
  pragma Import_Valued_Procedure
    (Get_Foreign,"LIB$GET_FOREIGN");

begin
  Get_Foreign(STATUS, GET_STR => TAIL,
                      OUT_LEN => LENGTH);
  if not Condition_Handling.success(
    STATUS) then
    -- should never happen, but if it does
    LENGTH := 0; -- no tail
  end if;
end Get_Command_Line;
```

```
-- Listing 61.

--              MORE.ada
--              Version 1
--              2 November 1988

--              Do-While Jones
--              324 Traci Lane
--              Ridgecrest, CA 93555
--              (619) 375-4607

-- Copyright 1989 by John Wiley & Sons, Inc.
--          All Rights Reserved.

with Get_Command_Line;
with VIRTUAL_TERMINAL, SCROLL_TERMINAL;
with ASCII_UTILITIES;
with TEXT_IO;
procedure More is
  TEXT     : string(1..200);
  FILENAME : string(1..68);
  LENGTH   : natural;
  FILE     : TEXT_IO.File_type;
  LINES    : natural;
  FINISHED : boolean;

  procedure Display(LINES    : natural;
                    FINISHED : out boolean) is
  begin
    FINISHED := FALSE;
    for i in 1..LINES loop
      if TEXT_IO.End_Of_File(FILE) then
        FINISHED := TRUE;
        return;
      end if;
      TEXT_IO.get_line(FILE,TEXT,LENGTH);
      SCROLL_TERMINAL.put_line(TEXT(1..LENGTH));
    end loop;
  end Display;

  procedure get(LINES    : out natural;
                FINISHED : out boolean) is
    C : character;
    X : natural;
    NEEDS_HELP : exception;
```

```
          procedure Help is
            use SCROLL_TERMINAL;
          begin
            new_line;
            put_line("These are your options:");
            new_line;
            put_line("<Carriage Return>"
              & "  1 more line  displayed");
            put_line("d (or <CTRL-D>)  "
              & " 11 more lines displayed");
            put_line("<Space Bar>       "
              & " 22 more lines displayed");
            put_line("<any integer N>  "
              & "  N more lines displayed");
            new_line;
            put_line("<Delete (or Control-E)>"
              & " to quit displaying");
            new_line;
          end Help;

        begin
          SCROLL_TERMINAL.put_line("--More--");
          VIRTUAL_TERMINAL.get(C);
          FINISHED := FALSE;
          case C is
            when ASCII.CR =>
              LINES := 1;
            when 'd' | VIRTUAL_TERMINAL.CTRL_D
                    | 'D' =>
              -- Note: Upper case D isn't UNIX
              -- standard, but I didn't want to annoy
              -- a user who happened to have the CAPS
              -- LOCK button down.
              LINES := 11;
            when ' ' =>
              LINES := 22;
            when '0'..'9' =>
              VIRTUAL_TERMINAL.put(C);
              X := ASCII_UTILITIES.Value(C);
              loop
                VIRTUAL_TERMINAL.get(C);
                if C in '0'..'9' then
                  VIRTUAL_TERMINAL.put(C);
                  X := 10 * X
                     + ASCII_UTILITIES.Value(C);
                else
```

```
                 exit;
               end if;
             end loop;
             LINES := X;
             SCROLL_TERMINAL.new_line;
         when VIRTUAL_TERMINAL.DELETE |
              VIRTUAL_TERMINAL.CTRL_C =>
             -- VIRTUAL_TERMINAL.DELETE
             -- is CONTROL_E.
             -- Also quit when the user enters the
             -- PANIC character, even though the
             -- Help message doesn't say so.
             FINISHED := TRUE;
         when others =>
             raise NEEDS_HELP;
       end case;
     exception
       when NEEDS_HELP =>
         Help;
         get(LINES,FINISHED);
     end get;

  begin
    Get_Command_Line(FILENAME,LENGTH);
    if LENGTH = 0 then
      SCROLL_TERMINAL.put("What file? ");
      SCROLL_TERMINAL.get_line(FILENAME,LENGTH);
    end if;
    TEXT_IO.Open(FILE,TEXT_IO.IN_FILE,
        FILENAME(1..LENGTH));
      LINES := 22;
    loop
      Display(LINES,FINISHED);
      exit when FINISHED;
      get(LINES,FINISHED);
      exit when FINISHED;
    end loop;
    TEXT_IO.Close(FILE);
  exception
    when TEXT_IO.NAME_ERROR =>
      SCROLL_TERMINAL.put("File """);
      SCROLL_TERMINAL.put(FILENAME(1..LENGTH));
      SCROLL_TERMINAL.put_line(
        """ could not be found.");
  end More;
```

```
-- Listing 62.

--              WRITE.ada
--              Version 2
--              17 July 1988

--              Do-While Jones
--              324 Traci Lane
--              Ridgecrest, CA 93555
--              (619) 375-4607

--  Copyright 1989 by John Wiley & Sons, Inc.
--         All Rights Reserved.

-- Version 2 includes help and recovery
-- routines.

with Get_Command_Line;
with SCROLL_TERMINAL, SCROLL_PRINTER, TEXT_IO;
procedure Write is
  TITLE               : string(1..79);
  FILENAME            : string(1..68);
  LENGTH              : natural;
  FILE                : TEXT_IO.File_type;
  PAGE                : positive;
  DOUBLE_SPACED       : boolean;
  LINES_LEFT_TO_PRINT : natural;
  TEXT                : string(1..250);
  KEY                 : character;

  procedure Get_File(FILENAME : out string;
                     LENGTH    : out natural) is
    use SCROLL_TERMINAL;
  begin
    get_line("What file? ",FILENAME,LENGTH);
  exception
    when NEEDS_HELP =>
      new_line;
      put_line("Please enter the name of the" &
               " file you want to print.");
      put_line("You may enter a complete path"
               & " name if you like.");
      put_line("Press CONTROL-C to QUIT.");
      Get_File(FILENAME,LENGTH);
  end Get_File;
```

```
procedure Get_Title is
  use SCROLL_TERMINAL;
begin
  TITLE := (others => ' ');
  TITLE(1..LENGTH) := FILENAME(1..LENGTH);
  put_line("Enter page TITLE, please.");
  get("", TITLE, TITLE);
exception
  when NEEDS_HELP =>
    put_line("What do you want written" &
             " at the top of each page?");
    Get_Title;
end Get_Title;

function First_Page return positive is
  TEXT : string(1..4);
  PAGE : positive;
  use SCROLL_TERMINAL;
begin
  get("Start numbering pages at page ",
    "1",TEXT);
  PAGE := integer'VALUE(TEXT);
  return PAGE;
exception
  when CONSTRAINT_ERROR | NEEDS_HELP =>
    new_line;
    put_line(
     "Please enter a number from 1 to 9999");
    return First_Page;
end First_Page;

function Double_Space_Input return boolean is
  RESPONSE : character;
  use SCROLL_TERMINAL;
begin
  get("SINGLE or DOUBLE spaced? (S/D) ",
    'S', RESPONSE);
  new_line;
  case RESPONSE is
    when 'D' | 'd' =>
      return TRUE;
    when 'S' | 's' =>
      return FALSE;
    when others =>
      raise NEEDS_HELP;
```

```
        end case;
     exception
       when NEEDS_HELP =>
         new_line;
         put_line("If you want the file printed" &
                  " SINGLE spaced, enter S");
         put_line("If you want it DOUBLE spaced,"
                  & " enter D");
         return Double_Space_Input;
     end Double_Space_Input;

begin
  Get_Command_Line(FILENAME,LENGTH);
  if LENGTH = 0 then
    Get_File(FILENAME,LENGTH);
  end if;
  TEXT_IO.Open(FILE, TEXT_IO.IN_FILE,
    FILENAME(1..LENGTH));
  Get_Title;
  PAGE := First_Page;
  DOUBLE_SPACED := Double_Space_Input;
  loop
    exit when TEXT_IO.End_Of_File(FILE);
    SCROLL_PRINTER.new_line(4);
    SCROLL_PRINTER.put_line(TITLE);
    SCROLL_PRINTER.new_line(3);
    LINES_LEFT_TO_PRINT := 50;
    loop
      exit when TEXT_IO.End_Of_File(FILE);
      if SCROLL_TERMINAL.Any_Key_Pressed then
        begin
          -- discard input
          SCROLL_TERMINAL.get("",KEY);
          -- may raise PANIC or NEEDS_HELP
        exception
          when SCROLL_TERMINAL.NEEDS_HELP =>
            null; -- help is always given
        end;
        -- help the user
        SCROLL_TERMINAL.put(ASCII.BEL);
        SCROLL_TERMINAL.new_line;
        SCROLL_TERMINAL.put(
          "Printing in progress.");
        SCROLL_TERMINAL.put(
```

```
              " Press CONTROL-C to abort.");
            SCROLL_TERMINAL.new_line;
          end if;
          TEXT_IO.get_line(FILE,TEXT,LENGTH);
          SCROLL_PRINTER.put_line(TEXT(1..LENGTH));
          LINES_LEFT_TO_PRINT
            := LINES_LEFT_TO_PRINT-1;
          if DOUBLE_SPACED then
            SCROLL_PRINTER.new_line;
            LINES_LEFT_TO_PRINT
              := LINES_LEFT_TO_PRINT-1;
          end if;
          exit when LINES_LEFT_TO_PRINT < 1;
        end loop;
        SCROLL_PRINTER.new_line(
          LINES_LEFT_TO_PRINT+3);
        SCROLL_PRINTER.Set_Col(30);
        SCROLL_PRINTER.put_line(
          integer'IMAGE(PAGE));
        PAGE := PAGE+1;
        SCROLL_PRINTER.new_page;
      end loop;
      TEXT_IO.Close(FILE);
      SCROLL_TERMINAL.put_line("Done.");
    exception
      when TEXT_IO.NAME_ERROR =>
        SCROLL_TERMINAL.put("File """);
        SCROLL_TERMINAL.put(FILENAME(1..LENGTH));
        SCROLL_TERMINAL.put_line(
          """ could not be found.");
      when SCROLL_TERMINAL.PANIC =>
        SCROLL_TERMINAL.put_line(
          "Program terminated by user.");
        SCROLL_PRINTER.new_page;
        TEXT_IO.Close(FILE);
    end Write;
```

```
-- Listing 63.

--              LINE.ada
--              Version 1
--              19 July 1988

--              Do-While Jones
--              324 Traci Lane
--              Ridgecrest. CA 93555
--              (619) 375-4607

--   Copyright 1989 by John Wiley & Sons, Inc.
--          All Rights Reserved.

with Get_Command_Line;
with SCROLL_TERMINAL, TEXT_IO, ASCII_UTILITIES;
procedure Line is
  TAIL      : string(1..79);
  FILENAME : string(1..68);
  SOURCE    : string(1..250);
  TAIL_LENGTH, NAME_LENGTH, SOURCE_LENGTH
    : natural;
  THIS_LINE, LINE_NUMBER : natural;
  FIRST_LINE, LAST_LINE  : positive;
  START_LINE             : integer;
  FILE                   : TEXT_IO.File_type;

  procedure Extract(TAIL        : string;
                    TAIL_LENGTH : natural;
                    FILE_NAME   : out string;
                    NAME_LENGTH : out natural;
                    LINE_NUMBER : out natural)
    is separate; -- file LE.ada

  procedure Get_File(FILENAME    : out string;
                     NAME_LENGTH : out natural)
     is
   use SCROLL_TERMINAL;
begin
   get_line("What file? ",FILENAME,
     NAME_LENGTH);
exception
   when NEEDS_HELP =>
     new_line;
     put_line("Please enter the name of the"
             & " file you want to print.");
```

```
            put_line("You may enter a complete"
                  & " path name if you like.");
            put_line("Press CONTROL-C to QUIT.");
            Get_File(FILENAME,NAME_LENGTH);
      end Get_File;

      procedure get(LINE_NUMBER : out positive) is
        TEXT : string(1..4);
        use SCROLL_TERMINAL;
      begin
        get("What line number? ",TEXT);
        LINE_NUMBER := integer'VALUE(TEXT);
      exception
        when CONSTRAINT_ERROR | NEEDS_HELP =>
          new_line;
          put("Please enter the number of the");
          put_line(" line you want displayed.");
          put_line(
            "(It must be in the range 1..9999.)");
          new_line;
          get(LINE_NUMBER);
      end get;

    begin
      -- Get the FILENAME and LINE_NUMBER from the
      -- command line.
      Get_Command_Line(TAIL, TAIL_LENGTH);
      Extract(TAIL, TAIL_LENGTH,
              FILENAME, NAME_LENGTH,
              LINE_NUMBER);

      -- If no FILENAME on the command line,
      -- ask the user for it.
      if NAME_LENGTH = 0 then
        Get_File(FILENAME, NAME_LENGTH);
      end if;

      -- Open the file (or raise NAME_ERROR
      -- while trying).
      TEXT_IO.Open(FILE, TEXT_IO.IN_FILE,
        FILENAME(1..NAME_LENGTH));

      -- If no LINE_NUMBER on command line,
      -- ask the user for it.
      if LINE_NUMBER = 0 then
        get(LINE_NUMBER);
```

```
    end if;

    -- Compute first and last line numbers.
    START_LINE := LINE_NUMBER-10;
    if START_LINE > 0 then
      FIRST_LINE := START_LINE;
    else
      FIRST_LINE := 1;
    end if;
    LAST_LINE := LINE_NUMBER+10;

    -- Read the file. Count each line as you read
    -- it. If the line is before FIRST_LINE, just
    -- throw it in the bit bucket and get the
    -- next one. When you finally get to the
    -- FIRST_LINE, print the line number and the
    -- text on that line. Keep doing this until
    -- you have printed the LAST_LINE.
    THIS_LINE := 0;
    while not TEXT_IO.End_Of_File(FILE) loop
      THIS_LINE := THIS_LINE+1;
      TEXT_IO.get_line(FILE, SOURCE,
        SOURCE_LENGTH);
      if THIS_LINE >= FIRST_LINE then
        SCROLL_TERMINAL.put(string'
          (ASCII_UTILITIES.Image(
            THIS_LINE,4)) & ' ');
        SCROLL_TERMINAL.put_line(
          SOURCE(1..SOURCE_LENGTH));
      end if;
      if THIS_LINE = LAST_LINE then
        exit;
      end if;
    end loop;

    -- All done, so close the input file.
    TEXT_IO.Close(FILE);
  exception
    when TEXT_IO.NAME_ERROR =>
      SCROLL_TERMINAL.put("I can't find """);
      SCROLL_TERMINAL.put(
        FILENAME(1..NAME_LENGTH));
      SCROLL_TERMINAL.put_line(""".");
  end Line;
```

```
-- Listing 64.

--              LE.ada
--              Version 1.0
--              25 September 1988

--              Do-While Jones
--              324 Traci Lane
--              Ridgecrest. CA 93555
--              (619) 375-4607

-- Copyright 1989 by John Wiley & Sons, Inc.
--          All Rights Reserved.

separate(Line)
procedure Extract(TAIL        : string;
                  TAIL_LENGTH : natural;
                  FILE_NAME   : out string;
                  NAME_LENGTH : out natural;
                  LINE_NUMBER : out natural) is
  I, FIRST, LAST, LENGTH : integer;
  BACKWARDS : boolean;
begin
  -- Assume no file name or line number.
  NAME_LENGTH := 0;
  LINE_NUMBER := 0;
  if TAIL'LENGTH = 0 then return; end if;

  -- There really is something on the command
  -- line. Use "I" as an index pointer that
  -- scans TAIL.
  I := TAIL'FIRST; -- always 1

  -- Skip over leading blanks (if any).
  while I <= TAIL_LENGTH
      and then TAIL(I) = ' ' loop
    I := I+1;
  end loop;

  if I > TAIL_LENGTH then return; end if;
  -- NAME_LENGTH and TEXT_LENGTH still = 0.

  -- Find the first field.
  FIRST := I;
```

```
I := I+1;
while I <= TAIL_LENGTH loop
  if TAIL(I) = ',' or
     TAIL(I) = ' ' then
    exit;
  end if;
  I := I+1;
end loop;
-- I is > TAIL_LENGTH or I points
-- to a terminator
LAST := I-1;

-- Convert the first field to a line number.
begin
  LINE_NUMBER
    := integer'VALUE(TAIL(FIRST..LAST));
  BACKWARDS := FALSE; -- arguments are in
                      -- correct order
exception
  when CONSTRAINT_ERROR =>
    BACKWARDS := TRUE; -- arguments are
                       -- reversed
    -- copy first field to the file name
    -- instead
    LENGTH := LAST-FIRST+1;
    NAME_LENGTH := LENGTH;
    FILE_NAME(FILE_NAME'FIRST..
      FILE_NAME'FIRST+LENGTH-1)
        := TAIL(FIRST..LAST);
end;

-- Skip over separating blanks (if any).
I := I+1;
while I <= TAIL_LENGTH
    and then TAIL(I) = ' ' loop
  I := I+1;
end loop;

if I > TAIL_LENGTH then return; end if;
-- LINE_NUMBER = 0

-- Find the second field.
FIRST := I;
I := I+1;
```

```
while I <= TAIL_LENGTH loop
  if TAIL(I) = ',' or
     TAIL(I) = ' ' then
    exit;
  end if;
  I := I+1;
end loop;
LAST := I-1;

if BACKWARDS then
  -- hope the second field is a number
  begin
    LINE_NUMBER
      := integer'VALUE(TAIL(FIRST..LAST));
  exception
    when CONSTRAINT_ERROR => -- it wasn't
      LINE_NUMBER := 0;
  end;

else -- correct order
  -- Copy the second field to FILE_NAME.
  LENGTH := LAST-FIRST+1;
  NAME_LENGTH := LENGTH;
  FILE_NAME(FILE_NAME'FIRST..
    FILE_NAME'FIRST+LENGTH-1)
      := TAIL(FIRST..LAST);
end if;

end Extract;
```

```
-- Listing 65.

--                    GCLBMIBM.ada
--                    Version 1.1
--                    25 September 1988

--                    Do-While Jones
--                    324 Traci Lane
--                    Ridgecrest, CA 93555
--                    (619) 375-4607

--   Copyright 1989 by John Wiley & Sons, Inc.
--            All Rights Reserved.

-- Meridian command line interface for IBM PC.

-- This procedure is NOT PORTABLE because it
-- uses some utility packages available from
-- Meridian Software Systems, Inc. These
-- packages are compatible with the Meridian
-- AdaVantage compiler, but are not included
-- with the compiler. (They must be purchased
-- separately.)

-- Revision 1.1 returns the whole command line.
-- It is based on a routine suggested by
-- Stephanie Leif.

with ARG, TEXT_HANDLER; -- Meridian utility packages
procedure Get_Command_Line(
    TAIL    : out string;
    LENGTH : out natural) is
  ARGUMENTS  : natural;
  TEMP_LINE  : TEXT_HANDLER.TEXT(80);

begin
  -- Find out how many arguments are in the
  -- line.
  ARGUMENTS := ARG.COUNT;

  if ARGUMENTS = 1 then
    -- the only thing there is the name of the
    -- program called. Return null string.
    LENGTH := 0;
```

```
      else
        -- Start with a null string.
        TEXT_HANDLER.SET(TEMP_LINE,"");

        -- Join the arguments in the command tail.
        for INDEX in 2..ARGUMENTS loop
          -- Declare a block to allow memory re-use
          -- when joining arguments.
          begin
            -- Catenate the next argument.
            TEXT_HANDLER.APPEND(
              ARG.DATA(INDEX),TEMP_LINE);
            -- Insert a space before the next
            -- argument.
            TEXT_HANDLER.APPEND(" ", TEMP_LINE);
          end;
        end loop;

        -- Assign out parameters.
        TAIL(1..TEXT_HANDLER.LENGTH(TEMP_LINE))
          := TEXT_HANDLER.VALUE(TEMP_LINE);
        -- Ignore the space at the end.
        LENGTH
          := TEXT_HANDLER.LENGTH(TEMP_LINE) -1;
      end if;

  end Get_Command_Line;
```

```
-- Listing 66.

--                      PCS.ada
--                      Version 2
--                      10 May 1988

--                      Do-While Jones
--                      324 Traci Lane
--                      Ridgecrest, CA 93555
--                      (619) 375-4607

--   Copyright 1989 by John Wiley & Sons, Inc.
--           All Rights Reserved.

package PLAYING_CARDS is

   CARDS_IN_A_DECK : constant := 52;
   CARDS_IN_A_HAND : constant :=  5;

   type Suits is (CLUBS, DIAMONDS, HEARTS,
     SPADES, NO_TRUMP);

   type Ranks is (TWO, THREE, FOUR, FIVE, SIX,
     SEVEN, EIGHT, NINE, TEN, JACK, QUEEN, KING,
     ACE);

   type Cards is private;
   type Hands is private;
   type Decks is private;

-- Exceptions

   DECK_ERROR : exception;
      -- Raised by Open_New(DECK) if the number
      -- of cards created for the deck doesn't
      -- match the constant CARDS_IN_A_DECK. This
      -- exception will only be raised if you
      -- modify the package body to create a
      -- Canasta or Pinochle deck and forget to
      -- change the constant CARDS_IN_A_DECK.

   DECK_EXHAUSTED : exception;
      -- Raised by Deal_A_Card if you try to deal
      -- from an empty deck.
```

```
   HAND_FULL : exception;
      -- Raised by Deal_A_Card if you try to deal
      -- a card to a hand that is already full.

-- Operations on Cards:

   function Suit_Of(CARD : Cards) return Suits;
      -- Tell the suit of the card.
   function Rank_Of(CARD : Cards) return Ranks;
      -- Tell the rank of the card.

-- Operations on Decks:

   procedure Open_New(DECK : out Decks);
      -- Create a new (unshuffled) deck.
      -- May raise DECK_ERROR.

   procedure Shuffle(DECK : in out DECKS);
      -- Shuffle the deck.

-- Operations on Hands:

   procedure Open_New(HAND : out Hands);
      -- Create a new (empty) hand.

   procedure Sort(HAND : in out Hands);
      -- Sort the hand by ranks, ignoring suits.

   function Peek(CARD_NUMBER : integer;
                 HAND        : Hands)
      return Cards;
      -- Look at a particular card in a hand.

   procedure Play(CARD_NUMBER : integer;
                  HAND         : in out Hands);
      -- Play a card from the hand.

   function Played(CARD_NUMBER : integer;
                   HAND        : Hands)
      return boolean;
      -- Tell if a card has already been played.

   function Filled(HAND : Hands) return boolean;
      -- Tells if the hand is filled.
```

```
    -- Operations on Decks and Hands:

    procedure Deal_A_Card(TO   : in out Hands;
                          FROM : in out Decks);
      -- Deal a card to a hand from a deck.
      -- May raise DECK_EXHAUSTED or HAND_FILLED.

  private

    type Cards is
      record
        SUIT : Suits;
        RANK : Ranks;
      end record;

    type Fans is
      array(integer range <>) of Cards;
    type Status is
      array (integer range <>) of boolean;

    type Decks is
      record
        CARDS_LEFT : integer;
        FAN        : Fans(1..CARDS_IN_A_DECK);
      end record;

    type Hands is
      record
        PLAYED : Status(1..CARDS_IN_A_HAND);
        FAN    : Fans(1..CARDS_IN_A_HAND);
      end record;

  end PLAYING_CARDS;
```

```
--  Listing 67.

--    PCB.ada
--    Version 2.0
--    10 May 1988

--    Do-While Jones
--    324 Traci Lane
--    Ridgecrest, CA 93555
--    (619) 375-4607

--  Copyright 1989 by John Wiley & Sons, Inc.
--          All Rights Reserved.

with RANDOM_NUMBERS, STANDARD_INTEGERS;
package body PLAYING_CARDS is

  function Suit_Of(CARD : Cards)
    return Suits is
  begin
    return CARD.SUIT;
  end Suit_Of;

  function Rank_Of(CARD : Cards)
    return Ranks is
  begin
    return CARD.RANK;
  end Rank_of;

  procedure Open_New(DECK : out Decks) is
    i    : integer := 0;
    CARD : Cards;
  begin
    for S in CLUBS..SPADES loop
      for R in Ranks loop
        CARD.SUIT := S;
        CARD.RANK := R;
        i := i+1;
        DECK.FAN(i) := CARD;
      end loop;
    end loop;
    DECK.CARDS_LEFT := i;
    if i /= CARDS_IN_A_DECK then
      raise DECK_ERROR;
    end if;
```

```
exception
  -- CONSTRAINT_ERROR or DECK_ERROR may be
  -- raised by this procedure if the number
  -- of cards in a deck does not equal the
  -- number of cards generated.
  when others =>
    -- convert all errors to DECK_ERROR
    raise DECK_ERROR;
end Open_New;

procedure Shuffle(DECK : in out Decks) is
  SEQUENCE : RANDOM_NUMBERS.Sequences
    (1..CARDS_IN_A_DECK);
  TEMP : Decks;
  INDEX : integer;
  use STANDARD_INTEGERS;
begin
  TEMP.CARDS_LEFT := CARDS_IN_A_DECK;
  SEQUENCE := RANDOM_NUMBERS.Deal
    (CARDS_IN_A_DECK, CARDS_IN_A_DECK);
  for i in 1..CARDS_IN_A_DECK loop
    INDEX := integer(SEQUENCE(Natural_8(i)));
    TEMP.FAN(i) := DECK.FAN(INDEX);
  end loop;
  DECK := TEMP;
end Shuffle;

procedure Open_New(HAND : out Hands) is
begin
  for i in 1..CARDS_IN_A_HAND loop
    HAND.PLAYED(i) := TRUE;
    -- hand is empty (all cards have
    -- been played)
  end loop;
end Open_New;

procedure Sort(HAND : in out Hands) is
  SORTED : boolean;
  TEMP   : Cards;
begin
  loop
    SORTED := TRUE;
    for i in integer
        range 1..CARDS_IN_A_HAND-1 loop
      if Rank_Of(Peek(i,HAND)) >
```

```
              Rank_Of(Peek(i+1,HAND)) then
                TEMP := Peek(i,HAND);
                HAND.FAN(i) := Peek(i+1,HAND);
                HAND.FAN(i+1) := TEMP;
                SORTED := FALSE;
            end if;
          end loop;
          exit when SORTED;
        end loop;
      end SORT;


      function Peek(CARD_NUMBER : integer;
                    HAND        : Hands)
        return Cards is
      begin
        return HAND.FAN(CARD_NUMBER);
      end Peek;


      procedure Play(CARD_NUMBER : integer;
                     HAND         : in out Hands) is
      begin
        HAND.PLAYED(CARD_NUMBER) := TRUE;
      end Play;


      function Played(CARD_NUMBER : integer;
                      HAND         : Hands)
        return boolean is
      begin
        return HAND.PLAYED(CARD_NUMBER);
      end Played;


      function Filled(HAND : Hands)
        return boolean is
      begin
        for i in 1..CARDS_IN_A_HAND loop
          if Played(i,HAND) then
            return FALSE;
            -- if any card is played, then
            -- hand is not filled
          end if;
        end loop;
        return TRUE;
        -- because no cards have been played
      end Filled;
```

```
   procedure Deal_A_CARD(TO   : in out Hands;
                         FROM : in out Decks) is
     X : integer := 0;
   begin
     -- find and empty slot in the hand
     loop
       X := X+1;
       if X > CARDS_IN_A_HAND then
         raise HAND_FULL;
        end if;
       exit when Played(X,TO);
     end loop;
     -- draw a card from the deck,
     -- and put it in the empty slot
     if FROM.CARDS_LEFT < 1 then
       raise DECK_EXHAUSTED;
     else
       FROM.CARDS_LEFT := FROM.CARDS_LEFT-1;
     end if;
     TO.FAN(X) := FROM.FAN(CARDS_IN_A_DECK
                 - FROM.CARDS_LEFT);
     TO.PLAYED(X) := FALSE;
   end Deal_A_Card;

end PLAYING_CARDS;
```

```
-- Listing 68.

--              DP2.ada
--              Version 2
--              13 May 1988

--              Do-While Jones
--              324 Traci Lane
--              Ridgecrest, CA 93555
--              (619) 375-4607

-- Copyright 1989 by John Wiley & Sons, Inc.
--          All Rights Reserved.

with PLAYING_CARDS, MONEY;
use PLAYING_CARDS;
procedure Draw_Poker is

   type Values is (NOTHING, TWO_PAIR,
    THREE_OF_A_KIND, STRAIGHT, FLUSH,
    FULL_HOUSE, FOUR_OF_A_KIND,
    STRAIGHT_FLUSH, ROYAL_FLUSH);

   STOCK        : Decks;
   PLAYERS_HAND : Hands;
   WAGER        : MONEY.Cents;
   VALUE        : Values;

   function "="(LEFT, RIGHT : MONEY.Cents)
     return boolean renames MONEY."=";

   procedure get(WAGER : in out MONEY.Cents)
     is separate; -- file DP2G.ada

   function Value_Of(HAND : Hands) return Values
     is separate; -- file DP2VO.ada

   procedure put(PLAYERS_HAND : Hands;
                 VALUE        : Values)
     is separate; -- file DP2P.ada

   procedure Discard_From(
     PLAYERS_HAND : in out Hands) is separate;
     -- file DP2DF.ada
```

```
    procedure Payout(VALUE : Values;
                     WAGER : MONEY.Cents)
      is separate; -- file DP2PO.ada

begin
   -- Open a new deck of cards.
   Open_New(STOCK);
   -- Let the initial default bet be $1.
   WAGER := MONEY.Type_Convert(100); -- cents

   loop
      -- Play as long as the user is willing
      -- to bet.
      get(WAGER);
      exit when WAGER = MONEY.Type_Convert(0);
      -- Shuffle before every deal.
      Shuffle(STOCK);
      -- Deal a hand to the player.
      Open_New(PLAYERS_HAND);
      for i in 1..CARDS_IN_A_HAND loop
         Deal_A_Card(PLAYERS_HAND, STOCK);
      end loop;
      -- Show him what he has.
      VALUE := Value_Of(PLAYERS_HAND);
      put(PLAYERS_HAND,VALUE);
      -- Let the player hold or draw each card.
      Discard_From(PLAYERS_HAND);
      -- Replace any cards he may have discarded.
      loop
         exit when Filled(PLAYERS_HAND);
         Deal_A_Card(PLAYERS_HAND, STOCK);
      end loop;
      -- Show him what he has now.
      VALUE := Value_Of(PLAYERS_HAND);
      put(PLAYERS_HAND,VALUE);
      -- Pay him if he won.
      Payout(VALUE,WAGER);
   end loop;
end Draw_Poker;
```

```
-- Listing 69.

--              DP2G.ada
--              Version 2.0
--              13 May 1988

--              Do-While Jones
--              324 Traci Lane
--              Ridgecrest, CA 93555
--              (619) 375-4607

-- Copyright 1989 by John Wiley & Sons, Inc.
--          All Rights Reserved.

with SCROLL_TERMINAL, ASCII_UTILITIES;
separate(Draw_Poker)
procedure get(WAGER : in out MONEY.Cents) is
  BET : string(1..4);
  NEGATIVE, TOO_SMALL, TOO_BIG : exception;
  use MONEY;
begin
  -- Let the default BET be the previous WAGER.
  BET := Image(WAGER, LENGTH => 4,
    PENNIES => FALSE);
  ASCII_UTILITIES.Left_Justify(BET);
  SCROLL_TERMINAL.get(
   "How much do you want to bet? ", BET, BET);
  -- Check for illegal bets.
  WAGER := MONEY.Value(BET);
  if WAGER < +0 then raise NEGATIVE; end if;
  -- see if player wants to quit
  if WAGER = +0 then return; end if;
  if WAGER < +100 then raise TOO_SMALL; end if;
  if WAGER > +99900 then raise TOO_BIG; end if;

exception
  when NEGATIVE =>
    SCROLL_TERMINAL.put_line(
        "You think to can make money"
      & " by betting a");
    SCROLL_TERMINAL.put_line(
      "negative amount and then"
      & " losing on purpose,");
    SCROLL_TERMINAL.put_line(
      "don't you?" & ASCII.LF);
```

```
      SCROLL_TERMINAL.put_line(
        "It's not going to work, Smarty!"
        & ASCII.LF);
      -- Try again with $1 default.
      WAGER := +100; -- cents
      get(WAGER);

   when TOO_SMALL =>
      SCROLL_TERMINAL.put_line(
        "Come on, Sport! Bet at least a buck!");
      -- Try again with $1 default.
      WAGER := +100; -- cents
      get(WAGER);

   when TOO_BIG =>
      SCROLL_TERMINAL.put_line(
        "Sorry, the house limit is $999.");
      -- Try again with $1 default.
      WAGER := +100; -- cents
      get(WAGER);

   when SCROLL_TERMINAL.NEEDS_HELP
      | CONSTRAINT_ERROR =>
      SCROLL_TERMINAL.put_line(ASCII.LF &
        "Enter $1 to $999 to keep playing.");
      SCROLL_TERMINAL.put_line(
        "ENTER 0 to quit." & ASCII.LF);
      -- Try again with $1 default.
      WAGER := +100; -- cents
      get(WAGER);
end get;
```

```
-- Listing 70.

--              DP2V0.ada
--              Version 2.0
--              10 May 1988

--              Do-While Jones
--              324 Traci Lane
--              Ridgecrest, CA 93555
--              (619) 375-4607

-- Copyright 1989 by John Wiley & Sons, Inc.
--          All Rights Reserved.

-- This revision recognizes that TWO, THREE,
-- FOUR, FIVE, ACE is a straight (but not a
-- royal flush). There are no real differences
-- between this version and the 30 DEC 1985
-- version, except the name of the function
-- Card_Number has been changed to Peek to
-- match the new PLAYING_CARDS package
-- specification.

separate (Draw_Poker)
function Value_of(HAND : Hands) return Values is

  PATTERN : string(1..CARDS_IN_A_HAND-1);
  X       : Hands;

  function Flush_In(HAND : Hands)
    return boolean is
  begin
    for i in
        integer range 1..CARDS_IN_A_HAND-1 loop
      if Suit_Of(Peek(i, HAND)) /=
         Suit_Of(Peek(i+1, HAND)) then
          return FALSE;
      end if;
    end loop;
    return TRUE;
  end Flush_In;

  function Straight_In(HAND : Hands)
      return boolean is
    -- HAND must be sorted for this to work
```

```
   begin
      if Rank_Of(Peek(1,HAND)) = TWO    and
         Rank_Of(Peek(2,HAND)) = THREE and
         Rank_Of(Peek(3,HAND)) = FOUR   and
         Rank_Of(Peek(4,HAND)) = FIVE   and
         Rank_Of(Peek(5,HAND)) = ACE then
           return TRUE;
      end if;
      for i in
          integer range 1..CARDS_IN_A_HAND-1 loop
        if Ranks'POS(Rank_Of(Peek(i,HAND))) /=
           Ranks'POS(Rank_Of(Peek(i+1,HAND)))-1
           then
           return FALSE;
        end if;
      end loop;
      return TRUE;
    end Straight_In;

 begin

    -- make a copy of the hand so it can be
    -- sorted
    X := HAND;
    SORT(X);
    for i in
        integer range 1..CARDS_IN_A_HAND-1 loop
      if Rank_Of(Peek(i,X)) =
         Rank_Of(Peek(i+1,X)) then
         -- adjacent cards have the SAME rank
         PATTERN(i) := 'S';
      else
         -- adjacent cards have DIFFERENT rank
         PATTERN(i) := 'D';
      end if;
    end loop;
    if Flush_In(X) and Straight_In(X) then
      if Rank_Of(Peek(4,X)) = KING then
        return ROYAL_FLUSH;
      else
        return STRAIGHT_FLUSH;
      end if;
    end if;
```

```
if PATTERN = "SSSD" or PATTERN = "DSSS" then
  return FOUR_OF_A_KIND;
end if;

if PATTERN = "SSDS" or PATTERN = "SDSS" then
  return FULL_HOUSE;
end if;

if Flush_In(X) then
  return FLUSH;
end if;

if Straight_In(X) then
  return STRAIGHT;
end if;

if PATTERN = "SSDD" or
   PATTERN = "DSSD" or
   PATTERN = "DDSS" then
    return THREE_OF_A_KIND;
end if;

if PATTERN = "SDSD" or
   PATTERN = "DSDS" or
   PATTERN = "SDDS" then
    return TWO_PAIR;
end if;

return NOTHING;

end Value_Of;
```

```
-- Listing 71.

--                 DP2P.ada
--                 Version 2.0
--                 10 May 1988

--                 Do-While Jones
--                 324 Traci Lane
--                 Ridgecrest, CA 93555
--                 (619) 375-4607

-- Copyright 1989 by John Wiley & Sons, Inc.
--           All Rights Reserved.

with SCROLL_TERMINAL;
separate(Draw_Poker)
procedure put(PLAYERS_HAND : Hands;
              VALUE        : Values) is
begin
  SCROLL_TERMINAL.New_Page;
  SCROLL_TERMINAL.put_line("You have:");
  for i in 1..CARDS_IN_A_HAND loop
    delay (1.0); -- for suspense
    SCROLL_TERMINAL.put_line(Ranks'IMAGE
      (Rank_Of(Peek(i,PLAYERS_HAND)))
      & " of " & Suits'IMAGE
      (Suit_Of(Peek(i,PLAYERS_HAND))));
  end loop;
  SCROLL_TERMINAL.new_line;
  if VALUE /= NOTHING then
    SCROLL_TERMINAL.put("You have ");
    case VALUE is
      when TWO_PAIR |
           THREE_OF_A_KIND |
           FOUR_OF_A_KIND =>
        null; -- no article needed
      when others =>
        SCROLL_TERMINAL.put("a ");
    end case;
    SCROLL_TERMINAL.put_line
      (Values'IMAGE(VALUE) & '!' & ASCII.LF);
  end if;
end put;
```

```
-- Listing 72.

--              DP2DF.ada
--              Version 2.0
--              10 May 1988

--              Do-While Jones
--              324 Traci Lane
--              Ridgecrest, CA 93555
--              (619) 375-4607

-- Copyright 1989 by John Wiley & Sons, Inc.
--          All Rights Reserved.

with SCROLL_TERMINAL;
separate(Draw_Poker)
procedure Discard_From(
    PLAYERS_HAND : in out Hands) is

  CURRENT_CARD : positive;
    -- This tells the exception handler where
    -- to begin.

  procedure Hold_Or_Draw(
      THIS_CARD : positive) is
    ACTION : string(1..4);
  begin
    ACTION := "HOLD";
    SCROLL_TERMINAL.get(Ranks'IMAGE
      (Rank_Of(Peek(THIS_CARD,PLAYERS_HAND)))
      & " of " & Suits'IMAGE
      (Suit_Of(Peek(THIS_CARD,PLAYERS_HAND)))
      & " --> ", ACTION, ACTION);
    case ACTION(1) is
      when 'H' | 'h' =>
        null; -- hold the card
      when 'D' | 'd' =>
        -- discard it
        Play(THIS_CARD,PLAYERS_HAND);
      when others =>
        raise SCROLL_TERMINAL.NEEDS_HELP;
    end case;
  end Hold_Or_Draw;
```

```
procedure Start_With(CARD_NUMBER : positive)
  is
begin
  for i in CARD_NUMBER..CARDS_IN_A_HAND loop
    CURRENT_CARD := i;
    Hold_Or_Draw(CURRENT_CARD);
  end loop;
end Start_With;

begin
  SCROLL_TERMINAL.put_line(
    "HOLD or DRAW each card.");
  Start_with(1);

exception
  when SCROLL_TERMINAL.NEEDS_HELP =>
    SCROLL_TERMINAL.put_line
      ("If you want to keep this" &
       " card, type 'H' or 'HOLD'.");
    SCROLL_TERMINAL.put_line
      ("If you want to replace it," &
       " type 'D' or 'DRAW'.");
    Start_With(CURRENT_CARD);
end Discard_From;
```

```
-- Listing 73.

--              DP2PO.ada
--              Version 2.0
--              10 May 1988

--              Do-While Jones
--              324 Traci Lane
--              Ridgecrest, CA 93555
--              (619) 375-4607

-- Copyright 1989 by John Wiley & Sons, Inc.
--         All Rights Reserved.

with SCROLL_TERMINAL;
with STANDARD_INTEGERS; use STANDARD_INTEGERS;
separate(Draw_Poker)
procedure Payout(VALUE : Values;
                 WAGER : Money.Cents) is
  PAYOFF : Natural_32; -- because Cents is
                       -- 32 bit integer

  use MONEY; -- to make "*" visible

begin
  case VALUE is
    when ROYAL_FLUSH     => PAYOFF := 250;
    when STRAIGHT_FLUSH  => PAYOFF :=  50;
    when FOUR_OF_A_KIND  => PAYOFF :=  25;
    when FULL_HOUSE      => PAYOFF :=   6;
    when FLUSH           => PAYOFF :=   5;
    when STRAIGHT        => PAYOFF :=   4;
    when THREE_OF_A_KIND => PAYOFF :=   3;
    when TWO_PAIR        => PAYOFF :=   2;
    when NOTHING         => PAYOFF :=   0;
  end case;
  if PAYOFF = 0 then
    SCROLL_TERMINAL.put_line(
      "Sorry, you lost.");
  else
    SCROLL_TERMINAL.put("You win ");
    SCROLL_TERMINAL.put_line
      (MONEY.Image(WAGER * PAYOFF) & '!');
  end if;
end Payout;
```

```ada
-- Listing 74.

--                  COSTEST.ada
--                  Version 1
--                  24 July 1988

--                  Do-While Jones
--                  324 Traci Lane
--                  Ridgecrest, CA 93555
--                  (619) 375-4607

-- Copyright 1989 by John Wiley & Sons, Inc.
--           All Rights Reserved.

with TEXT_IO, ASCII_UTILITIES, TRIG;
procedure Cos_Test is
  ANGLE  : TRIG.Deg;
  X      : float;
  OUTPUT : TEXT_IO.File_type;
  use TRIG;
    -- for "+" and "-" type conversions
begin
  TEXT_IO.Create(OUTPUT,TEXT_IO.OUT_FILE,
    "COS.DAT");
  TEXT_IO.put_line(
    "Writing output to COS.DAT");
  X := -5.0;
  while X < 370.0 loop
    ANGLE := Type_Convert(X);
    TEXT_IO.put(OUTPUT,
      ASCII_UTILITIES.Fixed_Image(X));
    TEXT_IO.Set_Col(OUTPUT,20);
    TEXT_IO.put_line(OUTPUT,
      ASCII_UTILITIES.Float_Image(
      TRIG.Cos(ANGLE)));
    X := X+1.0;
  end loop;
  TEXT_IO.Close(OUTPUT);
  TEXT_IO.put_line("Done.");
end Cos_Test;
```

```
-- Listing 75.

--                      COSDIF.ada
--                      Version 1
--                      26 September 1988

--                      Do-While Jones
--                      324 Traci Lane
--                      Ridgecrest, CA 93555
--                      (619) 375-4607


--   Copyright 1989 by John Wiley & Sons, Inc.
--            All Rights Reserved.

with TEXT_IO; use TEXT_IO;
with ASCII_UTILITIES;
procedure Cos_Dif is
  TEXT       : string(1..80);
  LENGTH     : natural;
  REF_ANGLE, REF_COS, TEST_ANGLE, TEST_COS
             : float;
  TEST, REF : File_type;
  MAX_ERROR : float := -100.0;
  MIN_ERROR : float := 100.0;
  MAX_ERROR_ANGLE, MIN_ERROR_ANGLE : float;
begin
  -- Open the two files the user wants
  -- compared.
  put(
   "What is the name of the REFERENCE file? ");
  get_line(TEXT,LENGTH); new_line;
  Open(REF,IN_FILE,TEXT(1..LENGTH));
  put("What is the name of the TEST file? ");
  get_line(TEXT,LENGTH); new_line;
  Open(TEST,IN_FILE,TEXT(1..LENGTH));

  -- Compare every line.
  while not End_Of_File(REF) loop
    get_line(REF,TEXT,LENGTH);
    REF_ANGLE :=
      ASCII_UTILITIES.Value(TEXT(1..10));
    REF_COS :=
      ASCII_UTILITIES.Value(TEXT(10..LENGTH));
    get_line(TEST,TEXT,LENGTH);
    TEST_ANGLE :=
```

```
     ASCII_UTILITIES.Value(TEXT(1..10));
   TEST_COS :=
     ASCII_UTILITIES.Value(TEXT(10..LENGTH));

   -- Check to make sure the angles are
   -- the same.
   if REF_ANGLE /= TEST_ANGLE then
     put_line("Files out of sync.");
     put("REFERENCE ANGLE = ");
     put_line(
       ASCII_UTILITIES.Fixed_Image(
       REF_ANGLE));
     put("   TEST ANGLE = ");
     put_line(
       ASCII_UTILITIES.Fixed_Image(
       TEST_ANGLE));
     exit;
   end if;

   -- Keep track of the biggest error.
   if TEST_COS - REF_COS > MAX_ERROR then
     MAX_ERROR := TEST_COS - REF_COS;
     MAX_ERROR_ANGLE := REF_ANGLE;
   end if;
   if TEST_COS - REF_COS < MIN_ERROR then
     MIN_ERROR := TEST_COS - REF_COS;
     MIN_ERROR_ANGLE := REF_ANGLE;
   end if;

end loop;

-- Print the largest error in each direction.
put("The maximum positive error was ");
put(ASCII_UTILITIES.Fixed_Image(
  MAX_ERROR,0,6));
put(" at ");
put(ASCII_UTILITIES.Fixed_Image(
  MAX_ERROR_ANGLE));
put_line(" degrees.");
put("The maximum negative error was ");
put(ASCII_UTILITIES.Fixed_Image(
  MIN_ERROR,0,6));
put(" at ");
put(ASCII_UTILITIES.Fixed_Image(
  MIN_ERROR_ANGLE));
put_line(" degrees.");
```

```
   -- Close the input files.
   Close(REF);
   Close(TEST);

end Cos_Dif;
```

```
-- Listing 76.

--              RNS.ada
--              Version 3
--              14 February 1988

--              Do-While Jones
--              324 Traci Lane
--              Ridgecrest, CA 93555
--              (619) 375-4607

--   Copyright 1989 by John Wiley & Sons, Inc.
--          All Rights Reserved.


-- Version 2 has the following improvements
-- over Version 1:
--     It works even on 16 bit machines.
--     It includes the Error and Noise
--     functions.


-- Version 3 includes the Random_Digit
-- function.

with STANDARD_INTEGERS; use STANDARD_INTEGERS;
package RANDOM_NUMBERS is

  type Sequences is
    array(Natural_8 range <>) of Positive_8;

  function Rnd return float;
    -- Return a random number X
    -- such that 0.0 <= X < 1.0.
    -- The implementation of the random number
    -- generator happens to generate only 2048
    -- different random numbers. Therefore, if
    -- you multiply Rnd by a number larger than
    -- 2048, "holes" will start to appear in
    -- the distribution.

    -- (Use Random_Digit to build random
    -- numbers bigger than 200.)

  function Roll(LIMIT : Positive_8)
    return Positive_8;
```

```
   -- Return a random number in the range
   -- 1..LIMIT. The pattern repeats after 2048
   -- rolls.

function Deal(NUMBER, LIMIT : Positive_8)
 return Sequences;
   -- Return a sequence of NUMBER random
   -- integers. Each integer in the sequence
   -- is in the range 1..LIMIT. No integer
   -- appears twice in the sequence.

function Error(LIMIT : float) return float;
function Error(LIMIT : Positive_8)
   return Integer_8;
   -- Return a random number in the range
   -- -LIMIT..+LIMIT. Since this is derived
   -- from Rnd, it would not be a good idea to
   -- let the LIMIT exceed 128 for the float
   -- version of this function.

function Noise(RMS : float) return float;
   -- Return a zero-mean gausian random number
   -- with a standard deviation of RMS. The
   -- sequence repeats after 2048 values.

procedure Set_Seed(X : Natural_32);
   -- Used to set the seed in the random
   -- number generator.

procedure Randomize;
   -- Set the seed in the Rnd function
   -- generator based on the current time of
   -- day.

subtype Numerals is integer range 0..9;

function Random_Digit return Numerals;
   -- This function returns a random digit in
   -- the range 0..9. Unlike the other
   -- subprograms in this package, the
   -- sequence does not repeat after 2048
   -- numbers. The price for this randomness
   -- is speed. It does, however, allow you to
   -- build as many random numbers as large as
```

```
         -- you please without repetition. Suppose
         -- you want a 9 digit random number. You
         -- can do this:
         --  X := float(Random_Digit);
         --  for i in 1..8 loop
         --    X := 10.0 * X + float(Random_Digit);
         --  end loop;

         -- X will be a floating point number in the
         -- range 000000000.0 .. 999999999.0.

end RANDOM_NUMBERS;
```

```
-- Listing 77.

--                    RNB.ada
--                    Version 3.0
--                    14 February 1988

--                    Do-While Jones
--                    324 Traci Lane
--                    Ridgecrest, CA 93555
--                    (619) 375-4607

-- Copyright 1989 by John Wiley & Sons, Inc.
--          All Rights Reserved.

with CALENDAR;
package body RANDOM_NUMBERS is

  SEED : Integer_32;

  type Digit_arrays is
    array(1..100) of Numerals;

  NUMBER_POOL : Digit_arrays;
    -- Contains 10 of every digit.
  POOL_INDEX : positive;
    -- Tells how many numbers in NUMBER_POOL
    -- have been used.

  function Rnd return float is
  begin
    -- Use the sequence generator from exercise
    -- 8.1 in "Programming in Ada" by John
    -- Barnes.
    if SEED mod 2 = 0 then
      SEED := SEED + 1;
    end if;
    SEED := (SEED * 3125) mod 8192;
    return float(SEED)/8192.0;
  end Rnd;

  function Roll(LIMIT : Positive_8)
      return Positive_8 is
    RANDOM : float;
  begin
    RANDOM := float(LIMIT) * Rnd;
```

```
      return Positive_8(RANDOM + 0.5);
end Roll;

function Deal(NUMBER, LIMIT : Positive_8)
 return Sequences is
   MAX           : Natural_8 := LIMIT;
   RS            : Sequences(1..NUMBER);
   SOURCE        : Sequences(1..LIMIT);
   RANDOM_INDEX  : Positive_8;
begin
   for i in Positive_8 range 1..LIMIT loop
     SOURCE(i) := i; -- SOURCE has 1 of
                     -- every number
   end loop;
   for i in Positive_8 range 1..NUMBER loop
     RANDOM_INDEX := Roll(MAX);
     -- pick a number
     RS(i) := SOURCE(RANDOM_INDEX);
     for j in Natural_8
         range RANDOM_INDEX..MAX-1 loop
       -- remove that number from SOURCE
       SOURCE(j) := SOURCE(j+1);
     end loop;
     -- there is 1 less number to choose
     -- from now
     MAX := MAX-1;
   end loop;
   return RS;
end Deal;

function Error(LIMIT : float) return float is
   X : float := Rnd;
begin
   return (X - 0.5) * 2.0 * LIMIT;
end Error;

function Error(LIMIT : Positive_8)
   return Integer_8 is
begin
   return Integer_8(Error(float(LIMIT)));
end Error;

function Noise(RMS : float) return float is
   SUM : float := 0.0;
   SCALE_FACTOR : float;
```

```
begin
   -- The Central Limit Theorem states that if
   -- enough random variables N with mean M
   -- and standard deviation S are added
   -- together, they will produce a random
   -- variable with mean N * M and standard
   -- deviation S * Sqrt(N).

   -- Dubes book, "The Theory of Applied
   -- Probability", says on page 306 that
   -- N = 3 or 4 give satisfactory results.
   -- N = 9 has the advantage that Sqrt(N)
   -- is a nice number.

   -- The random variable generated by the
   -- Error(1.0) function above has zero mean
   -- and standard deviation of 1.0 / Sqrt(3).
   -- Adding N of them together gives a random
   -- variable with Gausian distribution and
   -- mean of N * 0 and standard deviation of
   -- (1.0 / Sqrt(3)) * Sqrt(N). Since we want
   -- the standard deviation to be RMS, we
   -- must scale the result.

   for i in 1..9 loop
      SUM := SUM + ERROR(1.0);
   end loop;
   -- RMS * Sqrt(3) / Sqrt(9)
   SCALE_FACTOR := RMS * 0.57735;
   return SCALE_FACTOR * SUM;
end Noise;

procedure Set_Seed(X : Natural_32) is
begin
   SEED := Integer_32(X mod 8192);
end Set_Seed;

procedure Randomize is
   D : Duration;
begin
   D := CALENDAR.Seconds(CALENDAR.Clock);
   Set_Seed(Natural_32(D));
end Randomize;
```

```
   procedure Shuffle is
      INDEX : Sequences(1..100);
      TEMP : Digit_arrays;
   begin
      -- Let INDEX be a random sequence of
      -- numbers from 1..100 with each value
      -- appearing only once.
      INDEX := Deal(100,100);
      -- Fill TEMP with values selected from
      -- NUMBER_POOL using the random INDEX.
      for i in 1..100 loop
         TEMP(i) := NUMBER_POOL(positive(
            INDEX(Positive_8(i))));
      end loop;
      -- Replace NUMBER_POOL with shuffled copy.
      NUMBER_POOL := TEMP;
      -- No numbers have been drawn from the pool
      -- since it was last shuffled.
      POOL_INDEX := 1;
   end Shuffle;

   function Random_Digit return Numerals is
      X : Numerals;
   begin
      -- Consider NUMBER_POOL to be a deck of 100
      -- cards, with 10 zeros, 10 ones, etc. up
      -- to 10 nines. We deal 3 cards off the top
      -- of the deck, then shuffle it. The
      -- probability of dealing 3 identical
      -- numerals in a row should be 0.01. The
      -- fact that numerals are drawn without
      -- replacement biases the odds slightly
      -- against this happening. The odds are
      -- 9/99 * 8/98, which is 0.00742.
      X := NUMBER_POOL(POOL_INDEX);
      POOL_INDEX := POOL_INDEX + 1;
      if POOL_INDEX >= 3 then
         Shuffle;
      end if;
      return X;
   end Random_Digit;

begin
   -- Pick a seed at random.
   Randomize;
```

```
      -- Load the NUMBER_POOL with digits.
      for i in 0..9 loop
        for j in 0..9 loop
          NUMBER_POOL(10*i + j + 1) := j;
        end loop;
      end loop;
      -- Shuffle the digits in the NUMBER_POOL.
      Shuffle;
  end RANDOM_NUMBERS;
```

SOURCE CODE DISKS

If you want to use the source code shown in the listings and you don't want to type it all in by hand, you can purchase a pair of 5.25" IBM PC compatible disks. (Use the order form at the end of the book.)

DISK 1 contains these portable files

```
READ      ME      <----- IMPORTANT INFO !!!!!
DIR       TXT     Relates file name to listing
                    number
SIS       ADA     Listing 1. STANDARD_INTEGERS
GIU       ADA     Listing 2. INTEGER_UNITS
IUT       ADA                INTEGER_UNITS test
DI32      ADA     Listing 3. DIM_INT_32
GFU       ADA     Listing 4. FLOAT_UNITS
FUT       ADA                FLOAT_UNITS test
DFU       ADA     Listing 5. DIM_FLOAT Version 1.0
TS        ADA     Listing 7. TRIG specification
TRIGD     ADA                Trig_Demo
MATHD     ADA                Math_Demo
AUS       ADA     Listing 11. ASCII_UTILITIES
                             specification
AUB       ADA     Listing 12. ASCII_UTILITIES body
AUBFXI    ADA     Listing 13. ASCII_UTILITIES
                             .Fixed_Image
AUBFLI    ADA     Listing 14. ASCII_UTILITIES
                             .Float_Image
AUBII     ADA     Listing 15. ASCII_UTILITIES.Image
AUBV      ADA     Listing 16. ASCII_UTILITIES.Value
AUD       ADA                ASCII_UTILITIES demo
AUD       REF                ASCII_UTILITIES demo
                             output
VALDEMO   ADA                ASCII_UTILITIES.Value
                             demo
MS        ADA     Listing 17. MONEY_UTILITIES
                             specification
MB        ADA     Listing 18. MONEY_UTILITIES body
MD        ADA                MONEY_UTILITIES demo
MD        REF                MONEY_UTILITIES demo
                             output
VTS       ADA     Listing 19. VIRTUAL_TERMINAL
                             specification
VTT       ADA                VIRTUAL_TERMINAL test
VTT       REF                VIRTUAL_TERMINAL test
                             output
```

```
RNT        REF                  RANDOM_NUMBERS test
                                output
```

DISK 2 contains system specific files in individual directories.

DISK2 \MERIDIAN directory

```
DFU        ADA    Listing 6. DIM_FLOAT Version 1.1
TBMIBM     ADA    Listing 9. TRIG body
VTBMIBM    ADA    Listing 21. VIRTUAL_TERMINAL body
GCLBMIBM   ADA    Listing 65. Get_Command_Line body
AU         BAT               ASCII_UTILITIES
IU         BAT               INTEGER_UNITS
MONEY      BAT               MONEY
FU         BAT               FLOAT_UTILITIES
TRIG       BAT               TRIG
TRIGD      REF               Trig_Demo output
MATHD      REF               Math_Demo output
VT         BAT               VIRTUAL_TERMINAL
ST         BAT               SCROLL_TERMINAL
RN         BAT               RANDOM_NUMBERS
CL         BAT               Command Line programs
DP         BAT               Draw_Poker, Version 2
FT         BAT               FORM_TERMINAL
DP3        BAT               Draw_Poker, Version 3
VP         BAT               VIRTUAL_PRINTER
SP         BAT               SCROLL_PRINTER
```

DISK2 \ALSYS directory

```
TBAIBM     ADA    Listing 10. TRIG body
VTBAIBM    ADA    Listing 20. VIRTUAL_TERMINAL body
GCLBAIBM   ADA    Listing 58. Get_Command_Line body
NEWLIB                       Create a new library
SETDEF                       Set defaults
AU                           ASCII_UTILITIES
IU                           INTEGER_UNITS
MONEY                        MONEY
FU                           FLOAT_UTILITIES
TRIG                         TRIG
TRIGD      REF               Trig_Demo output
MATHD      REF               Math_Demo output
VT                           VIRTUAL_TERMINAL
```

```
ST                        SCROLL_TERMINAL
RN                        RANDOM_NUMBERS
CL                        Command Line programs
DP                        Draw_Poker, Version 2
FT                        FORM_TERMINAL
DP3                       Draw_Poker, Version 3
VP                        VIRTUAL_PRINTER
SP                        SCROLL_PRINTER
```

DISK2 \DEC directory

```
TBDEC     ADA   Listing 8. TRIG body
VMSS      ADA   Listing 48. VMS specification
VMSB      ADA   Listing 49. VMS body
VMSBI     ADA   Listing 50. VMS.INPUT
VMSBO     ADA   Listing 51. VMS.OUTPUT
VTSDEC    ADA   Listing 52. VIRTUAL_TERMINAL
                              specification
VTBDEC    ADA   Listing 53. VIRTUAL_TERMINAL body
VTTDEC    ADA               VIRTUAL_TERMINAL test
GCLBDEC   ADA   Listing 60. Get_Command_Line body
AU        COM               ASCII_UTILITIES
IU        COM               INTEGER_UNITS
MONEY     COM               MONEY
FU        COM               FLOAT_UTILITIES
TRIG      COM               TRIG
TRIGD     REF               Trig_Demo output
MATHD     REF               Math_Demo output
VT        COM               VIRTUAL_TERMINAL
ST        COM               SCROLL_TERMINAL
RN        COM               RANDOM_NUMBERS
CL        COM               Command Line programs
DP        COM               Draw_Poker, Version 2
FT        COM               FORM_TERMINAL
DP3       COM               Draw_Poker, Version 3
```

There are more files on the disks than there are on the listings because I have included some test routines, sample outputs, and compilation aides. The instructions telling how to use all these extra files are in the READ.ME file. Here's what READ.ME says.

```
READ.ME
```

```
Copyright (c) John Wiley & Sons, Inc. 1989.
All rights reserved.  Reproduction
```

These two disks contain the source code for
all the listings in "Ada IN ACTION" by
Do-While Jones, published by John Wiley &
Sons, Inc. DISK 1 contains all the portable
source code. DISK 2 contains three directories
called MERIDIAN, ALSYS, and DEC which contain
the unique source code for each system.

You can, of course, selectively copy individual
files and use them. I suggest, however, that you
follow a systematic plan that compiles and tests
all the listings that run on your system.

I have to assume that you already know how to
use your Ada compiler and the DOS operating
system. If you don't, read the manufacturer's
documentation on the compiler and operating
system. It will explain how to use them better
than I can.

I suggest you create a new directory called
ACTION on your hard disk, and let that be the
default directory.

```
C:\> MKDIR \ACTION
C:\> CD \ACTION
```

Insert DISK 1 into drive A:, then copy all the
source files from the the disk to this new
ACTION directory.

C:\ACTION> COPY A:*.*

Insert DISK 2 into drive A:, and copy all the
system specific source files, command files,
and reference output into the ACTION directory.

C:\ACTION> COPY A:\MERIDIAN*.*
   or
C:\ACTION> COPY A:\ALSYS*.*
   or
C:\ACTION> COPY A:\DEC*.*

Next, you need to create a program library. If
you are a Meridian user you should have
NEWLIB.BAT in a directory that is included in
your PATH statement.

Meridian: C:\ACTION> NEWLIB

If you are an Alsys user you probably have
written your own command file to get to the Ada
world and copy everything you need to the
virtual disk. I've included a "newlib" invoke
file in the ALSYS directory on DISK 2 to help
you create a new library in the ACTION directory.
It automatically links the Alsys math routines
to your new library. I've also included the
"setdef" invoke file I use to set all the
defaults whenever I go to the Ada world.

Alsys: C:\ACTION> (get into the Ada world)
       Ada.i newlib

If you are using DEC Ada on a VAX, you have to
get the source code onto the VAX. Presumably you
have some way to transfer ASCII files from a PC
to the VAX, or you would not have bought these
disks. I created a new directory on the VAX
($CREATE /DIR [MY_ROOT_DIRECTORY.ACTION]) and
used the Kermit server on the VAX and the

SMARTERM Kermit Send command on the PC to transfer the files. (Some Kermit implementations add a CONTROL-Z at the end of the source file. This confuses the compiler, so you have have to use the EDT editor to remove the CONTROL-Z.)

DEC: $ CREATE /DIR [your_dir.ACTION]
       $ (transfer from IBM PC ACTION
         directory to [your_dir.ACTION])
       $ ACS CREATE LIBRARY [your_dir.ADALIB]
       $ ACS SET LIBRARY [your_dir.ADALIB]

Now you should have all the files you need in the ACTION directory on the target system. Since most of the components depend on each other, I recommend you compile and test them all in the following order.

1. STANDARD_INTEGERS.

  Compile SIS.ada according to the directions for compiling source code for your compiler.

Meridian: C:\ACTION> ada SIS.ada

Alsys: Ada.c SIS.ada

DEC: $ ada SIS.ada

Just about everything depends on STANDARD_INTEGERS.Integer_32, so you must compile it first. It will be tested as a part of the ASCII_UTILITIES package.

2. ASCII_UTILITIES.

  Compile AUS.ada, AUB.ada, AUBFXI.ada, AUBFLI.ada, AUBII.ada and AUBV.ada, in that order. Compile AUD.ada and link AU_Demo. When you run AU_Demo you will get screen after screen of text that should look exactly like AUD.REF. You won't be able to read it as it scrolls by (unless you have a 300 baud modem, or are a really fast speed reader), so I suggest you

direct the output to the printer or a file. If
you direct it to AUD.OUT, then you can use the
TYPE command to display it, or use a file
comparison utility to compare it to AUD.REF.

Compile VALDEMO.ada and link VALDEMO. When you
run VALDEMO you will be asked to enter a real
number. Try any sequence of characters you like.
If the string you enter can be expressed as a
floating point number, then its value will
be displayed, and you will be asked to enter
another number. It will keep doing this until
you enter 'Q' or an invalid number (which raises
CONSTRAINT_ERROR and terminates).

There are some SHORTCUTS! If you have loaded
the Meridian files, there is a batch file called
AU.BAT which will compile and link everything
for you. If you have loaded the Alsys files,
there is an invoke file called AU that will
compile and link everything for you. If you have
loaded the DEC files, there is a command file
called AU.COM that will compile and link
everything for you.

```
Meridian: C:\ACTION> AU
          C:\ACTION> AU_DEMO > AUD.OUT
          C:\ACTION> TYPE AUD.OUT
          C:\ACTION> VALDEMO


Alsys: Ada.i AU
       Ada.s.AU_DEMO > AUD.OUT
       Ada.s.TYPE AUD.OUT
       Ada.s.VALDEMO


DEC:   $ @AU
       $ run AU_DEMO
       $ run VALDEMO
```

3. INTEGER_UNITS and DIM_INT_32.

Compile GIU.ada, DI32.ada, and the Integer
Units Test (IUT.ada), in that order. Link and
run IUT. You should get an output exactly like
IUT.ref.

There are shortcuts for all three systems.
Meridian has the IU.BAT batch file. Alsys has

the IU invoke file. DEC has the IU.COM command
file.

Meridian: C:\ACTION> IU
           C:\ACTION> IUT

Alsys: Ada.i IU
       Ada.s.IUT

DEC: $ @IU
      $ run IUT

4. MONEY.

   Compile MS.ada, MB.ada, and the Money_Demo
(MD.ada), in that order. Link and run
Money_Demo. You should get an output exactly
like MD.ref.
   There are shortcuts for all three systems.
Meridian has the MONEY.BAT batch file. Alsys has
the MONEY invoke file. DEC has the MONEY.COM
command file.

Meridian: C:\ACTION> MONEY
          C:\ACTION> MONEY_DEMO > MD.OUT
          C:\ACTION> TYPE MD.OUT

Alsys: Ada.i MONEY
       Ada.s.MONEY_DEMO > MD.OUT
       Ada.s.TYPE MD.OUT

DEC: $ @MONEY
      $ run MONEY_DEMO

MERIDIAN USERS NOTE: There is a bug in the
version 2.1 compiler that causes the MONEY_DEMO
to fail.

5. FLOAT_UNITS and DIM_FLOAT.

   Compile GFU.ada, DFU.ada, and the Float Units
Test (FUT.ada), in that order. Link and run FUT.
You should get an output exactly like FUT.ref.

There are shortcuts for all three systems.
Meridian has the FU.BAT batch file. Alsys has
the FU invoke file. DEC has the FU.COM command
file.

Meridian: C:\ACTION> FU
           C:\ACTION> FUT

Alsys: Ada.i FU
        Ada.s.FUT

DEC: $ @FU
       $ run FUT

6. TRIG.

Assuming you have successfully done step 5
above, you can compile TS.ada and the appropriate
body file (TBMIBM.ada for Meridian IBM,
TBAIBM.ada for Alsys IBM, or TBDEC.ada for DEC
Ada.) If you are using a compiler other than one
of the three just listed, you will have to figure
out how to modify one of those three TRIG
package body files for your system.
   Test the TRIG package by compiling TRIGD.Ada.
Link and run Trig_Demo. You should get an
output exactly like the file TRIGD.ref.
   Compile MATHD.Ada. Link and run Math_Demo. You
should get an output exactly like MATHD.ref.
   Compile COSTEST.ada, then link and run COS_TEST.
Compile COSDIF.ada, then link and run COS_DIF to
compare the output from COS_TEST (in COSTEST.DAT)
to COSTEST.REF.
   There are shortcuts for all three systems.
Meridian has the TRIG.BAT batch file. Alsys has
the TRIG invoke file. DEC has the TRIG.COM
command file.
   ALSYS USERS NOTE: The TRIG package requires the
user-supplied math library which was delivered
with version 3.2 of the Alsys compiler. If you
used the "newlib" invoke file to create the new
library, and it ran without error, you should
have all the files you need. You must also bind
MATH.LIB to your library. The last line of

"setdef" does this for you. If you have trouble,
read the notes in TBAIBM.ada

```
Meridian:  C:\ACTION> TRIG
           C:\ACTION> TRIG_DEMO > TRIGD.OUT
           C:\ACTION> TYPE TRIGD.OUT
           C:\ACTION> MATH_DEMO > MATHD.OUT
           C:\ACTION> TYPE MATHD.OUT
           C:\ACTION> COS_TEST
           C:\ACTION> COS_DIF
```
What is the name of the REFERENCE file? COS.REF
What is the name of the TEST file? COS.DAT
The maximum positive error was () at () degrees.
The maximum negative error was () at () degrees.

```
Alsys:  Ada.i TRIG
        Ada.s.TRIG_DEMO > TRIGD.OUT
        Ada.s.TYPE TRIGD.OUT
        Ada.s.MATH_DEMO > MATHD.OUT
        Ada.s.TYPE MATHD.OUT
        Ada.s.COS_TEST
        Ada.s.COS_DIF
```
What is the name of the REFERENCE file? COS.REF
What is the name of the TEST file? COS.DAT
The maximum positive error was () at () degrees.
The maximum negative error was () at () degrees.

```
DEC:   $ @TRIG
       $ run TRIG_DEMO
       $ run MATH_DEMO
       $ run COS_TEST
       $ run COS_DIF
```
What is the name of the REFERENCE file? COS.REF
What is the name of the TEST file? COS.DAT
The maximum positive error was () at () degrees.
The maximum negative error was () at () degrees.

7. VIRTUAL_TERMINAL.

   Since the VIRTUAL_TERMINAL is hardware
dependent, you have to do slightly different
things on different systems. When using DEC Ada
and a DEC CRT on VAX VMS, compile VMSS.ada,
VMSBI.ada, VMSBI.ada, VMSBO.ada, VTSDEC.ada,

VTBDEC.ada and VTTDEC.Ada. For IBM PC systems
compile VTS.ada and VTT.ada, then VTBMIBM.ada
(for Meridian) or VTBAIBM.ada (for Alsys).

After you have done that, the test procedure
is the same for all systems. Link VT_Test. Run
VT_Test and expect to see a screen just like
VTT.ref. (Note: If you direct the output to
a file or a printer, you will see something
similar, but not identical to, VTT.ref because
the control codes will probably get filtered
out. Don't try redirecting the output on this
test.)

Press the keys and see what they do. Normal
keys should echo. Arrow keys should move the
cursor anywhere on the screen (even outside the
box marked by 1,2,3 and 4). Attempting to move
the cursor off the screen should fail (no
automatic scroll up, scroll down, scroll left,
or scroll right). Special keys (TAB, BACK_TAB,
function keys, and so on) should echo a message.
Undefined keys do nothing.

There are shortcuts for all three systems.
Meridian has the VT.BAT batch file. Alsys has
the VT invoke file. DEC has the VT.COM command
file.

```
Meridian: C:\ACTION> VT
          C:\ACTION> VT_TEST

Alsys: Ada.i VT
       Ada.s.VT_TEST

DEC:   $ @VT
       $ run VT_TEST
```

IBM PC USERS NOTE: Be sure your system is
configured with the ANSI.SYS driver!

8. SCROLL_TERMINAL.

Compile STS.ada, STB.ada, and STBGR.ada, in
that order. Compile the SCROLL_TERMINAL
Demonstration (STD.ada), and then link and run
ST_DEMO. You should see something that looks

similar to STD.ref. It may not be exactly the
same, because your responses affect what it
does. You shouldn't direct this to a printer
because it is prompting you for inputs.
   There are shortcuts for all three systems.
Meridian has the ST.BAT batch file. Alsys has
the ST invoke file. DEC has the ST.COM command
file.

Meridian: C:\ACTION> ST
          C:\ACTION> ST_DEMO

Alsys: Ada.i ST
       Ada.s.ST_DEMO

DEC: $ @ST
       $ run ST_DEMO

9. RANDOM_NUMBERS.

   Compile RNS.ada, RNB.ada, and the Random
Numbers Test program (RNT.ada), in that order.
Link and run RNT. You should see something that
looks similar to RNT.ref. It won't be exactly
the same, because it is a random number
generator, and is different every time.
   There are shortcuts for all three systems.
Meridian has the RN.BAT batch file. Alsys has
the RN invoke file. DEC has the RN.COM command
file.

Meridian: C:\ACTION> RN
          C:\ACTION> RNT

Alsys: Ada.i RN
       Ada.s.RNT

DEC: $ @RN
       $ run RNT

10. Command Line interface programs (More and
Line).

   Compile GCLS.ada, GCLBxxx.ada (where xxx =
MIBM, AIBM, or DEC, depending on your system),

MORE.ada, LINE.ada and LE.Ada. Link and run MORE.
You can display any SOURCE file you like. (I
used MORE.Ada in the example.) Then link and run
LINE. Again, you can use any file and line
number. (I used line 13 of MORE.Ada.)

There are shortcuts for all three systems.
Meridian has the CL.BAT batch file. Alsys has
the CL invoke file. DEC has the CL.COM command
file.

DOS USERS NOTE: DOS already has a command
called MORE. You need to rename one or the other.
I recommend renaming MORE.EXE to DOSMORE.EXE
before compiling MORE. See section 4.1.8 for more
details.

DEC USERS NOTE: Reread section 4.1.6.2 and the
notes in GCLBDEC.ada explaining why you need to
create a symbol for the MORE and LINE programs to
get parameters from the command line. In the
example below I've pretended that your executable
code is in [your_dir.ACTION]. You will have to
substitute the real path name.

```
Meridian: (rename MORE.EXE to DOSMORE.EXE)
          C:\ACTION> CL
          C:\ACTION> MORE MORE.ADA
          (The source file MORE.ADA is displayed)
          C:\ACTION> LINE 13 MORE.ADA
          (Lines 3-23 of MORE.ADA are displayed)

Alsys: (rename MORE.EXE to DOSMORE.EXE)
       Ada.i CL
       Ada.s.MORE MORE.ADA
       (The source file MORE.ADA is displayed)
       Ada.s.LINE 13 MORE.ADA
       (Lines 3-23 of MORE.ADA are displayed)

DEC:   $ @CL
       $ MORE :== [your_dir.ACTION]MORE.EXE
       $ LINE :== [your_dir.ACTION]LINE.EXE
       $ MORE MORE.ADA
       (The source file MORE.ADA is displayed)
       $ LINE 13 MORE.ADA
       (Lines 3-23 of MORE.ADA are displayed)
```

11. Draw_Poker.

  Compile listing 66 through 73 in order. Link
and run DRAW_POKER. Play as long as you like.
  There are shortcuts for all three systems.
Meridian has the DP.BAT batch file. Alsys has
the DP invoke file. DEC has the DP.COM command
file.

Meridian: C:\ACTION> DP
          C:\ACTION> DRAW_POKER

Alsys: Ada.i DP
       Ada.s.DRAW_POKER

DEC: $ @DP
       $ run DRAW_POKER

12. FORM_TERMINAL.

  Compile listings 25 through 45 in order. Then
link and run Make_Form. Use it to create a form
and store it in JUNK.DAT. It doesn't really
matter what the form looks like. Just experiment
with it to get the feel of the program. Then link
and run Edit_Form to modify it. When you are done
you can delete JUNK.DAT.
  I modified the Draw_Poker program slightly to
use the FORM_TERMINAL instead of the
SCROLL_TERMINAL. Compile and link the files in
DP3 and run DRAW_POKER to see how the
FORM_TERMINAL works.
  There are shortcuts for all three systems.
Meridian has the FT.BAT and DP3.BAT batch files.
Alsys has the FT and DP3 invoke files. DEC has
the FT.COM and DP3.COM command files.

Meridian: C:\ACTION> FT
          C:\ACTION> MAKE_FORM
          (Make any form, use F10 to quit.
          Store the form in JUNK.DAT.)
          C:\ACTION> EDIT_FORM
          (edit the form in JUNK.DAT)

```
        C:\ACTION> del JUNK.DAT
        C:\ACTION> DP3
        C:\ACTION> DRAW_POKER
```

```
Alsys:  Ada.i FT
        Ada.s.MAKE_FORM
        (Make any form, use F10 to quit.
        Store the form in JUNK.DAT.)
        Ada.s.EDIT_FORM
        (edit the form in JUNK.DAT)
        Ada.s.del JUNK.DAT
        Ada.i DP3
        Ada.s.DRAW_POKER
```

```
DEC:    $ @FT
        $ run MAKE_FORM
        (Make any form, use F10 to quit.
        Store the form in JUNK.DAT.)
        $ run EDIT_FORM
        (edit the form in JUNK.DAT)
        $ delete /noconf JUNK.DAT;*
        $ @DP3
        $ run DRAW_POKER
```

13. VIRTUAL_PRINTER.

   Since the VIRTUAL_PRINTER is hardware
dependent, you have to do slightly different
things on different systems. If you using DEC
Ada on VAX VMS, you will have to talk to your
system administrator and hope he is
cooperative. If he will grant you access to
the printer, and will tell you what you need
to know to use it, then you can modify the
VIRTUAL_TERMINAL body file (VPBLPT1.ada) for
use on VMS. If you are using an IBM PC,
VPBLPT1.ada will work if your printer is
connected to the LPT1 port. If you are using a
different port for your printer, you will have
to modify VPBLPT1.Ada.
   Compile, link, and run VPS.ada, VPBLPT1.ada,
and VPD.ada. The file VPD.REF shows you what the
results should be.

There are shortcuts for the IBM PC systems
with printers on LPT1. Meridian has the VP.BAT
batch file. Alsys has the VP invoke file.

Meridian: C:\ACTION> VP
          C:\ACTION> VPD

Alsys: Ada.i VP
       Ada.s.VPD

   DEC USERS NOTE: If you have modified the
VPBLPT1.ADA file for use on the DEC, you can
copy the VP.BAT file to VP.COM and modify it
for use on VMS.

14. SCROLL_PRINTER.

   Compile SPS.ada and SPB.ada in that order.
Compile the SCROLL_PRINTER Demonstration
(SPD.ada), and then link and run ST_DEMO. You
should see something that looks exactly like
SPD.ref. Compile WRITE.ada. Link and run it to
make sure it works.
   There are shortcuts for the IBM PC systems.
Meridian has the SP.BAT batch file. Alsys has
the SP invoke file.

Meridian: C:\ACTION> SP
          C:\ACTION> SP_TEST
          C:\ACTION> WRITE (any filename)

Alsys: Ada.i SP
       Ada.s.SP_TEST
       Ada.s.WRITE (any filename)

   DEC USERS NOTE: If you have successfully ported
the VIRTUAL_PRINTER, you can copy the SP.BAT file
to SP.COM and modify it for use on VMS.

INDEX